THE

Revelation of Christ

TO HIS SERVANTS:

OF

Things THAT ARE,

AND

Things THAT SHALL BE."

BRIEF NOTES IN INTERPRETATION.

By F. W. GRANT.

WIPF & STOCK · Eugene, Oregon

Wipf and Stock Publishers
199 W 8th Ave, Suite 3
Eugene, OR 97401

The Revelation of Christ to His Servants
Of Things that Are, and Things that Shall Be:
Brief Notes in Interpretation
By Grant, F. W.
Softcover ISBN-13: 978-1-7252-7556-0
Publication date 3/30/2020
Previously published by Loizeaux Brothers,

PRESENT THINGS,

As Foreshown in the Book of Revelation.

THE PREFACE TO THE BOOK.

The Book and Its Subject. (*Chap.* i. 1-3)

THE book of Revelation is the one only book of New-Testament prophecy. As the completion of the whole prophetic Scriptures, it gathers up the threads of all the former books, and weaves them into one chain of many links which binds all history to the throne of God. As *New-*Testament prophecy, it adds the heavenly to the earthly sphere, passes the bounds of time, and explores with familiar feet eternity itself. Who would not, through these doors set open to us, press in to learn the things yet unseen, so soon to be for us the only realities? Who would not imagine that such a book, written with the pen of the living God Himself, would attract irresistibly the hearts of Christians, and that no exhortation would be needed for a moment to win them to its patient and earnest study?

It should be so, assuredly. How little it is so, the book in its first words is witness to us: for no book is so full of just such exhortation. And especially the first part, with which we are to be for the present occupied, abounds with solemn warnings to attention, regularly appended to its several sections: "He that hath an ear, let him hear what the Spirit saith unto the churches." Why is it that just here, where at first sight we have only addresses to the churches of far-distant times, these calls should be multiplied? Why but because there was just this danger to be guarded against? why but because the Spirit of God foresaw that a generation of men, most blind to their own interests when most wedded to them, would slight the very words of Christ Himself unless thus directly made over to them? What shall we say of those who with all this warning slight them still?

Scripture is thus ever prophetic, not in its plain predictions merely, but in its manner also. Why should *Peter* be the one to tell us that all Christians are "a holy priesthood," but in view of those who should misuse his name in after-times? or why should he be the one to announce to us that we are born again by the word of God, which is preached in the gospel, thus with two blows destroying ritualism to its foundations? or why should Mary never prefer a request to her Son and Lord but to be checked for it, save as an after-rebuke to those who should think to avail themselves of the Virgin's intercession?

So too is not the very title of this book, with its subject announced, and encouragement both to reader and hearer? How could words be better suited to rebuke the neglect, into which so many have fallen, in which so many still are found, of what is Christ's own "revelation," given to Him by God, "to show unto His servants things which must shortly come to pass"? Does a "revelation" hide, or *reveal?* Is that which is revealed to servants, to be kept (*v.* 3) by them in their service to their Lord, given in so doubtful a manner as to be more perplexity than guidance? Is not this an accusation of Him who has forbidden to His people doubtful paths, because "whatsoever is not of faith is sin"?

Strange is the mistake that "the Revelation of Jesus Christ, which God gave unto Him," means His "appearing," because His appearing is the central theme of the book! No doubt it is so, and that His appearing is spoken of elsewhere as His revelation; but here, that "which God gave unto Him, to show unto His servants things which must shortly come to pass," is plainly the book itself, and defines its character. It is not simply an *inspiration*, as all Scripture is, but something *revealed* for the instruction of the saints. Many are too little clear yet as to the difference between the two. But revelation is that in which is a direct communication from God to man—a fresh discovery of truth otherwise unknown; while inspiration is that which preserves from error, and assures that all that is written is for true profit and blessing to man.

"Jesus Christ's revelation" emphasizes the book before us, as what is from the Lord Himself in a peculiar way, of special importance and value where all is of value; and it is received by Him from God, as One who all through takes the place of Man, and as such is exalted of God, never exalts Himself. True pattern for His servants! He asks them to walk in no other path than He has trodden, and where they may have fellowship with Him.

This book is the servant's book. So it is plainly stated: "To show unto *His servants*." We may not expect, therefore, to be shown, except we come under this title; and indeed every child of God has the responsibility and privilege of service,—has something, no doubt, of the reality of it, as the Lord says, "He that hath My commandments and keepeth them, he it is who loveth Me" (Jno. xiv. 21). And so the apostle: "This is the love of God, that we keep His commandments" (1 Jno. v. 3). Both passages maintain that the only right measure of love is that of practical obedience. Emotional glow, warm feelings, are indeed to be desired,— nay, to be expected, from those conscious of redemption by the blood of Christ; but these vary with different natures, vary in the same person at different times, may even deceive very much the subject of them, while obedience is the test of the judgment-seat itself. Words and deeds we read of then as alone in question.

Yet there is need of a counter-check here too; for how much frequently goes under the name of service which is in truth even disobedience and self-will! How much there is also of legal drudgery and pretentious claim, which the light of God's holy presence will shrivel into nothing! "Lo, these many years do I serve thee" is the language of one to whom the music of the father's house was a strange and unaccustomed sound; and "I fast twice in the week, I give tithes of all that I possess" was said by one less acceptable to God by far than the despised publican, who could only groan out in His presence, "God be merciful to me the sinner!"

The service of love and the service of claim are opposites. "He died for all, that they which live should not henceforth live unto themselves, but unto Him who died for them and rose again." This is the moral power of Christianity—the fruit of grace, and only that. For if still there is a possibility of condemnation in the day of judgment, fear stirs me to self-interest, I work for myself to escape the condemnation. "Faith worketh by love"—an entirely opposite principle. Such service is necessarily freedom, the more so the more it rules me, and entire happiness. In exact proportion to love will be the desire to serve the object of our love: as we read of the "*work* of faith," so we do of the "*labor* of love." But earnest and self-sacrificing as this labor may be, it can never be drudgery, never aught but joy. If such is our service, the thankful offering of those knowing themselves washed from their sins in the blood of Christ, then Revelation, with its survey of the whole field of labor, and its communication of the mind of Christ as to all,—Revelation, with its windows open toward Jerusalem, and its eternal sunshine for our souls,—Revelation, with its throne of God and the Lamb, and the stimulation of its encouraging words to the overcomer,—is the very book for us, surely. We shall enter with rapt hearts into the truth of this: "Blessed is he that readeth, and they that hear the words of the book of this prophecy, and keep the things that are written therein."

It is the book for *all* servants. We have many and different fields of service, it is true; and happy as well as important it is to recognize this fact. There are high positions and lowly ones; positions before the eyes of multitudes, and positions hidden from almost all eyes, save His who are in every place. But every where it is a joy to know that we are accepted, not according to the place we are put in, but the way we fill it—the way we do the

Master's work there. Lowliness and obscurity will be no discouragement to those in the communion of the Father and the Son: they cease to have meaning there. And publicity and prominence are how unspeakably dangerous, if the soul is not correspondingly before God; like the tree which spreads its branches and lifts its top toward heaven, if its roots are not proportionately deep in the unseen depths below.

Whatever the field of service, the book of Revelation is for all. All need alike the warnings, all need alike the encouragement. From the most hidden retirement, He whom we serve in love would have our hearts with Himself, busy with all that is of interest to Him. In the place of intercession Himself above, He would have us in fellowship with Him below; our prayers rising up for all parts of the earth His Word is visiting, and where the true "irrepressible conflict" is going on between the evil and the good; our praises, too, returning to Him for all He is daily accomplishing. In Revelation is given us the one "mind of Christ" about all, that our prayers may be the intelligent guiding of the Holy Spirit, and our hearts giving their sympathies aright, our energies going forth in channels of His own making. Little indeed, in many of the systems of interpretation of this book, may be found, it is true, such help as this; and quite unable we may be to extract the spiritual blessing to be found in seals or trumpets which speak only of Alaric the Goth, or Attila the Hun: but for the simple ones who believe God, the mere direct label of this book for Christ's servants may certify that there is something deeper while simpler than all this for souls that seek it. There the words stand for faith to receive and rejoice in, —"Jesus Christ's revelation, which God gave unto Him, to show unto His servants things which must shortly come to pass." Join us in prayer, beloved reader, ere we pass on, that we may give His people from these pages real help and blessing drawn from this precious book!

"Things which must shortly come to pass." This would now no doubt impress us, as we look back from the end of eighteen centuries fulfilled since it was written, with the belief that already some, if not much, of what is here spoken of must already have come to pass. And this we shall find confirmed fully in the sequel. But two things we should guard here carefully,—the possibility on the one hand, and the profit on the other, of tracing with certainty, in the light of the prophetic Word, things which have *not* come to pass, and even will not while we are upon the earth. These two things, it is plain, hang very much together; for if there be not profit in it, it would seem clear that God would not enable us to do it; while of course there can, on the other hand, be no profit to us in a thing we cannot do.

But this impossibility of knowing can only be meant seriously as applying to details, and to a *certain extent* every Christian would allow this. Events are not so mapped out and put together for us as to make us able to see otherwise than "through a glass darkly"—the apostle's own emphatic word. We can see only as one behind a window, and in twilight, and are apt to fall into mistakes. Many have been thus made, which have thrown the study of future prophecy, for some, into utter disrepute. Yet who would say, or think the apostle meant to say, that "through a glass darkly " nothing, or nothing to the purpose, could be seen? The uncertainty applies mainly to the smaller features; there is much certain, much that grows always clearer as we look upon it. Who that would use the mistakes that have been made for discouragement from prophetic study *has ever been a student of it?* I dare to say, none. Granted, the mistakes: let us use them for humility, use them as arguments to more prayer, more careful searching, then, after all, they will be helpful in the end. We can see already why and how many of them came about; we can see how better to avoid them also in the future, and that the Word was not to blame, is not the less trustworthy, because we made them. We see that we trusted it too little, trusted ourselves too much.

Then as to the profit. All our blessings lie in the field of unfulfilled prophecy. What are all our promises but this? And then as to the earth, and what is to take place upon it, it is true that such interpretations as are common in many popular books leave one with the profound sense that they minister rather to spiritual dissipation than to profit. What can be supposed more unprofitable than the question if the antichrist is to come of the Napoleon family?—a great and grave point with many for years past; or whether the stars falling from heaven might be fulfilled in a shower of meteors? Such things seem to be utterly barren, and unworthy of a book so solemnly announced, so commended to us as is this.

Surely, " he that prophesieth speaketh to the church to edification and exhortation and comfort " might not be an inapt word to condemn such profitless speculation; and there is abundance of it in popular commentaries. But here the question is really not of fulfilled or unfulfilled prophecy. Such supposed fulfillment may be brought forward to vindicate Scripture—which has no need of it—or a certain system of interpretation, which it more justly would set aside. But unfulfilled prophecy, as we find it in the Word of God, even when it speaks of earthly events, and such as cannot be while we are upon the earth, always gives them morally; as what can be more practical for us than to trace out in the future, as men are constantly seeking to do, the results of the present? In this way we may find the *scriptural* fall of stars to have the deepest significance.

That all here is in the fullest way practical is very clear, from the blessing pronounced on those who "*keep* the things which are written" in the book. This "keeping" is observing them in such a way that our practical conduct shall be governed by them. Indeed we shall find that the wisdom of them we must be content to "buy," with what men would call many a sacrifice. There are costs to be counted if we would possess it really. And this is the demand that all truth makes upon us. It requires subjection to it as the first thing. We must not trifle with the words of our Lord and Saviour, nor set Him limits as to how far we shall obey Him. It is this, however little avowed, that darkens the minds of saints, diminishing all spiritual perception. It is this that is at the bottom of all doctrinal heresy. We will not have the truth, and seek out inventions to cover our nakedness; or at least we have not the soldier's "virtue," which is courage, and so cannot "add to" our "virtue knowledge."

I would warn my readers that the book of Revelation makes great demands upon those who keep its words. But I may assure them, on the other hand, that the more the demand the greater the blessing. Can it be otherwise when Christ it is who is speaking to us of that easy yoke and that light burden, in which, as we take them, we find rest to our souls? Will any that know their Lord charge Him with being a "hard man," or a taskmaster? Our givings up are here in reality only gains. We have that in Him which we are never called to give up, and which the more we prove the more its sufficiency is found for all conditions; the more we give up for it the deeper the endless joy.

But submission there must be. Absolute submission is what He rightly calls for; and it is well to search our hearts, to see if our desire and purpose are, to give Him that without reserve. How blessed to be among those who in uprightness of heart can say, "I esteem all Thy precepts concerning all things to be right, and I hate every false way" (Ps. cxix. 128)!

The Style and Character of the Book.
(Chap. i. 4-8.)

WE now come to the opening words of the book itself. It is in form a letter from the beloved apostle to "the seven assemblies which are in Asia." This Asia was the Roman province called by this name, being the west coast of what is now, for the sins of christendom, Turkey in Asia. The churches in it were even then, though traditionally the scene of John's as in the Acts of Paul's labors, already departing from the faith and spiritual power of Christianity; and this, as we may see more here-

THE PREFACE TO THE BOOK.

after, gives at once a certain character to the book. Whoever they were of whom Paul in his very last epistle says, "This thou knowest, that all they which be in Asia are turned away from me, of whom are Phygellus and Hermogenes," it is clear that Asia was thus the scene of a revolt from that "apostles' doctrine and fellowship" which it was a marked feature of the bright Pentecostal times to maintain.

The salutation shows at once the style of the book. It is not "grace and peace from God the Father, and our Lord Jesus Christ," but "from Him who is, and who was, and who is to come; and from the seven Spirits which are before His throne; and from Jesus Christ, the faithful Witness, and the First-born* of the dead, and the Ruler of the kings of the earth." Here, it is evident, we are not in the intimacy of children, but in the character of servants, according to what the previous verses have announced. The book is the book of the throne—of divine government; and that, not merely of the world, but of Christians no less. Indeed, where should divine government be more exemplified and maintained than among the people of God. "You only have I known of all the families of the earth," says God to His people of old; "therefore will I punish you for your iniquities." It is true that toward us now grace is fully revealed, and the throne is a "*throne* of grace," but its holiness is none the less inflexible. Would it *be* grace if it were not so? or do we desire to be de-

---

* As there are many (smaller or greater) inaccuracies in the common version of the book of Revelation, I take advantage of the difference here (though not a textual one,) to say that I follow, wherever it is possible, the new revision. Wherever I may not be able to do this, I hope to note the fact, and my reasons.

livered from the conditions of holiness, or from the sovereignty of God? No; grace enables for the conditions,—does not set them aside; and it sets God fully on the throne for us, makes the "shout of a King" to be in our midst. Children with the Father, where should there be whole-hearted, unreserved obedience if not among these?

The throne here is Jehovah's throne, for "who is, and was, and is to come" is just the translation of the covenant-name of Israel's God. "Grace and peace" salute us from this unchangeable One—this eternal God. The new revelation has not displaced, nor *mended*, (as rationalism would have it,) the God of Israel for us! It has *declared* Him: displaced shadows, filled in gaps, perfected the partial and fragmentary into the glorious God and Father of our Lord Jesus Christ! taught us to see in the older Scriptures themselves a fullness of meaning of which those who wrote them could have no possible perception. Do David's psalms yield us less than they yielded to faith of old? And if the New Testament has no corresponding book, is it not because, now that the Spirit of God is come, our psalmody is to be found in *every* book, which for us He has combined into one harmony of praise and triumphant joy?

Yes, the One who is *was*, and is to come. Our present God is He who from first to last abides, in every generation, amid all changes changeless; sitting on high above all water-floods; whose kingdom is an everlasting kingdom. What a resting-place for faith! "Lord, Thou hast been our dwelling-place in all generations!"

But not only are grace and peace breathed from this ever-living One, but also "from the seven

Spirits which are before His throne." We all recognize at once that these seven Spirits stand for the plenitude of the Holy Spirit; and in the fourth chapter they are represented as seven lamps of fire burning before the throne, while in the fifth they are the "seven eyes" of the Lamb, "sent forth into all the earth." This, again, evidently connects with Isaiah xi, where these seven Spirits are seen to be energies of the Spirit which are found in the Man, Christ Jesus, as reigning over the earth.

"Grace and peace," then, from these—how blessed! All the ministries of divine government upon the earth working in blessing toward us; all the course of things as guided and controlled by God, spite of all hindrances, all puzzles and perplexities, still working in one harmony of grace and peace toward His own. How easy to be bold and patient both, if we believe this!

Then also "from Jesus Christ, the *faithful* Witness, and the First-born of the dead, and the Ruler of the kings of the earth." "Faithful" is emphasized here, for our encouragement surely, if grace and peace are from such an One, but yet in contrast with other witness too, as that of the Church, so little faithful. Is it not a needed word for those oppressed with the sense of failure,—almost ready to give up what are *His* principles, because of the break-down of those who have undertaken to carry them out? In such a case, how good to remember that on the one hand we are servants and not masters, with no liberty to dispense with one even of His commandments, and on the other, that we serve One who Himself is faithful, however we have failed. Shall we go to Him and say, "Master, Thy principles are impracticable for a world and a time like this"? or shall we lack in courage when results are in His hand who has *never* failed, and never will, while He oftentimes submits to *apparent* defeat. Such was the cross, the victory of victories, and we must submit, here as elsewhere, to the rule of the woman's Seed. To this are we not in fact brought in the next words? "The First-born of the dead" unites us with Him as the later-born, and resurrection is the mode of His triumph over apparent defeat. But it is *divine* triumph, in which not alone evil is vanquished, but God is manifested in His resources and in His grace.

Grace and peace are ours from One who is conqueror over death, and who brings us into the place into which as Forerunner He has entered, while already He is, as risen, and on the Father's throne, Ruler of the kings of the earth,—the scene through which in the meantime we are passing. In a little while, when He takes His own throne, we shall share also in this.

Thus are we furnished at the outset for present service. Placed before the living and eternal God, the energies of His Spirit ministering to us, the Captain of our salvation cheering us on with the joy of already accomplished victory, the pledge of certainty as to our own. Now for the response of our hearts to this before we start: without our hearts are in tune, and we can go cheerily into the battlefield—for it is a battlefield into which we go, and not as spectators merely,—we should only expose ourselves there to our shame. The singers must be in the forefront of the Lord's army, as in Jehoshaphat's of old, and then there will be good success. So the saints' answer to their Captain's voice here is with a song:—

> "Unto Him who loveth us,
>   And hath washed* us from our sins
>   In His own blood,
>   And hath made us a kingdom,
>   Priests to His God and Father,—
> Unto Him be glory and might
> Unto the ages of ages.
>   Amen."

This is a sweet response of loyal hearts on the edge of the battlefield. It is the good confession of His name, and of the debt we owe Him, which has made us His own forever. Good it is, the open joyful maintenance of this, which at once separates us from the world that rejects Him, and puts us in the ranks of His witnesses and followers. "By Him therefore let us offer the sacrifice of praise to God continually, that is, the fruit of our lips, confessing His name." No such wholesome, invigorating, gladdening work as is confession.

"Unto Him who *loveth* us," not "*loved* us," as the common version reads. It is a present reality, measured only aright by a past work—"and hath washed us from our sins in His own blood." Let us take care we measure it ever so! Not by our own changeful feelings or experiences, as we are so prone to do, but by the glorious manifestation of itself thus: an infinite measure of an infinite fullness; for who knows aright the value of the blood of Christ?

"And hath washed us from our sins:" what an encouragement for those who have to go into a

---

*"*Washed* us," I believe, is right. The Revised Version puts it, however, into the margin, and "*loosed* us" into the text. Most of the modern editors agree with this, and it has the weight of the oldest MS. authority in its favor, although the great mass of MSS. give "washed." The latter seems more in the apostle's manner as 1 Jno. i. 7; Rev. vii. 14 (though in the latter case it is not persons, but robes).

world full of temptation and defilement! We have *known* sin as sin—known it as needing the precious blood of Christ to cleanse us from its guilt, and known ourselves too as thus cleansed. If we are "idle and unfruitful in the knowledge of our Lord Jesus Christ," it can only be because we have "forgotten that" we were "purged from" our "old sins."

But more: He has "made us a kingdom,* priests to His God and Father." Israel was promised, conditionally upon obedience, "Ye shall be unto Me a kingdom of priests, and a holy nation." (Ex. xix. 6.) They failed in obedience, and Levi's special priesthood was the consequence of their failure, while, as part of this failed people, not even the priesthood could pass within the vail. Grace has now given us as Christians that access to God to them denied, and to God fully revealed as the God and Father of our Lord Jesus Christ. He who has thus revealed God has given us our place in His presence—a happy, holy place of praise and intercession. "To Him be the glory and might unto the ages of ages!"

An "Amen" is added here, that we may as individuals join our voices to the voice of the Church at large. It is a blessed thing to be part of the innumerable company who have a common theme and a common joy; but it is also blessed to have

---

*All authorities, upon the warrant of the three oldest MSS. and some ancient versions, give this instead of the "kings and priests" of our common one. The reference to Exodus xix. is plain, but I do not see how in either passage we have the equivalent of the other reading. A "kingdom of priests" does not convey the thought of "*kings* and priests," which we have, however, undoubtedly, in chap. v. 10. Is it not rather a people who own God's sovereignty, instead of being a rabble of independent and rebellious wills, as once? Well may we praise Him who has done all this for us! Internal criticism, however, as opposed to authorities, might suggest the defensibility of the "Received Text." The MSS. are evidently here also in some confusion.

THE PREFACE TO THE BOOK. 17

our own distinct utterance and our own peculiar joy. The more distinct the better. Would the apostle have felt it the same thing to say, "Who loved *us*, and gave Himself for us," true as it might be, as to say, "Who loved *me*, and gave Himself for *me"?* Assuredly he would not. The "chief of sinners," realizing himself that, had something which was individual to himself, and which would not be lost or overlooked in the general song. And we have, each one of us surely, special experiences to call forth peculiar praise. Note, too, that the power of the life lived to God is associated by him with this individualization: "The life which I now live in the flesh I live by the faith of the Son of God, who loved *me*, and gave Himself for me."

Thus, then, the heart gives out its response to its beloved Lord. Now, then, it is qualified for testimony to Him. "If we be beside ourselves, it is to God; if we be sober, it is for your cause." The soul in company with Christ turns necessarily to the world with its testimony of Him: the Enoch-life is joined with the Enoch-witness. For it was he of whom it is written, "he walked with God, and he was not, for God took him," who "prophesied, saying, 'Behold, the Lord cometh with ten thousands of His saints, to execute judgment upon all.'" The Church it is who is called, like another Enoch, to walk here with Him whom she is soon to be called away to meet and be ever with; and the next verse in Revelation puts into her mouth her similar testimony:—

"Behold, He cometh with clouds, and every eye shall see Him, and they also which pierced Him, and all the tribes of the earth shall wail because of Him."

This is evidently not the Church's hope, but the

Church's testimony. It takes up the theme of the Old-Testament prophets, with direct appeal even to their prophecies; for Daniel saw of old the Son of Man come with the clouds of heaven, and Zechariah declares how Israel look upon Him whom they have pierced, and how the tribes of the land mourn for Him, as one mourneth for his only son, and are in heaviness as he that is in heaviness for his first-born." (Dan. vii. 13; Zech. x. 10, 12.)

I do not doubt that, while the words in Revelation repeat the very language of the older prophets, —for "kindreds" in the common version is literally "tribes," and "earth" and "land" are, both in Hebrew and Greek, but the same word,—yet that in the passage before us a wider application is to be made than this. Not only shall they see who have pierced Him, but "*every* eye." Naturally, therefore, not the tribes of the land only, but of the earth at large, shall wail on account of Him. The testimony is neither to nor of Israel only, though including these. And while the mourning in Zechariah is unto repentance, the word here is large enough to admit of the wail of despair as well as of repentance.

The Church's testimony is addressed to all. Christ is coming; the day of grace running out; judgment nearing with every stroke of the hour. A testimony which we know from Scripture, as we may realize every day around us, wakes only the scorn of "scoffers, walking in their own lusts, and saying, Where is the promise of His coming? for since the fathers fell asleep all things continue as they were from the beginning of the creation." *Whose*, then, is this Voice which here solemnly confirms the testimony of approaching judgment? It is surely none other than the voice of God Himself:—

"Yea, amen: I am Alpha and Omega, saith the Lord God, which is, and which was, and which is to come, the Almighty."

The "Yea, amen," are not, as our books give them, part of the seventh verse, but commence the verse following; and the words "I am Alpha and Omega, the Eternal, the Almighty," exhibit fully the One with whom men's unbelief brings them into controversy. *He* challenges all unbelief. Is He not doing so to-day, when on every side signs political, ecclesiastical, moral, and spiritual warn men, if they will but attend, that the Lord is at hand? Why, the cry itself is a sign—"Behold the Bridegroom!" Can they deny it has gone forth? Call it a mistake; call it enthusiasm; call it high treason to the world's magnificent and immense progress; still it stands written,—

"And at midnight there was a cry, 'Behold the bridegroom! go ye forth to meet him!' . . . And as they went to buy, the *bridegroom came*."

He who speaks is Alpha and Omega, whose word is the beginning and end of all speech: all that can be said is said when He has spoken; at the beginning, who spoke all things into being, and whose word, "It is done," will fix their eternal state.

He who speaks is Jehovah, the covenant-keeping God, unchangeable amid all changes, true to His threats and to His promises alike.

And He who speaks is the Almighty, lacking no power to fulfill His counsel. This is He who says, "Yea, amen," to the testimony that He who was crucified in weakness shall come again in power, and every knee shall bow to Him, and every tongue confess that Jesus Christ is Lord, to the glory of God the Father.

THE SON OF MAN AMONG THE CHURCHES.

(Rev. i. 9-20.)

WE come now to the vision which introduces the messages to the seven assemblies which with it constitute the first part of the book. The second part is similarly introduced by the vision of the fourth and fifth chapters. There is a very evident and characteristic difference between the stand-points of the two. In the one case it is John, companion with the saints in tribulation and endurance, and the scene is on earth; in the other case he is called up to heaven, and the scene is there.

The apostle writes, not as such, but as one in the common fellowship of the martyrs of Jesus, with whom testimony and suffering were linked necessarily together, the kingdom to be reached through tribulation. He being in Patmos for the word of God and for the testimony of Jesus Christ, the word of God is afresh communicated to him, and the testimony of Christ anew committed into his hands. Is it not the abiding principle, only in a more than usually eminent example, that "to him that hath shall more be given"? Did ever any one find himself so in Patmos without learning something of the revelations of Patmos? Surely it could not be. Joseph becomes in his prison the "revealer of secrets;" Moses in his wilderness banishment sees the burning bush; David in his affliction develops the sweet singer of Israel; Paul gives out the mystery of the Church from the place of his captivity; John follows only in the footsteps of these; and those who have followed him, though at a humbler distance, and with no fresh revelations because the Word of God is complete, have they no unfoldings of the Word, no nearer views of its Subject and Revealer, to more than compensate for the sorrow of the way—rhapsodies though they may seem to those of days of less demand and less enthusiasm?

Yet when the apostle puts himself down thus simply as "partaker with you in the tribulation and kingdom and patience in Jesus," does he not expect us also, and invite us, as it were, into this fellowship? and must we not in some true sense be there in order to profit aright by this communication? If we will be friends with the world, can we expect to understand or be in sympathy with the prophet of Patmos? And if it be a Christian world we think of, the words have nothing but an evil significance, if we take the significance from Scripture. But among the many tongues with which for our sins we are afflicted, how few are content to speak simply the language of Scripture!

"I *became* in the Spirit on the Lord's day," it should be. It was not simply in the right and normal Christian state in which John found himself, as so many think, but carried out of himself by the power of the Spirit; his senses closed to other things, his spirit awake to behold the things presented to him, and hear the voice that speaks to us also in him. The expression is found again in the beginning of the fourth chapter, at the opening of the vision there.

"On the Lord's day" does not mean, as some suppose, the prophetic "day of the Lord," for which there is a different expression, and which would not really apply at all to this first vision and what follows it. It is the Lord's day, the day of Christian privilege, in which in the joy of His resurrection we look back upon His death. Yet this does not surely shut out the looking forward to His coming: "ye do show forth the Lord's death till He come." This is the only right attitude for the Christian to be in, as one that expects his Lord. And this is indeed why, as it would seem, the voice that John hears speaks *behind* him, and he has to turn to see the One who speaks to him. His attention is to be directed to the present state of the Church; turned back, therefore, from the contemplation of the coming glory, to what to one so engrossed is a thing behind.

He turns, and sees seven golden candlesticks, or "lampstands," as the word is. They answer in number to the seven lamps of fire burning before the throne, the significance of which we have already seen. They represent, as we are told, the seven assemblies ($v.$ 20), and, plainly, as responsible to exhibit the light of the Spirit, during the night of the Lord's absence. The reference to the golden candlestick of the sanctuary is evident, and the contrast with it is as much intended for our notice, and should be as evident. The candlestick of the sanctuary was one only, its six branches set into the central stem, and it speaks of Christ, not the Church. The seven candlesticks are for lights, not in the sanctuary, where Christ alone is that, but in the world. And while there is a certain unity, as representing doubtless the whole Church, yet it is the Church seen, not in its dependent connection with Christ, but historically and externally, as "churches." Each lampstand is set upon its own base, stands in its own responsibility, as is manifest. To speak of the Son of Man in the midst as the invisible bond of union is surely a mistake. He is judging, not uniting.

Moreover, it is the Church in the larger, not the narrower sense here. Sardis as a whole is dead, and not alive. Christ is *outside* of Laodicea. Individually, they are local assemblies, which, as we shall see, stand each for the professing church of a certain epoch, or what in it characterizes the epoch. To see in them but Ephesus and its contemporary churches, as a large mass of interpreters still do, is indeed to be blind, and not see afar off; but the proof as to this comes naturally later. They are *golden* candlesticks, as set for the display of the glory of God (of which the gold speaks); but this is not what of necessity is displayed by them; they have the privilege and responsibility of it, but the candlestick may be, and in fact is, removed.

But the vision here is not simply, nor mainly, of the candlesticks—the churches; it is of One rather from whom alone they receive all their importance,—"One like unto the Son of man, clothed with a garment down to the foot, and girt about at the breasts with a golden girdle." The attire is that of a priest, but not in service, for the girdle is not about the loins, and the dress hangs loosely to the feet. As Priest, He is therefore a son of man, but He is more; and this the words, "One *like* unto the Son of man," indicate. Why "like unto" this, if He were indeed only this? The precise expression, moreover, is from Daniel, as what follows unites with it the features of the Ancient of days as pictured there. Thus it is the divine-human Priest, the true Mediator between God and men, as God and Man.

Yet He is not interceding. The characters which

follow show Him as when He comes to judge the world, and these are applied, in the third and fourth addresses, to the judgment of the churches. "His head and His hair were white as white wool, as snow;" this marks Him as the Ancient of days, the perfection of holy wisdom; "and His eyes were like a flame of fire"—with the same absolute holiness searching all things; "and His feet like unto white [-hot] brass, as glowing in a furnace*,"—judgment following, as inexorable against evil; "and His voice as the voice of many waters,"—the sound of that ocean which reduces man so easily to his native littleness and impotence.

Such is He who in grace has become the Son of man, but whose holiness is as unchangeable as His love is perfect. All judgment is committed unto Him, because He is the Son of man. The Church and the world alike are in His hand whose glorious uprising will bring, in a short time, summer to the earth. "And He had in His right hand seven stars; and out of His mouth goeth a sharp two-edged sword; and His countenance was as the sun shineth in its strength."

All this exhibits the Lord as just ready to come forth and take the kingdom; it is as if He had left the sanctuary, and were clothing Himself in the cloud with which He returns. And so Scripture, when urging our responsibility upon us, carries us constantly on to the day of His appearing, when the result of conduct will be brought out and manifested to all. There is a wide distinction always recognized between this and His coming to receive us to Himself, with which nothing but grace is as-

---

* On the whole, this seems the sense; but a word unknown to the lexicons perplexes the commentators.

sociated. *This* is the time when we receive the fruit of His work; and beautiful it is to see, and unspeakably comforting it is to realize, that first of all—before any thing else, His heart must have its way, and the sufficiency of His cross be shown to set the believer in full, unchallengeable possession of eternal blessedness, before ever a note of judgment has sounded, or a question as to *his* work been made. And this is plain from the fact of what the resurrection of the saint is stated to be. "It is sown in corruption"—the body of the dead saint;— "it is raised in incorruption: it is sown in dishonor; it is raised in glory: it is sown in weakness; it is raised in power." And we who are alive and remain unto the coming of the Lord, we shall be changed like them into the image of the heavenly, and caught up together with them, to meet the Lord in the air. Thus incorruption, glory, power, are ours before ever we see the face of the Lord or are manifested before His judgment-seat.

But with His *appearing* is associated the recompense of works; and thus all exhortations, warnings, encouragements, contemplate this. And so the Lord is seen in the vision here, though among the churches. In this way all is simple, and we cannot confound His being "in the midst of the assembly" with His being in the midst of the assembl*ies*, or seek for principles of gathering in what is of a totally different nature. "Who *walketh* in the midst of the seven golden candlesticks" is the Lord's own word to the church in Ephesus. How different is the thought of His *walking* in the midst from His being in the midst as the centre of gathering!

Principles of church-order and discipline are not

to be sought in the book of Revelation. It is most important to realize that God's Word, if it be beyond our systems, has a system of its own; and that He has so arranged His truth that His people may know where to look for it, and find it with more simplicity than in fact we do. Each book has its line of truth, distinct from, however much connected with, every other one. The first of Corinthians is the book of church-order and discipline. Revelation is the book of the throne, and divine judgment. And the simplest view of the vision before us agrees with this, which will only be more manifest the deeper we look.

The vision of glory overpowers the apostle: "And when I saw Him, I fell at His feet as dead. And He laid His right hand upon me, saying, 'Fear not.'" How the Christ of the gospel comes out here! What words more characteristic of Him than this, "Fear not"? "Perfect love casteth out fear," and such love is His who speaks, not alone to John in this, but to all who, realizing more His majesty than His grace, would put Him back into the distance and darkness from which He has come out to us. What *we* are is no more in question; the cross has manifested that fully: all for us lies now in what He is; and the cross has revealed that too. Word and deed witness for Him and unto us, and His right hand of power acts with His word: "Fear not; I am the First and the Last, and the Living One; and I was dead, and behold, I am alive for evermore, and have the keys of death and of hades."

Here again divine and human characters are mingled. The First is Cause of all; the Last, the end of all. "All things were created by Him and for Him:" no expression of divinity could be clearer or fuller than this. Then the Living One is necessarily also the *Source* of life,—living and life-giving. But this Living One has died, gone into death to become its Conqueror. Alive for evermore, He has the keys of death and of hades, —that is, of that which holds the body and that which holds the soul of the dead.* Thus man's condition is plumbed to the bottom, for death is the seal of that condition. Only that which meets the condition can break the seal of it.

He, then, who has been in death for us has turned its awful shadow into morning, not to bring back indeed out of its grasp the first creation, but to open for us the door into infinitely higher blessing. The gates of strength† have yielded to our Samson, and more: out of the eater comes forth meat, and out of the strong sweetness. How beyond measure is this love of One who, though the Living One, has been in death for us! How rich have we become through this voluntary poverty! And "He who descended is the same also who ascended up, far above all heavens, that He might fill all things."

He goes on:—

"Write, then"—with this assurance,—"the things which thou hast seen, and the things which are, and the things which shall be after these; the mystery of the seven stars which thou sawest in My

---

* A similar connection of death and hades is found in the twentieth chapter: "Death and hades delivered up the dead which were in them"— the one, the soul; the other, the body. "Hades" is never "the grave," as our common version sometimes renders it, and never "hell," which is its alternate rendering. "Thou wilt not leave My soul in hell," as spoken of the Lord (Acts ii. 27, 31), agrees with neither. The distinction in these terms shows very simply that it is the body only which really dies, or over which death has its proper empire.

† "Gaza" means "the strong."

right hand, and the seven golden candlesticks. The seven stars are the angels of the seven churches, and the seven candlesticks are the seven churches."

These words give us the division of the book. "The things which are" must needs apply to the seven assemblies and their state. "The things which shall be after these"—not "hereafter," which is too vague,—to the things which follow from the fourth chapter on. This is evident, whatever view we take of the interpretation of these sections. With the first of them only have we to do here,— "the things which are," or present things.

Present, then, in what sense? present at that time merely, and now long past? or, as many now consider, present still? Do the addresses to the churches give only such lessons for us here to-day as must necessarily be found in what is said to Christian gatherings of by-gone days by One who with perfect wisdom, knowledge, holiness, and love speaks to just such as we are? Or is there, beside all this, as many believe, a more precise, designed correspondence between these seven Asiatic assemblies and as many successive periods in the history of the Church at large—a prophetic teaching for all time, until the Lord come, and our path here is ended? Let us look briefly at what has been urged as to this latter view.

Against, it has been urged that the addresses are not given as a prophecy of the future, but simply *as* to churches then existing, now long passed away. This is undoubtedly the most forcible objection that has been made; for imagination is unholy license in the things of God, and the addresses have not the general style of prophecy, as must be admitted. We do right, then, to be watchful here.

But answer has been made to this: in the first place, that at the very beginning of the book, we have the whole of it called a *prophecy:* "Blessed is he that readeth and they that hear the words of the book of this *prophecy*, and keep the things that are written therein." It seems, therefore, that we *have* distinct warrant for holding the addresses to be prophetic, and that we should rather require it for refusing them this place.

Beside this, the disguise which confessedly they assume may be accounted for. The Christian's privilege and duty are, to be always expecting his Lord. He who says in his heart, My Lord delayeth His coming, is a "wicked servant." There was to be left room for this expectancy, as the best help against discouragement, the most effectual remedy against settling down in the world, the best means of fixing the eyes upon Christ and things above. This was not to beget false hope or encourage mistake, for the time of the Lord's return they were assured they did *not* know: "Watch, *for* ye know not when the time is." But thus to put before men a prophecy of a long earthly history for the Church would be to destroy what was to be a main characteristic of Christians, to take out of their hands the lamp of testimony to the world itself, the virgin's lamp lighted to go forth to meet her Lord.

And it is blessed to see that now, if, in the end of the days, the full meaning is being revealed, and we are shown how much of the road we have actually traveled, the effect is, after all the long delay, to *encourage* expectation, not to damp it. That we are nearing the end is sure; that any part of the road remains before us to be trodden, we have no assurance. The very thing which to past generations would have been an evil too fully to disclose is now for us as great and manifest a gain.

For the prophetic view is further urged the constant emphatic appeal to our attention with which every one of these addresses ends. Was it only for men of that day and place that it is written, "He that hath an ear, let him hear what the Spirit saith unto the churches"? No part of Scripture is so emphasized beside. Again, are there no candlesticks amid which Christ walks except those of these Asiatic churches? The very number 7 is characteristic of this book, as it is significant of completeness also. As the seven Spirits speak of the complete energy of the one blessed Spirit, do not the seven churches stand for the varied aspects of the one Church of God on earth?

And to them as representatives of this one Church is the whole book committed,—not for their own use merely, but for ours. As John is the representative servant, so the churches are representatives of the Church.

But the great proof of the correctness of the prophetic view is (what as yet it would be premature at any length to enter on,) the real correspondence between the picture given of the seven churches and the well-known history of the professing church. We have the successive steps of its decline—first hidden, then external; the judaizing process by which it was transformed from a company of saved and heavenly people into a mixed multitude uncertain of heaven, clinging to the certainties of earth; away from God, and committing the sacred things, for which they are too unclean, to an official class of go-betweens. Then open union with the world, once persecuting, now friendly, Balaam-teachers for hire promoting and celebrating it. Then the reign of Jezebel, inspired and infallible, her cup full of abominations and filthiness of her fornication. Then Protestantism, soon forgetting the things which it had heard, sunk into its grave of nationalism, though with a separate remnant as ever, dear to God. Then an era of revival and blessing, the Spirit of God working freely, outside of sectarian boundary-lines, uniting to Christ and to one another. Then, alas! collapse and threat of removal, Christ rejected and outside, the lukewarmness of water ready to be spued out of His mouth.

Such is the picture: does it appeal to us? In the midst of all this, in the central church, the centre of the darkness, *at midnight* surely, there begins a cry, faint though at first, but gathering strength as the time goes on, "Go ye out to meet Him!" In Thyatira first, "Hold fast till I come!" To Sardis, "I will come on thee as a thief." To Philadelphia, —more as in haste now,—" I come *quickly*." Then Laodicea, and the end!

Does this appeal to us? What follows then? Briefly: a scene in heaven, and a redemption-song before the throne; a Lamb slain, who as Judah's Lion unseals the seven-sealed book; churches no more on earth, but once more Jews and Gentiles; and out of these, a multitude who come out of the great tribulation; until, after the marriage of the Lamb has taken place in heaven, its gates unclose, and the white-horsed Rider and His armies come out to the judgment of the earth.

This to many even yet may read as strange as any fiction. I cannot of course enter on it now. But there are those who object that by this view the relative importance of events is quite inverted. Two chapters give us the whole course of christendom; the largest part of the book by far is taken up with the details of some seven years after the Church is removed to heaven: why so rapid a survey of what so immediately concerns us?—so lengthy a relation of what will not take place till after the saints of the present time have passed from the scene?

But how often are we mistaken in the relative importance of things! God seeth not as man seeth; and the common view which appropriates seal after seal to the succession of Roman emperors, trumpet after trumpet to the inroads of Goths and Vandals, vial after vial to the French revolution and Napoleonic wars, has surely missed His estimate of importance. But more: the events which fill so many chapters have indeed for us the very greatest significance. The time is that "end of the age" which is the harvest of the world; it is the judgment for which all around is ripening, and in which every thing comes out as He who judges sees it. Is it not for us of the greatest possible moment to see that final, conclusive end of what is now often so pretentious and delusive? Here we may surely gather, if we will, lessons of sanctification of the most practical nature. Indeed we are sanctified by the truth; and whatever is of the truth will sanctify.

THE ADDRESSES TO THE CHURCHES.

Ephesus, the Decline of the Church.
(Rev. ii. 1-7.)

IT is not in any wise as being the metropolitan church of Asia that we find Ephesus first addressed. This, which has been the thought of many, has assuredly no countenance from the Word. The Church of God, which is Christ's body, is not composed of churches, but of *members*, united together by that blessed Spirit which unites all to Christ the Head. Hence, the "churches," or "assemblies," are only local gatherings of so many Christians as find themselves, in the providence of God, actually together. Each of these is, according to Scripture, the Church in that place, as the true text reads invariably in these two chapters. This expanded would be, as in the epistle to the Corinthians, the "Church of God" in such or such a place. The place adds nothing to this title, nor is one gathering of its members superior or inferior in privilege or responsibility to any other.

It is true that the Church of God is not only designated as the body of Christ in Scripture, but also as the House of God—the place of His abode. But here, again, it is the Church at large that is so. There are not *bodies* of Christ, but "one body." Just so there are not *houses* of God, but "the house." In each place, the local assembly *represents* the Church at large, as being indeed the local Church, —what of the Church at large is in that place. And this may vary, from time to time, in numbers, spirituality, and many other ways: and thus there will be peculiar local responsibilities, differences, and privileges, as is recognized in the chapters before us; but the *standing* in each the same.

No doubt we must not forget, as indeed we are not allowed to forget, the immense difference between profession and reality. A dead Sardis could not be in reality of the body of Christ at all. But this is nevertheless what the Church means, if it means any thing according to Scripture. The professing church is this, or it is a lie; and how solemn a lie!

No, the reason why Ephesus stands at the head of those addressed here is of another nature. It is to be found, not in any external supremacy over the rest, but in its original spiritual eminency, and as the church to which the truth as to the Church had been first of all committed, and this, *not* as to its order upon earth, but as to its *heavenly character*.

The Ephesians had been addressed by Paul, as now at a much later date they are by the Lord Himself; and it is in comparing the tenor of these two epistles that we find the significance of its being Ephesus, and no other, with which we here begin. The epistle to the Ephesians is that which carries us up to the height of Christian position, quickened out of death in trespasses and sins as following the course of a world governed by Satan, —and quickened with Christ, raised up together, and seated together in heavenly places in Christ Jesus. This is individual, true of all believers, if there were no Church at all; but God has done more, and as united to Christ by His Spirit, we are members of His body, the fullness of Him who filleth all in all. Both as body of Christ and habitation of God, the apostle develops the doctrine of the Church in this epistle; while in the fifth chapter he carries us back to the beginning, and shows us once more the Church under the type of Eve, espoused to Him who will yet present her to Himself a glorious Church.

These are the truths, given to all saints, no doubt, but of which the Ephesian disciples were counted worthy to be the first recipients. And the apostle could write to them in this way as "faithful" ones, communicating what the spiritual state at Corinth or Galatia or among the Hebrews would have hindered his making known to them (1 Cor. iii. 1, 2; Heb. v. 11–14). If Corinth headed a list of churches declined from first love, we should not marvel; but can we fail to realize the significance of its being Ephesus, the special custodian of the truth of the Church itself, in its heavenly reality?

The style of the address is, at the very outset, a sign of distance, as unusual as full of significance on the part of the Lord toward His people. There can be no proper question that the churches are themselves addressed, for this is directly stated at the conclusion of each epistle: "He that hath an ear, let him hear what the Spirit saith unto the churches." Yet the Lord's words are, "To the *angel* of the church" in each case, and to this the style of the address fully corresponds. The responsibility of every thing that is wrong is ascribed to the angel; it is he that has them that hold the doctrine of Balaam, or of the Nicolaitanes; it is he that suffers the woman Jezebel; it is he who is threatened with the removal of his candlestick. It is quite plain that he represents the church in some way, and it is urged that the word "angel" has this force of a representative wherever it does not stand for the heavenly beings so called, who though higher naturally in the scale of creation, yet minister to the heirs of salvation.

The word "angel" means, as every one knows, simply "messenger," and is applied to the spirits of heaven as God's messengers to men. But it is plain that the messenger does *represent*, so far as his errand is concerned, the one who sends him. "He that receiveth whomsoever I send receiveth Me; and he that receiveth Me receiveth Him that sent Me." Thus this meaning of the word is easily derived from its original one.

However, the representative character of the angel here is plain. It is natural enough that the advocates of episcopal or presbyterian order should find, as they do with equal facility, the bishop or the pastor in this representative-angel. In Scripture elsewhere it is impossible to find either of these things, largely as they are now believed in, and therefore as impossible, if we cleave to Scripture, to read them in here. Apostles, prophets, evangelists, pastors, and teachers we read of as gifts to the Church at large, though a Peter might especially address himself to the circumcision as a Paul to the Gentiles. But where have we the apostle of this place or that? Just as little have we the pastor of this church or of that. Bishops and deacons, it is true, we do find with a local office; still, never the bishop of an assembly, but the bishops; with whom it is allowed that the elders were identical.* "They ordained them elders in every church" (Acts xiv. 23). The one representative

---
*Acts xx. 17, 28 ("overseers," the same word as "bishops"); Tit. i. 5, 7.

of each assembly supposed to be signified by the angel cannot be found in Scripture elsewhere.

Ephesus had its bishop-elders long before this, as we see in Acts xx. Its diocesan bishop at the time when this was written tradition makes the apostle John himself! He, then, cannot be the angel to whom he is told to write, nor will the search be more successful in other directions. All that can be truly urged is that this address to the angel is in accord with what we know to have been the state of things a century or so after the time of Revelation. And this is quite in accord with its sad significance.

We have epistles to individuals, as to Timothy and Titus, never to the church *through* these. We have the epistle to the saints in Christ at Philippi, *with* the bishops and deacons, not to the bishops and deacons for the church. The constant method of address is to the church as such; and suppose here the "angel" were to stand for the bishops of Ephesus, how evident would it make the contrast between the first epistle (perhaps of thirty-odd years back,) and this second one!

No more the direct address of familiar intimacy, though now from the very lips of the priestly Mediator. Yet His love has not changed; the change, then, has been in His people. The strange style is from One whom they have treated as a stranger. Sadly it tells of the close of the old intercourse which he who seeks will find as invited to, if it were Laodicea, "I will come in to him, and will sup with him, and he with Me." Turn to the Acts, and see how free, how tender, how as a thing of course—which deepens, not lessens, the wonder of it,—this intercourse can be. Or look back even to Genesis, if you will, and learn how truly God's last thought is His first thought. It is man who has driven back these approaches upon God's part, and forced Him into the cloud and darkness. The Church has but repeated the old history, though now, because the Light has come, the darkness is more strange and terrible.

But it is important to ask, Has He for our sins, then, given up His Church to this? and does the "angel" speak of distance maintained on His part toward even one, the least of all His saints? With whom, as with the angel, does He still speak face to face? Is it with an official class who interpret Him to those beneath them? Does the sun, as in winter-time, no longer reach the valley-bottoms, but only gild the tops of the hills with light? or is it to some gifted men that Christ reveals Himself, who, as planets, shed the little of His radiance they can reflect on others? Ah, no; it is not men of gift, still less an official class, who are indicated by the angel. The heart of those who know their Lord shall answer, It is not. No; nor, alas! is it any longer the church as a whole either; very far from that! Read the superscription "to the angel" in the light of the subscription, "*He that hath an ear, let him hear what the Spirit saith unto the churches,*" and you will find that still the question of who are nearest Christ is answered by another, who has ears and eyes and heart for Him. He still speaks as of old to those who as of old listen. His ways, His attitude, His heart, can know no change. The stars that shine in His firmament are the overcomers of the darkness, not of the world now merely, but of the church,—planets that know their orbit and are held by their centre, and shine by the light of Him who shines on them. "The

EPHESUS.

seven stars are the angels of the seven churches."

If to the opened ear Christ speaks, it is plain that the responsibility of hearing is as much as ever that of all. None are released from it. And yet it is not to the mass that He can speak any more, or the overcoming would not be in the church, as it clearly is. Already it is the few that listen, and the constraint in the Lord's manner is but the indication of His sense of this.

It may seem strange, however, that if the "angel" stands for these who listen to Christ's voice, He should hold them responsible, as we have already seen, for all the evil in the church with which they are connected. How, it may be asked, can He thus burden with the sins of the whole the few who have an ear to hear? The responsibility of an official class is more readily recognized than of those who may be, however spiritual, the feeblest possible to accomplish any change in the condition of things around them. But this is not the question. It is true we are powerless to alter the general state. The ebb-tide of ruin can be stemmed by no hand of ours, and this feebleness of ours may seem an available plea to withdraw us from responsibility as to it. But not so teaches the word of the Lord. Our associations are here distinctly recognized as part of our general condition. We are to "depart from evil," not be unequally yoked with unbelievers, purge ourselves from vessels to dishonor, and follow righteousness, faith, love, peace, *with* those that call upon the Lord out of a pure heart. For association with evil we are therefore ever responsible. It may be said that such principles, carried fully out, would involve a very narrow path and a wholesale giving up of spheres of usefulness. But be it so or be it not so, it is not ours to choose. Our path is defined for us. "To obey is better than sacrifice, and to hearken than the fat of rams; for *rebellion* is as the sin of witchcraft, and stubbornness as iniquity and idolatry."

Yes, "rebellion"! How gladly would we call an obedience limited by our own wills by some lighter name than that! Yet what else, in truth, was that which brought out Saul's true character, and lost the kingdom to him and to his seed forever? What he left undone was a mere trifle to what he did. And the sheep and oxen had been spared to sacrifice to the Lord. What fairer excuse have people now to offer for much disobedience—evil plausibly intended to bring forth good? And how hard is it to understand that while we may obey in much that in fact costs us little, the true test of *obedience* is just in that in which we are called to renounce our wills and our wisdom, perhaps to forfeit the esteem and companionship of others, by doing what has only the Word of God to justify it and must wait for eternity to find right appreciation!

But now to listen to His word to Ephesus, who "holdeth the stars in His right hand, and walketh in the midst of the seven golden candlesticks." The one point of the address is plain, and it is left to stand in sufficient, solemn, decisive contrast with all else that is unmingled commendation. Works, labor, patience, abhorrence of that which is evil, trying fearlessly those who put forth the highest claims, bearing for Christ's name's sake, and not fainting,—all this, put in the balance with one solemn charge: "Thou hast left thy first love." And this follows: "Repent, and do the first works, or else I will come unto thee, and will remove thy candlestick out of its place, except thou repent."

Let us look at these things more closely. Their interest for us is of the deepest, for upon this one root of evil has grown all that has ever been in the Church's long decline through the centuries which have intervened between that day and this. And this it is which, as we see, brings about her removal from the place of witness for Christ on earth. This it is too which is the secret of decline in every individual Christian. For us all, it should rouse the earnest, heart-searching inquiry, "Is it I?" For, if it can be truly said of any of us, "Thou hast left thy first love," it is vain for us to think that other things can be really judged. The single eye is wanted even to see them with. We must get back to this, or there is no real recovery. Two masters, the Lord says Himself, we cannot serve.

How much there was He could commend at Ephesus! "I know thy works" is commendation clearly. But not only had they works, they *labored*. Do you think there are really so many of whom it could be said, they *labor?* We have recognized, what is so precious to understand, that we have our different spheres of service, and that there is no mere secular work, if really done for Christ. But to labor is to work with energy—to "toil," as the Revision gives it. How many of us *toil* for Christ?

Then they had patience—endurance. Many begin well, like the Galatians, but in the face of unforeseen difficulties give way. It is the mark of divine work that it endures. Human energy quickly spends itself: faith draws upon a stock that never decreases. It was true faith that wrought in these Ephesian saints.

Patience, too, is apt to degenerate into a toleration, more or less, of evil. Finding it on every hand, and no where perfection, the very contact with it is apt to dull the spiritual sense. Charity would fain put also the mildest construction upon every thing. We are bidden to "*take forth* the precious from the vile," but we learn to tolerate the vile because of the precious. We become liberal where we have no right. The Lord praises the Ephesians for the opposite conduct: "Thou canst not bear them which are evil." And where there was the very highest assumption, they did not fear to test it: "Thou hast tried them which say they are apostles, and are not, and hast found them liars."

But more, it was true love to Christ which wrought in all this: "Thou hast patience, and hast borne for My name's sake, and hast not wearied." Yet here it follows: "Nevertheless I have against thee,"—not "somewhat," as if it were a little,—"that thou hast left thy *first* love."

But how dreadful a dishonor to Christ is this, to lose one's first love! It is as if at first sight He was more than He proved on longer acquaintance! Is not here the very germ of final apostasy? I do not, of course, mean that the Lord will allow any of His redeemed to be lost out of His hand. "*God* is faithful, who hath called us into the fellowship of His Son Jesus Christ;" and this faithfulness of God is our security: "the gifts and calling of God are without repentance." Nor only so; if we are born of God, we have that within us which cannot suffer us to become what we were before: "Whosoever is born of God doth not commit sin; *for his seed remaineth in him:* and he cannot sin, because he is born of God." Yet while this is true on the one side, in the child of God as identified with the divine nature by which he is such,—still, on the other side, it is no less true that in the believer also there remains yet the old nature. In him still there is that which lusts against the Spirit, and only if ye "walk in the Spirit, ye shall not fulfill the lust of the flesh."

Here is what makes the world to us such a battle-field. Capable, on the one hand, of enjoying all the joys of heaven; capable, on the other, of being attracted by that which lies under the power of the wicked one,—the eye affecting the heart,—day by day we are solicited by that which daily lies before us and from which there is no escape. Our danger here is first of all distraction, some gain to us which is not loss for Christ, or that dulling of the spiritual sense we just now spoke of; the dust of the way settles upon the glass in which Faith sees her eternal possessions. Our remedy is the presence of Him who with basin and towel would refresh His pilgrims, cleansing away the travel-stains that they may have part with Him.

Here alone first love is maintained. Here, in His presence, we learn His mind. The holiness of truth is accomplished in us. What is unseen but eternal asserts its power. The illusions of the prince of this world pass from us. The glory of Christ is revealed, and the eye here also affects the heart; He becomes for us more and more the light in which we see light, the Sun which rules the day, not only enlightening but life-giving: the light in which we walk is the "light of life."

Now here, as I have said, first love cannot but be maintained. Who could be daily in His presence, ministered to by Him, having part with Him, and yet grow cool in response to His love? It is impossible. Where this is the case, intimacy has not been kept up. We have not permitted the basin and towel to do its work. Assurance of heart before Him has been replaced by an uneasy sense of unfitness for His presence, the true causes of which we have not been willing fully to face, and for which the remedy has therefore not been found.

In this state there may be yet much work and labor and zeal, and true love at the bottom. Fruit may be on the tree, plentiful as ever, but not to the Master's taste as once, not *ripened* in the Sun. Form and bloom and beauty may be little lacking: this was the state at Ephesus. But the Lord says, "Repent, and do the *first* works."

What is the test, then, of "first love"? Not "work"—activity in outward service; this they had at Ephesus: not even "labor," for this too they had: no, nor yet "endurance"—though a more manifest sign than either of divine power in the soul. Not zeal against evil, nor boldness to examine and refuse the highest pretensions; not suffering even for Christ's name, and that unwearied. All this is good and acceptable to God, and the Ephesians had it all, and yet says the Lord, "I have against thee that thou hast left thy first love."

What, then, is the test of first love? It is in the *complete satisfaction of the heart by its object.* You know what power often there is in a new thing to take possession of one for the time being. And in first love, it is characteristic that it engrosses the subject of it. The Lord claims again and again the power to give this complete satisfaction of heart to His people. "He that drinketh of this water shall thirst again: but he that drinketh of the water that I shall give him shall never thirst; but the water that I shall give him shall be in him a fountain of water springing up unto eternal life." "He that cometh unto Me shall never hunger, and he that believeth on Me shall never thirst." "If any man thirst, let him come unto Me, and drink. He that believeth on Me, as the Scripture hath said, out of his belly shall flow rivers of living water."

Now this it is that will give a peculiar character to the life which nothing else will. It is of this the apostle speaks when he says, "The life which I now live in the flesh I live by the faith of the Son of God, who loved me, and gave Himself for me." It is this satisfaction with a heavenly object of which he is giving the effect when he says, "This one thing I do: forgetting the things which are behind, and reaching forth unto that which is before, I press toward the mark for the prize of the high calling of God in Christ Jesus." "What things were gain to me, those I counted loss for Christ. Yea, doubtless, and I count all things but loss for the excellency of the knowledge of Christ Jesus my Lord; for whom I have suffered the loss of all things, and do count them but dung, that I may win Christ."

This is the secret of happiness, who can doubt? That for which he counted all else dung and loss must have given him surpassing, supreme happiness. And happiness such as this, derived from nothing in the world, is power over the world. The back is upon it. The prize is elsewhere. The steps hasten upon a path that glows with the light of heaven. Holiness is found, as it only can be found, in heavenliness.

Such was the apostle, and Christianity is nothing else to-day. Blessed be God, it is not something either to be found far on in the Christian course, but at the beginning. It is *first* love which has these characteristics. In Christ Himself, at once for present need, all fullness is found, as His own words declare. "He that cometh to Me shall never hunger, and he that believeth on Me shall never thirst." It is in drinking of other streams that the old thirst comes back upon him who does so. "The lust of the flesh, the lust of the eyes, and the pride of life" are "all that is of the world." He that drinketh of this water shall thirst again. So the world holds its own by their very misery.

But we are not speaking of the men of the world. It is to Ephesus—to the saints there—the Lord is speaking: to those to whom the heavenly truth had been unvailed, the depositaries of it upon the earth, the representatives of the Church at large. And it is to the Church at large, through Ephesus, that this is now addressed. Can any doubt the truth of such an application? Would that it were even possible! but we have not to go beyond the New Testament itself to find the application confirmed, and to hear the prophetic announcement of still further departure even to the very end. The epistles of Paul, long before Revelation, reveal a state of things already beginning, such as it is hard to realize of those early days. In one of the very earliest comes the statement, "The mystery of iniquity doth already work," and "that day"—the day of the Lord—"shall not come, except there come a falling away first." The two epistles to the Corinthians are the next in time to those to the Thessalonians, and at Corinth there is sin such as was not named among the Gentiles, with divisions beginning, and some denying the resurrection of the dead. Next, Galatia is backsliding from Christ under the law, and receiving another gospel. Then, to the Romans he has to write, bidding them avoid those who cause divisions and offenses, contrary to the doctrine they have learned. His next epistles are written from a Roman prison: but here he has to say of those to whom he had written that their faith was spoken of through the whole world, "All seek their own, not the things of Jesus Christ." The epistles to Timothy may close the sorrowful picture: "At my first answer no man stood with me, but all forsook me:"—Paul ends his course like His Master. Not alone at Rome: "This thou knowest, that all they which are in Asia have departed from me.". But now all that will be vessels of honor, fit for the Master's use, are to purge themselves from the vessels to dishonor. Evil men and seducers shall wax worse and worse; and in the last days perilous times shall come, men throwing the Christian dress over their unchanged natures, having the form of godliness but denying the power thereof. From such they must turn away.

Peter, John, Jude, add each some fresh feature to the terrible picture; but we need not dwell upon it more. We see the professing church is ruined and doomed. The true-hearted are already a remnant. By the "many antichrists" then present, the latest apostle decides that it is the last time. We look beyond even the Ephesian epistle here to see the hopelessness of the thought of any general repentance. And the word abides, " I will take away thy candlestick out of its place, except thou repent."

The promise to the overcomer meanwhile rings out its words of cheer, "To him that overcometh will I give to eat of the tree of life which is in the midst of the paradise of My God." There is to be no yielding, however the difficulties of the way increase. God's stars shine by night as by day, and the darkness only makes them more apparent. It is no new thing, the darkness. The path of faith has been in all ages essentially alike. The incentive comes from beyond, and no sorrows of the way can mar the beauty of the paradise of God.

The tree of life in the garden of old meant clearly *dependent* life, which was to be ministered to Adam by its means. In himself, innocent as he was, there was no continuance apart from this. God would thus remind him of the essential mutability and dependence of the creature—a safe and wholesome lesson.

For us too, redeemed by the precious blood of Christ, and possessors of eternal life, this is still life in dependence; and herein is the secret of its eternity. It is life in Christ, in the Son who is alone essential Life. Of the fruits of this we shall partake forever. How suited an appeal to those in the state addressed in this epistle! It is failure in maintaining the place of dependence, in receiving out of His fullness in whom dwells all the fullness of the Godhead bodily, that is the very secret of their condition. The mind, the will, the heart, are in independence. He who keeps close to Christ overcomes. How suited, then, the encouragement to one who knows already the blessedness of this place, to look on to the time when in far other circumstances the full results of it shall be attained,—when eternally it will be ours to know the joy of that dependence which secures His ministry of love to us forever! "For of Him, and through Him, and to Him, are all things; to whom be glory forever. Amen."

Smyrna: the Double Assault of the Enemy.
(Rev. ii. 8-11.)

THE decline of the Church opens the way for the power of the enemy to display itself; and the assault is a double one—from without and within at the same moment. The result is, however, very different in the two cases. The outside assault is failure, for it is impossible that the Lord should leave His saints to be subdued by power beyond their own; while the defeat of Satan's wiles is another matter. Here they must put on the whole armor of God, that they may be able to stand in the evil day. We shall be able from this point to trace an instructive correspondence between the history of the kingdom as developed in the first four parables of the thirteenth of Matthew and that of the Church in the first four addresses here. There also the failure (or partial success) of the good seed is the first fact insisted on, and then follows the inroad of the enemy. The two are put in connection by the words, "*While men slept*, the enemy came and sowed tares among the wheat."

Here, as not in the parable, the open assault is connected with the secret and inward one, and we shall see, if the Lord permit, that the two are really parts of one whole, the one favoring the other. The roar of the lion is well calculated to frighten souls into the secret snare; and in this regard we could not say that it had no success. God, on the other hand, suffers it to alarm His people into their place of refuge; and with true souls this would be its effect. The test is permitted to manifest the condition of things, and it is His way to allow such tests ever, as in all dispensations we shall find to be the case. Alas, for the invariable result as to man! but He will be glorified through all.

Let us look briefly first at the open attack which, as it makes a figure in ecclesiastical history, gives us a date to attach to the period before us. Even those who do not see the historical application of these addresses generally admit a reference in the "tribulation ten days" to ten persecutions under the Roman emperors. That there were just so many can hardly be made out, and the expression need not be pressed so literally. It is quite plain, nevertheless, how the address to Smyrna suits this period, which lasted from Domitian's persecution now begun, right on to Constantine,—that is, for over two centuries. This was undoubtedly the martyr-age of the Church as a whole, although the persecution may have been more bitter locally in other periods. The power of Rome, absolute as it was throughout her wide-spread empire, when wielded against Christianity, left little room for escape any where, while as a heathen power it was antagonistic to all that professed the name. The address to Smyrna, therefore, comes exactly in place here; and the very name—"myrrh,"—used, as this was, in the embalming of the dead, reminds us of how "precious in the sight of the Lord is the death of His saints."

Indeed this is manifest all through the address. It is as "the First and the Last, who" yet "was dead, and is alive," that He speaks to them. In the voice of One who though divine stooped down to death and is come out of it, and who gives them thus only to drink of the cup of which He has drunk, and to be baptized with the baptism wherewith He has been baptized. How fully can *He* say, "I know thy tribulation"! and how sweet the commendation, "I know thy poverty, *but thou art rich*"! Yea, "blessed are ye when men shall revile you and persecute you, and say all manner of evil against you falsely for My sake: rejoice, and be exceeding glad."

The times are so changed, we look back with a shudder to the sufferings endured at these times, unable, as it would seem, to comprehend the blessedness of this link of sorrow with the Man of sorrows. And yet we can see, even through the lapse of intervening centuries, how the "Spirit of glory and of God" rested upon these sufferers. The Captain of their salvation was at all charges for them, and as the sufferings of Christ abounded in them, so their consolation also abounded by Christ. They had heard His voice saying, "Fear not those things which thou shalt suffer; be thou faithful unto death, and I will give thee a crown of life."

Multitudes were thus faithful; but we are apt to form a wrong estimate of the times gilded by the glory of this faithfulness. Just so, in the address to Smyrna, the Lord's undisguised and tender sympathy with His own under persecution hides from the eyes of many the evil which is pointed out by Him as there in terms of indignant reprobation. By most, "The blasphemy of those who say they are Jews and are not" is supposed to refer to the well-known and constant enmity of the unbelieving nation against the followers of their rejected Messiah. It is evident that they are treated as outside of those whom the Lord is here addressing, and that the "angel" is not, as elsewhere, charged with responsibility for their presence. But so neither are the Nicolaitanes, or the followers of Balaam at

Pergamos, or the woman Jezebel at Thyatira, addressed directly by the Lord, while no one doubts, nor can it be doubted, that they formed part of the respective assemblies. The question of responsibility is a more difficult one, and we shall be obliged to consider it a little later.

"Those who say they are Jews and are not" might be taken, no doubt, as parallel to the apostle's words that "they are not all Israel which are of Israel," and "he is not a Jew which is one outwardly." Still it would not seem that they would so much need to profess themselves such, if they were of the nation really; nor does it seem that so much would be made of the falseness of a profession for which there was after all a certain justification. If this, too, were really the character of those in question, there is no significance, that one can see, in the appearance here as regards any divine judgment of the churches.

The moment we realize the adversaries here spoken of as *Judaizers within* the professing church, we find that we have in them as much the formal root of decline as in first love left we had the internal principle. The mention of them at this point becomes a necessity really for the perfecting of the picture of what has in fact taken place. With the heart-failure first reproved, it is the key to the condition of things which is all around us, it characterizes the state of ruin which has come in. It is this which has robbed Christians of the enjoyment of their place with God; it is this which has put them back into the world out of which grace had called them; it is this which has built up once more a priestly hierarchy as necessary mediators between a mixed and carnal people and a far-off God. It is this which is indeed the triumph of the great adversary, although God be as ever sovereign above it; and no name could more fitly designate the instruments by which he has degraded the Church of God into the synagogue than the name by which the Lord brands them here—"the *synagogue of Satan.*"

The title precisely indicates the change accomplishing. The Church of God is indeed every way the precise opposite of Satan's synagogue. The word which we translate "church" is, as well known, properly "assembly,"—a title which, if it had been retained in our common version, would have prevented the possibility of some significant perversions. The assembly could not be confounded, for instance, with a material building, though spiritually indeed God's house. Nor could it be the clergy merely, as from Romanism, though by more than Romanists, it has been made to signify. These applications of the term are but indications of the very change of which we are now speaking. The assembly of God in Scripture is Christ's body, the fellowship of those who are His members, and of none but these. It is true that the responsibility of this place may be assumed by those who are not such, and so we find the assembly in Sardis pronounced by the Lord to be dead, and not alive. Yet in the divine thought this is what the assembly is, and at the Lord's table every one declares this: "we being many are one bread, one body, for we are all partakers of that one bread."

Thus it is the assembly, or gathering, of those who are Christ's members, *called out* by grace out of the world, and this is what the word used means.

"*Ecclesia*" is the assembly of those called out; while "*synagogue*" means merely a "gathering *together*," no matter of whom. The latter, of course, was the Jewish word, as the former the Christian; and they exactly express the difference between the respective gatherings. Christ died, "not for the nation [of Israel] only, but also that He might gather together in one the children of God which were scattered abroad." Outside of the Jewish fold He had sheep to bring in, and inside of it not all were His sheep. Judaism did not unite the children of God as such, as is plain, and its separation was not of believers from the world, but of Israel from the Gentiles. So, consequently, the children of God were not given their place with God, and had no Spirit of adoption—did not cry, "Abba, Father." God was saying, "I am a father to *Israel*"—and this which comes nearest to Christian knowledge shows in fact the contrast. Relationship was by birth, not *new* birth, and did not mean justification and eternal life, as it means now. Those who belonged to the family of God might perish forever, and those outside His family might be saved eternally.

Judaism decided the eternal state of none. As a dispensation of law, it could give no assurance, it could preach no justification. For if the law says on the one hand "the man that doeth these things shall live in them," it says also "there is none righteous—no, not one." And that was not merely the effect, but the designed effect: "We know that whatsoever the law saith it saith to them that are under the law, that every mouth may be stopped, and all the world become guilty before God." It was thus ordained for the probation of man, a probation necessary before grace could be proclaimed; but on this account it could but as a means of salvation bear witness to its own incompetency. The announcement of that *new* covenant under which Israel's sins and iniquities would be no more remembered was such a witness.

Thus, as the law could not justify, it could not bring to God. The unrent vail is the characteristic of Judaism as the rent vail is of Christianity. "Thou canst not see My face, for there shall no man see Me and live" is the contrasted utterance to His who says, "He that hath seen Me hath seen the Father;" as is "who can by no means clear the guilty" the opposite declaration to that of the gospel, that we "believe on Him who justifieth the ungodly." The darkness is passed from the face of God, and the true light—for God is light—shineth. We walk, therefore, in the light, as God is in the light, and have fellowship one with another, and the blood of Jesus Christ His Son cleanseth from all sin.

The Judaizing of the Church means therefore, first of all, the putting God back (if that were possible; possible for our hearts it is) into the darkness from which He has come forth; replacing the peace which was made for us upon the cross with the old legal conditions and the old uncertainty. Darker than the old darkness this, inasmuch as the Christ for whom they only looked is come, and come but to put His seal upon it all: come, and gone back, and declared little more, at any rate, than was said before, and only definitively shut out hope of any further revelation.

Thus in the Judaizing gospel confidence is presumption. "No man knoweth whether he is worthy of favor or hatred" is quoted as if from Paul instead of Solomon. In fact, is not Ecclesiastes scripture as well as Romans? and will you make scripture to contradict scripture? Did not Christ say, also, "I came not to destroy the law, but to fulfill"? and ought we not to follow Him?

Peace is of course lost, and in the dread uncertainty that every-where prevails, who can distinguish any longer between God's children and the world? Yet Judaism had its family of God, its ordinances which separated them from those around, its absolutions by the way which encouraged hope, while yet, as continually needed, they sanctioned no presumptuous assurance. The Christian family could still exist, baptism and the supper of the Lord take the place of the old Jewish ordinances, the Christian ministry conform to the Levitical priesthood, and the Church become more venerable by her identification with that of the saints from the beginning, and richer for the inheritance of all the promises from Abraham down.

This is assuredly the transformation that has taken place, and that began so early that we have but few traces of the manner of its accomplishment, or its agents either. We open the page of uninspired history, and the terrible transformation has been already achieved. In fact, so fully, that it presents the only difficulty in the application of the address before us to the period of heathen persecution. One would hardly suppose from the Lord's words here that (as it would appear) the witnesses for Him, faithful to death as they were, were nevertheless thoroughly implicated in this descent from Christianity to Judaism. It would hardly seem as if the "blasphemy" or slander of this Jewish party

SMYRNA.

had been directed against them, or that the Lord could ignore their reception of these satanic doctrines.*

The real question is, how far could we expect the history, meagre in proportion to its earliness, and which has come down to us through centuries of darkness and hostility to the truth, to reveal to us the struggle with these Jewish teachers, so generally successful as they were? I do not think we could expect it. An age which would forge the names of those in repute to spurious documents, often with the express design of giving authority to some favorite doctrine, would hardly hesitate to remove the too suspicious traces of opposition to prevalent views and practices from the history of the early church. That there should have been no such struggle is scarcely to be credited. And the words of our Lord here may well be taken as an encouragement rather to believe that there were even many who were doubly faithful in this time of trial; faithful amid the outside persecution, and faithful also against what could and did soon develop into no less bitter persecution within the professing church.

Of one thing we may be sure, that the true history of the Church remains to be written, or is written only before God. That which fills men's histories is hardly, save in responsibility, the Church at all. Solemn it is to realize the completeness of the ruin, almost from the first; and yet this has been the case in every dispensation. How long did our first parents live in paradise? Of the genera-

---

* For I cannot accept, as some do, that "but thou art rich" is a reproof. And the blasphemy against them surely should acquit them of complicity with those who slander them.

tion before the flood, what was the record? and what of Noah's sons? Of Israel in the wilderness, but two of all that as men left Egypt got into the land. In the land, how soon does Bochim succeed Gilgal! The priesthood fail on the day of their consecration. The first king falls on the battle-field, an apostate. The hands that have built the temple to the true God build the shrines of idols. The remnant brought back from Babylon murder one of their latest prophets (Matt. xxiii. 35), and the awful history of the chosen people closes with the crucifixion of the Son of God.

What hope, then, for the Church? And here the blessing bestowed only makes the ruin the more awful: the corruption of the best becomes the worst corruption. "The annals of the Church," says the Romish historian, "are the annals of hell." How solemn a witness to the application of the words here, "who say they are Jews, and are not, but are the synagogue of Satan"!

Not that we must brand with this name the masses who fell into the snare prepared for them, still less the generations afterward succeeding to the fatal heritage. It is applied, as we may easily see, to the earnest and active propagators of the heresy rather than to those whom they seduced to follow them. The Word of God, while teaching us to be open-eyed as to the character of things around us, teaches us carefully the need of making a difference as to those who may profess the very same principles. Indeed, as to persons, love will ever hope the best that it is possible to hope. It will not be blinded into putting good for evil, or sweet for bitter; and for evil principles it never can have even the smallest toleration: can it tolerate poison in that which is men's food? But it is another thing when the question of what is in the heart is raised. We are never really called to judge what is in the heart, while we are called to judge what is manifest in the life and ways. "I wot that through ignorance ye did it" was said to those who had had part in crucifying Christ; and it was but the echo of the Lord's own plea for them.

But whatever our judgment may be as to persons, the evil abides, and its effects are in the present day all around us. The Judaizing of the Church means the vail replaced before God, souls at a distance, in uncertainty and darkness; the Church and the world confounded, the children of God deprived of their place and privileges, the world made Christian in form, the Church more and more degraded to its level. The development we shall see at length in the after-addresses.

Nicolaitanism, or the Rise and Growth of Clerisy.
(Rev. ii. 6, 15.)

THE address to Pergamos follows that to Smyrna. This next stage of the Church's journey in its departure (alas!) from truth may easily be recognized historically. It applies to the time when, after having passed through the heathen persecution, and the faithfulness of many an Antipas being brought out by it, it got publicly recognized and established in the world. The characteristic of this epistle is, the Church *dwelling* where Satan's throne is. "Throne" it should be, not "seat." Now Satan has his throne, not in hell, which is his prison, and where he never reigns at all, but in the world. He is expressly called the "prince of this world." To dwell where Satan's throne is, is to settle down in the world, under Satan's government, so to speak, and protection. That is what people call the establishment of the Church. It took place in Constantine's time. Although amalgamation with the world had been growing for a long time more and more decided, yet it was then that the Church stepped into the seats of the old heathen idolatry. It was what people call the triumph of Christianity, but the result was that the Church had the things of the world now as never before, in secure possession: the chief place in the world was hers, and the principles of the world every-where pervaded her.

The very name of "Pergamos" intimates that. It is a word (without the particle attached to it, which is itself significant,)—really meaning "marriage," and the Church's marriage before Christ comes to receive her to Himself is necessarily unfaithfulness to Him to whom she is espoused. It is the marriage of the Church and *the world* which the epistle to Pergamos speaks of—the end of a courtship which had been going on long before.

There is something, however, which is preliminary to this, and mentioned in the very first address; but there it is evidently incidental, and does not characterize the state of things. In the first address, to the Ephesians, the Lord says, "But this thou hast, that thou hatest the *deeds* of the Nicolaitanes, which I also hate" (ii. 6). Here it is more than the "deeds" of the Nicolaitanes. There are now not merely "deeds," but "doctrine." And the Church, instead of repudiating it, was holding with it. In the Ephesian days, they *hated* the deeds of the

NICOLAITANISM. 61

Nicolaitanes; but in Pergamos, they "had," and did not reprobate, those who held the doctrine.

The question now before us is, How shall we interpret this? and we shall find that the word "Nicolaitanes" is the only thing really which we have to interpret it by. People have tried very hard to show that there was a sect of the Nicolaitanes, but it is owned by writers now almost on all sides to be very doubtful. Nor can we conceive why, in epistles of the character which we have seen these to have, there should be such repeated and emphatic mention of a mere obscure sect, about which people can tell us little or nothing, and that seems manufactured to suit the passage before us. The Lord solemnly denounces it: "Which thing I hate." It must have a special importance with Him, and be of moment in the Church's history, little apprehended as it may have been. And another thing which we have to remember is, that it is not the way of Scripture to send us to church histories, or to any history at all, in order to interpret its sayings. God's Word is its own interpreter, and we have not to go elsewhere in order to find out what is there; otherwise it becomes a question of learned men searching and finding out for those who have not the same means or abilities, applications which must be taken on their authority alone. This He would not leave His people to. Besides, it is the ordinary way in Scripture, and especially in passages of a symbolical character, such as is the part before us, for the names to be significant. I need not remind you how abundantly in the Old Testament this is the case; and in the New Testament, although less noticed, I cannot doubt but that there is the same significance throughout.

Here, if we are left simply to the name, it is one sufficiently startling and instructive. Of course, to those who spoke the language used, the meaning would be no hidden or recondite thing, but as apparent as those of Bunyan's allegories. It means, then, "*Conquering the people.*" The last part of the word ("*Laos*") is the word used in Greek for "the people," and it is the word from which the commonly used term "Laity" is derived. The Nicolaitanes were just those "subjecting—putting down the laity"—the mass of Christian people, in order unduly to lord it over them.

What makes this clearer is, that,—side by side with the Nicolaitanes in the epistle to Pergamos,— we have those who hold the doctrine of Balaam, a name whose similarity in meaning has been observed by many. "Balaam" is a Hebrew word, as the other is a Greek; but its meaning is, "*Destroyer* of the people," a very significant one in view of his history; and as we read of the "doctrine of the Nicolaitanes," so we read of a "doctrine of Balaam."

You have pointed out what he "taught" Balak. Balaam's doctrine was, "to cast a stumbling-block before the children of Israel, to eat things sacrificed to idols, and to commit fornication." For this purpose he enticed them to mixture with the nations, from which God had carefully separated them. That needful separation broken down was their destruction, so far as it prevailed. In like manner we have seen the Church to be called out from the world, and it is only too easy to apply the divine type in this case. But here we have a confessedly typical people, with a corresponding significant name, and in such close connection as naturally to confirm the reading of the similar word, "Nicolai-

NICOLAITANISM.

tanes," as similarly significant. I shall have to speak more of this at another time, if the Lord will. Let us notice now the development of Nicolaitanism. It is, first of all, certain people who have this character, and who (I am merely translating the word,) first take the place of superiors over the people. Their "deeds" show what they are. There is no "doctrine" yet; but it ends in Pergamos, with the *doctrine* of the Nicolaitanes. The place is assumed now to be theirs by right. There is a doctrine—a teaching about it, received at least by some, and to which the Church at large— nay, on the whole true souls, have become indifferent.

Now what has come in between these two things, —the "deeds" and the "doctrine"? What we were looking at last time—the rise of a party whom the Lord marks out as those who said they were Jews and were not, but who were the synagogue of Satan: the adversary's attempt (alas! too successful) to Judaize the Church.

We were looking but a little while since at what the characteristics of Judaism are. It was a probationary system, a system of trial, in which it was to be seen if man could produce a righteousness for God. We know the end of the trial, and that God pronounced "none righteous—no, not one." And then alone it was that God could manifest His grace. As long as He was putting man under trial, He could not possibly open the way to His own presence and justify the sinner there. He had, as long as this trial went on, to shut him out; for on that ground, nobody could see God and live. Now the very essence of Christianity is that all are welcomed in. There is an open door, and ready access, where the blood of Christ entitles every one, however much a sinner, to draw near to God, and to find, in the first place, at His hand, justification as ungodly. To see God in Christ is not to die, but live. And what, further, is the consequence of this? The people who have come this way to Him,—the people who have found the way of access through the peace-speaking blood into His presence, learned what He is in Christ, and been justified before God, are able to take, and taught to take, a place distinct from all others, as now His, children of the Father, members of Christ—His body. That is the Church, a body called out, separate from the world.

Judaism, on the other hand, necessarily mixed all together. Nobody there could take such a place with God: nobody could cry, "Abba, Father," really; therefore there could not be any separation. This had been then a necessity, and of God, no doubt; but now, Judaism being set up again, after God had abolished it, it was no use, it *is* no use, to urge that it was once of Him; its setting up was the too successful work of the enemy against His gospel and against His Church. He brands these Judaizers as the "synagogue of Satan."

Now we can understand at once, when the Church in its true character was practically lost sight of, when Church-members meant people baptized by water instead of by the Holy Ghost, or when the baptism of water and of the Holy Ghost were reckoned one, (and this very early became accepted doctrine,) how of course the Jewish synagogue was practically again set up. It became more and more impossible to speak of Christians being at peace with God, or saved. They were *hoping* to be, and sacraments and ordinances became means of grace to insure, as far as might be, a far-off salvation.

NICOLAITANISM.

Let us see how far this would help on the doctrine of the Nicolaitanes. It is plain that when and as the Church sank into the synagogue, the Christian people became practically what of old the Jewish had been. Now, what was that position? As I have said, there was no real drawing near to God at all. Even the high-priest, who (as a type of Christ,) entered into the holiest once a year, on the day of atonement, had to cover the mercy-seat with a cloud of incense that he might not die. But the ordinary priests could not enter there at all, but only into the outer holy place; while the people in general could not come in even there. And this was expressly designed as a witness of their condition. It was the result of failure on their part; for God's offer to them, which you may find in the nineteenth chapter of Exodus, was this: "Now, therefore, if ye will obey My voice indeed, and keep My covenant, ye shall be a peculiar treasure unto Me above all people; for all the earth is Mine; and ye shall be unto Me a *kingdom of priests*, and a holy nation."

They were thus conditionally offered equal nearness of access to God,—they should be *all* priests. But this was rescinded, for they broke the covenant; and then a special family is put into the place of priests, the rest of the people being put into the background, and only able to draw near to God through these.

Thus a separate and intermediate priesthood characterized Judaism, as on the other hand, for the same reason, what we should call now *missionary*-work there was none. There was no going out to the world in this way, no provision, no command, to preach the law at all. What, in fact, could they say? that God was in the thick darkness? that no one could see Him and live? It is surely evident there was no "good news" there. Judaism had no true gospel. The absence of the evangelist and the presence of the intermediate priesthood told the same sorrowful story, and were in perfect keeping with each other.

Such was Judaism; how different, then, is Christianity! No sooner had the death of Christ rent the vail, and opened a way of access into the presence of God, than at once there was a gospel, and the new order is, "Go out into all the world, and preach the gospel to every creature." God is making Himself known, and "is He the God of the Jews only?" Can you confine that within the bounds of a nation? No; the fermentation of the new wine would burst the bottles.

The intermediate priesthood was, on the other hand, done away; for all the Christian people are priests now to God. What was conditionally offered to Israel is now an accomplished fact in Christianity. We are a kingdom of priests; and it is, in the wisdom of God, Peter, ordained of man the great head of ritualism, who in his first epistle announces the two things which destroy ritualism root and branch for those who believe him. First, that we are "born again," not of baptism, but "by the word of God, that liveth and abideth forever;" and this, "the word which by the gospel is preached unto you." Secondly, instead of a set of priests, he says to all Christians, "Ye also, as living stones, are built up a spiritual house, a holy priesthood, to offer up spiritual sacrifices, acceptable to God by Jesus Christ." (ii. 5.) The sacrifices are spiritual, praise and thanksgiving, and our lives and bodies also (Heb. xiii. 15, 16; Rom. xii. 1); but this is to be with us true priestly work, and thus do our lives get their proper character: they are the thank-offering service of those able to draw nigh to God.

In Judaism, let me repeat, no one drew really nigh; but the people—the laity (for it is only a Greek word made English,)—the people not even as the priest could. The priestly caste, wherever it is found, means the same thing. There is no drawing nigh of the whole body of the people at all. It means distance from God, and darkness,— God shut out.

Let us see now what is the meaning of a *clergy*. It is, in our day, and has been for many generations, the word which specially marks out a class distinguished from the "laity," and distinguished by being given up to sacred things, and having a place of privilege in connection with them which the laity have not. No doubt in the present day this special place is being more and more infringed on, and for two reasons. One is, that God has been giving light, and, among Protestants at least, Scripture is opposing itself to tradition,—modifying where it does not destroy this. The other is a merely human one—that the day is democratic, and class-privileges are breaking down.

But what means this class? It is evident that as thus distinguished from the laity, and privileged beyond them, it is real and open Nicolaitanism, if Scripture does not make good their claim. For then the laity has been *subjected to* them, and that is the exact meaning of the term. Does Scripture, then, use such terms? It is plain it does not. They are, as regards the New Testament, an invention of later date, although, it may be admitted, as imported really from what is older than the New,—the Judaism with which the Church (as we have seen,) was quickly permeated.

But we must see the important principles involved, to see how the Lord has (as He must have) cause to say of the deeds of the Nicolaitanes, "Which I also hate." We too, if we would be in communion with the Lord in this, must hate what He hates.

I am not speaking of people (God forbid!): I am speaking of a thing. Our unhappiness is, that we are at the end of a long series of departures from God, and as a consequence, we grow up in the midst of many things which come down to us as "tradition of the elders," associated with names which we all revere and love, upon whose authority in reality we have accepted them, without ever having looked at them really in the light of God's presence. And there are many thus whom we gladly recognize as truly men of God and servants of God in a false position. It is of that position I am speaking. I am speaking of a *thing*, as the Lord does: "Which thing I hate." He does not say, Which people I hate. Although in those days evil of this kind was not an inheritance, as now, and the first propagators of it, of course, had a responsibility, self-deceived as they may have been, peculiarly their own. Still, in this matter as in all others, we need not be ashamed or afraid to be where the Lord is;—nay, we cannot be with Him in this unless we are; and He says of Nicolaitanism, "Which thing I hate."

Because what does it mean? It means a spiritual caste, or class,—a set of people having *officially* a right to leadership in spiritual things; a nearness to God, derived from official place, not spiritual power: in fact, the revival, under other names, and with various modifications, of that very intermediate priesthood which distinguished Judaism, and which Christianity emphatically disclaims. That is what a clergy means; and in contradiction to these, the rest of Christians are but the laity, the seculars, necessarily put back into more or less of the old distance, which the cross of Christ has done away.

We see, then, why it needed that the Church should be Judaized before the deeds of the Nicolaitanes could ripen into a "doctrine." The Lord even had authorized obedience to scribes and Pharisees sitting in Moses' seat; and to make this text apply, as people apply it now, *Moses' seat* had of course to be set up in the Christian Church; this done, and the mass of Christians degraded from the priesthood Peter spoke of, into mere "lay members," the doctrine of the Nicolaitanes was at once established.

Understand me fully, that I am in no wise questioning the divine institution of the Christian ministry. God forbid! for ministry in the fullest sense is characteristic of Christianity, as I have already in fact maintained. Nor do I, while believing that all true Christians are ministers also by the very fact, deny a special and distinctive ministry of the Word, as what God has given to some and not to all—though for the use of all. No one truly taught of God can deny that some, not all, among Christians have the place of evangelist, pastor, teacher. Scripture makes more of this than current views do; for it teaches that every true minister is a gift from Christ, in His care, as Head of the Church, for His people, and one who has his place from God alone, and is responsible in that character to God, and God alone. The miserable system which I see around degrades him from this blessed place, and makes him in fact little more than the manufacture and the servant of men. While giving, it is true, a place of lordship over people which gratifies a carnal mind, still it fetters the spiritual man, and puts him in chains; every where giving him an artificial conscience toward man, hindering in fact his conscience being properly before God.

Let me briefly state what the Scripture-doctrine of the ministry is—it is a very simple one. The Assembly of God is Christ's body; all the members are members of Christ. There is no other membership in Scripture than this—the membership of Christ's body, to which all true Christians belong: not many bodies of Christ, but one body; not many Churches, but one Church.

There is of course a different place for each member of the body by the very fact that he is such. All members have not the same office: there is the eye, the ear, and so on, but they are all necessary, and all necessarily ministering, in some way or sense, to one another.

Every member has its place, not merely locally, and for the benefit of certain other members, but for the benefit of the whole body.

Each member has its *gift*, as the apostle teaches distinctly. "For as we have many members in one body, and all members have not the same office; so we, being many, are one body in Christ, and every one members one of another. *Having then gifts*

NICOLAITANISM. 71

differing according to the grace that is given to us," etc. (Rom. xii. 4–6.)

In the twelfth chapter of first Corinthians, the apostle speaks at large of these gifts; and he calls them by a significant name—"manifestations of the Spirit." They are gifts of the Spirit, of course; but more, they are "manifestations of the Spirit;" they manifest themselves where they are found,—where (I need scarcely add that I mean,) there is spiritual discernment,—where souls are before God.

For instance, if you take the gospel of God, whence does it derive its authority and power? From any sanction of men? any human credentials of any kind? or from its own inherent power? I dare maintain, that the common attempt to authenticate the messenger takes away from instead of adding to the power of the Word. God's Word must be received as such: he that receives it sets to his seal that *God is true*. Its ability to meet the needs of heart and conscience is derived from the fact that it is "God's good news," who knows perfectly what man's need is, and has provided for it accordingly. He who has felt its power knows well from whom it comes. The work and witness of the Spirit of God in the soul need no witness of man to supplement them.

Even the Lord's appeal in His own case was to the truth He uttered: "If I say the truth, why do ye not believe Me?" When He stood forth in the Jewish synagogue, or elsewhere, He was but in men's eyes a poor carpenter's son, accredited by no school or set of men at all. All the weight of authority was ever against Him. He disclaimed even "receiving testimony from men." God's Word alone should speak for God. "My doctrine is not

Mine, but His that sent Me." And how did it approve itself? By the fact of its being truth. "If I speak the truth, why do you not believe Me?" It was the truth that was to make its way with the true. "He that will do God's will shall know of the doctrine, whether it be of God, or whether I speak of Myself." He says, "I speak the truth, I bring it to you from God; and if it is truth, and if you are seeking to do God's will, you will learn to recognize it as the truth." God will not leave people in ignorance and darkness, if they are seeking to be doers of His will. Can you suppose that God will allow true hearts to be deceived by whatever plausible deceptions may be abroad? He is able to make His voice known by those who seek to hear His voice. And so the Lord says to Pilate, "Every one that is *of the truth* heareth My voice." (Jno. xviii. 37.) "My sheep hear My voice, and I know them, and they follow Me;" and again, "A stranger will they not follow, but will flee from him; for they know not the voice of strangers." (Jno. x. 27, 5.)

Such is the nature of truth, then, that to pretend to authenticate it to those who are themselves true is to dishonor it, as if it were not capable of self-evidence, and so dishonor God, as if *He* could be wanting to souls, or to what He Himself has given.

Nay, the apostle speaks of "by manifestation of the truth commending ourselves to *every* man's conscience in the sight of God" (2 Cor. iv. 2); and the Lord, of its being the condemnation of the world, that "light is come into the world, and men loved darkness rather than light, because their deeds were evil" (Jno. iii. 19). There was no lack of evidence: light was there, and men owned its

NICOLAITANISM.

power to their own condemnation, when they sought escape from it.

Even so in the gift was there "the manifestation of the Spirit," and it was "given to every man to profit withal." By the very fact that he had it, he was responsible to use it—responsible to Him who had not given it in vain. In the gift itself lay the ability to minister, and title too; for I am bound to help and serve with what I have. And if souls are helped, they need scarcely ask if I had commission to do it.

This is the simple character of ministry—the service of love, according to the ability which God gives, mutual service of each to each and each to all, without jostling or exclusion of one another. Each gift was thrown into the common treasury, and all were the richer by it. God's blessing and the manifestation of the Spirit were all the sanction needed. All were not teachers, still less public teachers, of the Word; still in these cases, the same principles exactly applied. That was but one department of a service which had many, and which was rendered by each to each according to his sphere.

Was there nothing else than that? Was there no ordained class at all, then? That is another thing altogether. There were, without doubt, in the primitive Church, two classes of officials, regularly appointed, or (if you like) ordained. The deacons were those who, having charge of the fund for the poor and other purposes, were chosen by the saints first for this place of trust in their behalf, and then appointed authoritatively by apostles mediately or immediately. Elders were a second class,—elderly men, as the word imports,—who were appointed in the local assemblies as "bishops," or "overseers," to take cognizance of their state. That the elders were the same as bishops may be seen in Paul's words to the elders of Ephesus, where he exhorts them to "take heed to . . . . all the flock, over which the Holy Ghost hath made you *overseers*." There they have translated the word, "bishops," but in Titus they have left it— "that thou shouldest ordain elders in every city, as I had appointed thee; if any be blameless, ... for a *bishop* must be blameless." (Acts xx. 28; Tit. i. 5, 7.)

Their work was to "oversee," and although for that purpose their being "apt to teach" was a much-needed qualification, in view of errors already rife, yet no one could suppose that teaching was confined to those who were "elders," "husbands of one wife, having their children in subjection with all gravity." This was a needed test for one who was to be a bishop; "for if a man know not how to rule his own house, how shall he take care of the Church of God?" (1 Tim. iii. 1–7.)

Whatever gifts they had they used, as all did, and thus the apostle directs—"Let the elders that rule well be counted worthy of double honor, especially they who labor in the Word and doctrine (v. 17). But they might rule, and rule well, without this.

The meaning of their ordination was just this, that here it was *not* a question of "gift," but of authority. It was a question of title to take up and look into, often difficult and delicate matters, among people too very likely in no state to submit to what was merely spiritual. The ministration of gift was another thing, and free, under God, to all.

NICOLAITANISM.

Thus much, very briefly, as to Scripture-doctrine. Our painful duty is now to put in contrast with it the system I am deprecating, according to which a distinct class are devoted formally to spiritual things, and the people—the laity—are in the same ratio excluded from such occupation. This is true Nicolaitanism,—the "subjection of the people."

Again I say, not only that ministry of the Word is entirely right, but that there are those who have special gift and responsibility (though still not exclusive) to minister it. But priesthood is another thing, and a thing sufficiently distinct to be easily recognized where it is claimed or in fact exists. I am, of course, aware that Protestants in general disclaim any priestly powers for their ministers. I have no wish nor thought of disputing their perfect honesty in this disavowal. They mean that they have no thought of the minister having any authoritative power of absolution; and that they do not make the Lord's table an altar, whereon afresh day after day the perfection of Christ's one offering is denied by countless repetitions. They are right in both respects, but it is scarcely the whole matter. If we look more deeply, we shall find that much of a priestly character may attach where neither of these have the least place.

Priesthood and ministry may be distinguished in this way: Ministry (in the sense we are now considering) is to *men;* priesthood is *to God.* The minister brings God's message to the people,—he speaks for Him to them: the priest goes to God *for* the people,—he speaks in the reverse way, for them to Him. It is surely easy to distinguish these two attitudes.

"Praise and thanksgiving" are spiritual "sacrifices:" they are part of our offering as priests. Put a special class into a place where regularly and officially they act thus for the rest, they are at once in the rank of an intermediate priesthood,—mediators with God for those who are not so near.

The Lord's supper is the most prominent and fullest expression of Christian thankfulness and adoration publicly and statedly; but what Protestant minister does not look upon it as his official right to administer this? what "layman" would not shrink from the profanation of administering it? And this is one of the terrible evils of the system, that the mass of Christian people are thus distinctly secularized. Occupied with worldly things, they cannot be expected to be spiritually what the clergy are. And to this they are given over, as it were. They are released from spiritual occupations, to which they are not equal, and to which others give themselves entirely.

But this must evidently go much further. "The *priest's* lips should keep knowledge." The laity, who have become that by abdicating their priesthood, how should they retain the knowledge belonging to a priestly class? The unspirituality to which they have given themselves up pursues them here. The class whose business it is, become the authorized interpreters of the Word also, for how should the secular man know so well what Scripture means? Thus the clergy become spiritual eyes and ears and mouth for the laity, and are in the fair way of becoming the whole body too.

But it suits people well. Do not mistake me as if I meant that this is all come in as the assumption of a class merely. It is that, no doubt; but never could this miserable and unscriptural distinction

NICOLAITANISM.

of clergy and laity have obtained so rapidly as it did, and so universally, if every where it had not been found well adapted to the tastes of those even whom it really displaced and degraded. Not alone in Israel, but in christendom also, has it been fulfilled: "The prophets prophecy falsely, and the priests bear rule through their means, and *My people love to have it so!*" Alas! they did, and they do. As spiritual decline sets in, the heart that is turning to the world barters readily, Esau-like, its spiritual birthright for a mess of pottage. It exchanges thankfully its need of caring too much for spiritual things, with those who will accept the responsibility of this. Worldliness is well covered with a layman's cloak; and as the Church at large dropped out of first love, (as it did rapidly, and then the world began to come in through the loosly guarded gates,) it became more and more impossible for the rank and file of christendom to take the blessed and wonderful place which belonged to Christians. The step taken downward, instead of being retrieved, only made succeeding steps each one easier; until, in less than three hundred years from the beginning, a Jewish priesthood and a ritualistic religion were every-where installed. Only so much the worse, as the precious things of Christianity left their names at least as spoils to the invader, and the shadow became for most the substance itself.

But I must return to look more particularly at one feature in this clerisy. I have noted the confounding of ministry and priesthood; the assumption of an official title in spiritual things, of title to administer the Lord's supper, and I might have added also, to baptize. For none of these things can scripture be found at all. But I must dwell a little more on the emphasis that is laid on ordination.

I want you to see a little more what ordination means. In the first place, if you look through the New Testament, you will find nothing about ordination to teach or to preach. You find people going about every where freely exercising whatever gift they had; the whole Church was scattered abroad from Jerusalem except the apostles, and they went every where preaching (literally, evangelizing) the Word. The persecution did not ordain them, I suppose. So with Apollos: so with Philip the deacon. There is, in fact, no trace of any thing else. Timothy received a gift by prophecy, by the laying on of Paul's hands with those of the elders; but that was *gift*, not authorization to use it. So he is bidden to communicate his own knowledge to faithful men, who should be able to teach others also; but there is not a word about ordaining them. The case of elders I have already noticed. That of Paul and Barnabas at Antioch is the most unhappy that can be for the purpose people use it for; for prophets and teachers are made to ordain an apostle, and one who totally disclaims being that, "*of* men or *by* man." And there the Holy Ghost (*not* confers power of ordaining any, but) says, "Separate *Me* Barnabas and Saul for the work whereto I have called them,"—a special missionary journey, which it is shown afterward they had fulfilled. (See Acts viii, xi, xiii, xviii; 1 Tim., etc.)

Now, what means this "ordination"? It means much, you may be sure, or it would not be so zealously contended for as it is. There are, no doubt, two phases of it. In the most extreme, as among Romanists and ritualists, there is claimed for it in the fullest way that it is the conveyance, not merely of authority, but of spiritual power. They assume with all the power of apostles to give the Holy Ghost by the laying on of their hands, and here for priesthood in the fullest way. The people of God as such are rejected from the priesthood He has given them, and a special class are put into their place to mediate for them in a way which sets aside the fruit of Christ's work, and ties them to the Church as the channel of all grace. Among Protestants, you think perhaps I need not dwell on this; but it is done among some of these also, in words which to a certain class of them seem strangely to mean nothing, while another class find in them the abundant sanction of their highest pretensions.

Those, on the other hand, who rightly and consistently reject these unchristian assumptions do not pretend indeed to confer any gift in ordination, but only to "recognize" the gift which God has given. But then, after all, this recognition is considered necessary before the person can baptize or administer the Lord's supper,—things which really require no peculiar gift at all. And as to the ministry of the Word, God's gift is made to require human sanction, and is "recognized" on behalf of His people by those who are considered to have a discernment which the people as such have not. Blind themselves or not, these men are to become "leaders of the blind;" else why need others to be eyes for them, while their own souls are taken out of the place of immediate responsibility to God, and made responsible unduly to man? An artificial conscience is manufactured for them, and conditions are constantly imposed, to which they have to conform in order to obtain the needful recognition. It is well if they are not under the control of their ordainers as to their path of service also, as they generally are.

In principle, this is unfaithfulness to God; for if He has given me gift to use for Him, I am surely unfaithful if I go to any man or body of men to ask their leave to use it. The gift itself carries with it the responsibility of using it, as we have seen. If they say, "But people may make mistakes," I own it thoroughly; but who is to assume my responsibility if I am mistaken? And again, the mistakes of an ordaining body are infinitely more serious than those of one who merely runs unsent. Their mistakes are consecrated and perpetuated by the ordination they bestow; and the man who, if he stood simply upon his own merits, would soon find his true level, has a character conferred upon him by it which the whole weight of the system must sustain. Mistake or not, he is none the less one of the clerical body,—a minister, if he has nothing really to minister. He must be provided for, if only with some less conspicuous place, where souls, dear to God as any, are put under his care, and must be unfed if he cannot feed them.

Do not accuse me of sarcasm; it is the system I am speaking of which is a sarcasm,—a swathing of the body of Christ in bands which hinder the free circulation of the vitalizing blood which should be permeating unrestrictedly the whole of it. Nature itself should rebuke the folly—the enormous inference from such scriptural premises as that apostles and apostolic men "ordained elders"! They must prove that they are either, and (granting them that,) that the Scripture "elder" might be no elder at all,

NICOLAITANISM.

but a young unmarried man just out of his teens, and on the other hand was evangelist, pastor, teacher—all God's various gifts rolled into one. This is the minister (according to the system, indeed, *the* minister,)—the all in all to the fifty or five hundred souls who are committed to him as "*his* flock," with which no other has title to interfere! Surely, surely, the brand of "Nicolaitanism" is upon the forefront of such a system as this!

Take it at its best, the man, if gifted at all, is scarcely likely to have *every* gift. Suppose he is an evangelist, and souls are happily converted; he is no teacher, and cannot build them up. Or he is a teacher, sent to a place where there are but a few Christians, and the mass of his congregation unconverted men. There are no conversions, and his presence there (*according to the system*) *keeps away* the evangelist who is needed there. Thank God! He is ever breaking up these systems, and in some irregular way the need may be supplied. But the supply is schismatical and a confusion: the new wine breaks the poor human bottles.

For all this the system is responsible. The exclusive ministry of one man or of a number of men in a congregation has no shred of Scripture to support it; while the ordination, as we have seen, is the attempt to confine all ministry to a certain class, and make it rest on human authorization rather than on divine gift, the people, Christ's sheep, being denied their competency to hear His voice. The inevitable tendency is, to fix upon the *man* the attention which should be devoted to the word he brings. The question is, Is he accredited? If he speak truly is subordinated to the question, Is he ordained? or, perhaps I should say, his orthodoxy is settled already for them by the fact of his ordination.

Paul, an apostle, not of men, nor by man, could not have been, upon this plan, received. There were apostles before him, and he neither went up to them nor got any thing from them. If there were a succession, he was a break in the succession. And what he did he did designedly, to show that his gospel was not after man (Gal. i. 11), and that it might not rest upon the authority of man. Nay, if he himself preached a different gospel from that he had preached, (for there was not *another*,)—yea, or an angel from heaven (where the authority, if that were in question, might seem conclusive), his solemn decision is, "Let him be accursed."

Authority, then, is nothing if it be not the authority of the Word of God. That is the test—Is it according to the Scriptures? "If the blind lead the blind, shall they not *both* fall into the ditch?" To say, "I could not, of course, know: I trusted another," will not save you from the ditch.

But the unspiritual and unlearned layman, how can he pretend to equal knowledge with the educated and accredited minister devoted to spiritual things? In point of fact, in general he does not. He yields to the one who should know better; and practically the minister's teaching largely supplants the authority of the Word of God. Not that *certainty*, indeed, is thus attained. He cannot conceal it from himself that people differ—wise and good and learned and accredited as they may be. But here the devil steps in, and, if God has allowed men's "authorities" to get into a Babel of confusion, as they have, suggests to the unwary soul that the confusion must be the result of the obscurity of Scripture, whereas they have got into it by *disregarding* Scripture.

But this is every where! Opinion, not faith;—opinion to which you are welcome and have a right, of course; and you must allow others a right to theirs. You may say, "I believe," as long as you do not mean by that, "I know." To claim "knowledge" is to claim that you are wiser, more learned, better, than whole generations before you, who thought opposite to you.

Need I show you how infidelity thrives upon this? how Satan rejoices when for the simple and emphatic "Yea" of the divine voice he succeeds in substituting the Yea and Nay of a host of jarring commentators? Think you you can fight the Lord's battles with the rush of human opinion instead of "the sword of the Spirit, which is the Word of God"? Think you "Thus saith John Calvin, or John Wesley," will meet Satan as satisfactorily as "Thus saith the *Lord*"?

Who can deny that such thoughts are abroad, and in no wise confined to papists or ritualists? The tendency, alas! is, in the heart of unbelief ever departing from the *living* God,—as near to His own to-day as at any time through the centuries His Church has traveled on, as competent to instruct as ever, as ready to fulfill the word, "He that will do His will shall know of the doctrine, whether it be of God." The "eyes" are "of the *heart*," and not the *head*. He has hidden from wise and prudent what He reveals to babes. The school of God is more effectual than all colleges combined, and here layman and cleric are equal: "he that is spiritual discerneth all things," and he alone. Substitute for spirituality there is none: unspirituality the Spirit of God alone can remedy. Ordination, such as practiced, is rather a sanction put upon it, —an attempt to manifest what is the manifestation of the Spirit, or not His work at all, and to provide leaders for the blind, whom with all their care they cannot insure not being blind also.

Before I close, I must say a few words about "succession." An ordination which pretends to be derived from the apostles must needs be (to be consistent,) a successional one. Who can confer authority (and in the least and lowest theories of ordination authority *is* conferred, as to baptize, and to administer the Lord's supper,) but one himself authorized for this very purpose? You must, therefore, have a chain of ordained men, lineally succeeding one another. Apostolic succession is as necessary on the presbyterian as on the episcopalian plan. John Wesley, as his warrant for ordaining, fell back upon the essential oneness of bishop and presbyter. Nay, presbyterians will urge against episcopalians the ease of maintaining succession in this way. I have nothing to do with this: I only insist that succession is needed.

But then, mark the result. It is a thing apart alike from spirituality and from truth even. A Romish priest may have it as well as any; and indeed through the gutter of Rome most of that we have around us must necessarily have come down. Impiety and impurity do not in the least invalidate Christ's commission. The teacher of false doctrine may be as well His messenger as the teacher of truth. Nay, the possession of the truth, with gift to minister it and godliness combined, are actually *no part* of the credentials of the true ambassador. He may have all these and be none; he may want them all and be truly one nevertheless.

Who can believe such doctrine? Can He who is truth accredit error?—the righteous One unrighteousness? It is impossible. This ecclesiasticism violates every principle of morality, and hardens the conscience that has to do with it. For why need we be careful for truth if He is not? and how can He send messengers that He would not have to be believed? His own test of a true witness fails; for "he that speaketh of himself seeketh his own glory; but he that seeketh *his* glory that sent him, the same is true, and no unrighteousness is in him." His own test of credibility fails, for "If I *speak the truth*, why do ye not believe Me?" was His own appeal.

No: to state this principle is to condemn it. He who foresaw and predicted the failure of what should have been the bright and evident witness of His truth and grace, could not ordain a succession of teachers for it who should carry His commission unforfeitable by whatever failure! Before apostles had left the earth, the house of God had become as a "great house," and it was necessary to separate from vessels to dishonor in it. He who bade His apostle to instruct another to "follow righteousness, faith, love, peace, with those who call on the Lord out of a pure heart," could not possibly tell us to listen to men who are alien from all this, as His ministers, and having His commission in spite of all. And thus notably, in the second epistle to Timothy, in which this is said, there is no longer, as in the first, any talk of elders or of ordained men. It is "*faithful* men" who are wanted, *not* for ordination, but for the deposit of the truth committed to Timothy: "The things which thou hast heard of me among many witnesses, the same commit thou to faithful men, who shall be able to teach others also."

Thus God's holy Word vindicates itself to the heart and conscience ever. The effort to attach His sanction to a Romish priesthood or a Protestant hierarchy fails alike upon the same ground, for as to this they are upon the same ground. Alas! Nicolaitanism is no past thing—no obscure doctrine of past ages, but a wide-spread and gigantic system of error, fruitful in evil results. Error is long-lived, though mortal. Reverence it not for its gray hairs, and follow not with a multitude to do evil. With cause does the Lord say in this case, "Which thing I hate." If He does, shall we be afraid to have fellowship with Him? That there are good men entangled in it, all must admit. There are godly men, and true ministers, ignorantly wearing the livery of men. May God deliver them! may they cast aside their fetters and be free! May they rise up to the true dignity of their calling, responsible to God, and walking before Him alone!

On the other hand, beloved brethren, it is of immense importance that all His people, however diverse their places in the body of Christ may be, should realize that they are *all* as really ministers as they are all priests. We need to recognize that every Christian has spiritual duties flowing from spiritual relationship to every other Christian. It is the privilege of each one to contribute his share to the common treasury of gift, with which Christ has endowed His Church. Nay, he who does not contribute is actually holding back what is his debt to the whole family of God. No possessor of one talent is entitled to wrap it in a napkin upon that account: it would be mere unfaithfulness and unbelief.

"It is more blessed to give than to receive." Brethren in Christ, when shall we awake to the reality of our Lord's words there? Ours is a never-failing spring of perpetual joy and blessing, which if we but come to when we thirst, out of our bellies shall flow rivers of living water. The spring is not limited by the vessel which receives it: it is divine, and yet ours fully,—fully as can be! Oh to know more this abundance, and the responsibility of the possession of it, in a dry and weary scene like this! Oh to know better the infinite grace which has taken us up as channels of its outflow among men! When shall we rise up to the sense of our common dignity,—to the sweet reality of fellowship with Him who "came not to be ministered unto, but to minister"? Oh for *unofficial* ministry—the overflowing of full hearts into empty ones, so many as there are around us! How we should rejoice, in a scene of want and misery and sin, to find perpetual opportunity to show the competency of Christ's fullness to meet and minister to every form of it.

Official ministry is practical independence of the Spirit of God. It is to decide that such a vessel shall overflow though at the time, it may be, practically empty; and, on the other hand, that such another shall *not* overflow, however full He may have filled it up. It proposes, in the face of Him who has come down in Christ's absence to be the Guardian of His people, to provide for order and for edification, not by spiritual power, but by legislation. It would provide for failure on the part of Christ's sheep to hear His voice, by making it as far as possible unnecessary for them to do so. It thus sanctions and perpetuates unspirituality, instead of condemning or avoiding it.

It is quite true that in God's mode of treating it the failure in man's part may become more evident externally; for He cares little for a correct outside when the heart is nevertheless not right with Him, and He knows well that ability to maintain a correct outside may in fact prevent a truthful judgment of what is our real condition before Him. Men would have upbraided Peter with his attempt to walk upon those waves which made his little faith so manifest. The Lord would only rebuke the littleness of the faith which made him fail. And man still and ever would propose the boat as the remedy for failure, instead of the strength of the Lord's support, which He made Peter prove. Yet, after all, the boat confessedly may fail,—winds and waves may overthrow it; but "the Lord on high is mightier than the noise of many waters—yea, than the mighty waves of the sea." Through these many centuries of failure, have we proved Him untrustworthy? Beloved, is it your honest conviction that it is absolutely safe to trust the living God? Then let us make no provision for *His* failure, however much we may have to own that *we* have failed! Let us act as if we really trusted Him.

Pergamos: the Church united with the World.
(Rev. ii. 12-17.)

WE have seen, then, two main steps in the Church's outward decline, after the loss of first love had made any departure possible. First of all, the divine idea of the Church was lost. Instead of its being a body of people having, in the full and proper sense, eternal life and salvation, children of God, members of Christ, and called out of the world as not belonging to it, it became a mere "gathering together" of those for whom, indeed, the old names might in part remain, but who were, in fact, the world itself with true Christian people scattered through it. Children of God, no doubt, they might be by baptism,* and by it have forgiveness of sins also, but that was no settlement for eternity at all. They were confessedly under trial, uncertain as to how things would finally turn out,—a ground which all the world could understand and adopt, with sacraments and means of grace to help them on, and prevent them realizing the awfulness of their position.

Of course this immense change from Church to synagogue was not at once effected. Yet the church, historically known to us outside of the New Testament, is but in fact essentially the synagogue. The fire of persecution combined with the fidelity of a remnant to prevent for awhile the extreme result, and to separate mere professors from

---

* "The prodigal son answers," says Chrysostom, in his first homily on Repentance, "to those who fall after baptism: he does so inasmuch as he is called a *son;* for none are sons apart from baptism, with which are connected all the benefits of heirship, and a community of interests with the family. He is called, moreover, the brother of him who was approved; but there is no brotherhood without the spiritual regeneration" (baptism).

In another place: "Although a man should be foul with every vice—the blackest that can be named, yet, should he fall into the baptismal pool, he ascends from the divine waters purer than the beams of noon."

"As a spark thrown into the ocean is instantly extinguished, so is sin, be it what it may, extinguished when the man is thrown into the laver of regeneration."

I quote from Isaac Taylor's "*Ancient Christianity*," (Philadelphia edition, pp. 346, 325, 326,) on "the means of estimating the quality of the Nicene theology," where much else of the same character may be found. It is significant that the Nicene Creed, with all its Trinitarian orthodoxy, knows nothing but "one *baptism* for the remission of sins."

the confessors of Christ. Still, through it all, the leaven of Judaism did its deadly work; and no sooner was the persecution stopped than the world's overtures for peace and alliance were eagerly listened to, and with Constantine, for many, the millennium seemed to have arrived. Could the Church of the apostles have fallen into the world's arms so? Their voice would have rebuked the thought as of Satan, as indeed it was. "Ye adulterers and adulteresses, know ye not that the friendship of the world is enmity with God?"

The second step we saw in the rise of a clergy, a special priestly class, replacing the true Christian ministry, the free exercise of the various gifts resulting from the various position of the members in the body of Christ. The clerical assumption displaced the body of Christian people,—now a true laity,—as at least less spiritual and near to God: a place, alas! easily accepted where Christ had lost what the world had gained in value with His own. As Judaism prevailed, and the world came in through the wider-opening door, the distance between the two classes increased, and more and more the clergy became the channels of all blessing to all the rest. Practically, and in the end almost openly, they became the church; and the Church became, from a company of those already saved, a channel for conveying a sacramental and hypothetical salvation.

We now come to look at the issue of all this when circumstances favored. In Pergamos, the change in the Lord's position is noteworthy and characteristic. He presents Himself no longer in the tender and compassionate way which He exhibits toward His suffering ones in Smyrna. It is now "These things saith He which hath the sharp sword with two edges." His word is a word of penetrating and decisive judgment. It is with this two-edged sword that He by and by smites the nations (chap. xix.), so that there can be no question as to its meaning. And while it is of course true that it is not His own at Pergamos who are smitten with it, yet it is those whom He charges them with having in their midst (*v.* 16).

The characteristic thing in Pergamos is that they are dwelling where Satan's throne is. "Throne," not merely "seat," is the true word, though our translators, as it would seem, because of the strength of the expression, shrank from using it. To what it referred in the actual city, no commentator can tell us. Trench remarks, "Why it should have thus deserved the name of '*Satan's throne*,' so emphatically repeated a second time at the end of this verse—'*where Satan dwelleth*,' must remain one of the unsolved riddles of these epistles." But did the Lord bid him that hath an ear to hear what must remain an unsolved riddle? Assuredly not. It is one of the characteristics of the prophetic view in these epistles, that it delivers one from the necessity of waiting until some archæologist shall be found who can explain such things, and gives us one for our profit both clear and satisfactory, derived from Scripture itself. But not only so. The practical worth of the archæologic rendering would be very likely little, if it could be gained. Of what value would it be if we believed with Grotius that this expression had reference to the worship of Æsculapius, whose symbol was a *serpent ?* Surely of very little. Whereas the prophetic view flashes light upon the whole condition.

Satan reigns in hell, according to the popular belief; and Milton's picture, while it reflects this, has done much to confirm and make it vivid. But hell is a place of punishment, and Scripture is quite plain that he is not confined there. Then he must have broken loose, is the idea. God's prison was not strong enough! One might ask, How do we know, then, it will ever be? Think of the government which allows the chief malefactor to reign in his prison over those less evil than himself, and to break prison, and roam freely where he will! God's government is not chargeable with this. In hell, Satan will be, not king, but lowest and most miserable there; and once committed to it, no escape will be permitted. But this will not be till after the millennium, as Rev. xx. assures us.

But this idea permits people to escape from the thought—an appalling one, no doubt,—that he is still what the Lord designates him—"prince of *this world:*" "the prince of this world cometh, and hath nothing in Me."

True, He does speak so, some one may suggest; but does He not also say, when predicting the effect of His cross, "Now shall the prince of this world be cast out"? has he not, then, been cast out of his kingdom? and are we not "translated into the kingdom of our Lord Jesus Christ"?

The latter is true; but as to the former, the Lord only predicts the certain effect of the cross, and the "now" simply declares it to *be* the effect. Here one startling expression of the apostle Paul, going beyond even that which the Lord uses, is decisive as to the matter; he calls the devil—long after the cross—"the *god* of this world" (2 Cor. iv. 4).

And indeed the expression is stronger even than

this. For the margin of the Revised Version is assuredly right, and it is the word "age," not "world," which the apostle uses. "The god of this age" is surely a very solemn title to be given to Satan after the Christian dispensation, as we call it, had already begun. Yet there it stands; and "Scripture cannot be broken."

Yes, it is over the world, and in these Christian times, that Satan exercises this terrible sway, and this is what makes the expression here, "dwelling where Satan's throne is," so sadly significant.

For "*dwelling* in the world" is another thing from *being* in it. We are in the world perforce, and in no wise responsible for that, but to be a *dweller* in it is a moral state: it is to be a citizen of it, the condition which the apostle speaks of in Philippians as obtaining among professing Christians: "For many walk, of whom I have told you before, and now tell you even weeping, that they are the enemies of the cross of Christ; whose god is their belly, whose glory is in their shame, who mind earthly things: for our citizenship is in heaven, from whence we look for the Saviour, the Lord Jesus Christ."

Their characteristic is that they are enemies, not of Christ personally, but of the *cross*—that cross by which we are crucified to the world and the world to us. Their hearts were on earthly things, which, not satisfying them, as earthly things cannot, made their god to be their belly; their inward craving became their master, and made them drudge in its service.

The Christian's citizenship is in heaven. That delivers him from the unsatisfying pursuit of earthly things. But little indeed is this understood now. Even where people can talk and sing of the world being a wilderness, you will find that in general the idea is rather of the sorrows and trials of which the world is full, and which Christians are exposed to like the men of the world themselves. "Man is born to trouble as the sparks fly upward;" and pilgrimage in their minds is a thing perforce. The world passes away, and they cannot keep it; so they are glad to think that heaven is at the end. In the meanwhile, they go on trying (honestly, no doubt, if you can call such a thing honest in a Christian,) to get as much of it as they can, or at least as much as will make them comfortable in it.

But a pilgrim is not one whom the world is leaving, but who is *leaving it*. Otherwise the whole world would be pilgrims, as indeed they talk about the "pilgrimage of life." But this is the abuse of the term, and not its use. We can be pilgrims in this sense, and find all the world companions; and such, in fact, had got to be the idea of pilgrimage in the Pergamos state of the Church. They talked of it, no doubt, and built their houses the more solidly to stand the rough weather. *God said* they were dwelling where Satan's throne was.

It was the history of old Babel repeating itself. You may find the vivid type of it in Gen. xi., where men "journeyed," indeed, but not as pilgrims, or only as that till they could find some smooth spot to settle down in. They "journeyed," as colonists or immigrants on the look-out for land; from the rough hills beyond the flood, where human life began; "from the east"—with their backs, that is, toward the blessed dawn; "and they found a plain in the land of Shinar, and they *dwelt there."*

Such was, alas! the Church's progress—from the rough heights of martyrdom down to the level plain where there were no difficulties to deter the most timid souls. There the Church multiplied, and there they began to "build a city, and a tower whose top should reach to heaven." But "a city" was not Jerusalem, but Jerusalem's constant enemy; not the "possession of peace," but a city of "confusion"—Babel.

Yet it prospered: they built well. True, they were away from the quarries of the hills, and could not build with the "stone" they had there been used to. They did what they could with the clay which was native in that lower land. "They had bricks for stone, and bitumen for mortar." We have seen some of this work already. It looks well, and lasts in the fine climate of these regions quite a long time: human material, not divine,—"bricks," man's manufacture, "for stones," God's material. They cannot build great Babylon with the "living stones" of God's producing. Man-made Christians, compacted together, not by the cementing of the Spirit for eternity, but by the human motives and influences whereby the masses are affected, but which the fire of God will one day try. So is great Babylon built.

Now it is remarkable that the word "Pergamos" has a double significance. In the plural form, it is used for the "citadel of a town," while it is at least near akin to *purgos*, "a tower." Again, divide it into the two words into which it naturally separates, and you have *per*, "although," a particle which "usually serves to call attention to something which is objected to" (Liddell & Scott), and *gamos*, "marriage." Pergamos,—"a marriage though."

It was indeed by the marriage of the Church and the world that the "city and tower" of Babylon the Great was raised; and such are the times we are now to contemplate.

Before we proceed, however, let us to this double proof unite another, that the threefold cord may not be broken. The parallel between the first addresses to the churches and the first four parables of the kingdom in Matthew xiii. I have referred to before. The first parable gives the partial failure of the good seed, as Ephesus gives the initial failure of the true Church. The second parable gives the direct work of the enemy—the tares sown among the wheat, as the address to Smyrna does the "synagogue of Satan." But the tares and wheat are separate, and the view is, in the first two parables, an individual one; the third parable is entirely different in this respect. *One* seed stands here for the whole sowing, and what is seen is now the aspect of the whole together. The little mustard-seed produces, strange to say, a tree, in which the birds of the heaven lodge, and the tree is a type of worldly power. Turn to the fourth chapter of Daniel, and you will find in Nebuchadnezzar, king of Babylon, such a tree. Surely it is significant that in every direction in which we look from here there is a finger-post which points to Babylon! And here in Pergamos, as in the mustard-tree, it is the Church as a whole which is spoken of. It is established, as men triumphantly say: it is *fallen* is the lament from heaven.

For this is not the Church's establishment upon its Rock-foundation, where the gates of hades cannot prevail against it, but in the world's favor; and if Satan be the prince of this world, what must be the price of this?

As a consequence, we find not only Nicolaitanism fully accepted, but the doctrine of Balaam also. They are still what is called "orthodox." "Thou holdest fast My name, and hast not denied My faith, even in those days wherein Antipas was My faithful witness, who was slain among you where Satan dwelleth." For these are the Nicene times, the time of the first Christian council called (at Nicœa) by a Roman emperor, and which maintained the deity of Christ against Arianism. It was a sight, they said, to see at the council the marks of the confession of Christ in those who had endured the late persecutions. The Nicene period was that of two, at least, of the creeds substantially acknowledged by the faith of Christians every where since. But theirs was an orthodoxy which, while maintaining (thank God!) the doctrine of the Trinity, could be and was very far astray as to the application of Christ's blessed work to the salvation of men. Orthodox as to Christ, it was yet most unorthodox as to the gospel.

Where in the Apostles' Creed, so called, do you find the gospel. "The forgiveness of sins" is an article of belief, no doubt, but how and when? In the Nicene creed is acknowledged "one *baptism* for the remission of sins," but there is entire silence as to any other. In the Athanasian, it is owned Christ "suffered for our salvation," but how we are to obtain the salvation for which He suffered is again omitted. Practically, the belief of the times was in the efficacy of baptism, and so painful and uncertain was the way of forgiveness for sins committed afterward, that multitudes deferred baptism to a dying bed, that the sins of a lifetime might be more easily washed away together.

The Lord goes on to say, "But I have a few things against thee, because thou hast there them which hold the doctrine of Balaam, who taught Balak to cast a trap before the children of Israel, to eat things sacrificed to idols, and to commit fornication."

Balaam, the *destroyer* of the people, is a new graft upon Nicolaitanism. A prophet, in outward nearness to the Lord, while his heart went after its own covetousness,—a man having no personal grudge against the people, but whose god was his belly, and so would curse them if his god bade:—one whose doctrine was to seduce Israel from their separateness into guilty mixture with the nations and their idolatry round about. The type is easily read, and the examples of it distressingly numerous. When the Church and the world become on good terms with one another, and the Church has the things of the world with which to attract the natural heart, the hireling prophet is a matter of course, who for his own ends will seek to destroy whatever remains of godly separateness.

It is one step only in the general, persistent departure from God never retraced and never repented of. Solemn to say, however much individuals may be delivered, such decline is never recovered from by the body as such. At every step downward, the progress down is only accelerated. "Have ye offered Me slain beasts and sacrifices by the space of forty years in the wilderness? Yea, ye took up the tabernacle of Moloch, and the

PERGAMOS.

star of your god Remphan, figures which ye made to worship them; and I will carry you away beyond Babylon. There were many reformations afterward, more or less partial, but no fresh start.

So with the Church. Men talk of another Pentecost. There never was another. And the first lasted for how brief a season! "Unto thee, goodness, if thou *continue* in His goodness; otherwise thou also shalt be cut off."

From Constantine's day to the present, world and Church have been united in christendom at large; and wherever this is found, there in truth is Babylon, though Rome be the head of Babylon, as indeed she is.

Let us look about us with the lamp the Lord has given us, and see whereabouts we are with regard to these things. How far are we individually keeping the Church and the world separate? How far are we really refusing that yoke with unbelievers which the passage in 2 Cor. vi. so emphatically condemns? Our associations are judged of God as surely as any other part of our practical conduct; and "Be not unequally yoked together with unbelievers" is His word. He cannot, He declares, be to us a Father as He would, except we come out and be separate! Solemn, solemn words in the midst of the multiplicity of such confederacies in the present day! Can we bear to be ourselves searched out by them, beloved brethren? Oh, if we value our true place as sons with God, shall we not be only glad to see things as they are?

Now this "yoke" forbidden has various applications. It applies to any thing in which we voluntarily unite with others to attain a common object. Among social relations, marriage is such a yoke;

in business relations, partnerships and such like; and in the foremost rank of all would come ecclesiastical associations.

To take these latter, now: There are certain systems which, as we have already seen, mix up the Church and the world in the most thorough way possible. All forms of ritualism do:—forms wherein a person is made by baptism "a member of Christ and a child of God." Where that is asserted, separation is impossible; for no amount of charity, and no extravagance of theological fiction, can make the mass of these baptized people other than the world.

All national churches in the same way mix them up by the very fact that they are national churches. You cannot by the force of will or act of parliament make a nation Christian. You can give them a name to live, while they are dead. You can make them formalists and hypocrites, but nothing more. You can do your best to hide from them their true condition, and leave them under an awful delusion, from which eternity alone may wake them up. That is much to do indeed, and it is all in this way possible.

All systems Jewish in character mix them up of necessity. Where all are probationers together, it is not possible to do otherwise. All systems in which the church is made a means to salvation, instead of the company of the saved, necessarily do so. When people join churches in order to be saved, as is the terrible fashion of the day, these churches become of course the common receptacle of sinners and saints alike. And wherever assurance of salvation is not maintained, the same thing must needs result.

Systems such as these naturally acquire, and rapidly, adherents, money, and worldly influence; and among such, the doctrine of Balaam does its deadly work. The world, not even disguised in the garb of Christianity, is sought, for the sake of material support. Men that have not given themselves to the Lord are taught that they can give their money. It is openly proclaimed that God is not sufficient as His people's portion. His cause requires help, and that so much, that He will accept it from the hands of His very enemies. There is an idolatry of means abroad. Money will help the destitute; money will aid to circulate the Scripture; money will send missionaries to foreign parts; money will supply a hundred wants, and get over a host of difficulties. We are going to put it to so good a use, we must not be over-scrupulous as to the mode of getting it. The church has to be maintained, the minister to be paid. They do not like the principles that "the end sanctifies the means"—but still, what are they to do? God is in theory of course sufficient, but they must use the means, and the nineteenth century no longer expects miracles.

But why go over the dreary round of such godless and faithless arguments? Is it a wonder that infidelity bursts out into a triumphant laugh as Christians maintain the impotence of their God, and violate His precepts to save His cause from ruin? Nay, do you not in fact proclaim it ruined —irredeemably, irrecoverably ruined, when His ear is already too dull to hear, and His arm shortened that it cannot save?

Money will build churches, will buy Bibles, will support ministers,—true. Will it buy a new Pentecost? or bring in the millennium? Will you bribe the blessed Spirit to work for you thus? or make sheer will and animal energy do without Him? Alas! you pray for power, and dishonor Him who is the only source of power!

But what is the result of this solicitation of the world? Can you go to it with the Bibles you have bought with its own money, and tell it the truth as to its own condition? Can you tell them that "the whole world lieth in wickedness"?—that "all that is in the world—the lust of the flesh, and the lust of the eyes, and the pride of life—is not of the Father, but is of the world"? Can you maintain the separate place that God has given you, and the sharp edge of the truth that "they that are in the flesh cannot please God"? Of course you cannot. They will turn round upon you and say, "Why, then, do you come to us for our money? You ask us to give, and tell us it will not please Him our giving! It is not reasonable: we do not believe it, and you cannot believe it yourselves!"

No: the world does not believe in giving something for nothing. Whatever the Word of God may say, whatever you may think of it in your heart, you must compromise in some way. You must not maintain the rigid line of separation. Balaam must be your prophet. You must mix with the world, and let it mix with you; how else will you do it good? You must cushion your church-seats, and invite it in. You must make your building and your services attractive: you must not frighten people away, but allure them in. You must be all things to all men; and as you cannot expect to get them up to your standard, you must get down to theirs. Do I speak too strongly? Oh, words can hardly exaggerate the state of things that may be every-where found, not in some far-off land, but here all around us in the present day. I should not dare to tell you what deeds are done in the name of Christ by His professing people. They will hire singers to sing His praises for admiration, and to draw a crowd. They will provide worldly entertainments, and sit down and be entertained in company. And as more and more they sink down to the world's level, they persuade themselves the world is rising up to theirs; while God is saying, as of His people of old, "Ephraim, he hath mixed himself among the people: Ephraim is a cake not turned. Strangers have devoured his strength, and he knoweth it not,—yea, gray hairs are here and there upon him, yet he knoweth it not. And the pride of Israel testifieth to his face; and they do not return to the Lord their God, nor seek Him for all this" (Hos. vii. 8–10).

It is a downward course, and being trod at an ever-increasing pace. Competition is aroused, and it is who can be the most successful candidate for the world's favors. The example of one emboldens another. Emulation, envy, ambition, and a host of unholy motives are aroused; and Scripture, the honor of Christ, the jealous eyes of a holy, holy God—ah, you are antiquated and pharisaic if you talk of these.

There is one feature in this melancholy picture I cannot pass by briefly thus. *The ministry*, or what stands before men's eyes as such, how is it affected by all this? I have already said that Scripture does not recognize the thought of a minister and his people. Upon this I do not intend to dwell again. But what, after all, in the present day has got to be the strength of the tie between a church and its ministry? Who that looks around can question that money has here a controlling influence? The seal of the compact is the salary. A rich church with an ample purse, can it not make reasonably sure of attracting the man it wants? The poor church, however rich in piety, is it not conscious of its deficiency? People naturally do not like to own it. They persuade themselves, successfully enough, no doubt, that it is a wider and more promising field of labor that attracts them. But the world notoriously does not believe this; and it has but too good reason for its unbelief.

The contract is ordinarily for so much money. If the money is not forthcoming, the contract is dissolved. But more, the money consideration decides in another way the character of man they wish to secure. It is ordinarily a *successful* man that is wanted, after the fashionable idea of what is success. They want a man who will fill the church, perhaps help to pay off the debt upon it. Very likely the payment of his own salary depends upon this. *He will not be likely most to please who is not influenced by such motives;* and thus it will be only God's mercy if Balaam's doctrine does not secure a Balaam to carry it out. But even if a godly man is obtained, he is put under the influence of the strongest personal temptation to soften down the truth, which, if fully preached, may deprive him of not only influence, but perhaps even subsistence.

Will the most godly man be the most popular man? No; for godliness is not what the world seeks. It can appreciate genius, no doubt, and eloquence, and amiability, and benevolence, and utilitarianism; but godliness is something different from the union of even all of these. If the world can appreciate godliness, I will own indeed it is no longer the world. But as long as the lust of the flesh and the lust of the eyes and the pride of life still characterize it, it is not of the Father, nor the Father of it. And then, why in that passage does the apostle say "the *Father*"? Is it not because in thinking of the Father's relation to the world, we must needs think of the *Son?* As he says again in another place, "Who is he that overcometh the world, but he that believeth that Jesus is the *Son of God?*" And why? Because it is the Son of God the world has crucified and cast out; and that the cross, which was the world's judgment of the Son of God, is, for faith, *God's* judgment of the world.

Was Christ popular, beloved friends? Could He, with divine power in His hands and ministering it freely for the manifold need appealing to Him on every side,—*could He* commend Himself to men His creatures? No, assuredly. But you think perhaps those peculiarly evil times: they understand Him better now, you think. Take, then, His dear name with you to men's places of business and to their homes to-day, to the workshop and the counting-houses, and the public places—do you doubt what response you would get?

"In the churches?" Oh, yes, they have agreed to tolerate Him there. The churches have been carefully arranged to please the world. Comfortable, fashionable, the poor packed in convenient corners, eye and ear and intellect provided for: that is a different thing. And then it helps to quiet conscience when it will sometimes stir. But oh, beloved, is there much sign of His presence whose own sign was, "*To the poor* the gospel is preached"?

Enough of this, however; it will be neither pleasure nor profit to pursue it further. But to those with whom the love of Christ is more than a profession, and the honor of Christ a reality to be maintained, I would solemnly put it how they can go on with what systematically tramples His honor underfoot, yea, under the world's foot,—falsifies His gospel, and helps to deceive to their own destruction the souls for whom He died. The doctrine of Balaam is every where: its end is judgment upon the world, and judgment too upon the people of God. If ministers cannot be supported, if churches cannot be kept up without this, the honestest, manliest, only Christian course is, let the thing go down! If Christians cannot get on without the world, they will find at least that the world can get on without them. They cannot persuade it that disobedience is such a serious thing when they see the light-hearted, flippant disobedience of which it is so easy to convict the great mass of professors, while it is so utterly impossible to deter them from it. "Money" is the cry; "well, but we want the money." Aye, though Christ's honor is betrayed by it, and infidels sneer, and souls perish. Brethren, the very Pharisees of old were wiser! "*We may not put it into the treasury,*" they whispered, "*because it is the price of blood.*"

It will be a relief to turn to Scripture, and to examine what we have there upon this subject. It is very simple. There was no organized machinery for supporting churches; none for paying ministers; no promise, no contract upon the people's part, as to any sum they were to receive at all. There were necessities, of course, many, to be provided for, and it was understood that there was to be provision. The saints themselves had to meet all. They had not taken up with a cheap religion. Having often to lay down their lives for it, they did not think much of their goods. The principle was this: "Every man as he is disposed in his heart, so let him give; not grudgingly, or of necessity; for God loveth a cheerful giver." It was to be to God, and before God. There was to be no blazoning it out to brethren, still less before the world. He that gave was not to let his left hand know what his right hand was doing.

It is true there were solemn motives to enforce it. On the one side, "he that soweth sparingly shall reap also sparingly, and he that soweth bountifully shall reap also bountifully;" but on the other side, most powerful, most influential of all, was this: "Ye know the grace of our Lord Jesus Christ, who, though He was rich, yet for your sakes became poor, that ye through His poverty might become rich."

Such was the principle, such was to be the motive. There was no compulsory method of extraction if this failed. If there was not heart to give, it was no use to extract.

So as to the laborer in the Word,—it was very clearly announced, and that as what God had ordained, that "they which preach the gospel should live of the gospel," and that "the laborer is worthy of his hire." But although here also God used the willing hands of His people, it was not understood that *they* "hired" him, or that he was *their* laborer. What they gave, it was to God they gave it, and *his* privilege was to be Christ's servant. His responsibility was to the Lord, and theirs also. They did not understand that they were to get so much work for so much money. They did not *pay*, but "*offered.*" There is a wonderful difference; for you cannot "pay" God, and you do not "offer" (in this sense of offering,) to man. The moment you *pay*, God is out of the question.

Do you think this is perhaps a little unfair on both sides? that it is right that there should be something more of an equivalent for the labor he bestows,—for the money you give? That is good law, bad gospel. What better than simony is it to suppose after this fashion—"that the gift of God can be purchased with money"? Would you rather make your own bargain than trust Christ's grace to minister to your need? or is it hard for him that he who ministers the Word should show his practical trust in the Word by looking to the Lord for his support? Ah, to whom could he look so well? and how much better off would he be for losing the sweet experience of His care?

No; it is all unbelief in divine power and love, and machinery brought in to make up for the want of it. And yet if there is not this, what profit is there of keeping up the empty profession of it? If God can fail, let the whole thing go together; if *He* cannot, then your skillful contrivances are only the exhibition of rank unbelief.

And what do you accomplish by it? You bring in the Canaanite (the merchantman) into the house of the Lord. You offer a premium to the trader in divine things,—the man who most values your money and least cares for your souls. You cannot but be aware how naturally those two extremes associate together, and you cannot but own that if you took the Lord's plan, and left His laborers to look to Him for their support, you would do more to weed out such traffickers than by all your care and labor otherwise. Stop the hire, and you will banish the hirelings, and the blessed ministry of Christ will be freed from an incubus and a reproach which your contracts and bargainings are largely responsible for.

And if Christ's servants cannot after all trust Him, let them seek out some honest occupation where they may gain their bread without scandal. In the fifteenth century before Christ, God brought out a whole nation out of Egypt, and maintained them forty years in the wilderness. Did He? or did He not? Is He as competent as ever? Alas! will you dare to say those were the days of His youth, and these of His decrepitude?

So serious are these questions. But the unbelief that exists now existed then. Do you remember what the people did when they had lost Moses on the mount awhile and lacked a leader? *They made a god of the gold which they had brought out of Egypt with them, and fell down and worshiped the work of their own hands.* History repeats itself. Who can deny that we have been looking on the counterpart of that?

Is there any measure, it may be well to ask here, of the Christian's giving, for one who would be right with God about it?

The notion of the tithe or tenth has been revived, or with some two tithes, as that which was the measure of an Israelite's giving. Jacob has been propounded to us as an example, as he stood before God in the morning after that wonderful night at Bethel, when God had engaged to be with him and to be his God, and to multiply his seed, and bring him again into the land from which he was departing. "If God will be with me," he says, "and will keep me in the way that I go, and will give me bread to eat and raiment to put on, so that I come again to my father's house in peace; then the Lord shall be my God; and this stone, which I have set for a pillar, shall be God's house, and of all that Thou shalt give me, I will surely give the tenth unto Thee."

God's ways are so little like our ways, His thoughts so little like our thoughts, it is not very wonderful man does not understand them. But surely Jacob does not here enter into the blessedness of God's thoughts.

I need not dwell now upon his case, but only notice it to say that for a Christian at least the whole principle is a mistake. You are not to ransom nine-tenths from God by giving one. You are bought with a price—you and yours. In a double way, by creation and redemption too, you belong, with all you have, to God. Many people are acting upon the perfectly wrong idea that whether as to time, money, or whatever else, God is to have His share, and the rest is their own. They misunderstand the legal types, and do not realize the immense difference that accomplished redemption has brought in with it.

Before "Ye are bought with a price" could yet be said, it was impossible to deduce the consequences that result from this. Grace goes beyond law, which made nothing, and could make nothing, perfect. The very essence of the surrender of the life to God is that it must be a voluntary one. Like the vow of the Nazarite, which was a vow of separation to the Lord, and which reads, "When any one *will* vow the vow of a Nazarite," that surrender must be of the heart, or it is none. Nor is it a contradiction to this that there were *born* Nazarites—Nazarites from the womb, as Samson and the Baptist. We are all *born* (new-born) to Nazariteship, which is implied and necessitated (in a true sense) by the life which we receive from God. But the necessity is not one externally impressed upon it; it is an internal one. "A new heart will I give you," says the Lord; but the new heart given is a heart which chooses freely the service of its Master.

A legal requirement of the whole then would have been unavailing, and a mere bondage. "Not grudgingly, or of necessity," is, as we have seen, the Scripture rule. But that does not at all mean what people characterize as "cheap religion." It does not mean that God will accept the "mites" of the niggard as the Lord did those of the woman in the Gospels. Christ does not say now, Give as much or as little as you please: it is all one. No: He expects intelligent, free surrender of all to Him, as on the part of one who recognizes that all is really His.

If you will look at the sixteenth chapter of Luke, you will find the Lord announcing very distinctly this principle. The unjust steward is our picture here,—the picture of those who are (as we all are as to the old creation) under sentence of dismissal from the place they were originally put in, on account of unrighteous dealing in it. Grace has not recalled the sentence, "Thou mayest be no longer steward." It has given us far more, but it has not reinstalled us in the place we have thus lost. Death, in fact, is our removal from our stewardship, although it be the entrance, for us as Christians, into something which must be confessed "far better."

But grace has delayed the execution of the sentence, and meanwhile our Master's goods are in our hand. All that we have here are *His* things and not ours. And now God looks for us to be faithful in what is, alas! to men as such (creature of God as indeed it is,) "the mammon of unrighteousness,"—the miserable deity of unrighteous man.

Moreover, grace counts this faithfulness to us. We are permitted to "make *friends* of this mammon of unrighteousness" by our godly use of it, whereas it is naturally, through our fault, our enemy and our accuser. It must not be imagined that the "unjust steward" is to be our character literally all through. The Lord shows us that this is not so when He speaks of "faithfulness" being looked for. No doubt the unjust steward in the parable acts unjustly with his master's goods, and it must not be imagined that *God* commends him: it is "his lord" that does so,—man as man admiring the shrewdness which he displayed. Yet only so could be imaged that conduct which in us is *not* injustice but faithfulness to our Master,—grace entitling us to use what we have received, for our own true and eternal interests, which in this case are one with His own due and glory.

But then there are things also which we may speak of as "our own." What are these? Ah, they are what the Lord speaks of as, after all, "the true riches." "If ye have not been faithful in the unrighteous mammon, who will commit to your trust the true riches? And if ye have not been faithful in that which is Another's, [not 'another *man's*,' but of course God's,] who will give you that which is *your own?*"

Thus our own things are distinct altogether; and I must not tell Christians what they are. I need only remind you that if you have in your thoughts as men down here, a quantity of things, your own possessions, to be liberal with or to hoard up,—in both cases you misapprehend the matter. You have as to things here your *Master's* goods, which if you hoard up here, you surely lose hereafter, and turn into accusers. On the other hand, you are graciously permitted to transfer them really to your own account, by laying them up amid your treasure, where your treasure is—"in heaven."

The rich man in the solemn illustration at the end of the chapter was one who had made his Lord's "good things" his own after another fashion, and in eternity they were not friends, but enemies and accusers. "Son," says Abraham to him, "remember that thou in thy lifetime receivedst thy good things." That was all, but what a solemn memory it was! How once again the purple and fine linen and sumptuous fare met the eyes they had once gratified and now appalled! Lazarus had been at his gate, but it was not Lazarus that accused. And oh, beware of having things your own down here! There was a man who had "his good things" here, and in eternity what were they to him?

I know this is not the gospel. No, but it is what, as the principle of God's holy government, the gospel should prepare us to understand and to enter into. Have you observed that the most beautiful and affecting story of gospel grace, the story of the lost son received, is what *precedes* the story of the unjust steward? The Pharisees who in the fifteenth chapter stand for the picture of the elder son are here rebuked in the person of the rich man. Will not the prodigal received back to a Father's arms be the very one who will understand that he owes his all to a Father's love? Is not "Ye are bought with a price" the gospel? But then "ye are *bought:* ye are not your own."

Put it in another way. You remember that when God would bring His people out of Egypt, Pharaoh wanted to compromise,—of course by that compromise to keep the people as his slaves. Three separate offers he makes to Moses, each of which would have prevented salvation being, according to God's thought of it, salvation at all. The first compromise was, "Worship *in the land*."

"And Pharaoh called for Moses and for Aaron, and said, 'Go ye, sacrifice to your God in the land.'"

And still the world asks, "Why need you go outside it? You are entitled to your opinions, but why be so extreme? Why three days' journey into the wilderness? Why separate from what you were brought up in, and from people as good as you?" Ah, they do not know what that three days' journey implies, and that the death and resurrection of Christ place you where you are no more of the world than He is! Egypt,—luxurious, civilized, self-satisfied, idolatrous Egypt,—and the wilderness! what a contrast! Yet only in the wilderness can you sacrifice to God.

Then he tries another stratagem:—

"And he said unto them, 'Go, serve the Lord your God; *but who are they that shall go?*'

"And Moses said, 'We will go with our young and with our old, with our sons and with our daughters, with our flocks and with our herds we will go; for we must hold a feast unto the Lord.'

"And he said unto them, 'Let the Lord be so

with you, as I will let you go and your little ones: look to it, for evil is before you. Not so: go now ye that are *men*, and serve the Lord; for that ye did desire.'"

By their little ones he had them safe, of course,—a perfectly good security that they would not go far away. And so it is still. How many are brought back into the world by the children they did not bring with them *out of* the world!

One last hope remains for Pharaoh:—

"And Pharaoh called unto Moses, and said, 'Go ye, serve the Lord; *only let your flocks and your herds be stayed:* let your little ones also go with you.'"

"Leave your possessions," he says; and how many leave their possessions! Themselves are saved: but their business, their occupation, these are still not sacred things, they are secular; what have these things to do with the salvation of the soul?

But God says, No: bring them all out of Egypt: yourselves, your families, your property,—all are to be Mine.

And in point of fact, His it must be if we would ourselves keep it, for we cannot keep it of ourselves. The man out of whom the devil went is our Lord's own illustration of the fact that an empty house will never lack a tenant. The sweeping and garnishing and all that, will not keep out the devil, but perhaps only make him more earnest after occupation. Nothing will save from it but the positive possession of it by another, who will not and need not give it up. So we must bring Christ into every thing, or by that in which He is not we shall find we have but made room for another,—Christ's opposite. The parable has application in many ways and in many degrees to those who are Christ's people, as well as to those who are not. Our really idle hours are not idle. Our useless occupations have a use, if not for Christ, then against Him. Our so-called recreations may be but the frittering away of energy, as well as time, and not only distraction, but the seed of worse distraction.

We are in a world where on every side we are exposed to influences of the most subtle character; where corruption and decay are natural; and where all thus is not permeated by divine life, it becomes the necessary and speedy subject of decay and death. To a beleaguered garrison, a holiday may be fatal. We cannot ever here ungird our loins or unbuckle our armor. It is not enough to withstand in the evil day; but having done all, still you must stand. So if you leave Christ at the door of the counting-house, you will have to contend alone with (or give place to) the devil within the counting-house.

Does this startle you? does it seem to require too much? It requires that you should be with Christ in constant companionship, at all times and on all occasions. Is that narrow,—a rigid, an uncomfortable view of matters? Does it distress you to think of giving Him such a place as that? There are those who believe that *he* is the picture of a converted man, who complains he never got a kid to make merry with his friends. Do you realize that? Do you sympathize with such a view? Have you friends that you would like to run away to for a while out of Christ's scrutiny or company? Beloved, when you think of heaven, is it of a long *monotony* of being "ever with the Lord"? You startle at that suggestion; and no wonder. But if you will find eternal joy then, and now can think of it as that, to be ever with Him there, is it less happy to think of being always with Him here?

At any rate, you cannot alter the reality by all your thoughts about it. None of our thoughts can change the nature of things. You cannot find in all this world a clean corner in which you can be apart from Christ and yet apart from evil. And if you could, the very idea of being so would of itself pollute it with evil. No; Christ must be a constant Saviour as to every detail of our walk and ways. Communion with Him is the only alternative of communion with evil. The wisdom that has not Him in it, will be "earthly, sensual, devilish;" if it come not from above, come it will from below.

Thus you see how important it is to be right here. It is not a mere question of points of detail; it is a question of truth of heart to Him, which affects every detail,—the whole character and complexion of our lives indeed. So you must not wonder at a question of *cattle* being concerned with a deeper question of "salvation" itself; looking at salvation as not merely being from wrath and condemnation, but of salvation from the sin also which brings in these. God gives it us thus in the typical picture here, and it is not a blot or deformity in the picture, but rather an essential part. Be persuaded of it, beloved friends, that only thus can we find, in the full power of it, what salvation is.

We have been looking at this from the side of responsibility. Surely it is good to look at it also from the side of salvation. Until you are clean delivered in these three respects, you cannot be happily with God, nor even safe. Of course I am not talking about reaching heaven; you may be safe in that respect. But whatever you have that is not Christ's, that is the world's still, and it will drag you back into the world. You are keeping it back from Him; you have a divided interest; how can this but affect all your intercourse, all your happiness (or what you ought to have) with Him? Can you go to your business and shut the door upon Him and He not feel it, and *you* not feel it? Can you say to Him, "Lord, Sunday is Yours and Monday is mine," or "Lord, there is Your tenth, and these nine are mine," and feel perfectly satisfied that all is right with Him?

And practically, it gets to be much less. He gets a part of our superfluity, and that is all. We must dress like our neighbors, live up to our rank of life, put a little by for a "rainy day," and something for our children. "We must be *just* before we are generous," we think. And then, with some reserve for recreation, and some for miscellaneous trifles, *all the rest shall be the Lord's*. It may be but a "mite," but did not He accept a mite? *So the very narrowness of our dole to the Lord who has saved us links us with her who had His special commendation.*

Better keep it all back than give it in that fashion. For the amount given just hinders from realizing where we are. We give it ungrudgingly, perhaps: we think it has the Lord's approval therefore. We do not think *how much it is* that we can give ungrudgingly.

Ungrudgingly it must be. Love it must be. Though I give all my goods to feed the poor, except it be love that does it, it will be utterly contemned. But if our love is measured by what we give to Him, how serious is the question raised!

In this great world of sorrow and of evil, Christ has interests dear to His heart,—how dear, no one of us has perhaps a notion of. Souls lie in darkness to whom His Word would give light, and in bondage to whom it would bring deliverance. He says to us, "I count upon My people to do this." How can we answer to Him for this confidence He has placed in us? Shall we say, "Lord, I have had to keep up with my neighbors, to provide for the future, to do a great many things, which I thought of more importance"? or shall we say, "Lord, Thou art so great, so high, so powerful, Thou surely canst not want my help in a matter like this!" or, again, "Lord, Thou art so gracious, I am sure Thou wilt accept any thing I may bring: I would not suppose Thee a hard Master, to want me to bring Thee much"? Alas, what shall we say? Shall we not rather own with broken hearts how little we have valued *Him?*

The "doctrine of Balaam" thrives upon the heartlessness of God's own people. Do not let us imagine, because we denounce the mercenary character of what is current all around, that we can have no share in upholding what we denounce. It is far otherwise. If we have given cause, are giving cause, to those who sneer at the advocates of "cheap religion," we are giving it the most effectual possible support. In words, you denounce; in deeds, you justify. You tell them that it is vain to trust to the power of Christ's love in Christians,—that your own barn is practically dearer to you than all God's house; and they can point to you triumphantly as proof of the necessity of all that they contend for.

Beloved, I have done. I have spoken out my heart, and I must pray you bear with me. Who that looks around with a heart for Christ upon all the abominations practiced in His name but must be led to ask, Did not all this evil spring out of the failure of His own people—of those who at heart loved Him? And further, how far are we perhaps now unsuspectingly helping on the very evils we deplore? Do we not pray for Him to search out our hearts? and shall we shrink from having them searched out? If the search detects nothing, we need not fear it: if it shows us unanticipated evil, it is well to realize that the truthful judgment of the evil is ever the truest blessing for our souls. It will cost us something, no doubt, to walk in what is ever a narrow way. A race, a warfare, call for energy and self-denial. But ah, beloved, it will cost us more, much more, to have Christ walk as a stranger to us because our paths and His do not agree. How few, when they speak of cost, put this into their balance-sheet! Yet, "if I wash thee not," He says, "thou hast no part with Me." Are there not many trying to keep up appearances, when that is the inward trouble of their souls?

But the door is open, beloved, to came back. He has never shut it. The one thing so greatly lacking now is whole-hearted integrity;—so few without some secret corner in their hearts that they would not like to have searched out by Him. That corner *must* be searched out, for He must be a Saviour after His own fashion; and if we would not have it, we can have little apprehended the fullness and reality of His salvation. Not alone does He save from wrath: He saves from *sin*. It is in subjection to His yoke that we find rest. From our own will and ways and thoughts, in His blessed will, His thoughts, His love.

God grant it to us for His name's sake, even now.

Pergamos: the Promise to the Overcomer.
(Rev. ii. 17.)

THE promise to the overcomer in Pergamos claims our deepest attention. As always in these epistles, it emphasizes the condition of those to whom it is addressed; and we have seen that this is not merely a past condition, but a stage in the development of what is all around us to-day; so that the exhortations and warnings suited to it have for us no less force than ever. In fact they should have more, as we stand face to face with that development,—as the fruit, ripe and multiplied, is before our eyes.

But the promise to the overcomer, while reminding us of the departure and decay already so far gone, is not shrouded with the gloom of this. On the contrary, it is bright with hope, and full of the joy which for the Christian can spring out of whatever sorrow. It breathes the spirit of what the apostle speaks of as our portion ever, "not the spirit of fear, but of power and love and of a sound mind." It is Christ's word of encouragement for those who in the strife of the battle-field look to the Captain of their salvation; and it carries us beyond the scene of strife to the inheritance already sure to us, although through trial and suffering is the path by which it is ordained to reach it.

The promise has two parts, which are in beautiful relation to one another. The *manna*, as is evident, speaks of Christ Himself, and of *our apprehension of Him;* the *white stone* is a sign, on the other hand, of *His appreciation of us.* How blessed is the interchange of affection thus expressed! How touching the appeal to it where the heart of His beloved is so manifestly wandering away from Him! The manna is wilderness food: it fell only there, in Egypt it was not yet known; arrived within the borders of the land, it ceased. It was divine provision for those to whom God was an absolute necessity, whom He had brought into a place where was no natural provision, where they were wholly cast upon Him. It was this necessity which was their claim upon the tender compassion of their great Deliverer. He had, indeed, made Himself responsible to answer to it, and all their varied need was thus to draw out new witness of divine resources,—riches of glory—power and love alike.

The wilderness does not speak of any natural condition. Egypt is the natural condition, and Egypt is a very fruitful land. There were many drawbacks there, no doubt, which would in general be freely acknowledged. Plagues smote there as elsewhere, and an oppressive tyranny brooded over it: but the one, they might hope individually to escape; the other, they bore in company with a multitude. But the productiveness of the soil no one could question: "We remember the fish which we did eat in Egypt freely; the cucumbers, and the melons, and the leeks, and the onions, and the garlic: and now our soul is dried away, there is nothing at all but this manna before our eyes."

The promise of the manna is, then, for the wilderness, but it is the *overcomer* in Pergamos who alone knows the need of the wilderness. Those who have settled down in the world proclaim by the fact how little they find the world such; and this character of the overcomer confirms our view of the state spiritually of Pergamos itself. Here it was no longer the state of individuals merely, but of the mass; and not even a secret state, but avowed openly in deed if not in word. Thus, then, the Lord speaks to him who, true to his calling, finds in Himself his one necessity and satisfaction, "Bread shall be given him, his water shall be sure." Yea, "meat which endureth unto everlasting life," and water which shall "be in him a *spring* of water, springing up to everlasting life."

And this may remind us that the manna, of which the Lord speaks in the promise here, although it be the manna of the wilderness, is not, nevertheless, what was partaken of in the wilderness. The "*hidden* manna" was that put by command of God into the ark, and carried into the land, that after-generations might see the bread wherewith He had fed them in the wilderness." In this case it was, of course, not eaten; but the Lord promises to the overcomer here that he shall eat it; clearly in the blessed place which for us has in the highest degree the character attributed to the land of Canaan, —a place "where the eyes of the Lord are continually:" the wilderness food is still to be enjoyed when the wilderness is passed forever. The hidden manna was the memorial sample of what had fallen long before: it is typically the abiding remembrance of what we once tasted,—the fresh taste in eternity of Christ as enjoyed by faith down here.

We may thus see (and it is good to see,) how closely connected the life to come is with the present. Do we not miss much by separating them as widely as we sometimes do? and by supposing that, apart from all experiences and attainments here, all elements of blessing will be found in equal degree in the cup of eternal joy, when our lips are once at its brim? by imagining that if "when that which is perfect is come, that which is in part shall be done away," then all present effects of lack of communion, or of that knowledge which results in and implies communion, will be necessarily passed also; not allowed to abate in any wise the eternal portion? Is this what the words of the apostle indeed assure us of?

For each one of us, no doubt, the state will be perfect, the partial condition will be done away. That is surely so. When the bud is ripened into the flower, the perfect condition is reached; it is a bud no longer. Does it follow from this at all that the flower is in no wise *dependent* upon that bud which is passed away? We know it *is* dependent. So when it is no longer a condition of faith, but of sight,—no longer seeing through a glass, darkly, but face to face, the present *knowing**—not the knowledge itself, but the manner of it—will have passed. We "shall know," not as afar off any longer, but in the presence of the things known. That is, "as we are known," as He to whom all

---

*"Knowledge," in 1 Cor. xiii. 8, may be here better rendered "knowing" ($\gamma\nu\tilde{\omega}\sigma\iota\varsigma$). When it is added, "Then shall I know even as also I am [or rather *have been*] known" (*v.* 12), a compound form is used ($\dot{\epsilon}\pi\iota\gamma\iota\nu\tilde{\omega}\sigma\kappa\omega$). This last perfectly suits the apostle's comparison of seeing face to face instead of through a glass. It is intensive,—a knowing founded upon knowledge, and thus often used for "recognition" and "acknowledgment."

things are present knows us. It does not speak of the *measure* of knowledge, but of the *manner* of it; for who could suppose the measure of it to be God's omniscience? And it is of the manner of it —face-to-face knowledge—the apostle speaks.

Rather will the limits of our knowledge there be defined, and we shall be conscious of them,—spared thus the strain of searching into the unsearchable, and delivered from the temptation of aspiring to what is beyond our sphere. There will be, of course, complete satisfaction with the limits whatever they may be.

But this, then, removes the thought of any necessary equality of knowledge among the redeemed themselves. The "new name written, which no man knoweth saving he that receiveth it" is a proof of this in the words before us. And the hidden manna is another proof. For the partaking of that which fell in the wilderness is only possible as a recalling of experience once known. It is not a fresh experience, but a past experience enjoyed afresh. Christ is no more there the humbled One of which the manna speaks; and the hidden manna was carried into Canaan, not belonged there. It was strictly a memorial of the past, and as this, has its significance. The experience which we gain here is gained forever; the joy is not for a moment, the meat endures unto eternal life: the fruit of the sorrow we pass through is not reaped all amid the sorrow, but reaped above all, there where the harvest is an abiding one. Blessed be God, it is so.

Some imagine a common height of blessing to which grace lifts in result all partakers of it, which leaves no practical issue for eternity of whatever difference in the life and ways on earth. Others would cut off, as contrary to the grace which remembers our sins and iniquities no more, the very memory of them within us, as if it would spoil the eternal blessedness. Others, again,—and this is a most common mistake,—would confound the fruits of grace, which we enjoy in common, with the rewards of grace, which have respect to responsibilities fulfilled. All these are alike errors, and lead to practical consequences which are of grave importance.

Sonship, heirship, membership in the body of Christ, are alike pure gifts of divine grace, and in no wise of work. They are ours once for all, and never withdrawn from us. How blessed to realize that these are, after all, our very chiefest blessings, which we have in common! How much less, comparatively, must the reward of *our* work be, and the reward of Christ's work, which they all are! How precious to know that every child of the Father's love shall be clasped to the Father's heart alike,—that there shall be no more distance for one than for another! Yet it is not every one who is clear as to salvation who is clear as to this. But were it otherwise, who could, without presumption, anticipate any nearness at all? But the many mansions of the Father's house have room for all, and the Father's heart has surely no less room. "What manner of love hath He" indeed "bestowed upon us, that we should be called the sons of God!" But it is *His* love, and let us enjoy it to the full without a remnant of fear. Let not one shadow of legality darken the joy of it. And this love shall be justified in its fullest expression also, for "we shall be"—one as much as another,—"like Christ, for we shall see Him as He is."

It is not, perhaps, wonderful that as we contemplate such blessings as these we should be tempted to think that there surely cannot be left room for any difference whatever. To be like Christ!—all altogether like Him! Think of it, ye His beloved, the fruit of His work, the purchase of His precious blood! Who could imagine, indeed, that the fruit of *our* work could make any difference here! For whom could it be but in the most absolute wonderful love, with power to accomplish its desires in us? Shall any thing hinder that accomplishment, then? No, nothing! What is stronger than what manifested itself in the cross? What can rob it of its glorious reward?

Yet unspeakably great as all this is, still he that has an ear to receive the Scripture testimony will surely find that, beside the common blessing which every one of Christ's own shall get, there are distinctive and individual blessings, which are not, therefore, the same for all. "To reward every one according as his work shall be."—"Rule thou over ten . . . rule thou over five cities."—"Hold that fast which thou hast, that no man take thy crown." These passages, and such as these, are unmistakably clear also. Nor can it be urged that it is only in temporary not in eternal awards that such distinctions can have place. The hidden manna and the white stone are not of this character, and they both speak of what is the result of the earthly walk.

And again, it is in no wise true that the very sins of which God says, "I will remember them no more" shall not come up before the judgment-seat of Christ. They surely shall. "God," says the Preacher, "shall bring every work into judgment, with every secret thing, whether it be good or whether it be evil." "We must all be manifested before the judgment-seat of Christ, that every one may receive the things done in his body, whether it be good or whether it be evil."

Are these things contradictory? They are equally parts of God's perfect and eternal Word. Nor is there the slightest difficulty even as to their reconciliation, if we may speak of reconciliation as needful. God will indeed remember our sins no more; but does any one imagine that His memory will fail in the least as to one of them? *Against us* He will not remember them. No displeasure on their account shall ever darken His glorious face. Never will He upbraid us with them. It is *we* who shall "give *account of ourselves* to Him." Shall it be only of whatever *good*, little or much as it may be? Shall we present ourselves as sinless ones, who have had no need of redeeming blood? Standing in the glory and perfection of Christ's likeness as we then shall be, our memories shall be fully alive with all the past, so as to give a faithful record of it before the throne of truth. All mists, all uncertainties, all errors, will be gone forever. How blessed to be clear of them! Then how bright will God's grace appear! how perfect His wisdom! Not, surely, with reference to an angel's course, but to that of a fallen, erring, yet redeemed man. And the memories of our sins, would we be then without them, when without them the whole world would be an impenetrable darkness still, and the very song of redemption could not itself be sung!

And it is declared of some who build upon God's foundation gold, silver, precious stones, wood, hay, stubble, the day shall declare it, for it shall be revealed with fire, and the fire shall try every man's work of what sort it is. If any man's work abide which he has built thereon, he shall receive a reward; if any man's work be burned up, he shall suffer loss; yet he himself shall be saved, yet so as through the fire. No matter of what class of believers this speaks, the principle announced is plain: reward to some, to others loss, while yet both alike are saved ones.

Thus the promise of the hidden manna appeals solemnly, while most encouragingly, to us. Our present life is not cut off by so broad a division from the eternal one as some would have it, while yet there is a division as plain as it is serious. The days of human responsibility end with the life here. It is for the things done in the body that they are judged or rewarded, and for these only. Thus these days exercise an irreversible influence over the life to come: the hidden manna and the white stone are eternal recompenses of the present time. In another sense, as to the hidden manna, it is but that "the meat" that faith lives on now is but the "meat that endureth to everlasting life." So that the spiritual experiences of the present pass on as memories into the eternal joy beyond. But as memories with none of the dullness which attaches to such things now; for then is the day of manifestation and of recompense, and the memory then will far outdo the experience now.

We pass through trial and adversity, through a world in truth a wilderness, a place of utter dependence, in which faith feels, amid the darkness, for the strength of the everlasting arms. And here we learn, as no where else could we learn, the grace that is come down to us. We are like those that go down to the sea in ships, and that have their business in the deep waters,—men that see the works of the Lord, and His wonders in the deep. "A brother is born for adversity," and in adversity we learn the touch of a brother's hand; yea, "there is a Friend that sticketh closer than a brother," and how blessed to realize in Him who sticks so close the very Lord of glory Himself! Not a kindly and gracious Protector merely, from His own sphere of unchanging blessedness, but One hand in hand, traveling the same road, ministering of His own cup of consolation, displaying sympathies which have been developed in the self-same path, but of sorrows voluntarily endured that He might so minister to us.

Precious humiliation, upon which the heavens once looked down in wonder! but of which none can know in truth the deepest meaning, save those who have drunk of the cup of the pilgrim, and in actual poverty been enriched by a greater poverty of Him for our sakes come into it. It is this which makes the hidden manna so impossible to be tasted except by one who has tasted the manna in that wilderness where alone it fell. After-generations in Israel might indeed *see* the food wherewith the Lord fed them in the wilderness, but that was all. He who had been *in* the wilderness alone could say of it, "I know its taste." When the people were despising it as light food, in touching appeal to us the Lord through the historian describes its taste. We can little indeed describe a taste; only at all by comparing it to some other familiar one, and so here: "its taste was as the taste of *fresh oil*,"—the ministry of the Holy Ghost; but in another place, "it was like wafers made with honey:" *that* speaks of Him whom the Holy Ghost declares to us.

The land promised to Israel was described in its riches as a "land flowing with milk and honey." It is the figure of natural sweetness; very sweet, but not to be partaken of too freely, nor allowed to be put into that which was offered to God. But the manna was not honey, and though having the sweetness of it, could be fed upon continually. All the sweetness of human affection and intimacy is found in the "Son of Man," but with no element of corruptibility in it. Honey easily ferments and sours, but in this sweet intimacy there is absolute stability: it is a love which can be relied on at all times, where the human has become one with the divine,—the divine makes itself realized in what we can apprehend and enter into as most truly human.

This is the taste; but to know it, you must taste it. No description will convey it rightly to you; and to know the grace of Christ's humiliation, you must have been in the wilderness, and there learned to say, "All my fresh springs are in Thee." If "a brother is born for adversity," it is only adversity that can rightly make you know that "brother." In the land, amid all its glories, the *manna* was "the *hidden* manna." In the wilderness it was not hidden; and to those who had gone the journey through the wilderness, the manna, even in the land, was not really hidden. In the glory of heaven we shall know in the Man, Christ Jesus, some steps (and surely wonderful ones) of His surpassing condescension; nay, a "Lamb, as it had been slain," will call forth the unceasing homage of all there; but the manna gives the personal application of this grace to a need which in heaven will no longer exist: it must be enjoyed there as knowledge gained in quite other circumstances. And here the wilderness will at last yield its harvests to us, the desert left behind will blossom as the rose.

For how will those spiritual experiences so full of joy to us here bloom in the sunlight of eternity into glorious recollections, when all that hinders shall be forever removed; when the divine ways shall be seen in all their holiness, all their wisdom, all their grace! Our senses are here at the best so dull, the power of the Spirit so little known, Christ is after all so little in His transcendent beauty enjoyed! Then, face to face with His glory, seeing Him as He is, and able to measure somewhat truly the depths of His descent from the heights before us, how will the King in His beauty, our blest Lord and Saviour, be revealed!

But it is time to turn round upon ourselves, is it not? and to ask of ourselves, How much material for this joy hereafter are we gathering here? And this suggests another question: How much need have we of Christ day by day? how much hunger and thirst have we after Him? These are very strong terms, as they are evidently also the terms of Scripture. All the labor of man is for the mouth. Hunger and thirst are controlling things. Yet says the Lord, "Labor *not* for the meat that perisheth, but for that meat which endureth unto everlasting life." Do we indeed by comparison not labor for the one as we labor for the other? and *which* one is it—in calm, sober, reality—that we labor for?

We have life, perhaps,—eternal life,—salvation. Blessed to have these. With the rest thus gained, have we started for the goal outside the world? or are we practically living much as others in it,—the days filled up with a routine of things imposed by the various masters (customs, men's thoughts of us, the claims of society, and what not) which rule there? It is one thing or other; outside the world, and in opposition to it, or in it, and floating with its stream.

In this last case, there will either be no felt need, or none that Christ can be counted on to meet. Much may be pleaded as to duties, which are merely artificial, and untruly covered with so fair a name. But whatever may be the plea, the daily need and ministry of Christ is a thing unknown. *Great* needs may demand Him, but life is not made up of these.

Briefly to consider now, however, the second part of the promise—the "white stone":—

The two parts of the promise are inseparably connected with one another. The appreciation of Christ by the soul is the necessary basis of His answering approbation. The white stone speaks, as has been said, of this approbation. It was the token of approval, dropped by voters into the urn of old, with the name of the candidate approved upon it. But the name here is a *new* name, known only by Him who gives and by him who receives it.

The name, in Scripture, is always significant and descriptive of the one who bears it. To know God's name is just to know what He is, to know His character; and the new name here speaks of the character for Christ of him upon whom it is conferred, some character which He approves. It is a peculiar link between the Lord and the one approved, a peculiar something that we are for Him.

It implies some trial, as the former part of the promise, and speaks of His estimate of how it has been endured,—of something especially noted as pleasing to Himself. It is not publicly noted or rewarded, however. Such rewards, of course, there are; but this is another and a deeper thing. Still more than the hidden manna is it an individual joy, not shared by the general company of the redeemed,—the one secret link, as it would seem, between the Lord and the individual saint.

Is it worth seeking, this approbation of His? Is any thing else in comparison? Is it not marvelous that we can barter the priceless eternal joys for things which perish in the using, even if they did not also entail upon the soul a feebleness from which oftentimes there is here no recovery. We pity the inebriate, possessed by his passion for what rivets upon the ever-increasing load which will at last destroy him; but oh what sorrow should we have for the Nazarites of God, endowed with the limitless possession of the Spirit of God, to know the things that are freely given to us of God, yet drunk with the spirit of the world, His enemy, and squandering the precious gifts of God for the husks of the swineherd! We have no words that are worthy or of power to rebuke it; but let us hear the apostle:—

"Ye adulterers and adulteresses, know ye not that the friendship of the world is enmity with God? Wherefore, whosoever will be a friend of the world is the enemy of God."

"Love not the world, neither the things that are in the world. . . . For all that is in the world, the lust of the flesh, and the lust of the eyes, and the pride of life, is not of the Father, but is of the world. And the world passeth away, and the lust thereof; but he that doeth the will of God abideth forever."

"Wherefore awake, thou that sleepest, and arise from the dead, and CHRIST shall give thee light."

"For ye are all the children of the light, and the children of the day: we are not of the night, nor of darkness. Therefore let us not sleep, as do others; but let us watch and be sober. For they that sleep sleep in the night, and they that are drunken are drunken in the night; but let us, who are of the day, be sober, putting on the breastplate of faith and love; and for a helmet, the hope of salvation. For God has not appointed us unto wrath, but to obtain salvation through our Lord Jesus Christ, who died for us, that, whether we wake or sleep, we should *live together with Him*."

Yes, and that life is now begun with us; the eternal life has for us begun. May the words ring in our ears at least until they lay hold completely of our hearts and lives: "To him that overcometh will I give to eat of the hidden manna, and will give him a white stone, and on the stone a new name written, which no man knoweth saving he who receiveth it."

"Overcometh"—not in the world merely, but now in the church; not in circumstances in which he is *not*, but in the precise circumstances in which he is;—"overcometh:" do you, do I, know well, and from quite familiar experience, what it is to *overcome?*

Thyatira: the Reign of the World-Church.
(Rev. ii. 18-29.)

OUR course has been hitherto continually downward. The church to which we have now come forms no exception to this rule, and in a certain sense it is the end of the course that we reach in it. In Thyatira, our eyes are no more toward the past, but toward the future—the coming of the Lord: there is no more the call to repentance and doing the first works; the word is now, "I gave her space to repent, and she did not repent." The opportunity of repentance is therefore over: henceforth there can only be judgment—judgment which has accumulated terribly during the long delay: "I will cast her into a bed, and them that commit adultery with her into great tribulation, except they repent of her works; and I will kill her children with death."

But on this account we find a remnant in Thyatira distinguished from that upon which judgment is to fall; a remnant guilty indeed for their toleration of what the Lord has devoted to destruction, but which He cannot for a moment confound, nevertheless, with it. This remnant is exhorted to hold fast until He comes. "And to him that overcometh, and keepeth My works unto the end, to him will I give power over the nations, and he shall rule them with a rod of iron; as the vessels of a potter shall they be broken to pieces, even as I received of My Father; and I will give him the morning star."

We have reached, then, in this line, the final development, as I have said. Thyatira goes on, substantially, unchanged until the coming of the Lord.

What, then, is the character of Thyatira? It is characterized by the suffering of one who calls herself a prophetess,—that is, claims for herself divine inspiration,—and who by her name, Jezebel, carries us back to the idolatry of the worst days of Israel, and the bitter persecution of the saints and

THYATIRA.

servants of God by her who, stranger as she was, exercised royal authority in the midst of the professed people of the Lord. "And she teacheth and seduceth My servants to commit fornication, and to eat things sacrificed to idols."

We have already compared the opening parables of the thirteenth of Matthew with the first three of these addresses to the Asiatic churches, and we cannot but be here most powerfully impressed with the appearance of the "woman" alike in the fourth parable of this series and the fourth address to which we have come. It is a new figure in each case. When we come to examine it, we are made to realize without any doubt that the two women are in fact but one. And that in spite of various and discordant interpretations which have been given to these passages. Let us look, then, first at the parable, and then compare it with our Revelation chapter. They are both the words of our Lord Himself.

"Again, the kingdom of heaven is like unto leaven, which a woman took, and hid in three measures of meal, till the whole was leavened."

The common interpretation of this we are all familiar with. It is applied to the universal spread and final triumph of the gospel, which, diffusive as leaven in its nature, is thus to make its way among the nations of the earth, and subject them to its beneficent influence. And at first sight there is much plausibility in this view. It may be urged for it that if the *kingdom of heaven* be like unto leaven, this settles the question of the leaven itself as to be taken in a good sense, and then undoubtedly it is the *kingdom* which spreads throughout the world. But a brief examination will assuredly remove all the appearance of truth in this, and force upon us an entirely different conclusion from the common one.

In the first place, to meet the strongest point of the argument:—*is* the kingdom of heaven here intended to find its symbol in the leaven itself? At first sight, it may be granted that it seems so, but if we compare the style of similar parables, we shall more than hesitate to assert this. To take the second parable of the same chapter, is the kingdom of heaven meant to find its likeness in the Sower of the good seed? or rather, is it not in the whole story of the different seed, and of the issue? Again, in the fifth, if the treasure hid in the field be the kingdom, and not the man who finds it,—yet in the sixth it would be *not* the pearl itself, *but* the man who finds it.

The truth is, it is the whole parable that is the likeness, and not any one point in it; and then also this does not decide that the meaning shall be good rather than bad: for the kingdom is not as it will be—set up in power and in the hands of Him whose right it is, but as now with the King absent, intrusted to the hands of others. Thus, *while men sleep*, the enemy can sow his tares among the wheat, and the proof is conclusive that in the first three parables there is a progressive growth of evil: the first showing the partial failure of the good seed; the second, the success of the bad seed, the enemy's work; the third, the tree-like worldly power which results from the sowing of the least of all seeds; and the fowls of the air, the evil powers of the first parable, securely lodged within it. If, then, the fourth parable shows the universal spread of the gospel, the whole course of things is changed, and the most perplexing contradiction arises, not only to the view presented in what goes before, but also to the view given by Scripture as a whole.

On the other hand, simply interpret Scripture by Scripture, and not only is there consistency throughout, but there is found a definiteness and precision of meaning which is itself a convincing proof of its truth. Every part of the parable becomes full of light. We have not, as before, to omit or interpret at hazard essential features of it, (as the three measures of meal, for instance,) and to claim in defense of it that "no parable goes on all fours," though this may be really true, instinct as it is with a life higher than bestial, as with a spirit more than human.

There should be no question that the key of the parable has been rightly found in the second chapter of Leviticus. The "three measures of meal" refer to the "fine flour" of the *meal-offering*, as the Revised Version very well styles it, into which the leaven was *never* to be put (Lev. ii. 11). The essential point is, that the woman is doing *what was expressly forbidden to be done*. This at once brings the similitude of the kingdom here into harmony with what has gone before. The process of deterioration which we see going on in the first three only assumes in the fourth a character of more decided evil. For the meal-offering is Christ the bread of life, the food of the *priestly people* of God, and the mixture of the leaven means the adulteration of Christ as this at the hands of the woman, the professing church.

We must, for its importance, look at this more closely, however. And here the feast of unleavened bread, so peremptorily insisted on in connection with the passover-feast, shows at once the perfect familiarity of the figure to the mind of the Jews whom our Lord was here addressing, and the way in which it could scarcely fail to be apprehended by them. Leaven in meal was to them undoubtedly a thing of evil significance and not of good. The positive word, "For whosoever eateth leavened bread from the first day until the seventh day, that soul shall be cut off from Israel" (Ex. xii. 15), was well known and rigidly held by the mass of the people in our Lord's day. The ordinance as to the meal-offering was scarcely less familiar to them, and the prohibition of leaven in any offering to the Lord made with fire was very clear in attaching to leaven as a type the thought of evil abhorrent to the Holy One.

The general use of leaven in Scripture, it is allowed, perfectly corresponds with this. There is no exception, if it be not found in the passage bebefore us; and here, the connection of the parable with what precedes necessitates an evil significance.

But there is a specific application of the figure by the Lord Himself, and in this gospel which defines it in a way completely in agreement with the parable before us: He applies it to "the *doctrine* of the Pharisees and Sadducees" (chap. xvi. 12).

Now Christ as the food of our souls is ministered to us in the way of doctrine. The Word is constantly, in Scripture, spoken of as food to be eaten, or appropriated by faith to the personal need. Christ is the "Truth," and in the truth we apprehend Him. The doctrine of the Pharisees and Sadducees is error presented in its common types of an external and self-righteous formalism, or of an unbelieving rationalism. The leaven in either case is the rejection of Christ as God presents Him and as faith enjoys Him. If to these we add what in the gospel of Mark (viii. 15) is added—"the leaven of Herod," or the court-party, then we have fully the great triumvirate of evil—the flesh, the devil, and the world—as corrupting influences of the truth of Christ.

But why "*three measures*" of meal? Upon any other interpretation of the meal, I know not. We find the same thing in the provision made by Abram for his heavenly guests; and both there and here, if we see Christ before us, it is not hard to realize the meaning. It is the *Son of Man* who gives us the "meat which endureth unto everlasting life;" as *man*, He becomes our necessary food: but what is the measure of the "Man, Christ Jesus"? *Three* is the *divine* measure, the number of the Trinity—of the fullness of God; and "in Him dwelleth all the fullness of the Godhead bodily." Lesser or lower measure would not fit the truth presented to us here.

Into these "three measures of meal" the woman, then, is putting leaven. But who is the woman? Undoubtedly the Church is in Scripture symbolized by a woman, and this whether it be the true or the nominal professing body, which so readily passes into the shape of the woman "Babylon," the false church of this book of Revelation. Between these two, in view of the other features of the parable, there is not the least difficulty in deciding as to which is before us. In the preceding parable, we have already found the Babylonish character,— the kingdom of heaven, becoming in its earthly administration of the pattern of the kingdoms of the world, the figure of the tree corresponding specifically, moreover, to that under which the power of Nebuchadnezzar is depicted. Thus here it is the reigning world-church, which as possessing empire must make its laws and promulge its doctrines. Necessarily the leaven comes then into the meal. All features cohere in a picture startling in its vividness.

The woman has in her hands the doctrine of Christ—the Christian doctrine; she has authority over it; she can knead and mould it at her will; she can add her traditions, her unwritten law, equal in authority to the written Word; she can interpret and fix its meanings. Here is the leaven: it is the leaven of Church-teaching, the essential error which wherever found, in whatever modified forms, quenches the Spirit of God, deforms and mutilates the Word of God, gives the conscience another master than the Lord Jesus Christ, and does all this cunningly in His name and by His authority, so that the souls of His people even bow to the forged decrees and shudder at the thought of resistance. For this is "Mystery, Babylon the Great, the Mother of harlots and abominations of the earth;" and her merchants are the great men of the earth, and by her sorceries are all nations deceived.

Turn we now to this other picture that we have in the address to Thyatira,—a picture by the same master-hand,—and put side by side the woman of the fourth parable and the woman Jezebel of the fourth Asiatic church. Who will deny that they are one? This Jezebel, who calls herself a prophetess, and teaches and seduces Christ's servants to commit fornication and eat things sacrificed to idols, is she any other than the leaven-hiding woman of the parable "writ large"? or than the woman Babylon of the later character? But we will take up the address in its due order; we will listen to Christ's words as the Spirit of truth has given them to us; we would not miss the least detail, or the impression that the "due order" should make upon us.

"And unto the angel of the church in Thyatira write, These things saith the Son of God, who hath His eyes like unto a flame of fire, and His feet are like fine brass." It is no longer, as in Pergamos, "He that hath the sharp sword with two edges." That sword is the Word of God as the word of penetrating judgment; for "the word that I have spoken," says the Lord, "the same shall judge [him that receiveth them not,] at the last day" (Jno. xii. 48). And so, in the nineteenth chapter of this book, men are slain with the sword proceeding out of His mouth.

But in the meanwhile the Word precedes and anticipates this judgment, and in Pergamos it is still there to appeal to, to warn of coming wrath, to separate between joints and marrow, and soul and spirit, and bring men into the presence of Him with whom we have to do, before whom all things are naked and opened. Plenty of perverters of the Word there are too in Pergamos, as we have seen; but the Word is also there witnessing for itself against them. In Thyatira it *remains no longer:* we hear of Jezebel's doctrine, and the word of the living prophets, clearer and more decisive, as her followers claim, has superseded practically the Scriptures. With the Church's word men may be more safely trusted than with the word of God.

Thus it is no more "He that hath the sharp sword with two edges," but the "Son of God," who has to assert His authority as a divine Being over the Church, rising into a sphere where she dare not pretend to be. With Him alone are the "eyes as a flame of fire," the really infallible and holy insight, which the "feet like fine brass" accompany with irresistible judgment.

And He needs to assert His claim, for she who claims to be His bride, in her own self-assertion, is doing what she can to lower it. She has taken the grace of His incarnation to subject Him to His human mother; or if she remember His divine title, it is to raise Mary into the "Mother of God." Systematically Rome degrades Him amid a crowd of saintly mediators and intercessors with God, all more accessible than Himself, foremost of whom is this "queen of heaven" with her woman's heart, more tender than His!

Here, then, He speaks as Son of God to those who would confound the Church's authority with His. Has she His eyes of fire? Has she His feet of brass? If that which she binds on earth is bound in heaven, will she bind with her decrees the throne of God itself? Will His all-conscious wisdom stutter in her infant's speech? or His holiness attach itself to error and frailty and sin?

It is well known, and shortly to come before us, how Rome escapes from such perplexity; and it is safe to assert there is no other way. But to all assertors of Church-authority alike, the Lord here maintains His distinctive place. *He* alone is the "*Son of God*," in a place unapproachable by His people, and His glory will He not give to another. He alone is the governing

THYATIRA.

Head; the Church His body, in a wondrous relationship to Him as that, but perfectly distinct and wholly subject.

As "Son of God," also, He now sits upon the throne—His Father's throne,—that of pure deity, which no creature could possibly share. His words to Laodicea afterward bring out the force of the assertion here,—"To him that overcometh will I grant to sit with Me in My throne, even as I also overcame, and am set down with My Father in His throne" (chap. iii. 21). As Son of man the apostle has seen Him in the vision with which the book commences; as Son of man He will presently take a throne which He can share with men, His redeemed. Till then, they are in the field of conflict, to overcome as He overcame, and this is the manifest answer to the dream of authority in the world which in Thyatira possesses the false church. Rome would reign before Christ reigns, or reign upon the throne of God with Him. Thus His claim to be the Son of God is here of the greatest possible significance.

This is as to authority over the *world*, and in this way, of course, "whatsoever ye shall bind on earth shall be bound in heaven" cannot possibly apply. The passage in Matthew connects it with the maintenance of discipline among the saints, with care for the holiness which His people are to exhibit. It is not founded on relationship to Him, save as disciples to a Master, and then of obedience to Him which they are under responsibility to enforce. In the fulfillment of this responsibility He is surely with them: what they bind He binds; but apart from His word they bind nothing, nor are they even the authorized exponents of it.

Themselves subject to that Word, He is for them in all true subjection. It is the Word that has authority, not they; and let it be shown that the Word has not guided them, then Christ cannot bind upon His people *insubjection to the Word:* it would be to be a party to His own dishonor.

And all claim of ecclesiastical authority other than this is real rebellion against Christ Himself. Here as elsewhere, "no man can serve two masters." The conscience is to be before God alone, and this is a first principle of all holiness, all morality. Swerve from it by a hair's breadth, right is no longer right, nor wrong wrong; all lines are blurred; the unsteady tremulousness of the soul warns but too surely of the approach of spiritual paralysis.

Yes, the "eyes of fire" are still with the "Son of God" alone. Let us take heed how we hear and what! But clear and holy as they are, they are the eyes of the priestly Son of Man, full of an infinite pity and tenderness none can fathom. How blessed to have to do with Him! How full of joy to stand before Him! And even in Thyatira—amid the awful corruption of that "mystery of iniquity," Rome,—still His words to His own recognize all He can:—

"I know thy works and love and faith and service, and thy patience, and thy last works to be more than the first." We must remember that a remnant is distinctly separated in Thyatira, and that neither Jezebel nor her children are included here. Then it will not be hard to realize this testimony on the Lord's part to what He has seen in them. Little, too, do we know of the hidden lives of those who amid the assumption and pride of the days of

Romish tyranny walked humbly and in secret with their God. Comforting it is to realize how fully Christ could appreciate and how openly He will yet acknowledge them. Like the devil-coats put upon their victims by the Inquisition of old, how many falsehoods have besmirched the memories often of those who in the day of manifestation will receive their crown of righteousness from the Lord the righteous Judge! Of how many Naboths has Jezebel suborned her witnesses that they have "blasphemed God and the king," because they would not surrender their inheritance for a price! Here is the record, that they are not forgotten, those nameless ones, or of dishonored names: "works and love and faith," how tested! "and service," amid what discouragement! "and thy patience," marked and emphasized in the language used,—that long endurance!

And then comes, last of all, that sweet witness of real divine energy, which does not flag as what is merely human does,—" and *thy last works to be more than the first.*" Not simply the *same* as the first,— that would be much to say, as it should seem, amid all the opposition, continuous, unrelenting, of all that held power on earth. But here it is "*more* than the first," for the works recorded are fruits of the life eternal, which, implanted within us, is a *growth*, a living energy, which, thank God! can burst all bands and defy all imprisonment. We have all remarked how the might of a living tree will break up and burst through the stones around its roots, as it forces its way up into the light of heaven. How much more will the energy of that eternal life whose nature is spirit, and which the Spirit of God sustains, develop itself in the face of whatever hindrances. "They go from strength to strength" is said of God's pilgrims through the valley of Baca; for it is Christ's strength perfected in human weakness.

If we study the record which we have of those dark days also, we shall be inclined too to believe that there was in the line of those patient witnesses, looked at as a whole, a growth in vigor as the days went on. They come more into the light; they take bolder place; the coming Reformation has its precursors; the torch of truth, as it drops from one hand, is taken up by another. Above all, separation becomes more decided,—a great point, one of the greatest; for we see that what the Lord has against these saints of His is declared to be their tolerance of the woman Jezebel. The evil, it is true, was rampant, and might seem supreme; none the less, but the more, became the duty of open testimony against it. It was by such a testimony, in the face of overwhelming odds naturally, the Reformation established itself; and where it was the Word openly preached, God rallied round it defenders of it.

"Notwithstanding I have against thee, that thou sufferest that woman Jezebel, who calls herself a prophetess; and she teaches and seduces My servants to commit fornication, and to eat things sacrificed unto idols. And I gave her space to repent of her fornication, and she will not repent."

Here is the distinctive evil of Thyatira,—an evil so frightful that the Lord calls it further on "the depths of Satan." Beyond it we do not get in this direction. It closes the development of the Church's departure from God in true succession from its germ in the beginning. Afterward, we find a fresh work of God has commenced, although it too is shortly, and indeed when first it comes before us, declined and passing. But as the woman closes the first series of the parables of Matt. xiii., so does the woman close the first series of the Asiatic churches. We shall speedily find, as has been already stated, that these two women are in fact one and the same,—the woman, "Babylon the Great, the Mother of harlots and abominations of the earth."

Her name is at once significant, and is a striking exemplification of the pregnant speech of Scripture, which with a single word will illuminate a subject with a flood of light. The name, with its attached history, adds features to the picture which carry us far beyond the mere assembly in Asia to which first the Lord spoke, and identically the "woman" in question in the plainest way possible.

Thus she is described here simply as one that calls herself a prophetess, and the effect of her false prophecy is given as seducing to fornication and idolatry; but the history referred to by no means gives us Jezebel as a prophetess. She is a *queen*, and an idolatrous queen, but this the Jezebel of Thyatira was surely not. Yet in the promise to the overcomer we have evident allusion to a reign over men on earth, which helps us easily to understand that the thought of queenly power is really meant to be implied in the name as used. For the promise, as we see in all these cases, has reference to the state of things in which the overcoming is to be. Here he who overcomes waits in fruitful patience, till he shall reign with Christ. How significant if in that scene which is the full realization of what is in the Lord's mind here, the false church is reigning! Babylon, too, in the after-churches reigns a queen, and thus these two passages are linked together.

Babylon also is red with the blood of the saints and with the blood of the martyrs of Jesus; and here again is a character of the woman which we could not expect to find in the Thyatiran assembly. But the name "Jezebel," interjected in the address, recalls at once to our minds the persecutor. And we need all this to bring out the full meaning of the address. On the other hand, the fourth parable of Matthew says nothing of the queen or of the persecutor, while it speaks clearly of the self-assumed prophetess. Thus the address to Thyatira binds together these two other prophesies, and the three throw their concentrated light upon the solemn reality which is presented to us.

Rome it surely is, drawn with the few bold strokes of a master-pencil,—Rome as the Lord Himself sees and judges it. Good it is, and necessary, to take our estimate of her from the Word of God itself rather than from the judgments of men, shifting and unstable as they have ever proved. The judgment of God abides, and the day that is coming will only affirm its decisions, unutterably solemn as indeed they are. How dare we indulge the false liberality so common in this day in presence of the awful threatenings of the passage before us?

"And I gave her space to repent of her fornication, and she repented not. Behold, I will cast her into a bed, and them that commit adultery with her into great tribulation, except they repent of her deeds. And I will kill her children with death; and all the churches shall know that I am He that searcheth the reins and hearts; and I will give to every one of you according to your works."

Thus the pitiless persecutor of God's people shall find sure doom from His hand at last; and with that judgment all heaven will be in sympathy: "I heard as it were the voice of a great multitude in heaven, saying, 'Halleluiah! Salvation and glory and power unto the Lord our God, for true and righteous are His judgments; for He hath judged the great whore, which did corrupt the earth with her fornication, and hath avenged the blood of His servants at her hand.' And again they said, 'Halleluiah!' And her smoke riseth up forever and ever."

No true charity can possibly soften down the terms of divine judgment here pronounced, but will rather echo the call of mercy in the meantime: "Come out of her, My people, that ye be not partakers of her sins, and that ye receive not of her plagues."

Yet it is quite possible to judge Rome without hesitation, and to partake, nevertheless, in what are the works of Rome. We must remember, therefore, that Rome is the "*mother* of harlots and abominations of the earth." Principles can be received and followed which are essentially Romish, while we reject the full development of them in the canons of the Council of Trent or the creed of Pope Pius IV. The features of popery, if carefully noted here, will often be found under the guise of Protestantism. And there is a tendency in them to reproduce themselves together. Take Irvingism, in which, in the most startling manner, all the doctrines of popery (without the pope) have sprung up into a precocious maturity: and here, even the claim of infallibility is found, though the pope is not: there is the voice of the woman calling herself a prophetess, whether the woman's name be "Jezebel" or not.

But in modified forms, the features of Rome may be found where there is no pretension to infallibility, and none at all to worldly supremacy for the Church as such. Wherever the teaching of the Church is maintained as authoritative, though it be over a body of Christians who make no claims to catholicity, or to succession after the Romish manner, and who do not propose to add to the Word of God, but to be guided by it,—still, even here the voice of the woman is heard, although the woman's name be certainly *not* "Jezebel." Yet here, not only the churches of the Reformation, but all churches almost, stand. Nay, it is considered even that there is no sure guarantee for orthodoxy where this is not so. And indeed it cannot be denied that the abolition of creeds has been very often loudly urged by those who desired latitude as to the most positive doctrines of the Word itself. The deniers of eternal punishment have contended for it; the men who put the inspiration of Scripture on the same footing with the inspiration of Shakespeare; the people who to retain Christianity must leave out Christ. All these, in their various pleas against the stiffness of a creed that they refused, have furnished the most convincing arguments for its necessity. Nor do I now propose to deal with these arguments; they will come before us properly elsewhere. It is nevertheless true that, according to Scripture, the Church never teaches. God teaches by His Spirit, and the one authoritative teaching is that of the inspired Word,—truly authoritative, because absolute truth itself. This much is true in Jezebel's false claim, that infallible teaching alone can demand obedience, as alone it can implicit faith. Allow that the guide may lead astray, and how can you require men to follow her? "If the blind lead the blind, shall they not both fall into the ditch?"

But the creeds are to be submitted to because they may be proved by Scripture, "by most certain arguments," it is said. Well, if Scripture be so certain and so authoritative, what need of any thing else? I believe indeed that it is certain and all-sufficient, and thus the argument proves too much. Why seek to make certain what is already so, or give authority to what is already and only authoritative? In so doing, Scripture is dishonored in the very method by which you would honor it. Its own testimony is, that it is "given by inspiration of God, and profitable for doctrine, for correction, for reproof, for instruction in righteousness; that the man of God may be perfect, *thoroughly* furnished unto all good works." But the authoritatively imposed creed actually takes away the appeal to Scripture, becoming itself the only permissible appeal. If there be error in the creed, it will have to be maintained as carefully as the truth in it. If there be defect in the creed, the Scripture cannot be allowed even to supplement it. It is, in short, completely displaced from its rightful supremacy over men. The conscience is not allowed to be before God, and the most godly are just those who will be forced most into opposition against the human rule thus substituted for the divine.

This we shall have to look at further at another time, however. But it is evident that Jezebel is right thus far, in that she connects her right of rule over the people of God with the infallibility of the prophetess. She displays, however, the falsity of her pretension by her refusal to submit her claims in this respect to be judged by that which she owns herself to be the Word of God. Her infallibility must not be tested, but received: whereas Scripture itself, with a claim no less absolute, *on that very account* submits to every possible test, assured that the more complete the test, the more will this claim be manifested and made good. The true coin fears not the test which would at once expose the counterfeit. Faith in Rome is credulity and superstition only: faith in Scripture is intelligent, reasonable, and open-eyed.

In Scripture, the Church does not teach at all. The prophets speak, and the rest "judge." The Word itself is the rule by which all is judged, and the conscience is kept directly in the presence of God Himself. All are exercised as to what is spoken: they are to take heed *what* they hear, as well as *how* they hear. This exercise is necessary to maintain the soul in vigor and in dependence. Vigilance, the constant habit of reference to God, and walking before Him are to be ever emphasized and insisted on. We tend continually to follow human authorities and traditional teachings, which God has continually to break through for us, sending us afresh to His Word, that our faith may not stand in the wisdom of men, but in the power of God. Thus alone true spiritual health is realized and preserved.

Church teaching is one mark, then, of what in Rome has only come to full maturity. The seed is scattered widely, and found in the most diverse places. Another thing often to be met with independently is yet, quite similarly to this, the germ of what is fully developed only in Rome. This is, the claim for the Church of rightful supremacy over the world.

In Rome, it is outspoken and defiant. Jezebel reigns as a queen, and is no widow, and shall see no sorrow. With her foot upon the necks of kings, she can apply to herself the words which belong to Christ,—" Thou shalt tread upon the lion and the adder; the young lion and the dragon Thou shalt trample underfoot." This needs, of course, no comment; but how many are there, on the other hand, who sincerely believe that Christians should have their place in the government of the world,—nay, should control it! Who, in fact, so fitted? and what could be so desirable for the world itself?

They do not see that the world is never to be subject to Christ until He take possession of it with the rod of iron; that Satan is its prince and god, never to be cast out until the Lord comes Himself from heaven; that the world remains, therefore, in steadfast opposition to what is of God, and Christianity, if it root itself in it, only becomes corrupted by it, and not its purifier. The yoke with unbelievers, which these principles of necessity bring about, is what at the start forfeits for the child of God the enjoyment of the child's proper place. "For what fellowship hath righteousness with unrighteousness? or what communion hath light with darkness? or what concord hath Christ with Belial? or what part hath he that believeth with an unbeliever? and what agreement hath the temple of God with idols? For ye are the temple of the living God, as God hath said, 'I will dwell in them and walk in them, and I will be their God, and they shall be My people. Wherefore come out from among them, and be separate; and touch not the unclean thing, and I will receive you, and will be a Father to you; and ye shall be My sons and daughters, saith the Lord Almighty.'"

In Jezebel, the full maturity of these principles is reached, and the Church attains its rule over the world; but in so doing, *it has entirely changed its character*. It is no longer the true Church, but the false, although in historical succession with the true. The world's principles have leavened it; it shelters the unclean "birds of the air," the followers of the "prince of the power of the air;" the true followers of Christ are hunted down and destroyed; and their only hope is here the coming of the Lord Himself, which now for the first time in these addresses becomes the Star of promise. "But unto you I say, even unto the rest in Thyatira, as many as have not this doctrine, and which have not known the depths of Satan, as they speak; I will put upon you none other burden: but that which ye have already hold fast *till I come*. And he that overcometh, and keepeth My works unto the end, to him will I give power over the nations: and he shall rule them with a rod of iron; as the vessels of a potter shall they be broken to shivers; even as I received of My Father. And I will give him the morning star."

Here is, plainly, the attitude of faith declared in contrast with Jezebel's claim of rule. Rule! yes, we are to have it when the Lord comes,—not before. The reign of the saints is to be with Christ, and although it is true that He now reigns, it is upon the Father's throne—a throne which cannot be shared with men. It is impossible, therefore, that Christians can reign now. When as Son of Man He takes His own throne, then indeed they shall be associated with Him. This is in the promise to the overcomer in Laodicea: "To him that overcometh will I grant to sit with Me in My throne, even as I also overcame, and am set down with My Father in His throne."

It is in that day the rod of iron will be in His hands, which, as we see here, He promises to share with His people. This is a direct reference to the second psalm, where Christ is seen, as in the purpose of God, "set" upon the "holy hill of Zion." It is not a heavenly, but an earthly, throne. And thereupon Christ's own voice is heard declaring the decree which establishes Him in possession of the earth: "I will declare the decree; the Lord hath said unto Me, 'Thou art My Son, this day have I begotten Thee. Ask of Me, and I will give Thee the heathen for Thine inheritance, the uttermost parts of the earth for Thy possession.'" This is often quoted to show the gradual spread of the gospel over the earth, but how, in fact, is Christ's claim upon the nations to be made good? "Thou shalt rule them with a rod of iron; Thou shalt dash them in pieces like a potter's vessel."

This is plainly not the grace of the gospel. It is as plainly the exercise of the power in which He associates the saints with Himself. It is again referred to, when in the nineteenth chapter of this book the white-horsed Rider, whose name is called the Word of God, comes forth from heaven, attended by His armies, to the judgment of the nations banded still, as in the second psalm, "against the Lord and against His Christ." "And out of His mouth goeth a sharp, two-edged sword, that with it He should smite the nations, and He shall *rule them with a rod of iron*, and He treadeth the wine-press of the fierceness and wrath of Almighty God."

Thus the time of this rule is fixed definitely, and its character it would seem impossible to mistake. Till then, "overcoming" is in patience and long-suffering, keeping Christ's works unto the end.

But the promise of the morning-star goes beyond this, even; and we must look at it with corresponding attention. We have here the Lord's own interpretation, and in the same book. When the whole roll of prophecy has been unfolded and come to an end, He returns to explain to us this significant word. "I Jesus have sent Mine angel to testify unto you these things in the churches. I am the Root and the Offspring of David, and the bright and *Morning-Star*." The Revelation, and thus the New-Testament as a whole, closes with this announcement. It is striking, therefore, to find the *Old* Testament closing, in Malachi, with a contrasted announcement, which yet applies to the same glorious Speaker, who thus takes His place in connection with the promises of both parts of the Word. The Old Testament, with its earthly promises, closes with this: "Unto you that fear My name shall the *Sun of Righteousness* arise with healing in His wings." The New Testament, with its heavenly promises, speaks, not of the Sun of Righteousness, but of the Morning-Star.

The Old-Testament promise may seem the fuller thing. It is more to have the sun rise, surely, one would say, than the morning-star,—to have the *day* than the *promise* of the day. And this is true from the Old-Testament point of view: the star shines out of heaven, does not brighten the earth at all; but *in its own sphere* it is bright nevertheless. And

THYATIRA. 159

this is the key to its New-Testament use. The Star shines its welcome for us out of those heavenly places in which our blessings as Christians are. Christ is coming to bring the day to the whole earth. The glory of the Lord, like the solar radiance, is going to cover it, as the waters cover the sea. It shall rise upon Israel, and the Gentiles come to the light, and kings to the brightness of its rising. But before this, our eyes shall have beheld Him; and when this comes, our higher, better place shall be already with Him. For His promise to us is, " I will come again, and receive you unto Myself, that where I AM,"—in His own eternal home,—"there ye may be also."

How beautiful this reminder, then, here, where the glitter of earthly rule and dignity seeks to attract and insnare the saints of God! Like the Lord's words to the seventy when they returned to Him again with joy, saying, "Lord, even the devils are subject unto us through Thy name!" With His face toward the very scenes of which we have been speaking, He replies, "I saw Satan as lightning fall from heaven! Behold, I give you power to tread on serpents and scorpions, and over all the power of the enemy; and nothing shall by any means hurt you. Notwithstanding,"—and here is the parallel so complete,—"in this rejoice not, that the spirits are subject unto you, but rather rejoice *because your names are written in heaven.*"

Though our reign be over the earth, and when He appears we shall appear with Him in glory, yet our "mansions"—our abiding-places, as the word means,—are not on earth, but in the Father's house, of which the temple, with its "patterns of things in the heavenlies," was the type and presentation upon earth. "My Father's house" was Christ's name for the temple. This had its temporary apartments for the priests, as they came up in their courses to fulfill their service at Jerusalem. And is it not in designed contrast that our Lord designates our places in the Father's house above, not as *temporary*, but *abiding*-places? To "abide," "continue," is one of the characteristic words in John's gospel, and it is in perfect harmony with the gospel of Christ's deity that it should be so; all that belongs to Deity *abides;* and here, in the place of the presence of God, are our not temporary but eternal *abodes*.

But "the Morning-Star" is more than our abode. The abode we shall have, to enjoy it, but Himself it is we are called to enjoy. "*I* am the bright and Morning-Star." "Father, I will also that those whom Thou hast given Me be with Me where I am; that they may behold My glory, which Thou hast given Me; for Thou lovedst Me before the foundation of the world."

How blessed to be forever where this glory is displayed, and where the eye will be perfect to let in the light! "We know that, when He shall appear, we shall be like Him, for we shall see Him as He is." And in order to see Him as He is, we must be like Him. The passage is often read the reverse way; as if it were the sight of Him that would change us into His likeness: but I do not believe that to be the thought. The truth is, that as we must have the divine nature to know God, so we must be in Christ's moral image to apprehend Him. Man knows man by reason of the common nature; here, where all obstruction is at last removed, and we enter into life as our abiding and exclusive condition,—the "body of death" gone forever,—here we shall be at last face to face with Christ indeed. And this will seal and perfect the blessedness of a life always in us essentially dependent. We shall still and ever, now with no inner obstruction to prevent its realization, be "complete" (or "filled full") "in Him."

The Morning-Star anticipates the day, and we shall be gathered up to Christ before He appears for the judgment yet deliverance of the earth. *Then*, those who have suffered will reign with Him. When judgment shall return to righteousness,—the rod, no longer a serpent, returns to the hand of that great Shepherd of whom Moses was but the fore-shadow,—we shall be with Him, to take joyful part in that "restitution of all things" which He comes to effect. When the Sun of Righteousness arises, " then shall the righteous shine forth *as* the sun, in the kingdom of their Father." The rod will then be the irresistible "rod of iron," but how beneficent shall be its sway! "Then, judgment shall dwell in the wilderness, and righteousness remain in the fruitful field; and the work of righteousness shall be peace; and the effect of righteousness, quietness and assurance forever. And My people shall dwell in a peaceable habitation, and in sure dwellings, and in quiet resting-places." For now, as never yet, "a King shall reign in righteousness, and princes shall rule in judgment. And a Man shall be as a hiding-place from the wind, and a covert from the tempest; as rivers of water in a dry place, as the shadow of a great rock in a weary land."

The word, then, to the overcomer is, "Hold fast till I come!" The night-watch is not over; nor will the failed Church recover itself. The watchword of comfort is, "Until I come." The true are but a remnant, and Rome's *catholicity* is but a decisive proof of the general departure. Revivals there may be, but no return. Good it is for those who accept humbly the lesson, which stains forever the glory of man. "The corruption of the best thing is the worst corruption." We have had God's "best thing" nearly two thousand years in hand: what have we done with it? Shall we do better now? It is easy to judge Rome; to judge, *in* Rome, our own utter and ruinous failure, is that to which God calls, and in which alone blessing is. Then, blessed be God, the Morning-Star rises in the darkened sky: "At midnight there was a cry made, 'Behold, the Bridegroom! go ye out to meet Him.'"

"He that hath an ear, let him hear what the Spirit saith unto the churches!"

Sardis: Sleeping Among the Dead.
(Rev. iii. 1-7.)

In the address to the Church at Thyatira, we have found the Lord announcing His coming, and bidding His saints wait to share with Him then the authority which the false church was assuming to have already. Thyatira presents us thus with a phase of things which goes on at least till the Lord comes for His saints; not, indeed, till the rising of the Sun of Righteousness upon the world, but until He comes as the Morning-Star, the herald of the day before the day appears.

In Sardis, we have, therefore, not a development of the Thyatira condition, but in many respects, as it is easy to see, what is in entire opposition to it.

Thyatira, or popery, is the last phase of the church in its Jewish hierarchic and ritualistic growth; and although there has been all through a remnant different in spirit, and becoming finally more or less distinctly separate, even outwardly, as among the Waldensian and kindred bodies, yet up to this point there has been in fact a certain unity: it could claim to be, before the eyes of men at least, the Catholic church.

True, there had been already a separation; not now of others from it, but of this latest development itself from others. Rome had separated herself from the churches of the east—the Greek and Syrian churches, which remained in the condition we have traced at Pergamos. The Catholic church of the west had become the *Roman* Catholic. Yet, in character, the system was the same throughout; here more, there less, developed—that was all. But now we come to a new thing,—a breach and a new beginning. There is now in Sardis, not the claim of infallibility, not (as what is prominent) corruption of doctrine, not persecution of the saints, not the exercise of authority in the same sense,— none of these things characterize Sardis. What characterizes is sufficiently definite in the Lord's charge here: it is lack of spiritual power,—nay, in the body as such, of life itself. "Thou hast a name to live, and thou art dead."

Yet they had "received and heard," and are bidden to "hold fast" this, "and repent." Just as Ephesus had been, at the commencement of decline, called back to remember their first state, so here there has been a fresh beginning in God's grace, a recovery of His word and truth, a new beginning, from which (alas!) already there is decline. Again, they have not answered to His grace, and those things which remained among them from this revival were languishing and ready to die. And no wonder, when the charge against them is considered. The body addressed is a professing but unconverted one: with a *name to live*, it is *dead*.

There is but too little difficulty in applying this. A breach with Rome, a restoration of the Word of God, a fresh revival of truth, ending, however, in a system or systems characterized by a fatal defect of spiritual power, and churches with an unconverted membership, God's saints being scattered through the mass,—living themselves, but unable to vitalize it: such are the characteristics, easily to be read, of the *national churches* which sprang out of the Protestant Reformation.

Let it be well understood: it is not the Reformation itself that is depicted here. So far as it was this, the Reformation was the blessed work of God, and the Lord does not judge, and can never need to judge, His own work. He refers to what His grace had done for them—to what they had received and heard. Their responsibility was, to take heed to it, and hold it fast; and already they had failed in doing so. This was therefore the ground of judgment.

Notice how Christ is represented here. He has "the seven Spirits of God, and the seven stars." There is no failure in the fullness of spiritual energy on His part, no possibility of failure in His love and care for His people. Yet this power is not found practically in that which has sprung out of the seed sown by the Reformation. With more pretension than before, for they have now a *name to live*—a name assumed to be in the book of life, the actual condition of the mass is that of death: not feebleness merely, but death.

Yet there are exceptions: not simply those alive, but still more—that have not defiled their garments; and of these the Lord speaks in the warmest terms of praise. "They shall walk with Me in white, for they are worthy." Indeed, these are only "a few names." Others may be alive, but in a scene of death (and the defilement which results from contact with the dead is emphasized in the symbols of the Old Testament) the many of those alive even are defiled. But the mass are dead altogether—dead, with a name to live.

In His promise to the overcomer, the Lord further refers to this: "He that overcometh, the same shall be clothed in white raiment, and I will not blot his name out of the book of life." The book of life is understood by the majority of people to be only in the Lord's hands, and all the names written in it to be written by Himself. Hence, those ignorant of the gospel stumble over this blotting out of the book of life, as supposing it is the blotting out of the names of those once saved. But there is no such thought here. There is not the slightest hint that those mentioned ever had life at all: they had a "*name* to live"—only a name.

On the contrary, you find in Rev. xiii. 8 the very opposite thought as to those "written," as we ought to read it, with the margin of the Revised Version, "from the foundation of the world in the book of the Lamb slain." There, this fact of their being written in the book *from the foundation* of the world is given as their security from being deceived by and worshiping the beast. Sovereign grace, that is, is their only and sufficient security.

Here, on the other hand, the book has got into man's hand, and he writes names in it as he pleases. It is a figure, of course, all through. The Lord, in His own time, corrects the book, and then He blots out the names of those to whom only the name belongs.

Now the "name to live" has a very special meaning in connection with Reformation times. The putting people's names into the book of life (while here on earth) is in no way characteristic of popery. *Saints*, for them, are only the dead, and not the living. The living she warns that "no man knows whether he is worthy of favor or hatred," and that it is not safe to be too sure. Her pardons, indulgences, sacraments, only show by their very multiplicity how difficult a thing she believes salvation is. Darkness is the essence of her system, and she thrives upon it.

On the other hand, the Reformation recovered the blessed gospel, and the word of reconciliation was preached with no uncertain sound. The doctrine of assurance was maintained with the utmost energy, and was stigmatized by the Council of Trent as "the vain confidence of the heretics." They even pushed it to an extreme, asserting (at least, some of the most prominent reformers did,) that assurance was of the very essence of saving faith itself, and that unless a man *knew* himself to be forgiven, he might be sure that he was *not* forgiven.

It is plain, then, that Protestantism put a man's name in the book of life in a way that popery did not at all.

Two immense things the Reformation gave us, which have never since been wholly lost,—an open Bible, in a language to be understood; and on the other hand, the gospel, at least in some of its most essential features. These are inestimable blessings, which would that we had hearts to value more.

Of the men, too, who were the dear and honored instruments in handing them down to us we cannot speak with enough affection and esteem. God honored them—how many!—taking them to Himself in fiery chariots, from which their voices come, thrilling us with the accents of the heaven opening to receive them. Those who disparage them will have to hear, one day, their names confessed and honored by Him they served, as those of whom the world was not worthy.

But on the other hand, we must not make, as many are doing, the Reformation the measure of divine truth. They are not loyal to the Reformation really who accept any thing beside Scripture as the measure and test of this. The broken and conflicting voices which are heard the moment it is a question no longer of the gospel but of the church and its government, assure us that if here Scripture has spoken, the churches of the Reformation do not in the same sense convey to us its utterances. Lutherism is not Calvinism, the Church of England is not the Church of Geneva here. We must needs, whether we will or not, take Scripture to decide amid claims so conflicting; and when we do so, we find, with no great difficulty, that no one of these takes us back to the Church as it was at the beginning—the body of Christ, or the house of living stones—at all.

Instead of this, as is well known, the churches of the Reformation were essentially national churches. Not in every country, of course, able to attain the full ideal,—as in France, where Rome retained its ascendency by such cruel means,—but always of that pattern. Rome had herself prepared the way for this. The nations of Europe were already professedly Christian nations, and it was not to be expected that those who escaped from Jezebel's tyranny would give up their long hereditary claim to Christianity. The adoption of an evangelical creed did not and could not change the reality of what they were. They learned the formula, put their names upon the church-books as Protestants, learned to battle fiercely for the gospel of peace, and how could you deny their title to be Christians? Yet, as to the many, it was but the "name to live."

We must learn to distinguish two elements in the ecclesiastical revolution of those times. There was, first of all, a most mighty and most manifest work of God. The Scriptures, released from their imprisonment in a foreign tongue, began to speak to responsive human hearts with the decision and persuasiveness that the Word of God alone can have. Christ began once more to teach as one having authority, and not as the scribes. The blessed doctrine of justification by faith every where brought souls held fast in bondage into liberty and the knowledge of a Saviour-God. The ecclesiastical yoke could not hold any longer those whom the truth had freed; and where Christ had become thus the soul's rightful Lord, the yoke of Rome was but the tyranny of Antichrist.

This was the first and most powerful element in Protestantism; not a political movement, but a movement of faith. Luther, solitary at Worms, in the presence of the mightiest political power in Europe, was the testimony that the work was of

Him. His strength was manifest in human weakness. Had that place of weakness been retained all through,—had but God been allowed to show that power was of Him alone, how different would have been the result! And it is due to the foremost name of Protestantism to acknowledge that, as far as carnal weapons were concerned, Luther would have rightly refused them a place in a warfare which was God's. At any rate, to think of Protestantism as essentially a political movement is to do it glaring injustice, and to contradict the plainest facts.

On the other hand, we cannot ignore the political element which so soon entered into it. Rome had made the nations every where feel the iron hand of her despotism, and the national reaction against her was the natural result of her intolerable and insolent oppression. The notorious wickedness of her chiefs had long destroyed all real respect. Her power stood now in an excessive and degrading superstition. She lived upon men's vices and their fears; and where the light fell and removed the darkness, the fears were removed also, where the vices were not. Men learned to look upon the power they had cringed to with contrary feelings, deep in proportion to their depth before. Their interests, political and otherwise, coincided with the spiritual movement which divine power had produced. Soldiers, politicians, governments, made common cause with the men of faith. It was hard not to welcome such apparently God-sent allies, when on every side persecution raged. The movement increased in external power and importance, but its character was in just that proportion lowered and perverted.

And now there was need of defined principles to give cohesion to elements which the Spirit of God no longer sufficed to bind together. Outside, there was the pressure of Rome, a compact and immensely powerful body, armed, drilled, and intensely hostile. Organization was soon a necessity; but of what or whom? To proclaim the true Church would have been to cast off their allies, to insure the continuance of persecution and reproach, to leave Rome unchecked, triumphant. I do not say that the true thought of the Church ever dawned upon them; but I do say that their alliance with the world was a sure means of hindering their seeing it. There were formed instead national churches, with evangelical creeds, used as pieces of state-craft, and political power to back them, not divine.

It is simple enough, that if a creed had been a necessity for His Church, the wisdom of God could easily have given us an infallible one, and His love could not have failed to do so. On the contrary, He has given us that which He testifies to as able to furnish the man of God thoroughly unto all good works, but which people feel at once to be as different from a creed as can be.

Why do people want a creed? As something more plainly and easily read than Scripture. Scripture is infinite: the creed must be definite. Of Scripture, every one makes what he likes; what is wanted is something different—something that shall not be capable of two meanings, plain to all—spiritual and unspiritual, Church and world alike.

It has been before contended that Scripture is clearer, plainer really, than any word of man; and so indeed it is; beside being, in divine wisdom, written so as to meet, as nothing else can meet, with perfect foresight of the future, all the thoughts of men. It is thus the only sufficient guard and protection against heresy to the end of time. And yet it is no contradiction to this to own that there is some truth from the point of view taken by those who contend for this, between the creed and Scripture.

From their point of view. For the apostle's words limit us somewhat when we speak of the intelligibility of Scripture. "All Scripture is given by inspiration of God, and is profitable for doctrine, for reproof, for correction, for instruction in righteousness,"—but for what?—"that the MAN OF GOD may be perfect, thoroughly furnished unto all good works."

So that Scripture, profitable for doctrine as it is, does need a certain state of soul for its proper apprehension. It needs not indeed great attainments, human learning, deep research,—although all these have their use, and are not despised by it; but it absolutely requires (what may be found in the lowest and poorest just as well,) *devotedness*—that we be *God's men:* what by possession and profession all Christians are, but alas! not what all, even of true Christians, always practically are. This is the single eye, which we must have for the body to be full of light.

But this being so, we can easily see that the Bible is not just the book for a court of law, and it is not the suited thing for a national creed. The truth is not meant to be accessible to the merely natural mind. Nay, "the natural man receiveth not the things of the Spirit of God; for they are foolishness unto him; neither can he know them, because they are spiritually discerned." The Bible is not crystalized for us into doctrines, but its truths are exhibited and only known as living realities to those who are in the true sense alive. It is so essentially unlike a creed, that we may be assured that nothing like a creed was in God's design. He did not mean to give what might serve as a motto for political partizanship, or a banner for any other than spiritual warfare.

Nationalism, then,—the union of the living and the dead—was never in His mind. He meant spirituality to be a first necessity, and an absolute one, for the discernment of His thoughts: and men, when they substitute in this respect the blessed word of God for their plainer creed, show really that herein they are at cross purposes with Him.

"Thou hast a name that thou livest, and art dead," is the exact moral description, as it is the plain condemnation of nationalism. Of more this, no doubt, but still of this. It is not the idea of the Church of God at all, but a Christianized world, with Christians scattered through it: a place so defiling, that but few indeed can keep their garments undefiled. Connected with the truth, as popery is not, such a system betrays the truth which it professedly upholds. The character of the last days is developed by it: "Men shall be lovers of their own selves, covetous, proud, blasphemers," the retaining all that is natural to them under the garb of Christianity; "having a form of godliness, but denying the power thereof." The direct command is, "From such, turn away."

This is the effect of popularized truth,—popularized as God never meant His truth to be. Of course this is to be distinguished from the *preaching* of His truth, than which nothing assuredly is more in accordance with His mind. His gospel is to go forth to every creature, and the blessings of an open Bible we could scarcely exaggerate. But by "*popularized* truth" is meant, what we have already been speaking of, truth made into a party badge, so as to be accepted by those with whom Christ is not; for He was never really popular, and still is not.

Popularized truth means, truth that has lost its power. It may be that for which martyrs died, and which when first given of God, or when afresh given, was full of quickening power. Popularized, it is so far lifeless. No exercise of soul in receiving it; no cross in professing it; men have got from their fathers what their fathers got from God: to their fathers it was shame, to them it is honor. There is nothing to test conscience, nothing to make them ask, Dare I take this without human sanction to commend—nay, in the face of all human discountenance? Yet only thus have we got it truly from God. The martyrs they talk of took it thus and suffered for it: *they* take it from their fathers—a principle which would have *condemned* the martyrs; and they take it without the slightest thought of *being* martyrs.

Truth is proclaimed as powerless by the unholy lives of its professors, while unholiness is recommended by the practice of those who are orthodox as to truth. And thus truth tends to die out of itself, as valueless, remaining all the while in the national creed, embalmed as a memorial of the past. "Be watchful, and strengthen the things which remain, which are ready to die; for I have not found thy works perfect before God." This has been long experienced with regard to all national systems too manifestly to need more than a bare allusion.

It is a system designedly adapted to worldly minds, and to be worked by political machinery. The Word of God is no necessity to it, except, it may be, to furnish a table of lessons; for the *authoritative* standard is the creed. The Spirit of God is not necessary to it; for colleges can manufacture preachers, and ecclesiastics ordain and send them forth apart from this. Christians are not necessary to it; they are too uncertain as a constituent part of a nation or its government to be capable of being reckoned on; nor is there any means of certainly determining who they are. A sacrament,—baptism or the Lord's supper,—takes here the place of less manageable tests.

And the grieved and insulted Spirit may be besought to breathe upon the lifeless mass, and fill the sails of the ship of state. But He must keep within the bounds prescribed by ritual, hierarchy, and parliament, or He will be treated as schismatical. And it must be remarked how often in this case a schism springs out of a large and manifest revival. Souls brought near to God, and made to feel the value of His Word, are not made thereby the more docile servants of a state-religion. The new wine will not be held in the old bottles. Statesmen are not thus favorable to such fresh enthusiasm, and no wonder: it divides the house which it is to their interest to keep as one.

But is not here the history of the churches of the Reformation—of Protestantism, in fact,—during the three centuries of its existence? Is not this the true account of its divisions, for which it is reproached? The Spirit of God is not, indeed, the author of confusion, but of peace,—of unity, and not disunion. But when people talk of schism, they should remember to what that term applies. As found in Scripture, it is "schism in the *body*" that is reprobated, and the *body of Christ* is not a national church. When men have joined together the living and the dead,—when they have subjugated consciences to formularies instead of Scripture,—to hierarchies instead of God, or to hierarchies in the name of God, what have they forced the blessed Spirit to do but to draw afresh the line they have obliterated between the living and the dead, between man's word and God's, between human authority and divine?

And His mode of doing this has been constantly to bring out of the inexhaustible treasure of His Word some fresh or forgotten truth, which would do that which the popularized truth in the creed had almost ceased to do—would test the souls of His people as to whether they were indeed the descendants of those who confessed Him of old, whose tombs they built, and whose memories they had in honor. The fresh truth calls for fresh confession; costs, and is meant to cost, something; brings its confessors into opposition to the course around them, and separates them at once from those whose only desire is to go with the stream, and with whom the profession of Christ and the cross are widely separate.

Doubtless the division may separate between true Christians themselves; and this is in itself an evil, that true Christians should be separated; but the responsibility rests with those who are not quick-eared enough to hear God's call when it comes,—not single-eyed enough to discern the path in which the Lord is leading His own. We are bound, by the honor we owe to Him, to maintain that He cannot possibly be leading His own in contradictory paths—cannot possibly refuse the needed light to walk aright, however simple or ignorant the soul may be. No one strays and no one stumbles because God denies him light. But "the light of the body" practically "is the eye"— the inlet of it, and there the hinderance is. Thus a severance, sorrowfully enough, is made between real Christians; but the sin of it is *not* with those who separate from that which God has shown them to be evil, but with those who remain associated with the evil which is forcing out the true in heart. Separation from evil, so far from being a principle of division, would, if honestly followed, make for unity and peace, as leading upon a path where God's Spirit, ungrieved, could really unite and strengthen His people. With evil He cannot unite; and this, indeed, therefore, wherever admitted, is a principle of division.

I am not, therefore, upholding or making light of schism. The divisions of Protestantism are its shame, and to glory in them is to glory in one's shame. Error is manifold, contradictory, schismatic. Truth, however many-sided, is but one. Sects, in their multiplicity, may accommodate, no doubt, the religious tastes of man; but that only would show how purely human they are, how little divine.

The unity of the Spirit may be maintained, and allow indeed for growth in knowledge, and in unity of judgment as to many things. The Church of God has room for all that are God's, of whatever stature—fathers, young men, and babes. It can allow of—nay, insists upon the largest charity for those who differ from us in aught that would not link the name of Christ with His dishonor. But that is a very different thing from what is implied in a creed, and indeed I may say, is its fundamental opposite. For the creed defines, in a way that, if rigidly adhered to, *shuts out* toleration as to points of confessedly minor importance, where the Spirit of God would teach, not indifference, indeed, but the largest charity,—forcing its definitions upon all in a way *most* felt by the *most* conscientious. It is as necessary, as far as the creed goes, to believe in a child's being regenerate when baptized as it is to believe in the Son of God Himself. I grant there may be practical laxity, but for a soul before God that does not do. For such an one, with his eyes open, the subjection to human institutions in the things of God is just what he cannot and dare not yield.

"Schism in *the body*," then, is always wrong. *Separation from evil*, at all costs, is a necessity, and always right. And from this have been gathered the freshness and power which have plainly characterized so many movements of this kind at the beginning. They began in self-judgment and devotedness. The evil at least they saw, and were exercised about, and the measure of truth they had was held in power. It was soon systematized, and in that proportion its power began to fail. The founders, if you look at their lives, were men of faith and power, suffering and enduring. The manners of the adherents were chastened, simple, primitive. Organized, popularized, with a large following, the freshness waned; and in the third or fourth generation, another sect had taken its place among the many, boasting of a history which it did not discern to be a satire upon its present condition.

The organization, the creed, are to preserve the truth. But did these give them the truth they are anxious to preserve? Surely not, as they must own. God in His love, God in His power, has given what man had proved his incompetency to retain. They cannot trust Him to retain it for them, after He has given it. He has used His Word to minister it; they turn round and use, for that blessed Word of His, a creed of their own manufacture to preserve it. The generations after follow their fathers' creed, and not the Word. The truth popularized is gone as "Spirit and Life." God has to work afresh and outside of what a little while ago He had Himself produced.

And the spiritual life of the time has come more and more to manifest itself in "revivals," which, so far as they are really such, are the protests of the Spirit of God against prevailing death continually creeping over every thing; and oftentimes connected with fresh statements of truth, when the old have lost their power. The Lord's warning to Sardis points out this constant tendency to death. "Be watchful, and strengthen the things that remain, which are ready to die." "Remember therefore how thou hast received and heard, and hold fast and repent."

It is scarcely too much to say that every true revival, whatever the blessing for individuals,—nay, I might even say, in proportion to the blessing for individuals,—weakens the national system; and this for reasons we have been considering. The Spirit of God must needs work in opposition to

SARDIS. 179

the death produced by the system, and therefore against the system which produces the death. Souls quickened by the Spirit of God cannot go on contentedly under deadly and unchristian teaching, comforting themselves with the assurance of the article that "the evil" who sometimes "have chief authority in the ministration of the Word and sacraments" do yet "minister by Christ's commission and authority;" nor will they always be able to accept the ecclesiastical "yoke with unbelievers," because the system requires "every parishioner" to communicate, irrespective of any other security as to his conversion than his baptism and confirmation may imply.

It will be no marvel, then, to find, what any one with spiritual understanding must own, that at least the large proportion of those who could be said to "have not defiled their garments" in the history of Protestantism have been in some way or other dissenters from the national system. The first generation of English reformers were dissenters from Rome, and Rome did her best to keep them pure, in the fires she kindled for them. In the second and third generation from these, a people began to be separated, who from their honest endeavor to be right with God were nick-named "Puritans." I need not tell you what great names, which after-generations have learnt to love and honor, are found among this class,—a class with whom fine and pillory and imprisonment were familiar things. Every body knows that Bedford gaol was the "den" in which John Bunyan dreamed his memorable dream. In Scotland, the attempted enforcement of prelacy gave a succession of martyrs and confessors to the Presbyterian name, with whom, as elsewhere, their time of persecution was their time of real blessing, while the Episcopalianism which was riding rough-shod over them had gone already more than half way back to Rome.

With the movement under Wesley and Whitefield, nearer to our own times, we are naturally still more familiar; and that which issued in the Free Church of Scotland is still within the memory of a generation not yet passed away. All these, and many others, will exemplify the truth of what I have been saying; until, in our own days, the national systems are showing evident signs of decrepitude and breaking up; and Romanists and infidels are beginning their pæans on the downfall of Protestantism. We who are able to see it all in the light of Scripture can easily understand why all this is, and see only the truth of God's Word more and more manifested in it. Christianity flung as a cloak over a corpse can surely not warm it into life. Corruption will go on underneath, eating away the *form* of life, the only thing it ever had, until at last the cloak will more or less fall off, and what was all along true become apparent.

When the Protestant churches shall be gone altogether, or gone as such, their *protest* will not be gone, but only transferred to another court. Heaven will take up what they have dropped. Babylon the Great will fall under divine judgment; and apostles and prophets, and God's people everywhere, will rejoice at her fall.

A few words now about another thing.

If the Church reigns in the absence of Christ, what then? Why, then there must be something representing Him down here;—He must have a vicar. He is not present (even the world cannot mistake that), except spiritually. He is at God's right hand. That is the common faith of Christianity, and it is the faith even of Rome. Although, in spite of that, her altars are continually proclaiming Him corporally present, the faith of Christianity is that Christ is away.

But a visible kingdom requires a visible head; and I need not tell you that such they have given it. The pope is, for Rome, Christ's vicar; and this is only the natural development of the thought of church-government which historically preceded and led on to it, and which extends far beyond Rome. Presbyterianism, prelacy, popery, are but three steps in the same direction. Apostles are no more; and the Church is orphaned, if not governed in a visible manner. Hierarchial government in some form is a necessity to it.

Now the Lord has indeed a Vicar during His absence—a perfect, infallible Guide for His people, as well as a guide-book absolutely perfect. The Church has not only a perfect body of discipline, but One also who is the Interpreter and Administrator of it. It is the characteristic of God's people that "as many as are *led* by the Spirit of God, they are the sons of God." So distinctive and so wonderful a blessing is the presence of the Holy Ghost with us now, that, although the disciples in our Lord's day were blessed, by the fact of His presence with them, beyond all the generations previous, yet He could say to them, "It is expedient for you that I go away: for if I go not away, the Comforter will not come unto you; but if I depart, I will send Him unto you."

His presence in the believer makes even his body

the temple of the Holy Ghost. So His presence in the church makes it also "the temple of the living God." Looking at the Church, again, as the body of Christ, He is the one Spirit animating the body. As all the members move under the control of the spirit in the natural body, so in the body of Christ also: if the members do not understand and move in harmonious subjection to the spirit, we speak of it as disease; and it is not less, but more truly, so in the body of Christ.

If we open the Acts, we shall find every where His presence—greater than apostles, higher than the highest there. From the day of His descent at Pentecost, He is supreme over all; and that supremacy becomes the harmony of action, the unity of spirit in the lower sense. Sovereignly, He calls instruments as He will, and as sovereignly uses whom He calls. "Separate Me Barnabas and Saul," He says to the prophets and teachers at Antioch, "to the work whereunto I have called them. . . . And they, being sent forth by the Holy Ghost, departed into Seleucia." How strange to read as power conferred on man to convey office what is really the naming of individuals by the Spirit Himself, as called and sent forth by Him: one of them being the man who asserts his own apostleship to be, "not *of* men, nor *by* man"! *Gal. 1-1 (Paul)*

"Now when they had gone throughout Phrygia and the region of Galatia, and were forbidden of the Holy Ghost to preach the Word in Asia, . . . they assayed to go into Bithynia, but the Spirit suffered them not." "And finding disciples, we tarried there seven days; who said to Paul by the Spirit that he should not go up to Jerusalem." Not ordinarily, indeed, perhaps not often, was the bidding of the Spirit expressed as audibly; but the manner of communication was but circumstantial, and not of the essence of the matter. *He* was present, Comforter, Guide, Teacher, Witness; Spirit of the body, "dividing to every man severally as He will;" a divine Person, with divine power and divine authority.

Yet unseen! I grant the fatal flaw in all this for most. The Bible they can see, but it is not definite enough. The Spirit of God they cannot see, and, alas! cannot believe in, in a practical way. "Whom the world cannot receive," says the Lord Himself, of the Holy Ghost, "because it seeth Him not, neither knoweth Him." And when the line between the Church and the world is gone, who can wonder that this unbelief should be permeating the mass of what is professedly Christ's? It is not only Rome that refuses to the blessed Spirit the place He has come to fill. The unbelief which has denied the sufficiency of Scripture, and supplemented it by creeds which come soon to supplant it, has denied in the same way the sufficiency of the Holy Ghost, and supplemented His authority with hierarchical governments to which (whatever the theory) He is practically unnecessary.

If you ask people what they mean by "church-government," you will get various answers, no doubt; but they will all agree substantially in one thing. That one thing is, in an omission of what is, indeed, the key-stone of the arch. They will tell you, some, that they believe in an episcopal form of government, some a presbyterian, some a congregational. And if you ask them further, Where do they put the Holy Ghost? you will find the mass of people even denying any special presence of the Holy Ghost as characterizing this dispensation. They will tell you (so far, truly,) that the Spirit of God has always been acting in the world, from the creation of it; that the new birth has always been His work, from Abel, or from Adam, to this time. They believe, too, in certain special gifts at the day of Pentecost, and for some time thereafter. A distinctive "coming" in the place of Christ, a coming so important in character that it was expedient for Christ to go away that we might have it, they do not understand and do not believe in. One well-known man, an evangelical divine, Dr. Hugh McNeile, of Liverpool, when he had to admit that a personal "coming" of the Holy Ghost after the ascension of Christ was taught in the Word, could only account for it by the supposition that during the Lord's lifetime upon earth all the operation of the Spirit was limited to Himself alone, so that the three and thirty years of our Lord's presence were years in which no conversions could take place at all,— a barren time in the world's history, a unique and utter desolation otherwise of spiritual influences!

And thus you will find that the *practical* faith in the Holy Ghost's presence now is scarcely faith in a *Person*. It is "influence," like rain, or dew, or gentle breeze,—and these are true and scriptural figures so far, but quite impersonal. They talk of a "measure of the Spirit," and every fresh stirring of heart they find is a fresh "baptism" of the Spirit. The evident and necessary result is that they lose the first requisite for faith in Him as One come down to take charge for Christ on earth, to dwell as God in the house of God, to animate and govern the body of Christ, as the spirit in man guides and governs the natural body.

Hence church-government, in people's minds, has nothing to do really with His presence here. Bishops, priests, and deacons may need, and of course do need, His influences. So, in theory, does the pope. But practically the ordering of things is (within certain limits, whether of church-tradition or of Scripture, so far as Scripture is supposed to serve,) in human hands, and subject to human wills. "The Church has power to decree rites and ceremonies, and authority in controversies of faith." "And those [ministers] we ought to judge lawfully called and sent which be chosen and called to this work BY MEN who have public authority given unto them in the congregation to *call and send* ministers into the Lord's vineyard." But the Holy Ghost may not have "called or sent" them! Well, that, of course; and that is provided for: for "although in the visible church the evil be ever mingled with the good, *and sometimes the evil have chief authority in the ministration of the Word* and sacraments, yet forasmuch as they do not the same in their own name, but in Christ's, and DO MINISTER BY HIS COMMISSION AND AUTHORITY, we may use their ministry both in hearing of the Word of God and receiving of the sacraments"!!

Thus they may have Christ's commission although the Holy Ghost hath *not* "called or sent" them: Christ and the Holy Ghost are made to be at issue, and the Church can go on ordering and ordaining in despite of the Spirit Himself!

And this is *order;* while those who desire to yield subjection to the Word and Spirit of God alone are convicted of being rebels against proper authority, and sure to end in confusion and (as some have said,) in "atoms"! Yet faith will follow where

God leads, owning indeed that in His path all will be confusion that is not subjection; and that, leave Him out, we at least have no resource. Let it be so: we will abide the issue.

But let us contemplate a little while now the other side of things. We have had before us what is intensely sorrowful, more provocative of tears than Jezebel's corruption. There, the very malignity of the evil roused the whole soul against it: here, there is the fruit of what was in the beginning a movement of God. He can speak of what they had seen and heard, and exhort to hold it fast. There are still "things that remain," although "ready to die." And how can we but sorrow intensely over what was so fair in its earliest promise, and received its baptism in the blood of martyrs?

Yet the word to the overcomer, once again recurring here, comforts us with its recurrence. It links us, if we have ears to hear, with the same little remnant that has ever been finding its way, through storm and flood, to Him from whose love neither tribulation, nor distress, nor persecution, nor famine, nor nakedness, nor peril, nor sword can separate, and in which they have approved themselves, through Him, more than conquerors. The overcoming may be now in a new sphere, and separation may have to be from brethren, in some sense, of a common faith, heirs of great names in faith's records. Yet, in the *overcoming*, only *overcomers* are their true successors. Not those who, in our Lord's days, built the sepulchres of the prophets, represented them, or were linked with them, in His account, but those whom He sent forth to be persecuted by these same admirers of antiquity.

And God must teach us independence, even of one another,—that rightful independence which springs from real and lowly dependence upon Him. In His presence, what were even the greatest of His followers? How can I say to another, "Rabbi, Rabbi," when I must take the honor from Him that I deck another with? If I had not Him, it were lowliness; if I have Him, it is dishonor to Him.

It is not schism, this separate path, when not my own will leads me, but His Word and Spirit! It is not separation in heart from brethren, if Christ be dearer to me still than they. Nay, love to them approves itself only thus, as the apostle teaches us, "when we love God and keep His commandments." (1 Jno. v. 2.)

Faith's victories are not in applause wrung from a multitude, but in the path of One, true Joseph, separated from His brethren; and God has overruled the presence of evil (which, I need not say, He has not caused) to the giving us a path, at least in its circumstances, the more Christlike. We are not left to the subjection to evil: He calls us to rise above it. The difficulties of the path are only to carry us through them all. Every encouragement throughout these epistles is held out simply to the overcomer. The Lord give us only the needed energy. The time is short: the end is at hand. The grace that is now sufficient for all daily need will soon be manifested in the crowning of the conquerors. Then those that are poor shall have the kingdom; the mourners shall be comforted; the meek shall have the inheritance; the hungerers and thirsters after righteousness shall be filled; above all, the pure in heart shall see God—the God whom sin for the time has banished from the earth He made.

Philadelphia: the Revival of the Word of Christ, and the Brotherhood of Christians.

(Rev. iii. 7-13.)

WE come now to a phase of the Church's history of the deepest interest and of the greatest possible importance to us. How great it must be to realize a condition which the Lord can commend and only commend! For in this address to Philadelphia there is no word of reproof throughout. Warning there is, and of this we shall have to take special note; but reproof there is none! How blessed a condition to be in, when the "Holy" and the "True" can smile upon us thus with not a cloud to obscure His love! It should be, of course, the condition of Christians always; and sweet it is to remember that thus, all through the ages of its course, when as a phase of its history Philadelphia yet was not, the Church had its *Philadelphians* nevertheless. Manifestly it had when John was instructed to write this epistle; and if the general character of things around, even in an apostle's days, did not answer to this, only the greater would be the Lord's approbation of the few who were thus faithful. Overcomers they are whom He is commending; and the adverse condition of things around can never, let us mark it well, be really *adverse to the overcoming.* They furnish, rather, some of the conditions of it. If we have but the *spirit* of the overcomer, all the evil, whether in the world or in the Church itself, will only make us this the more.

Before we take up the details of the address before us, let us seek to get hold of the character of the church in Philadelphia. And for this we must remember in the first place what we have seen to be represented by that in Sardis. Sardis undoubtedly stands for the national churches of the Reformation, in which masses of peoples, Christianized externally, not truly, possessed a "name to live," and yet were "dead." Among these, indeed, though few comparatively, were those not only living, but faithful,—men who walked in spirit apart, and did not defile their garments;—men of whom their Lord says, "They shall walk with Me in white, for they are worthy." Yet their presence did not alter the general character of that in which they were—in it, but not of it.

Sardis, then, is the world, Christianized as far as possible to be still the world, with Christians scattered through it. Philadelphia stands with its principle of "brotherly love," in essential contrast with it as that in which the brotherhood of saints is found and recognized. *It represents the movement of the Spirit, therefore, to recover the true Church*, lost amid the confusion of Sardis, uniting the members of Christ together in one, outside the mere profession. This, if once fairly considered, will be evident. It is not meant, however, by this that this movement has any proportionate success as might seem thus assured. It is one of our strange and sorrowful yet familiar experiences, that Christians can grieve, limit, quench, the Spirit in its action, and all the history of the Church that we have been examining is the reiterated assurance of this. Moreover, in the address to Philadelphia itself we have a very impressive warning to the same effect.

It has been already said, and is plain enough in it, that the Lord's message in this case contains no rebuke, but the sweetest possible sanction and encouragement. Not that there is Pentecostal energy or blessing indeed. "Thou hast a *little* strength" negatives such a thought, if we were disposed to entertain it. Still this is commendation, and not blame, and blame there is none. On this very account there seems a difficulty, which presses for solution. For the final blessing is assured, in this as every other of these epistles, to the *overcomer:* "Him that *overcometh* will I make a pillar in the temple of My God, and he shall go no more out." And here the reference is plainly to such pillars as Jachin ("He shall establish") and Boaz ("In which is strength") in the temple of old, and on the other hand to the "little strength" before ascribed to Philadelphia. He who has little strength becomes in the end a pillar of strength, and the true Philadelphian (it is inferred here,) is in fact the overcomer. Philadelphia is but the company of such.

But then it returns upon us with double force, what can be this *overcoming?* For in every case beside, but one, throughout these churches, it is plain that the overcoming is of things *inside* the church: in Ephesus, the failure of first love; in Pergamos, the settling in the world; in Thyatira, the doctrines and deeds of Jezebel; in Sardis, defilement with the dead; in Laodicea, the lukewarm condition. In Smyrna, indeed, though there is a Judaizing party there, yet the direct promise seems to refer more to the threatening of death from without, although it cannot be denied that the Judaized Christianity found easier escape from this, and Satan's open violence might therefore well drive many (it can hardly be doubted, *did*,) into his secret snare.

But in Philadelphia, rich with the Lord's approval, yet with no such front of persecution to endure, it does require answer,—Where, then, the overcoming? By which, moreover, every true Philadelphian seems as much to be characterized as every Smyrnean was. Not every Ephesian was this, still less every one at Pergamos, or Thyatira, or Sardis, or Laodicea. The Philadelphian was such, as he *overcame*. But what peril then, or difficulty, or opposition? The answer is only one; the question admits no other.

There is nothing but commendation in the address,—that is, no *blame*. But there is warning, and in this warning is pointed out the danger that threatens. It is the *only* danger pointed out, and therefore clearly makes known to us what is to be overcome. The warning word is, "*Hold fast that which thou hast, that no man take thy crown.*" Here, then, must be the overcoming. The danger is, of letting slip the Philadelphian character. And it is a real and pressing danger,—so pressing, that upon the mastery of it all blessing is suspended. It is the point of peril.

Philadelphia represents the Spirit of God working in living energy to deliver from that which is engulfing the people of God in a flood of worldliness. Alliance with the world is the forfeiture of Christian position practically, and of enjoyed privilege. So the Word of God definitely declares. The unequal yoke,—the yoke with unbelievers,—must be refused, or the unclean thing forbids the Lord Almighty to be to His people the Father that He is (2 Cor. vi. 17, 18). Separation from the world is not any the more schism because this has been falsely called the Church; nor will "the lust of the flesh, the lust of the eyes, and the pride of life," its moral characteristics, be purged out by the adoption of the Christian name. Thus the state religions are directly accountable for the divisions which have always marked them from the beginning of their history. Every revival tends to break them up. Where there is none, there we find continual gravitation to a lower level, which no orthodoxy of the creed can really avert.

The work of the Spirit, then, will necessarily bring about dissent from the national church. And it will be found that, at their beginnings at least, such movements have been very largely marked by a new fervency of spirit, a zeal and earnestness which have made their first generations men of power. The movement, purified by the opposition it has necessarily to endure, discovers and brings together the most spiritual. Consciences are exercised, the Word is felt and opened, Christ's presence becomes more necessary and more real, the fellowship of saints is valued. In a word, the character of the movement manifests itself as Philadelphian.

It is the voice and person of Christ which are here controlling, and he who is thus controlled is upon a path of unlimited progress and unspeakable blessing. The clue-line is in his hand which will lead him out of all entanglements, from truth to truth, from strength to strength. There is but one condition here, and that is, manifestly, that he "*holds fast*" *the clue-line*. If he drops this, progress is at an end, his path becomes devious. Alas! is it a rare thing for those who have begun in the Spirit to be made perfect by the flesh?

Asshur went out from Babylon,—so far, well;

but only to found Nineveh, Babylon's rival and counterpart. And this is the history of much that was spiritual in its beginning, and since has grown great. At first there was simplicity and faith, and Christ the Leader of true pilgrims. Now they are but conservators of a tradition of the past, and their glory is a golden age gone from them. They are often in this case earnest in holding fast, but not to a living Leader: they have dropped the clue of progress, and lost their crown to others. No wonder, then, at the emphasis laid upon this warning in the epistle.

This, then, is, in brief, what Philadelphia is. The application in particular may and will be differently made according to what we are and where we are ourselves; and we have special need of care to test ourselves truly by it. For to test *ourselves* is surely the use that we are called to make of so solemn and yet so blessed a word as this is. We are bound to ask, Are we such as keep Christ's word and do not deny His name, and who keep also the word of His patience? Blessed, thrice blessed for us if we are!

Let us look, then, with something like suited care, into the details of the Saviour's message.

It has been often observed, and is evidently true, that the person of the Lord is more prominent in this address than in any of the others. It is a beautiful testimony that He is being Himself sought after with a new earnestness, to which He with a full heart responds. And the character in which He displays Himself is that of holiness and truth; for there is no way of nearness to Him but **by separation from the evil that He hates, and be-**

ing formed by the truth which He reveals. The Word is separative and formative. The mark of its reception is, the abandonment of *all* iniquity, marked as such, not by the common conscience of men, but by the Word itself. This is the sign of entrance into the sanctuary—of the presence of the Lord realized, when in *His* light we see light.

Absolute truthfulness is rare indeed. The penalties attending it are so many, often to be escaped by so slight a swerving from the strict path,—a path often so lonely and without sympathy, and so barren as it might seem in its isolation. Even to Christians, Christ often appears to have deserted it. And then after all to break down there! and what so likely as to break down? In this way we may connive at self-deception; for what do all these reasonings amount to, but that the path is to be a path of faith to us now as it ever was, and difficulties are to be as ever the test of faith?

Here, then, is conscience challenged as we enter on this address to Philadelphia. Have we indeed the "courage of our convictions"? or, perhaps, have we the courage to *expose ourselves* to possible conviction?

And note that the "holy" goes before the "true." There may be "truth," or "*genuineness*," as the word means, where after all *holiness* is not maintained. Satan succeeds by some puzzle for the mind in diverting many from a true issue. *Authority* may be pressed and bowed to as from God, and the soul awed into subjection to what it dares not approach near enough to recognize in its true character. Conscience may act, but blindfold, at the bidding of another than its "one Master." With Him, on the other hand, the "*holiness*" it is that guarantees the "truth."

He who thus declares Himself invites after all to no path of uselessness: He has the key of David, is Ruler over the kingdom absolutely, opens and no one shuts, and shuts and no one opens; and to those whom He addresses, pledges an open door, plainly for service, as the whole tenor here implies, and as the apostle three times over uses the expression (1 Cor. xvi. 9; 2 Cor. ii. 12; Col. iv. 3). Who could be in Christ's company without finding on the one hand His rejection, on the other how human hearts recognize their Lord? Here is no contradiction, but what every page of the gospels bears witness of to us.

Assuredly faith will still be necessary, and a judgment by results will be often much mistaken. If we wait for these to authenticate our course to us, we must in the meanwhile walk doubtfully, and not in faith. These words are an assurance rather to those who may be pursuing what to sense seems doubtful enough as to its issue. *He* affirms it to them. If they have the character here,—if they are with the Holy and the True,—holy with the Holy, true with the True,—then precisely because of this assurance, they need not ask, Will this be fulfilled— is it being fulfilled to us? Our eyes must be upon the path and the Leader. Success, where it seems fullest, must yet be tested rather by the future than the present—rather by eternity than time; and he who follows it most will be most distracted by other voices than His who speaks here. What tempter lures indeed the servants of Christ like this? For how many does *success*, rather than the Word of God, sanction their measures, while alluring them into direct opposition to the Word! If even gained in true obedience, how often does the flattery of great achievement unbalance a soul which adversity could only school to more endurance! These things are but common-places of experience; and in view of them, we need not wonder if God has, in general, been sparing in measuring out to His people great success.

And yet finally the success is great indeed, as it is certain to those who conform to the rule laid down as of old to Joshua: "This book of the law shall not depart out of thy mouth; but thou shalt meditate therein day and night, that thou mayest observe to do according to all that is written therein: for then thou shalt make thy way prosperous, and then shalt thou have good success." Alas! how much oftener is this thought to be insured by a supple and worldly wisdom than by a close and undeviating adherence to the Word of God!

The Lord now gives here, as elsewhere, what He approves in them: "For thou hast a little strength, and hast kept My word, and hast not denied My name."

A little strength He marks and approves; yet it is but a little. No Pentecostal energy revived, no faith that can move mountains, shall we find here. The "day of small things," in the Christian as in the Jewish history, is not at its beginning, but at its close. It is a great mistake to confound the day of Ezra with the day of David. And although it may be said, and truly, that eternal life and the power of the Spirit know no decrepitude, yet our day and generation leave their imprint on us. They should not; we are not blameless in it; yet they do. Still "a little strength" is here approval.

And how is this marked? Surely in what follows,—"Thou hast kept My word, and not denied My name." It is not in gifts restored to the Church, as some claim now; it is not in ecclesiastical position, nor in numbers, nor in place among men;—in none of these things is there strength before God, but in *obedience and devotedness.*

We have seen in Thyatira Jezebel's word claimed as inspired and authoritative; we have seen, too, in Sardis, a separation from and refusal of such claim: yet the Church, though no longer inspired, teaches still. There is, as men say, an open Bible, (blessed be God for it!) and with this, a certain necessary diffusion of light. The Reformation creeds insist upon the fundamental truths of the gospel, and these have been sealed by the lives and deaths of the martyrs. At the first, also, these creeds are in harmony with the convictions of those who subscribe them, although very soon dissent has to be embodied in a separate creed. Then a strife of creeds begins which has been the shame and reproach of Protestantism,—which has added schism to schism and sect to sect.

For the creed in Protestantism,—the pretension to catholicity, as in Rome, being gone,—*means* sectarianism. Who that has the thought of Christ's Church would undertake to frame a confession or constitution for it? Hence all such things now are local, and professedly for a part only. It is a fencing off of a greater or less number from the rest. If you cannot agree, you are at best dismissed to go elsewhere, and find or make a party for yourself.

But he who will keep Christ's word can bind himself to none,—must preserve his individuality of conscience, subject to one Master only; as much so as if there were no other Christians but himself on earth: and in a true walk with God, the knowledge of Himself, acquaintance with His Word increases with each step of the way. The light brightens to the perfect day, and in this brightening light we are called to walk, true to it, and to Him whose light it is. An immense thing it is, in a day like this, to be keeping, with an exercised heart, the word of Christ! Not a word here and there; not following it until the cost may be too much; but through honor and dishonor, through evil report and good report. For is there right obedience *any where*, when there is not in our purpose obedience *every* where? Can He whom we serve accept a compromise to His own dishonor, when we really tell Him we will do this, but not that, at His bidding? Solemn questions these, which may His grace keep ringing in our ears, until they wake up only harmonies of joy and peace within our souls, and not self-accusation.

Let us understand that keeping Christ's word means, if it mean any thing, honest subjection to the whole of it: to that of which we may not even perceive the importance, as if we did; calling nothing little which He enjoins—of what has equal authority with the weightiest to emphasize it for us. Herein is often the truest test of a right spirit in us, when we obey not in uncertainty, but in darkness; and go out upon His leading, not knowing where.

We have need to remember, too, that our own contrary wills are often the most effectual hinderances to receiving what is really Christ's word. How solemn it is to think that of the mass of things in which we differ from each other as Christians, this contrariety must needs account for very much the larger part. The Lord's words are plain enough, and universally applicable, that "if any one will do God's will, he *shall* know of the doctrine whether it be of God." It is due to Him to own that as the blessed Spirit of God could not lead into contradictory beliefs, these differences must be of us, and not of Him. But then, found as they are in so many whom we must esteem as godly men, what a warning they give us of how much that is not of God,—of real insubjection—may be found even in such. So far as we have indeed whole-heartedly followed Him, who can doubt that He has led us right? But then how little really unreserved following of Him there must be after all!

And who can measure the loss even now? and who then can measure the eternal loss, when we thus let slip communion with Himself? And how many are trying to win it back, or make up for its absence by filling their hands with work for Him, as if they were almost persuaded that "to obey is" *not* "better than sacrifice, and to hearken than the fat of rams."

How plainly perceptible it is when a soul reaches the barrier line beyond which he *will* not go! Activities may go on, and the whole *outward* man be no other than it was, yet there is something gone from the soul which at once one with God will discern as hindering fellowship. How sorrowful to lose one another's company this way, while yet perhaps the feet go on together! But if we lose Christ's companionship, what shall replace it?

Naturally and necessarily connected, then, with "Thou hast kept My word," is this: "and hast not denied My name." Christ's name expresses what He is. "They shall call His name 'Emmanuel,' which being interpreted is, 'God with us.'" And to fulfill this, He is named "Jesus"—"Jehovah saving;" for save He must, that God may dwell among us. Thus, again, He is "Christ," the Anointed One, to fill the Mediator's place,—with God for us, with us for God. Who that knows it would deny this blessed name?

What does it express, what does it emphasize for us but communion with God? He hath come out after us, left His place and glory, to let the light of that glory in upon our hearts. It is in Him, this glory, in—

"The person of the Christ,
Enfolding every grace."

Justified we must be, to be able to draw nigh; and without sanctification "no man shall see the Lord;" but the Lord Himself is thus the end and sum of all. "Christ is all," says one whose life spake with his lips; and "I count all things but loss for the excellency of the knowledge of Christ Jesus my Lord; for whom I have suffered the loss of all things, and do count them but dung, that I may win Christ, and be found in Him."

It is, as often said, what gives the peculiar glow to the picture of Philadelphia here, that it is Christ personally who fills the scene of their vision, and who associates them with Himself. This is what gives them their name, surely, in its spiritual power and value; for never was Christ welcomed into a heart but He made room in it for all His people. This is true linking with one another when we are united by the Centre,—when our association is first of all with Christ, and this determines the measure and character of all other associations. For indeed there is much, even among the people of God, that is not Philadelphian, but only a corrupt and evil counterfeit. If our "part" is first of all to be with

Christ, let us hear Him say, "Except I wash thee, thou hast no *part with Me*." And this is not spoken of the first general "washing" when we are born anew, which the Lord expressly distinguishes from this washing of the feet, the cleansing from all defilement by the way. If *He* washes, there can be no compromise with defilement; our feet must be in His hand; there must be surrender to Him at all points, so that He may be able to show us *all* that is evil in His sight. Thus alone can we have part with Him; and therefore in this way only can we have rightly part with one another.

To this such union as can be obtained by compromise is in essential contradiction. It is mere *confederacy*, whatever may be the end proposed. God has one method for us by which we may walk together according to His mind, and only one. We are to "follow righteousness, faith, love, peace, with those who call on the Lord out of a pure heart." By taking the same road, we are necessarily brought together. The road is guaranteed to us by its four decisive marks; and here there can be no compromise, we must not give up any one of these. Moreover, it is thus by a path in the strictest sense *individual* that we find our *company;* yet it is wide enough to contain "*all* that call upon the Lord out of a pure heart." Its characters are, first of all, "righteousness," and this must be maintained before we can properly speak of "faith" at all. But *then* "faith" marks the conscience in the presence of a living Lord, as well as a heart confiding in Him; and so it is only that we can have this restful, practical confidence, as we walk in conscious recognition of and obedience to His will. Here "love" then comes in due place,—we can now let our hearts out; and in this atmosphere love will develop itself. While lastly, "peace" characterizes it in view of opposition and conflict and trouble: the Lord is over all the uprising of the waterfloods.

In all this, it may be said, there is nothing but the most complete individualism; yet here it is we find the divine law of association. There is no confederation, no agreement, no prescription of terms to one another. One Master prescribes to every one his place, and in accepting that place we find the true law of co-operation with one another. United to Him as members of His body, we are, to begin with, "members one of another." This is not a question submitted to us, whether we shall be one; and to form other unions, while it may be ignorance, is none the less complete opposition to His will. Alas! in our day it is not "union is *obedience*" that is the motto, but "union is *strength;*" and for whatever purpose men may have, they *combine*. Strength of a certain sort is found, no doubt; but it is not where he found it who says, "When I am *weak*, then am I strong;" "I can do all things through Christ, who strengtheneth me."

Individuality is thus lost, a majority decides for the remainder; for the advantage gained, certain things which we do not approve must be acquiesced in. Conscience, at first uneasy, becomes more tolerant. More demands made upon it find less and less the power of resistance. Christ's word is given up, and what is due to His name forgotten. How many have thus lost in their souls the sensitiveness to sin they once had; yet the apostle insists, "Let him that nameth the name of the Lord depart from iniquity." Blessed, thrice blessed are they who, if they have but a little strength, yet have kept His word, and do not deny His name.

The next verse seems somewhat strangely to connect Philadelphia with Smyrna: "Behold, I will make them of the synagogue of Satan, which say they are Jews and are not, but do lie; behold, I will make them to come and worship before thy feet, and to know that I have loved thee." Here again comes before us that class through which Satan had wrought the downfall of the already declining Church. Judaism, set aside by God, is now one of Satan's best weapons and most subtle snares. Great Babylon has built her superstructure upon this foundation, and displaced with the ritualism, the sacerdotalism, and the legalism of an earlier time, the simplicity and open speech, the equal priesthood and completed sacrifice, the free grace and full salvation, of Christianity. It is not after all so strange, therefore, that if in Philadelphia we find the heart fresh awakened after Christ, His Word preached with fresh energy and held with more appreciation, on the other hand Satan's old attempt should be renewed. And this the words here seem to indicate. They assure us also, no doubt, that for the true Philadelphian it will end only in defeat, and the acknowledgment of their enemies that they are objects of Christ's special love, yet this does not assume that the onset will have no success. God permits these things for the trial of His own, and there was only One who could say, "The prince of this world cometh, and hath *nothing* in Me."

In fact, if we look at the history of the movement which has been for years going on, we shall find that along with revived study of the Word, and energetic evangelizing, and the drawing of Christians to one another, there has been an undoubted revival of ritualism also, and that not in Rome where it never had slept, but in Protestantism. The Puseyite or Tractarian movement, as it used to be called, had all the freshness and energy of a revival, and its success was marked. At the present time, it is less noted only because its influence is become a thing of course; and Protestant Episcopalianism is largely leavened with it.

This may be thought outside Philadelphia, according to our definition of it, but it is one of the things it is called to meet. Nearer home, however, in less developed forms, the same spirit is manifesting itself. The fruits of many a revival and separation from the church-establishments of Protestantism have been blighted by a spirit of conformity to that which had been left. The chapels have become churches, the ministry a priesthood, the congregations multitudinous and indiscriminate under this influence; and the desire for Christian union has been perverted into a desire for *denominational* union, a more or less ignoring of differences which were once matters of conscience for the soul, but have become rather matters of dispute left to the champions of conflicting creeds.

Even for those most widely removed (as it might seem) from all this, the same influences are at work, and should be no less dreaded. Ecclesiasticism, clerisy, the substitution of corporate for individual conscience,—these are all elements of a return-movement, the ebb of the tide which once seemed as if it could not so soon fail. But they are elements also of that Judaism with which man's mind, if it slip away from God, so readily assimilates. In fact it is all that is natural to man, and of himself he never gets beyond it.

Let us take heed, then, that we be true Philadelphians. Tested we shall be assuredly all round, and in different *forms* if the spirit be not different. The Word here is the assurance, is it not? for the faith that might quail and question as the results of the trial become apparent. Not now, but by and by, things shall be manifested, and where Christ's heart is shall come out openly.

Meanwhile there is another promise: "Because thou hast kept the word of My patience, I also will keep thee out of the hour of temptation which shall come upon all the world, to try them that dwell upon the earth."

Here is still the keeping of Christ's word: all blessing lies in the track of obedience; but it is now a peculiar character of that Word, and as manifesting a character of Christ Himself,—His *patience*, or *endurance*. It was of course a character of His on earth; it is also a character that He is manifesting where He sits now, upon the throne of heaven. He has but to ask, and the rod of iron shall be His to dash to pieces all opposition, like a potter's vessel. Yet He waits; not unobservant of the trials of His saints, not surely as unsympathetic with them. But He waits, that God's purpose may be fully wrought and the discipline of His people fully accomplished. It seems to me another mark of Philadelphia herself being tested by that of which the previous verse has spoken. They have needed patience: they have learnt it in the apprehension of that patience of His who Himself exercises it, with power in His hands which could change the face of things as in a moment. They have *kept* that word of His patience,—feeling the trial, but learning the consolation. Then, when the hour of trial for the dwellers upon earth shall come, they shall be out of it! Suited all this is, surely. And that word even, "dwellers upon earth," suits exactly the Judaized synagogue of Satan of which the Lord has spoken. For the expression has a moral force, like that where Pergamos is described as *"dwelling* where Satan's throne is." The hour is the hour of terrible tribulation, which, involving Israel first (Matt. xxiv. 21), will extend also to the Gentiles (Rev. vii. 14, *R.V.*), and reap with its scythe of destruction the tarefield of Christendom; God's wheat having been removed from it.

Into this time of judgment no saint, indeed, of the present time can come. And this has been with some an objection to such an interpretation of the words before us. But it would be only be that, if they were to be *confined* to Philadelphia, which is not the case. The promise to Smyrna is equally such to every child of God that ever was. Will any of these be hurt of the second death? Assuredly no; and yet not the less suited to the sufferers in Smyrna was that word of comfort. So here: doubtless God's people have all been in various ways made to apprehend the word of Christ's patience, and will be kept out of the hour of trial for apostate Christendom.

But the word is suited especially here, because that which separates the saints from it, and from the possibility of sharing its judgments, is at hand. More decisively now He announces, "I come *quickly*." The day of grace is running out with the day of patience. Soon it shall be Christ's presence and glory. The centuries of delay have come to years, the years are soon to be months, the months days, the days moments. "I come quickly:" this is to be shown in its power for the soul by its keeping the exhortation, "*Hold that fast which thou hast, that no man take thy crown.*"

But all shows it to be a time of drift,—a time of declensions as well as revivals: overcomer is he only who holds fast. The Spirit of God moving, the Word manifesting its power, conscience responding; yet every where the ebb after the flow, the trial which sifts, separates, individualizes. By and by comes the terrible *back*-flow of Laodicea. Think not Philadelphia is a haven of refuge where we may lie at anchor and never feel it. Not so,— oh, not so: this is the fatal delusion of Laodicea itself: "Hold that fast which thou hast!" The tug, if it has not come, is coming: *hold thou fast!*

But to what?—hold *what* fast? The *word*, and the *name*, and the *patience* of Christ. Not the word of even the leaders of God's raising up. The truth must ever commend the man, *never the man the truth*. One great danger is, lest, having begun with the former principle, we slip into the latter. Even the truth they teach is not truth received till it has been gotten at the Master's feet and in communion with Himself,—till you can hold it, not with the eyes *shut*, but with eyes open,—till you can maintain it for truth against the very instrument used of God to give it you, if need be. "If WE, or an angel from heaven, preach any other gospel unto you than that ye have received, let him be accursed."

Then, HOLD FAST! When it is no longer a question if it be the truth, but only of its consequences. Hold fast: though those who have held it with you, or before you, give it up; though it separate you from all else whomsoever; though it be worse dishonored by the evil of those who profess it; though it seem utterly useless to hope of any good from it: in the face of the world, in the face of the devil, in the face of the saints,—"hold fast that which thou hast, that no man take thy crown!"

For many a crown has been lost, and many a crown will be lost, if the Lord should tarry. Yet he who will hold fast shall find Christ's arms underneath him, Christ's hands upon his hands. He shall not only keep, he shall be kept; in the might of Christ's victory he shall stand, and the crown given he shall cast before the Giver of it as a trophy of His own conquest, and the fruit of His grace.

"Him that overcometh will I make a pillar in the temple of My God; and he shall go no more out. And I will write upon him the name of My God, and the name of the city of My God, which is New Jerusalem, which cometh down out of heaven from My God, and I will write upon him My new name."

A fixed eternal place in the sanctuary of God; identification with the display of God as revealed in Christ forever; identification with the abiding-place of His affections, in which heaven and earth shall meet at last in an eternal embrace of love; identification with the manifestation of Christ in His new eternal relationship to this whole scene:— this is what seems to be expressed in the promise here. But who shall give it proper utterance? What an end for the weak one who under trial still holds fast to Christ and His word! How blessed the stability of this scene by which He would establish our hearts amid the perpetual flux by which we are surrounded. How sweet the identification with Himself of the feeble one who has but owned on earth the authority of Him whom heaven and earth will own in joy in but a moment! It is a text to be expounded by the Holy Ghost to the heart of the overcomer, rather than to be spread out upon the page here. It is a sanctuary word, and the ear receives but a little thereof.

Laodicea: What Brings the Time of Christ's Patience to an End.

(Rev. iii. 14-22.)

WE come now to the solemn close of these addresses, the Lord's last word to the churches; and it is very striking that we come to that close here, just after that epistle to Philadelphia, in which we have seen recognized a certain real return of heart to Christ, and a true revival by His Word and Spirit. Now, there are, on the contrary, prostration and collapse: and the most serious thing is that these are the infallible signs of the failure on the part of Philadelphia itself. *Laodicea springs out of Philadelphia.* The blessing there leads to the judgment here.

In the states of the professing church which these addresses have already pictured, there is not only historical succession, but development. Even Protestantism sprang out of the bosom of Romanism, as Philadelphia out of Protestantism. In neither case is the one absorbed into the other, however. Romanism continues, outside the Reformation. The signs of a remnant are unmistakable in Philadelphia. Moreover, "overcomers" are implied in each case until the coming of the Lord. In Thyatira, thus, they are exhorted to "hold fast till I come; and he that overcometh, and keepeth My works unto the end, to him will I give power over the nations." In Sardis, "If therefore thou shalt not watch, I will come upon thee as a thief." In Philadelphia, "I come quickly." In this way, Protestantism, springing out of Romanism, runs henceforth side by side with it to the end. Philadelphia springs out of Protestantism, and similarly accompanies it. And so Laodicea, we may conclude, springs out of Philadelphia, and runs its course parallel with the rest.

But there is more positive proof. For if in Sardis there has been the absolute coldness of death, in Philadelphia, the glow of revival, in Laodicea there is the fatal lukewarmness which shows at once the effect (and the limited effect) of one upon another. And this is why the cold of Sardis itself is preferable to the lukewarmness of Laodicea. All God's grace has been spent in vain upon it.

Laodicea gives us, then, the failure of Protestantism, as Thyatira of that which assumes to be the Catholic Church. It is the complete failure of Christendom the second time; and now, in the full light of an open Bible, and after repeated intervention of God in wide-spread and protracted revival and blessing. The full end of patience has at last been reached, and the time to display also the results of the divine work, which no failure or opposition of man can in any wise hinder.

But before entering upon the details of this address to Laodicea, let us inquire as to the name itself. It was given to the city by Antiochus II., after his enlargement of it, in honor of his wife Laodice, and is a compound of two words—*laos*, "people," and *dike*. "*Dike*" is given by the dictionaries as having the three meanings, closely connected together, (1) of "manner, custom, usage;" (2) of "right;" (3) of "requirement," and so "vengeance," punitive justice. We have thus three possible meanings: "custom of the people," "people's right," "judgment of the people." And these three things have equally plain and solemn connection with one another.

For it is indeed the "people's custom" that is here unfolded. If under popery it is rather the usurpation of the leaders that is the question, in Protestantism, with its open Bible, the *people* are tested as never before. The earliest ages of Christianity, dependent upon the toilsome labor of copyists for the multiplication of copies of the Word, had in no wise the privileges of which the Reformation, with its providentially furnished printing-press, at once came into possession. Hence, also, responsibilities as great, and brought home to the door of every man. People may still be ignorant, but it is now assuredly a willing ignorance. They may still seek to cast responsibility upon others, and blindly follow still leaders as blind, but this has necessarily now another character from what it had before. Hence it is the *people* who are now being manifested,—their way which is being made apparent; and judgment, however delayed, must at last follow with proportional energy. Thus two significant applications of this word "Laodicea" are made evident.

But again, and connected with this, there is a feature of the last days which Scripture puts prominently forward,—the self-assertion which indeed on man's part has never been lacking, but which now pervades, in a manner not before seen, the masses of the population. That Protestantism has favored this, is one of the reproaches of the Romanists. And it is undeniably true that in one sense it *has* favored it. The breaking of ecclesiastical yokes,—the yoke of a tyranny more prostrating than any other,—with that awaking of the mind of man which is ever found where the light of the Word of God has penetrated,—has produced a state of things in which, if Christ's yoke be not accepted, man's will will assuredly assert itself as never before. And so it has proved; and so Scripture long before declared that it would be. "Laodicea," in its third sense, as "people's *right*," has become, morally, spiritually, and politically also, the watchword of the times. On the one hand, there is an immense march of civilization, a predicted running to and fro, and increase of knowledge; on the other, an uprise of what threatens civilization, and is ominous of an approaching end of the whole state.

"People's right!" The rights of the masses! and which the masses themselves mean to define and pronounce upon. Here is that condition of things which Hobbes, more than two centuries since, declared to be the natural condition, and which he rightly said *meant universal war*. For who is to judge as to these conflicting interests? and who is to enforce the judgment? Class will disagree with class,—nay, individual with individual: every man's hand will be against his brother; might will make right upon a scale the world has never seen, until out of this surging sea a power rises strong enough to command once more. Then they that will be lords shall have a lord, and they that will not receive Christ shall have Antichrist.

So the Word of God declares. For this ominous watchword, "people's rights," in the end of centuries of divine long-suffering, is a terrible claim in the ears of a God, strong, if yet so patient, and who is provoked every day.

It is a claim which denies the fall, and the sentence confirmed by countless individual sins,—the claim of a world which has refused and crucified the Son of God come into it in simplest loving mercy;—which would take the earth out of its Maker's hand, and enrich itself at His cost and to His dishonor. What wonder if they should quarrel over the spoils of victory, and the nations be quaking, as they are, over the success of their policy of liberty and equal rights? When democracy meant only the curbing of the despotic power of rulers, when it meant still respect for wealth and rank, and law and order, they could rejoice over it, and cite it as the evidence of morally improved times. Arbitrary power only was to be restrained: there was to be equal justice, and quietness and assurance as the effect of righteousness. Certainly the abuse of power had been great enough to provoke reprisals, and make the downfall of absolutism an apparent real advancement. But man was and is the same; and the mistake has been ever to suppose that alterations of this kind could really heal or touch a moral state which was the essence of the trouble. The leprosy, skinned over here, would only break out elsewhere, for it was deeper than the surface,—in the blood, in the vitals of humanity itself.

Who can say where the movement for men's rights shall stop? If they be rights, must it not be unrighteousness to stop any where? Who can say to the restless, resistless, surge of the sea. Come no further! here shall thy waves be stayed? There were, there are, most real and gigantic evils,--tyrannies which no form of government yet devised has taken into account, or probably can take. What does every man's right to his own imply? What is "his own"? How can you take from wealth the power which wealth implies? or allow power without allowing the abuse of it? Settle all inequalities, make one general plain of all the mountains upon earth, you have stopped the fertilizing rivers also which the mountains roll over the plains and in the valleys which you deprecate, but for whose benefit, spite of all, they rise.

Rights! what scale have you of rights? Listen to the voices from a lower level than you desire, which will interpret for you, and enforce their interpretation,—socialism, communism, nihilism,— dread names, not merely for the monarch, but for the man of property also, and for the law-abiding citizen. People's rights are already in terrible conflict with one another, and in their name how many wrongs may be inflicted yet! This Laodicea of politics is destined to be the rock upon which all governmental reform will end in anarchy and chaos. He who can read the great typical book of nature may read the scriptural presages upon a scroll written with lamentation and mourning and woe: "And there shall be signs in the sun, and in the moon, and in the stars; and upon the earth, distress of nations, with perplexity; the sea and the waves roaring; men's hearts failing them for fear, and for looking after those things which are coming upon the earth: for the powers of the heavens shall be shaken" (Luke xxi. 25, 26).

But the removal of the things that can be shaken will only make way for a kingdom, not such as they anticipate, absolute beyond all the tyrannies of old, a "rod of iron," which shall break as potsherds all the opposing powers of man, yet be the shepherd's rod under which the poor of the flock will lie down at last in peace, and none shall make them afraid. How refreshing to turn from what has been engaging us to contemplate such a rule as the world has never seen!

"He shall judge Thy people with righteousness, and Thy poor with judgment. The mountains shall bring peace to the people, and the little hills by righteousness. He shall judge the poor of the people; He shall save the children of the needy, and break in pieces the oppressor. . . . In His days shall the righteous flourish, and abundance of peace as long as the moon endureth. He shall have dominion also from sea to sea, and from the river to the ends of the earth. All kings shall fall down before Him; all nations shall serve Him" (Ps. lxxii. 2-4, 7, 8, 11).

But, it may be objected, this is altogether political: what has this to do with Laodicea *as a condition of the churches?* It would have little indeed to do with it if only the Church realized its separation from the world. As it is, it has very much indeed to do,—so much, that in Christendom a political Laodicea involves, as a matter of course, an ecclesiastical one. The world and the Church are so allied, so mingled, so permeate each other now, that ideally alone will they endure separation. And as a matter of fact, "people's rights" has become scarcely less an ecclesiastical than a political watchword. In this sphere, the masses are rising up against the long rule of their spiritual leaders, and claiming their rights at their hands. The oldest and best established oligarchies are accepting popular methods and forms upon all sides. The few must yield to the many. They choose their pastors as they choose their lawyer or their doctor, and insist upon having what they pay for. What can be a better "right" than that? Thus, however, it is clear, they "heap to themselves teachers," if you must not assume that they have "itching ears." But, in truth, the ear it is that is largely consulted; and necessarily so, where the very idea at the bottom is a commercial equivalent, and popular majorities rule, as quantity instead of quality. Even in the Church, and at its best, the most spiritual have never been the larger number. How much less in churches demoralized by heterogeneous mixture, competing for power and popularity!

Think of it, however, as we may, there is no doubt that, in church as well as state, "liberal" thoughts are prevailing,—democratic forms are succeeding to the old aristocratic ones. And here certainly Philadelphia has prepared the way for Laodicea. Distinctive priesthood, and the vested rights of clerisy, have in measure yielded to the free evangelization going on, and the equality of Christian brotherhood, and it is impossible not to rejoice that this should be so. But yet who can doubt that the overthrow, such as it is, of these ecclesiastical superstitions has favored claims that are no more of God than they? The laity may dispossess the clergy, and dominion pass from one class to another without reverting to the hands to which it really belongs. Christ is alone Master, not clergy, and not people. Ministers are indeed servants, as the very name imports, yet not servants of *men*,—a thing against which the apostle so vehemently contends. "Ye are bought with a price; be ye not the servants of men: if I yet pleased men, I should not be the servant of Christ." Thus these two things are in essential opposition. Christ needs to be in His true place,—a thing which so marks Philadelphia, but from which Laodicea excludes Him as does Thyatira. Bring Christ in, and the ministers are *His* servants. Bring Christ in, and the people are *His* people. His service, on the part of all alike, is true and equal freedom at once to all.

But the spiritual phase of Laodicea we are now to follow. May we do it honestly, with hearts open to receive rebuke; remembering that, not ecclesiastical place, but spirit, is in question. It is an old deceit to pride one's self on possession of the truth, while yet the sanctification by the truth is unknown. And this indeed makes a large part of the character of what is before us.

The Lord presents Himself here as the One who amid the general failure is "the Amen, the faithful and true witness:" *He* has not failed.

He is the Amen: "For the Son of God, Jesus Christ," says the apostle, "who was preached among you by us, even by me and Sylvanus and Timotheus, was not yea and nay, but in Him was yea. For all the promises of God in Him are yea, and in Him Amen, to the glory of God by us" (2 Cor. i. 19, 20). No uncertainty, no doubtfulness, is there in Christ or His Word. He is always simple, positive "Yea," speaking one thing, absolutely to be depended on. If we have but a word of His, it is a blessed reality, given us in God's infinite love, which we may rest our souls on for eternity, and which can never fail us. This is a resource which the denial of verbal inspiration would completely take from us; but His own assurance is, "Scripture cannot be broken" (Jno. x. 35). If it be a question, as in the case which the Lord is speaking of here, of but a title applied by an inspired writer to a certain class of men, there must be perfect suitability and divine wisdom in the application. "If he called them gods to whom the word of God came, *and Scripture cannot be broken.*" How precious is this assurance! Coming where it does, is it not itself a significant warning, this claim of His as "the Amen, the faithful and true Witness" to such a generation as the present? Does He not in it challenge the unbelief so common all around us?

But this presentation of Himself as a true and faithful Witness is in contrast with the failure of the Church, which has been any thing but that. He is just about to remove the candlestick because it has been unfaithful and untrue. But His people's shortcoming is not His own. Infidelity may seek to justify itself by the failure of Christians; and even Christians, alas! are almost capable of taking it as in some sort a reflection upon Himself. But "if we are unfaithful, he abideth faithful," as the Rev. Ver. rightly puts it now (2 Tim. ii. 13). And He is just ready to rise up and bring in that day in which, with the revelation of all things, this faithfulness of His will appear abundantly. In the general wreck, this only now remains to Him.

He proclaims Himself with this: "The Beginning of the creation of God." The old creation, spoiled by sin, is passing away; its history is nearly completed; its judgment has been long since pronounced in the cross, and in Christ risen from the dead is begun all that God owns as really His,—first and always in His thought, and for which the ruin of the old only prepared the way.

When the Psalmist lifted up his eyes to heaven, and in view of God's glorious handiwork there exclaims, "What is man, that Thou art mindful of him? or the son of man, that Thou visitest him?" the answer is, "Thou hast made him a little lower than the angels; thou hast crowned him with glory and honor; Thou madest him to have dominion over the works of Thy hands; Thou hast put all things in subjection under his feet." But of whom is he speaking? As the apostle in the second of Hebrews assures us, not of the first, but of the Second Man. "We see Jesus, who was made a little lower than the angels for the suffering of death, crowned with glory and honor." It is Christ in whom the true ideal of man is realized, and of whom the first Adam was but the fleeting image, and in many respects the contrast.

Now in Laodicea, with Christ outside, it cannot be the new creation in which their riches are. Yet they say they are rich, and increased with goods, and have need of nothing. Thus there are things which are gain to them which they have not counted loss for Christ.

It is an exceedingly solemn thing that the very truth which with all its grace judges and sets aside man most thoroughly is the very truth which he is prone to take and use for the purpose of self-gratulation. Take the law: God gave it "that *every* mouth might be stopped, and all the world become guilty before God" (Rom. iii. 19). But how has man used, and how is he using it? Always to establish his own righteousness by it. The large part of the Christian world, so called, to day is taking the "strength of sin" (1 Cor. xv. 56) to accomplish holiness by it, and are taking salvation itself to be, "not" indeed "by the *merit* of works, but" yet "by works as a condition."

So, exactly, with Christianity: God has brought in the truth of new creation, the world before Him lying under death and judgment. Yet man takes the blessed truth of Christianity to patch up the world with it, and make it better if he can. And in the very presence of the ruin and break-up of things on every side, men are vaunting the success of the effort. On the eve of judgment, they are fulfilling the Scripture-portents of such a time by their smooth auguries of prosperity and peace.

No doubt God's Spirit is really and largely working; but His end and man's thought are diverse, in that, while He is converting souls to "deliver them *out of* this present evil world," man's thought is an improved world, a Christian world: the effect of which is, to amalgamate Christians and the world, and spoil the scriptural character of Christianity altogether.

But in these last days God has given many to recognize the truth of the Word as to this. He has revived the truth of new creation, and revealed to us the practical and fruitful consequences which result from a place in Christ, where He is, in the heavens. But the question for us is, What are we doing, then, with the truth we recognize? Shall we talk of being in Christ a new creation, old things passed away, and all things become new, and yet cling to what has in it all the moral elements that make up the world—"the lust of the flesh, the lust of the eyes, and the pride of life"? Is it theory with us, or practical reality, to have "put on the new man, who is renewed in knowledge after the image of Him that created him: where there is neither Greek nor Jew, circumcision nor uncircumcision, barbarian, Scythian, bond nor free; but Christ is ALL, and in all"? Has the Lord need to appeal to us as the One who is "the Beginning of the creation of God"? If so, is not Laodiceanism with us in that proportion?

To Laodicea, as to the rest, He says, "I know thy *works.*" Here is the test,—the only true one. "I know thy works, that thou art neither cold nor hot: I would that thou wert cold or hot. So, then, because thou art lukewarm, and neither cold nor hot, I will spew thee out of My mouth." This is the certain and near end of professing Christendom. Of course He will not spew His own beloved people out of His mouth. He must take these first of all to Himself before He can reject the whole mass as nauseous. And we have already seen, in the address to Philadelphia, that the Lord tells them He will keep them out of the hour of temptation which shall come upon all the world:—not merely out of the temptation; He might hide them in the desert so, but out of the *hour* of it. For this, He must take them out of the world altogether. And that is what the "I come quickly" connected with this also intimates.

Here, then, we have the brief, solemn pause before the Lord takes His people to Himself. He must do this before the professing body can be spewed out of His mouth. He cannot so reject even the poorest, weakest, most wayward of His own. And it is important to insist upon this, because there is abroad a view according to which only a class of better than ordinary Christians will be taken up when the Lord comes, while the rest will be left upon earth to go through the tribulation which follows this, when the earth is enduring the vials of His wrath. They point to the promise to Philadelphia as in this way the promise to a special class; and the ten virgins of our Lord's parable they maintain to be all Christians, as they bring forward the fact of their being "virgins" to prove;— only foolish ones, unwatchful and unready, with indeed the oil of the Spirit in their lamps, but no *extra* supply in their "vessels." Thus their lamps, which had been burning, cease to burn at last, and the fresh supply of oil they get is obtained too late for admission to the marriage. The Lord rejects them only as the *bride:* they lose their place in this, and are shut out to be purified by tribulation, and made ready for the kingdom afterward.

But how many precious realities must be denied in order to hold this view! Is it our faithfulness, then, that gives us a place among those who are admitted to the dignity of the bride of Christ? Is the Lord when He comes indeed going to discriminate in this way between less and more faithfulness? —between ordinary and extraordinary Christians? What an engine is this for turning the blessed and purifying hope into a means of self-occupation and despair! If things are so, where is the line of acceptance to be drawn? and on what side of it are we? Is my joyful expectation of this blessed time to be based on the belief in my own superiority to many of my brethren? What comfortable Pharisaism, or what legal distress must such a view involve!

If true, why should such a discrimination be made between the living saints alone? Why should it not equally affect the dead? And then, is there to be a purgatory to purify these?

As to Scripture, the support it gives to any such view is only apparent, and results from an interpretation of single passages, which is at issue with its whole doctrinal teaching. The coming of the Lord to remove His saints is not in Scripture ever connected even with our responsibilities and their adjudication, but with the fulfillment of the hope with which grace has inspired us. Our responsibilities and the reward of our works are connected with that which is called the "appearing" or "manifestation" or "revelation of Christ,"—His coming *with* His saints, not *for* them. At the door of the Father's house to which He welcomes us when He comes, no sentry stands, no challenge is required. We go into it as purged by the precious blood of Christ, and in Christ. Already are we not only entitled, but "*meet* to be partakers of the inheritance of the saints in light."

When He comes to the world, and His people take their places with Him as associated with Him in government, then dignities, honors, rewards of work, will find their place. It will be "Have thou authority over ten"—"be thou also over five cities." But salvation, righteousness, the child's place with the Father, membership of the body of Christ, our relationship to Christ as His bride,—nay, even our being kings and priests unto His God and Father, are things which, as they are not gained, so they are not lost by any work of ours at all. Christ has procured them for us, and grace bestows them,—grace, and grace alone.

When, therefore, the Lord descends from heaven with a shout, with the voice of the archangel and the trump of God, is there discrimination among those in Christ?—of the dead who shall be raised? of the living who shall be changed? Nay, but the "dead in Christ shall rise first, then we which are alive and remain shall be caught up with them in the clouds to meet the Lord in the air; so shall we be ever with the Lord." Blessed words! how they pierce and scatter the chilling fogs of legalism, and make the "blessed hope," not a means of sorest perplexity and doubt, but hope indeed!

Nor are the passages which these writers build upon in contradiction with this at all. The promise to the overcomer at Philadelphia is one of a class which, as the eye runs over them throughout these apocalyptic addresses, show plainly that they apply more or less to every true believer. Take the promise to him at Ephesus, and ask, Will any believer *not* "eat of the tree of life which is in the midst of the paradise of God"? Take that to Smyrna, and ask, Will any "be hurt of the second death"? And so on through the remainder. Their special significance in relation to the overcomer in the cases there pointed out is not in the least diminished by their general application to all believers.

Again, as to the ten virgins, it is a mistake to suppose that in that character (*according to the parable,*) Christians are represented as espoused to Christ at all. Those who go forth to meet the bridegroom are not the bride; and to make them this, disjoints the parable. According to the whole tenor of the prophecy in these chapters, the Jewish people and the earth are in the foreground, and the parable of the virgins only parenthetically brings in the connection of Christians with these. According to the common language of the Old-Testament prophets, the Lord is coming to take a *Jewish* bride; and on His way to do this, His people of the present time are called up to meet Him and return with Him. So much is implied in the expression in the Greek. It is thus when He is come *to earth* that the foolish virgins are rejected, and cast out of His kingdom altogether. The parable is a parable of the *kingdom;* and the kingdom, in all the parables, speaks of earth, not heaven, and of the whole field of profession. "Virgins," "servants," and the like titles, merely intimate responsible profession, not necessarily the truth of it. *He* was a servant who had laid up his lord's money in a napkin, and never really served at all. He was a servant, but a wicked one; and so with these "foolish" virgins.

Oil they are explicitly stated not to have; and though their lamps are only represented as "*going* out," when the cry is raised, "Behold, the bridegroom!" this is the constant style of these parables, in which the inner thoughts of the soul are mirrored and exposed, not dogmatic truth taught. In their own imaginations, the Pharisees were the "ninety and nine just persons who need no repentance;" not in dogmatic reality. Moreover, the Lord's words of rejection, "I know you not," are decisive from One who "*knoweth* them that are His," and can never disown them.

No, He cannot spew His own out of His mouth, but must have them with Him out of the world before the first drops of the storm of judgment fall. Even then it will be made manifest, before He rejects the public professing body, that they have on their part rejected Him. Christendom ends in open apostasy. The day of the Lord will not come except there come a falling away first, and the man of sin be revealed. Popery, evil as it is, and antichristian too, is not the last evil, nor the worst. It is the sinful *woman*, not the *man*. It has been revealed over three hundred years as this, and the day of the Lord is not yet come. *The* Antichrist will deny the Father and the Son alike.

How solemn to contemplate the last end of what began so differently! How above all solemn to consider that both at the beginning and the end, the sin and failure of the true people of God it is which initiates and completes the ruin! Who can doubt that Christians themselves are largely taking up this self-complacent assumption—"rich, and increased with goods, and in need of nothing"?

Even by some who deem the time of harvest drawing near we are invited to consider the fact that if the tares are ripening for it, yet the wheat must be *ripening too;* and that this means that the present generation of Christians is spiritually in advance of every other! We are bidden observe the great awakening of the missionary spirit, the restoration of gifts of healing to the Church, and so on. Surely we are rich, and increased with goods, if this be our condition! And is there not a creed, connected very much with the latter claim, and largely professed among those who naturally take their place as the very leaders of the Christianity of the day, which comes very near indeed to Laodicean profession? How could the claim to be rich and increased with goods be more really made than by those who profess what they will not indeed call "sinless" and yet do assert for it what ought to be a still loftier title,—that of "*Christian* perfection."

Christian perfection is of course the very summit—the *ne plus ultra* of Christianity. Higher than this no one can hope to go: with such a condition God Himself must be completely satisfied. As Christ is, (so they apply it,) so are they in this world. Perfect knowledge, perfect wisdom, they do not suppose they have, but "perfect *love*" is the term which exactly fits and describes their condition. They perfectly obey the divine law, and for a large class there remains in them no corruption of nature even, although many would not go as far as that. There are many grades of the doctrine, and correspondingly it affects very distinct classes of Christian profession. Its wide acceptance is a very noticeable thing in these days, an unmistakable sign of the times.

For the term "perfection," and that as applied to Christians, there is scripture, of course. The devil, in deceiving the people of God, will always, if he can, use scripture to accomplish his object. But the term there does not mean what in the dialect of the "higher life" it is made to mean. Take one of the strongest texts used, "Be ye perfect, even as your Father which is in heaven is perfect"—the context shows decisively what is meant. We speak of a thing as perfect which has all its parts, without at all regarding the finish of its parts. So the Lord tells us that as children we must resemble our Father, and for this exhibit all the features of our Father's character. We must not only love those who love us, but as He makes His sun to rise on the evil and on the good, and sends His rain on the just and on the unjust, we must exhibit this feature of His character also: "Love your enemies, and pray for them which despitefully use you and persecute you, that ye may be the children of your Father which is in heaven." (Matt. v. 44, 45.)

"Perfection" is also used for the mature Christian condition, as a glance at the margin of Heb. v. 14 will show. The term there—"of full age"—is in the margin rendered "perfect," just as in 1 Cor. xiv. 20, "be *men*" is in the margin rendered "be perfect," or "of a ripe age." It is used thus with two applications: in Hebrews, Christianity itself is perfection, or maturity, in contrast with Judaism, which was a state of childhood. But again, among Christians there are those perfect, or mature, in contrast with being babes; and the apostle Paul, in the third of Philippians, in which he *disclaims* the having attained, or being already perfect, (as a consummation which he would not reach until with Christ in glory,) classes himself immediately after among those who *had* in another sense "attained:" "Let us therefore, as many as be perfect, be thus minded."

There are many texts which I cannot now go through; but this should prevent the catching at a word, as people are prone to do. Plenty about perfection there is, no doubt, in Scripture; but if we set up *any* standard short of walking as Christ walked, we are really lowering it. If, on the other hand, we can measure ourselves with Christ, and yet feel no rebuke, we must be indeed inordinately, if not incredibly, self complacent.

Mischief is wrought in two ways by the idea.

In the first place, sin must be palliated, excused, covered by misleading names. Lust is called temptation, and sometimes even daring dishonor done to Christ Himself by the insinuation that He too was in like manner tempted. So people quote, "He was in all points tempted like as we are, *yet* without sin," as if it meant that *He* had such inward desires, only restrained them, so that there was no positive outbreak. This, the actual blasphemy of Irving and Thomas, in milder and less pronounced forms infects many in the present day. The text they quote in the common version favors these views too much. And the Revised Version unhappily perpetuates the error. There is properly, as any one may see by the italics (Heb. v. 15), no word in the original representing "yet." "He was tempted in all points, like as we are, apart from sin" is the true rendering. You must not imply sin in any way in the Holy One of God. Sin it is that produces lust, as the seventh of Romans decisively teaches, as on the other hand lust, again, brings forth the positive outward sin. *He* had neither; no inward incitement as no sin in act, and herein was our total opposite, who, as Scripture assures us, "in *many* things offend, *all*." (Jas. iii. 2.)

But again, the character of holiness is sadly spoiled by this perfectionism. In the lips of many, "holiness" means "perfection," and nothing else, and so does "sanctification." And yet in fact holiness itself is marred and perverted by this claim as made. It becomes self-occupation, self-assertion. "Seraphic" men are held up to admiration. And how much of Christ really do you find in the experience so largely boasted of by those who advocate the doctrine? It may be in words—is it in reality, "not I, but Christ liveth in me"? or is it in fact a glorified, transfigured, but very self-conscious I, that lives and reigns throughout them? They do not see that, as the natural life in a state of health does not engross or claim the attention,—as the heart's pulsation, or the lung's work is not furthered, but disturbed, by thinking of it,—as the man in hospital it is who talks of his good days, because they are scarce, and as the dyspeptic it is who "feels" his stomach,—so this aim at a self-conscious holiness produces but a poor, degenerate, sickly Christianity at best. Is it far off from that which says, I am rich and increased with goods, and have need of nothing; and knows not that it is wretched, and miserable, and poor, and blind, and naked?

"I counsel thee," says the Lord to Laodicea here—"I counsel thee to buy of Me gold tried in the fire, that thou mayest be rich; and white raiment, that thou mayest be clothed, and that the shame of thy nakedness may not appear; and anoint thine eyes with eye-salve, that thou mayest see."

Three things are here which they are exhorted to "buy." So wealthy are they, the Lord will not talk of *giving* to them. And indeed it would be a happy thing for them to exchange their riches for them,—false glitter for true gold. This is the first thing: *gold*. A frequent symbol this is, we know, in Scripture, and pure gold (as here, "tried in the fire,") for what is divine. In the ark of the testimony, and in the furniture of the holy places generally, gold covered all. The apostle, I believe, gives us the exact meaning, when he speaks of the *golden* cherubim as the "cherubim of *glory*, shadowing the mercy-seat. This "glory" is the display of what God is. God glorifies Himself when He shines out in the blessed reality of what He is; and Christ is the true ark in which two materials are found together—gold and shittim-wood. The radiance of divine glory is the gold; the shittim-wood, the precious verity of manhood.

Can we not see why to Laodicea "gold tried in the fire" is the first requisite? Their riches were but paper money, manufactured out of the rags of self-righteousness, and of merely conventional, not intrinsic value. Christ was what they lacked: divine glory in the only face in which it shines undimmed. This is the power of Christianity, its essence and its power alike, and this is what their false, pretentious Christianity lacked so terribly: occupation with Christ,—discernment of what and where all that is true and valuable in Christianity is to be found. To know where this is, is to have it. Faith that finds this treasure is welcome to its enjoyment. To be without it, is to be poor indeed.

The next thing is, "white raiment, that thou mayest be clothed, and that the shame of thy nakedness do not appear." This is, no doubt, practical righteousness of life and walk. There is a connection between this and the former, which when we have their meaning becomes evident enough. Unless you have the divine glory in the face of Jesus shining for your soul, you will find no ability to live and walk aright. The "white" is the full, undivided ray of light; and God is light. How is our life to be the reflection of this, except as "God, who commanded the light to shine out of darkness," is shining in our hearts, "to give out the light of the knowledge of the glory of Christ in the face of Jesus Christ?" Leviticus must precede

Numbers ever. We must go in to see God in the sanctuary before we can possibly come out and walk with Him in the world.

Finally, we have here, "and anoint thine eyes with eye-salve, that thou mayest see." Thus there was utter blindness,—the condition of the Pharisees over again. *They* did not realize it. They said, "We see," and thus their "sin remained." For the consciously blind, there is with Christ effectual healing; but they, alas! needed not the physician.

These characters, taken in their full extent, reveal a state which is assuredly not Christian. We must not, however, on this account suppose, as some have done, that Laodicea thus represents merely the unbelievers among the Christian profession. Of Sardis it is distinctly said, "Thou hast a name to live, and thou art *dead*," and yet there are owned among them those who are not only alive, but "have not defiled their garments." This shows that we must beware of ascribing the characteristics of the mass to all the individuals in it. It is a state of things as to which all found in association with it have the gravest responsibility; but to say it is only to be applied to the unconverted is to deprive the warning given of all its power. It is to enable every consciously converted man to wash his hands of the responsibility. Whereas all around us, not only are the signs of Laodiceanism growing continually more manifest, but the infection also of Christians with its spirit. And here again also it is apparent how Philadelphia may open the way to Laodicea itself.

Philadelphia proclaims the brotherhood of Christians, seeks the true Church, insists upon the evil of division, and the maintenance of individual conscience in consistency with the recognition of the one body of Christ in all its members. Laodicea—Satan's counterfeit—proclaims also that the church is one, that union is strength, in order to bring about a grand confederacy in which truth shall be sacrificed for company's sake, and the power conferred by numbers. To the eyes of men, Laodicea becomes thus only the true carrying out of the Philadelphian idea,—itself a better and grander Philadelphia. Here Christ may in the very *name* of Christ be put outside the door,—a development of principles which are far and wide leavening men's minds, and preparing the way for the dark and dread apostasy in which the dispensation is announced of God to end.

Confederacy is, politically and socially, a character of the times. In mercantile affairs of every kind, companies are getting to be more and more every where the rule. The strength realized by union is here well recognized. In the rise of the popular element, combination is not merely an advantage; it is an imperative necessity. By its means alone can the poor man make his voice be heard upon nearer equality of terms with the capitalist, the laborer with his employer. Yet here the true individuality which God would have,—the individuality of conscience with which alone real uprightness of conduct can be maintained,—has to be lost and give way to the will of the majority.

No power can be attained by the body at large thus except by ruinous self-sacrifice on the part of its members. It must have unity, the unity of a machine, or nothing can be effected; but for this, heart and conscience must be leveled down to wood and iron. It is essential that freedom of individual action there should be none; and thus there is no tyranny so great as the tyranny often here exercised,—no more ruthless treading down of the most sacred and personal rights than with those in whose mouths the cry of "People's rights!" is oftenest and loudest.

Religious associations may seem often in their laxity as opposite to this as can be, and yet the laxity itself be as contrary to God, and bind me as much to His dishonor. What seems the largest liberality may thus be the very spirit of disobedience, and to this it is that every thing in the present day is tending. Satan can press upon us the evil of division just there where division is *not* an evil, but a right and godly separation from evil; and he can point out good to be accomplished, to make us little careful as to the means by which it is proposed to accomplish it. A united Christian church which should become so by making it a matter of indifference whether Christ were God or only the highest kind of man would certainly be his greatest achievement. The startling thing to-day is, that men considered evangelical can accept associations of this kind; and the platform upon which they stand widens continually: what would have been liberality a short time since is now narrowness. The world moves; but the unbending word of God which moves not, against this it will dash itself only to its destruction.

Amid this concourse and confederacy of men, communion with God becomes continually more restricted: "Behold, I stand at the door, and knock: if any man hear My voice, and open the door, I will come in to him, and will sup with him, and he with Me." This door is plainly individual,—not of the church, but of the heart. But then it is as plain that the church-door is shut against Him; not that He has shut it, or Himself spewed the church out of His mouth. He is still lingering in His love,—still saying, "As many as I love, I rebuke and chasten: be zealous, therefore, and repent." But they do not repent. He is as when at Nazareth in the days of His earthly ministry (rejected by those who should have known Him best,) it is written of Him, "And He could there do no mighty work, save that He laid His hand upon a few sick folk, and healed them." He could not do what He would; He would do what He could: "And He marveled at their unbelief; and He went round about the villages, teaching." So here, rejected by the body at large, He tries one door after another, in this solemn pause before the end. He would not judge in the mass; so He tries in detail. And *if* any heart responds,—for all seem to have shut Him out, but He will not take it yet as final,—then He will come in there, and sup: that soul shall yet to its everlasting joy entertain its Lord.

But the time hastens, and the nearness of the end is shown by the closing promise to the overcomer: "To him that overcometh will I grant to sit with Me on My throne, even as I also overcame, and am set down with My Father on His throne." He speaks, as He appears to the apostle, as Son of Man here. It is His kingdom as Son of Man He is about to take: that special throne from which as with a rod of iron He will break in pieces all opposition, and bring every thing into subjection to God. For it is His to do this. He has laid the foundation in the work of the cross: His hands shall finish it. All judgment is His, because He is the Son of Man. And judgment itself now is the only work left for mercy to accomplish. So there comes—most terrible of all wrath, the *wrath of the Lamb*,—the wrath of love itself: the wrath of Him who has been watching all these patient centuries the oppression of the meek, in whose ears have been the cries of the fallen in the terrible strife; He of whom the wicked hath said in his heart, He will not require it; yet who beholdeth mischief and spite to requite it with His hand; to whom the poor committeth himself, who is the Helper of the fatherless. HE now riseth up. "For the oppression of the poor, for the sighing of the needy, now will I arise, saith the Lord: I will set him in safety from him that puffeth at him."

In a word, the present day of grace is in this promise marked as just at its end. And with this the Church, as the vessel of the testimony of that grace, is being removed from the earth. The "present things" at which we have been looking are just over. The Christian dispensation has run its course. The saints removed to heaven, the rest that are left are but reprobate, and fall soon into utter apostasy. Then comes the earth's great trial-time, the time of Jacob's trouble, out of which yet he shall be delivered; the heading up of unbelief in gigantic forms of evil, dimly (and but dimly) now looming up amid the shadows of the horizon. Beyond it yet the glory of a brighter day, when the redeemed of the Lord shall come with singing unto Zion, and everlasting joy shall be upon their head; when a King shall reign in righteousness, and princes shall rule in judgment; and a MAN shall be as a hiding-place from the wind, and a covert from the tempest; as rivers of water in a dry place, as the shadow of a great rock in a weary land. And the earth shall be full of the knowledge of the Lord as the waters cover the sea.

Sweeter than all and brighter the joy above, when in the mansions of the Father's house that promise shall be fulfilled, "I will come again, and receive you unto Myself; that where I am, there ye may be also."

F. W. G.

"Things that Shall Be:"

An Exposition of Revelation IV.—XXII.

PART I.

Introductory.

(1) *Prophecies Leading Up to These.*

OUR title to the following pages indicates our adherence in some sense to the interpretation of the book of Revelation which makes the body of it—the nineteen chapters upon which we are entering—apply to what is still for us future. Those who so apply it, whatever differences in detail there may be among them, are on this account called "futurists," in contrast with the large school of "Presentists" or "Historicalists," who find in it a progressive history of the Church from the beginning, and interpret it naturally by that history.

They are usually and strongly opposed to one another, as might be expected, although there is no *necessary* opposition in the views themselves. Both may be held, and have been held together, by some who hold that there is an incipient, real, though incomplete fulfillment of divine prophecy, as well as a final exhaustive one; the first being often an assurance and help to the meaning of the latter. And this I accept for myself as at least generally true, and true in the case before us, and that (to use the words of another) "they are both alike *practically* wrong who have slightingly rejected the one or the other [application], and thus respectively deprived the Church of each."

But while I thus would keep in mind and seek to profit

by this double interpretation, the latter is what I desire, as God may enable me, to develop and insist upon, and this for more reasons than one, but especially just because it is that which is alone complete and final, and still lying in the future for us; whereas the historical interpretation occupies us largely with the past,—a past still fruitful for us assuredly, but less full of personal appeal. This will indeed be questioned, and it is not yet the time to answer the question.

Clearly the first point now is to prove, if it can be proved, the futurity of the fulfillment of the prophecies which we are to examine,—that such fulfillment is required by the inspired language of the book itself, and by a comparison with other Scripture. This ascertained, we can look better at objections which have been made to it, and realize also the profit of what is to engage us.

The first principle to be got hold of is that given us by the apostle Peter, that "no prophecy of the Scripture is of any private interpretation" (2 Pet. i. 20). It is *prophecy* that is in question here, not, all Scripture, as the Romanists would apply it. But also "private interpretation" is literally "*its own* interpretation." No single prophecy must be read alone,—as if it stood apart from the rest; but in connection with the whole plan of it in the Word. "For prophecy came not in old time by the will of man,"—is not therefore the expression of the many minds of men; "but holy men of God spake as they were moved by the Holy Ghost:"—there is One perfect mind throughout it.

Now the violation of this will be found to be largely the cause of the failure of expositors. They neglect a rule which the apostle emphasizes as of first importance —"knowing this *first*." It is comparatively easy to find some plausible application of a single passage; it is quite another thing to make this fit with a general prophetic testimony. Comparison of passage with passage on this

INTRODUCTORY.

subject is what we are invited and compelled to therefore, if we would have truth instead of theory, realized certainty rather than conjecture. What we hold must be tested and retested by the application of similar scripture, so that at least "in the mouth of two or three witnesses every word" may "be established."

Moreover, it will be plainly of importance to find some comprehensive prophecy connecting itself with some fixed point, or points, on Scripture, with which others may be then securely connected. Such prophecies we may find again and again in the book of Daniel, a book in the closest relation also to the book of Revelation, as all expositors of whatever school are agreed absolutely. Turn we, then, in the first place, to the second of Daniel.

We have here Nebuchadnezzar's vision of the four Gentile empires under the symbol of a great image, which is brought to an end by the sudden descent of a stone cut without hands out of a mountain; the stone becoming then a great mountain which fills the whole earth. This stone is interpreted for us as the kingdom of God, which is seen thus in victorious opposition to the kingdoms of the world, suddenly and totally destroying them. It is after this only that it grows and fills the earth. The world-kingdoms are not pervaded or "leavened" by the kingdom of God, but run their course first, and are then at once destroyed by it. This fall of the stone is one of those fixed points for which we are looking, and it is future without doubt.

In the seventh chapter the prophet has a vision of these same four empires, now seen very differently as four wild beasts, while the kingdom of God is introduced by the coming of the Son of Man in the clouds of heaven. And here it is, if possible, still more plain that this kingdom only *commences* with the destruction of the former ones. There is no possibility of any side by side development. Of the "little horn" of the last beast it is said : " And he shall speak great words against the Most

High, and shall wear out the saints of the Most High, and think to change times and laws, and they shall be given unto his hand until a time and times and the dividing of time; but the judgment shall sit, and they shall take away his dominion, to consume and destroy it to the end. And the kingdom and dominion and the greatness of the kingdom under the whole heaven shall be given to the people of the saints of the Most High, whose kingdom is an everlasting kingdom, and all dominions should serve and obey Him."

Thus it is evident that the kingdom of God here is that which will be set up only when the Lord returns in the clouds of heaven; that till then the kingdoms of the Gentiles continue, and then they are once for all broken and set aside. In connection with the last beast, moreover, we have just before the end the rise of a power which shows itself a blasphemous and persecuting one, and which by this brings judgment down upon itself and the beast, or empire, with which it is connected. This horn lasts, moreover, (in this character) just three and a half prophetic times, and then the judgment sits, and his dominion is taken away.

Carrying, then, these things with us, let us now go on to the ninth chapter, a prophecy which, for intelligence in the general plan of divine wisdom, is central in importance, and, interpreting as little as we can help, let us put this in connection with what we have already seen.

It is the well-known prophecy of the seventy weeks. In it we have an answer to Daniel's confession of his sin, and the sin of his people Israel, and his supplication for the holy mountain of his God; and he is told—

"Seventy weeks are determined upon thy people and upon thy holy city, to finish the transgression, and to make an end of sins, and to make reconciliation for iniquity, and to bring in everlasting righteousness, and to seal up the vision and prophecy, and to anoint the Most Holy."

INTRODUCTORY.   5

The meaning should be plain, that at the end of seventy determined weeks, *Jerusalem's* trausgression would be finished, and her sins would be at an end, her iniquity being purged,* and everlasting righteousness brought in for her; and her holy place, now desecrated, be once more anointed. At the same time vision and prophecy would be sealed up † by a fulfillment in which it would reach its end and disappear. This last statement alone is enough to show that we have to do with what is future still.

The angel goes on to give Daniel more in detail the events of these seventy weeks. "Know, therefore, and understand that from the going forth of the commandment to restore and to build Jerusalem unto Messiah the Prince, shall be seven weeks and threescore and two weeks: the street shall be built again, and the wall even in troublous times."

There is no need for our purpose to inquire for the exact beginning of this time. We are not tracing exactly its fulfillment. It is enough for us that the prophecy itself assures us that at the end of sixty-nine weeks, Messiah shall come. The weeks must be weeks of years, therefore, as almost all orthodox commentators agree,— all, in fact, who recognize in them any real specification

---

* *Kapper*, with the simple objective, speaks of atonement taking effect upon the object.

† "The figure of sealing is regarded by many interpreters in the sense of confirming, and that by filling up, with reference to the custom of impressing a seal on writing for the confirmation of its contents; and in illustration these references are given: 1 Kings xxi. 8, and Jer. xxxii. 10, 11, 44. But for this figurative use of the word to seal, no proof-passages are adduced from the Old Testament. Add to this that the word cannot be used here in a different sense from that in which it is used in the second passage. The sealing of the prophecy corresponds to the sealing of the transgression, and must be similarly understood." (Keil.) To "make an end of sins" is literally to "seal up sins."

The words "vision" and "prophecy" (literally "prophet") Keil says, "are used in comprehensive generality for all existing prophecies and prophets. Not only the prophecies, but the prophet who gives it,— *i.e.* not merely the prophet but the calling of the prophet must be sealed. Prophecies, and prophets are sealed when, by the full realization of all prophecies prophecy ceases, no prophets any more appear." (Keil on Daniel.)

of time at all.* And with year-weeks the Jews were, as we know, perfectly familiar. The whole period is thus ten jubilees.

Four hundred and eighty-three years, then, from the commencement of this period Messiah comes, and but seven years remain in which the full blessing should come in. It is this which has doubtless stumbled many as to the fulfillment to Israel and Jerusalem which the first words of the angel yet so clearly promise. Startling it is to have to recognize a break of over eighteen centuries in a period of time which seems so strictly defined. The next verse, however, prepares us for this, and accounts for it. Messiah comes to His own, and His own receive Him not. Thus the blessing is delayed, although, of course, the purposes of God are unrepenting.

"And after *the* threescore and two weeks"—as the Hebrew reads,—"shall Messiah be cut off, and *shall have nothing:*" so rightly the margin and the *R. V.* give. Instead of reception by a willing people, He finds rejection and a cross, does not therefore yet receive the promises. The city is not restored, but desolated: "And the people of the prince that shall come shall destroy the city and the sanctuary." All agree here that there is the destruction of the city by the Romans; most, therefore, assume that Titus is the "prince that shall come," but against this there are many reasons. For why in this case should the *people* be mentioned at all? Would it not be enough to say that the prince shall destroy—it being a matter of course that it would be through his people? Is it not plain that while the people and the prince are both emphasized for us, it is the *people* alone that are said to do this, only they are the people of the prince that shall come?

What importance attaches to Titus that he should be given this prominence, and in so concise a prophecy, in

---

* Keil regards the numbers as to be symbolically interpreted, which I do not doubt, while this does not in the least affect their chronological character.

which every word seems measured out with greatest economy? Certainly no where else does he appear at all. Why, too, the "prince that shall come"? against the city? but this would be strange tautology for the word of God! Of course if he were a leader of the host he would come against the city. But the expression is the very one which would be used to point out some great person predicted to arise, of whom Daniel had heard before.

But there is another mark attached to this person: "And his end shall be in the flood." Here our common version has indeed "the end thereof." But the end of what then? Not of the destruction of the city? Not of the city, for this is feminine in Hebrew, and would not agree with the pronoun. Not of the sanctuary, which could not be detached from the city in this way. Moreover, the article with flood—"*the* flood," as it should be—speaks again of some definite and known catastrophe. The whole passage is to be regarded as some relative clause, and connected with "shall come:" "the people of the prince that shall come and find his destruction in the flood." (Keil.)

This, of course, it is impossible to apply to Titus. Let us see how it does, in fact, apply.

The "*people* of the prince that shall come" we know historically as the Romans; the fourth beast or empire of the seventh chapter, it is conceded by the mass of interpreters, and susceptible of the most abundant proof, was also *Roman*. And now, looking at the prophetic history of the empire, surely it is not difficult to recognize in the little horn, whose actions bring judgment upon the beast, the prince that shall come whose end is in the flood. The closing statements in the chapter seem as if they should make doubt as to this really impossible.

We return for a moment, however, to what characterizes the rest of the period. The *R. V.* renders it well: "And even unto the end shall be war; desolations shall be determined."

The last verse of the prophecy now gives us, in connection with the doings of this little horn, the last of the seventy weeks: "And he shall confirm a covenant with the many for one week; and in the midst of the week he shall cause the sacrifice and oblation to cease; and on account of the wing of abominations there shall be a desolator; even until the consummation, and that determined shall be poured upon the desolate."

I have made in the translation some small and yet important alterations, which will be justified as we proceed. The first point to notice is that the last week is here divided in half, and that a half week of years—three and a half years—gives us another link which seems decisive with the history of the little horn. For "a time, times, and the dividing of a time" are times and laws given into the hands of this blasphemous and persecuting power, and here he causes sacrifice and oblation to cease for what is evidently this very period. This surely is a striking example of how times and laws have been given into his hands. And as the whole seventy weeks are determined upon Israel and Jerusalem, we see that the sacrifices must have been restored there. This naturally carries us back to the previous clause: "He shall confirm a covenant with the many for one week." It is not *the* covenant but *a* covenant: the definite article, misplaced here, has made people think of God's covenant with His people, and thus given aid to a false conception of its being Messiah that confirms it. But the antecedent to the pronoun "he" is certainly "the prince that shall come" as every other mark points in the same direction. On the other hand the article does stand before "many," making it "*the* many,"—*i.e.*, the mass of the Jewish people. The covenant becomes thus a political agreement with the mass of the Jewish nation for seven years; but in the week. he breaks it, changes times and laws, and his tyranny begins.

Why he makes sacrifices and oblation to cease is easily

seen from the seventh chapter. Every detail fits in the most exact way possible. The little horn speaks great words against the Most High, and wears out the saints of the Most High. It is as sacrifice to God that he stops the Jewish service. And in perfect agreement we read here: "And on account of the wing of abominations there shall be a desolator." This is quite literal, as our common version is not. The *R. V.* differs from it by translating "*upon* the wing," which is the more usual rendering of the pronoun, my own being simply the equivalent of "for" in that with which we are familiar, "For the protection of idols" is, I do not doubt, the sense sufficiently. A desolator comes in consequence of idolatry introduced, and this lasts until the decreed time expires—until the full end of the seventy weeks.

Notice another point where the seventh chapter not only confirms but explains the ninth. We have seen that the latter declares that at the end of the determined time the blessing comes for Israel. But the details of the seventy weeks show nothing but disaster and evil, right down to their expiration. *How* the blessing comes it does not show; but this the seventh chapter already supplies. The horn prevails against the saints for the three and a half times or years of either prophecy; but this is "*till* the Ancient of Days" comes (*v.* 22), which in a moment changes all. Let the reader only turn to Zech. xiv., and see how, in the very midst of Israel's distress, the Lord appears: "For I will gather all nations against Jerusalem to battle; and the city shall be taken, and the houses rifled, and the women ravished; and half of the city shall go forth into captivity, and the residue of the people shall not be cut off from the city." And why? "Then shall the Lord go forth and fight against those nations as when He fought in the day of battle. And His feet shall stand in that day upon the Mount of Olives, ... and the Lord my God shall come, and all the saints with Thee."

We see, then, how, as in a moment, the desolation ends.

There is entire harmony thus far, and this in itself is one of the most convincing arguments for the truth of that which unites and harmonizes these different statements. But we have not yet completed the review of Daniel's testimony, for in the final prophecy (chap. x.-xii.) we have what again in the clearest way supplements and confirms what has been gathered from the previous ones. We take it indeed from the long prophetic history with which it is connected, as yet not able even to glance at this, but trusting to the clearness of its own evidence for the relation it bears to what we have just been looking at :—

"And arms shall stand on his part, and they shall pollute the sanctuary of strength, and shall *take away the daily sacrifice,* and they shall *place the abomination that maketh desolate*" (chap. xi. 31).

"And I heard the man clothed in linen, which was upon the waters of the river, when he held up his right hand and his left hand unto heaven, and swore by Him that liveth forever that it shall be for a *time, times, and a half;* and when he shall have accomplished to scatter the power of the holy people, all these things shall be finished.

"And from the time that the daily sacrifice shall be taken away, and the abomination that maketh desolate set up, there shall be a thousand, two hundred and ninety days. Blessed is he that waiteth and cometh to the thousand, three hundred and five and thirty days. But go thou thy way until the end be, for thou shalt rest and stand in thy lot at the end of the days" (chap. xii. 7, 11-13).

Here it is clear that we have an equal period to the time, times, and a half, if taken as three and a half years, as we have already taken them;* that first thirty and then forty-five days more are added successively to this period; the twelve hundred and ninety days date from the setting up of the abomination, and therefore we may conclude that

---

* The year, of course, is to be calculated according to the Jewish reckoning, at 360 days.

the twelve hundred and sixty also do this; and that at the end of the longest period Daniel stands in his lot, implying surely that the resurrection of the saints has taken place. Thus all of these dates are connected with the end as were the former ones—with the coming of the Lord, and the setting up of His kingdom.

And the taking away the daily sacrifice and setting up the abomination of desolation which is connected with these dates, interprets clearly the causing sacrifice and oblation to cease, and the desolation on account of the wing of abomination, of the ninth chapter. It is a confirmation of what has already been our conclusion from the previous prophecy alone, which one may well believe irresistible to any unprejudiced mind. And yet it is far from all that Scripture has to give us with regard to a period to which evidently it attaches the very greatest importance.

(2) *Prophecies of the New Testament.*

WHAT we have gathered, then, from these different prophecies is this:—

1. That the times of the Gentiles—of the Gentile empires—are closed in sudden overthrow by the kingdom of God established in the hands of One who, as Son of Man, comes in the clouds of heaven.

2. That the last form of Gentile power,—the Roman,— ends in blasphemous opposition to God and to His saints —opposition which brings the judgment down.

3. That this opposition displays itself in a special way in connection with the Jews, who, in the security of a covenant with the last head, have re-established their temple-worship at Jerusalem. Three and a half years from the end—a half-week of years—he breaks this covenant, causes the worship of Jehovah to cease, and replaces it by an idolatry which brings in desolation, a scourge from God, lasting until this period expires.

Deliverance for the saints, and the end of Gentile dominion, come together with the sudden appearance of the Lord from heaven.

In all this the simple comparison of scripture with scripture has set aside the need of any labored interpretation. The time, times, and dividing of a time of the little horn's prevalence (Dan. vii.) correspond so in every feature with the last half week of the seventy in chap. ix., and the time, times, and a half of the twelfth chapter, that to force them asunder would seem almost manifest perversion. The successive prophecies agree with the preceding ones in the most perfect way, while adding each something of its own. The one mind of the Spirit runs evidently through them all.

We are now going to add in the same manner some New-Testament prophecies to the Old, and see if still Scripture will not speak for itself, and become its own interpreter,—if as definite certainty cannot be reached as to the main features of unfulfilled prophecy as with regard to any other part of inspired testimony.

And the first passage we naturally take up proclaims its own connection with what we have been looking at in Daniel. I refer, of course, to the great prophecy of Matt. xxiv. Read in the light of the prophecies to which it refers, it becomes as clear and intelligible as can be.

The Lord has announced to His disciples the impending overthrow of the temple. They thereupon put two questions to Him, which in their minds were no doubt more closely connected than they would be in ours: "Tell us when shall these things be? and what shall be the sign of Thy coming, and of the end of the age?"

As to the first question, which of course refers to the destruction of the temple, we have little to do with it just now. The answer will be found more fully given in Luke xxi., in which the destruction of Jerusalem, which took place more than thirty-five years afterward, is explicitly announced. In Matthew it will be found that the Lord deals rather with the second, double question, where they seem evidently to identify the coming of the Lord with "the end of the age"—for "world" it is not, either here or in the thirteenth chapter, where the same expression is to be found. Literally, it is the "consummation of the age."

Now, remembering Daniel, and that these were Jewish questioners, with at present none but Jewish hopes, but owning Jesus as their Messiah,—with no thought of the long interval which was in fact to elapse before His still future coming, it is plain that the age of which they spoke was the age of law—of Judaism as it then was. Of a Christian dispensation they could have no thought. The "coming" of which they spoke was doubtless connected with, if not derived from, the coming of the Son of Man of which Daniel had spoken. The "end of the age" we have found portrayed there in fact, in terms to which the Lord refers; but while they would necessarily think of it as the end of a Jewish age, most Christians would as naturally from their stand-point think of it as Christian.

For us, Judaism is gone forever, and it is a strange thing to speak of its revival; yet we have seen that Daniel shows us a week of special divine dealings with Judah and Jerusalem, cut off from the sixty-nine preceding by an unknown interval in which plainly Christianity has prevailed. And in this last week we find the temple-services again going on until their interruption by the head of Gentile power.

It is to this interruption the Lord refers, directly citing Daniel: "When ye therefore shall see the abomination of desolation, spoken of by Daniel the prophet, stand in the holy place, (whoso readeth, let him understand;) then let them which be in Judæa flee into the mountains; let him which is on the housetop not come down to take any thing out of his house; neither let him which is in the field return back to take his clothes."

In Luke, where the taking of Jerusalem by the Romans,

eighteen centuries ago, is prophesied, while the same injunction to flee to the mountains is given, the sign is different—"Jerusalem compassed with armies;" and these latter directions are omitted,—they would be plainly out of place. No such rapid and instant flight as is here spoken of was needed to escape the desolating hosts. It is merely therefore said, "Let them which are in Judæa flee to the mountains, and let them which are in the midst of it depart out, and let not them that are in the countries enter thereinto."

But here, the enemy is in the midst, the saints are the objects of special enmity, and there must be no delay: "And woe unto them that are with child, and to them that give suck in those days; but pray ye that your flight be not in the winter, neither on the Sabbath day." Here it is plain that Jews under the full rigor of Jewish law are contemplated.

And now comes another reference to Daniel. In his last prophecy we find that "at that time shall Michael stand up, the great prince that standeth for the children of thy people; and there shall be time of trouble such as never was since there was a nation even to that same time; and at that time thy people shall be delivered, every one that shall be found written in the book." (Chap. xii. 1.)

Thus it is the great day of Jewish deliverance which is at hand, and they are delivered out of a time of unequaled trouble. The Lord's words echo and emphasize the words of Daniel: "For then shall be great tribulation, such as was not since the beginning of the world to this time, no,—nor ever shall be. And except those days shall be shortened, there should no flesh be saved; but for the elect's sake those days shall be shortened."

The precise time of the tribulation is given by the Old-Testament prophet—three years and a half; and we see by the Lord's words that it is impossible to apply here the year-day theory, which would extend it to twelve hundred and sixty years. This certainly would not be shortening the days in any sense.

He follows with the announcement of false Christs and false prophets as characterizing this period,—an addition to the Old Testament of the greatest significance, and which we shall find developed in succeeding prophecies : "Then, if any man shall say unto you, Lo, here is Christ, or there, believe him not. For there shall arise false Christs and false prophets, and shall show great signs and wonders, insomuch that, if it were possible, they shall deceive the very elect. Behold, I have told you before. Wherefore if they shall say unto you, Behold, He is in the desert! go not forth; Behold, He is in the secret chambers! believe it not. For, as the lightning cometh out of the east, and shineth even unto the west, so shall also the coming of the Son of Man be. For wheresoever the carcass is, there will the eagles be gathered together."

As in Daniel also, it is by this coming that the time of trouble is closed: "Immediately after the tribulation of those days shall the sun be darkened, and the moon shall not give her light, and the stars shall fall from heaven, and the powers of the heavens shall be shaken; and then shall appear the sign of the Son of Man in heaven; and then shall all the tribes of the earth mourn, and they shall see the Son of Man coming in the clouds of heaven with power and great glory."

For our purpose, it is not necessary to go further. The agreement with former prophecies is clear and conclusive. A latter-day remnant is seen in Jerusalem, distinctly Jewish in character, yet listening to Christ's words, and owned of God; and the end of the age of which the disciples inquire is identified with the broken-off last week of Daniel's seventy. The temple is again owned as "the holy place," though in the meanwhile defiled with idolatry, and this before the Lord's coming in the clouds of heaven. We necessarily ask ourselves, Where, then, is Christianity ? and what does this presence once more of a *Jewish* "age" imply as to the present Christian dispensation?

To this, Scripture gives no undecided answer. It shows us that the Christian dispensation (properly so called,) is over then; that the Church, Christ's body, is complete; that all true Christians have been caught up to Christ, and are with Him; that the rest of the professing church has been spewed out of His mouth, according to His threatening to Laodicea; that the Lord is now taking up again for blessing His people Israel and the earth, and we are again in the line of Old-Testament prophecy, and going on to the fulfillment of Old-Testament promises.

That these promises belong to Israel, literally,—His kinsmen according to the flesh,—we have the unexceptionable witness of the apostle to the Gentiles (Rom. ix. 4), who also warns the Gentile professing body, that they stand only by faith, and if they abide not in the goodness of God which He has shown them, shall be cut off; and Israel, abiding *not* in unbelief, should be graffed back again into her own olive-tree. He tells us also that this receiving of them back shall be "life from the dead" to the nations of the world; that blindness in part is happened unto Israel, only till the fullness of the Gentiles is come in; and then *all* Israel—the nation as a whole—shall be saved. And he adds that while, as regards the *gospel*, they are [treated by God as] enemies for our sakes, as touching the election they are yet beloved for the father's sakes; because the gifts and calling of God are without repentance. (Rom. xi. 13-29.)

Thus the wonderful change which Matt. xxiv. exhibits is fully accounted for. The Jews and Judaism once more owned, shows that the *Christian* "gospel," having completed its full gathering of Gentiles as designed by God, is going out no longer. Heaven (though we must make a certain exception which we shall by and by consider,) —heaven is full. The gathering for earth and blessing there is now commencing.

The Lord has spoken of false Christs and false prophets in connection with that time. Let us turn now to the apostle John's description of Antichrist. He warns us indeed that already in his time there were many; already there was the character of the "last time." He speaks of them as apostates, issuing from the professing church itself, never really Christians, though among them. (1 Jno. ii. 18, 19.) But he goes on to describe one special form, "*the* liar," "*the* antichrist," as his words really are. "Who is the liar," he asks, "but he that denieth that Jesus is the Christ?" And then he adds, "He is the antichrist that denieth the Father and the Son." (*v.* 22.)

It will be found that there are here two forms of unbelief, which in this wicked one unite in one. The first is the Jewish one that denies that Jesus is the Christ. They do not deny that there *is* a Christ, but they deny Jesus to be this. The full Christian belief is not only that Jesus is the Christ, but that He is also the Son of the Father. "Whosoever denieth the Son, the same hath not the Father,"—there are many of these now, as the Unitarians so called; but they deny the Son to make much of the Father: the full climax of unbelief in this great head of it is here, that he denieth both the Father and the Son.

Thus the antichrist denies Christianity altogether; but he owns Judaism, for the very denial that *Jesus* is the Christ implies, however, that there *is* Christ. And this is the complete *anti*christ, who is not only *against* Christ, but takes His place. And so the Lord speaks of "*false* Christs." These are, by profession, then, Jews, and the antichrist is a Jew.

How naturally the antichrist belongs, then, to a time when Christianity is gone from the earth, and a revived Judaism is in its old seat, and they are in expectation (as almost necessarily they would be,) of the speedy fulfillment now of the promise of Messiah. When the Lord came in the flesh, there was just such an expectation, and just such fruit of it in the appearance of false Christs. And the words in Matthew show that such a time there will be again; only now with a peculiar power of deception which only the elect escape. Among these blasphemous pretenders is the full prophetic antichrist.

Let us turn to another picture, which the apostle puts before the Thessalonians. (2 Thess. ii. 1-12.) Here we shall find what unites John and Matthew, connecting the developed evil of apostate Christendom with the revival of Judaism which the Lord's own words foreshow. And I quote from the Revised Version, which is in many respects an improvement upon the common one:—

"Now we beseech you, brethren, touching the coming of our Lord Jesus Christ and our gathering together unto Him, to the end that ye be not quickly shaken from your mind, nor yet be troubled, either by spirit, or by word, or by epistle as from us, as that the day of the Lord is now present: let no man beguile you in any wise; for it will not be except the falling away come first, and the man of sin be revealed, the son of perdition, he that opposeth and exalteth himself against all that is called God or that is worshiped; so that he sitteth in the temple of God, setting himself forth as God. . . . For the mystery of lawlessness doth already work, only there is one that restraineth now until he be taken out of the way. And then shall be revealed the lawless one, whom the Lord Jesus shall slay with the breath of His mouth, and bring to naught by the manifestation of His coming: even he whose coming is according to the working of Satan, with all power and signs and lying wonders, and all deceit of unrighteousness for them that are perishing; because they received not the love of the truth that they might be saved. And for this cause God sendeth them a working of error, that they should believe a lie; that they all might be judged who believed not the truth, but had pleasure in unrighteousness."

Thus the solemn end of Christendom is revealed. And already in the apostle's days the leaven of evil was at work, which but for a divine restraint upon it would before this have permeated the whole mass of profession. But the apostasy will come, if even now rather it is not begun, of which the issue and final head will be this lawless one, who will sweep away with him to common ruin all that receive not the love of the truth. They will believe a lie—literally, it is "*the* lie,"—and "who is *the* liar, but he that denieth that Jesus is the Christ?" He opposeth and exalteth himself against all that is called God or worshiped: certainly therefore "denieth the Father and the Son." But not only so: he sitteth in the temple of God, setting himself forth as God." How can we forbear to think of that abomination of desolation standing in the holy place, which the Lord has called our attention to from Daniel?

But here is a notable instance of the need we have of the apostle's warning that "no prophecy of the Scripture is to be interpreted by itself." To those rooted in the idea that Judaism is gone forever, and that the Christian Church is now the only "temple of God," what more natural and necessary than to interpret this of the pope? Nor do I for a moment say that he is not in the direct line of development; prophecy has oftentimes these incomplete anticipative fulfillments, which answer for the full and exhaustive one which is to come. But in the light of all that has preceded, we may be quite sure that any application to the head of Catholicism is only partial and anticipative. Popery has existed for too many centuries to be a sign of the coming day of the Lord; and one sitting as God in the temple of God is too simply explicative of the abomination of desolation in the holy place to make the application difficult or doubtful.

This wicked one, like the little horn of the fourth beast, finds his end also at the coming of the Lord. I do not mean by this that they are the same person, for they are not; but they belong to the same time, and are closely connected.

Thus, then, the New Testament agrees perfectly with the Old in its representation of the end of the age. But we have not examined yet its fullest and most decisive testimony, which we find, just where we would expect to find it, in the book of Revelation. But of this we propose a more extended examination; and we have been gathering together the Scripture-testimony elsewhere only as introductory to this which lies before us. May the Lord Himself direct our inquiries and govern our hearts by the truth of His Word. It is not a mere intellectual study that we propose. We seek to have for our souls the spiritual power of what is unseen,—the future as light for the present,—the judgment of the Lord in the day of the Lord, in order to self-judgment now,—the joy of heaven for present communion. May He who alone can purge from our sight the dullness and drowsiness that so cling to us, our eyes anointed with His eye-salve, that we may see!

THE THRONE IN HEAVEN.

(Rev. iv 1-3.)

WE come, then, to our theme, the book of Revelation. Our glance at prophecy has been for the purpose of putting this last and fullest of all in connection with the earlier ones, that we might not make it of "private interpretation." And when we come so to connect it, we find unmistakable evidence that a large part of the book is occupied with that predicted last week of Daniel, the events of which we have been considering. That the last "beast" of Daniel appears again in Rev. xiii. and xvii. is acknowledged, and must be, by all. But there is noticed as to it here, what history has made plain to us, that it was not to continue without interruption from its first commencement to its overthrow. It was to have its period of non-existence, and then come up again in greatly altered character as "from the bottomless pit." This is the blasphemous form in which we have seen it to end at the coming of the Lord; and the exact time of its prevalence in this way is given us as in Daniel—"forty and two months," or three years and a half (chap. xiii. 5).

And again and again this period confronts us. In the eleventh chapter, we find it as the time of sackcloth testimony of the two witnesses; in the twelfth chapter, stated as in Daniel, as "time, times, and a half," and again as "a thousand, two hundred, and threescore days," as that of the woman's nourishment in the wilderness from the face of the serpent. Much before this also we hear of an immense company of Gentiles as "come out of *the* great tribulation" (chap. vii. 14, *R.V.*)—quite evidently that spoken of in Daniel and in Matthew, the only one that could be, in view of what is said there, announced as "*the* great" one. Thus from the seventh to the seventeenth chapters the last of the seventy weeks is clearly before us. But this implies, as we have seen, much. It shows that when this large portion of Revelation shall be fulfilled, the Christian dispensation will have passed away, Christians will be forever with the Lord, and the earthly people will be again those owned of Him, whatever the sorrows they may have yet to pass through, before their full blessing comes.

The *appearing* of the Lord in the clouds of heaven we find only in the nineteenth chapter, but then (as the apostle says,) "we shall appear with Him in glory" (Col. iii. 4). Our removal from the earth will therefore necessarily have taken place before: and thus he writes to the Thessalonians, that "the Lord shall descend from heaven with a shout, with the voice of the archangel, and with the trump of God: and the dead in Christ shall rise first; then we which are alive and remain shall be caught up together with them in the clouds to meet the Lord in the air; and so shall we be ever with the Lord" (1 Thess. iv. 16,17).

Here it is plain how "those that sleep in Jesus God will bring with Him." There is no promiscuous resurrection of the dead; there is no picking out by judgment of sheep from goats, such as the twenty-fifth of Matthew very plainly teaches *will* take place when the Son of Man comes in His glory and be sitting on the throne of His glory. Here, on the contrary, we find but one company of raised and glorified saints caught up to meet and be with Him. Scripture is clear as to this blessed fact, which in itself affirms and emphasizes the gospel assurance that those who have Christ's word, and believe on Him who sent Him, shall not come into judgment. (Jno. v. 24, *R.V.*) This is, by such a text, made clear and certain enough.

But from this no one would understand that between this gathering up of the saints to meet the Lord and His appearing in glory with them there should be an interval of months and years of earthly history. Nor can one be blamed, therefore, for being slow to assent to such a statement as this. Yet it is the truth ; and one which can be perfectly well established from Scripture, although there is no single text which states it. And here is the place to give this some final consideration.

We have seen elsewhere that as the Old Testament ends with the promise of the "Sun of Righteousness," so the New Testament ends with that of the "Morning Star." Christ Himself is both, and in both His coming is intimated, but, as is plain, in very different connections. The sun brings the day, flooding the earth with light, and this is in suited connection with the blessing of an earthly people, whose the Old-Testament promises are (Rom.ix.4). The morning-star *heralds* the day, but does not bring it : it rises when the earth is still dark, shining as it were for heaven alone. And this to us speaks of our being with Christ before the blessing for the earth comes.

In the promise to Philadelphia also we find the assurance, "Because thou hast kept the word of My patience, I will also keep thee out of the hour of temptation, which shall come upon all the world, to try them that dwell upon the earth." Here, out of a universal hour of trial some saints at least are to be kept. How simply explicable this in their being taken out of the world to be with their Lord before the hour commences ! how difficult to understand in any other way !

Accordingly, in those pictures of the world's trial which we have had before us, we have had no trace of the presence of Christians. All, as we have seen, speaks of Jews and Judaism as once more recognized,—a thing inconsistent with the existence of Christians and Christianity at the same time. As long as the present gospel goes out, "they are enemies for your sakes." (Rom. xi. 28.)

So also the antichristian snare, in the form it assumes, shows the same thing. Christ is looked for in the desert, or in the secret chambers, as appearing not from heaven, but in the midst of the people; and the false Christ, when he comes, sits with divine honors in the temple of God.

Explicitly is it stated also in Isa. lx., that when the Lord arises upon Israel, and His glory is seen upon them, "*darkness* shall cover the earth, and *gross* darkness the peoples," a thing impossible if Christianity existed at the same time, yet perfectly plain in what we have been looking at. Indeed, the difficulty with these passages has been to realize the fact of such darkness as succeeding the present day of gospel light.

Again, the important scene in Matt. xxv., so misconceived by most interpreters even now, and for centuries taken as a picture of the general judgment, becomes thus perfectly intelligible, as it is only consistent with this view. It is the judgment of the living upon earth, after the Lord has come and set up His throne here; and the passage in Thessalonians, cited but a while ago, makes it absolutely certain that Christians will not be among the nations upon earth then. The dead are not in question either. There is no hint of resurrection, and *they* have their separate judgment, at the end of the thousand years of blessing, when the earth and the heavens flee away from before the face of Him that sits upon the throne (Rev. xx. 12).

But if the Lord called up the saints to meet Him in the air, and then immediately came on to the judgment of the earth, there *could* be no "sheep" to put upon His right hand. Universal judgment alone could follow. The fact of an interval between these two, such as we have been considering, at once clears the whole difficulty.

But the most convincing proofs of such an interval we find in the chapters that are now to engage our attention. Coming as they do between the history of the dispensation with which the addresses to the churches have already made us familiar, and the prophecies of the last week of Daniel, which follow so promptly and occupy so much space in the latter portion of the book. All through the later addresses the announcement of the Lord's coming sounds with more and more urgency. In Thyatira, for the first time, they are exhorted, "Hold fast till I come." In Sardis, He is coming upon them as a thief, and they shall not know what hour He comes upon them. In Philadelphia, it is now, "I come *quickly*." And finally, Laodicea is ready to be spued out of His mouth, the last individual appeal being given, when the church as a whole has now rejected Him. In the fourth chapter, the "things that shall be after these" begin, and the apostle is at once caught up to heaven.

But we are now to proceed more leisurely. In so precious and wonderful a communication of divine grace we would gladly ponder every word, and allow nothing to escape us. But we are absolutely dependent upon the Spirit of God for aid, lest, after all, the very essence of them be lost. The various and contradictory interpretations that they have received may well teach us self-distrust, but not shake our confidence, that in proportion to our real simplicity and real desire to be taught of God, His truth will be discovered to us. He that seeks shall find. He will not for bread give us a stone, nor for a fish a serpent.

The "things that are" have come to an end. The voice that spake on earth is silent, but presently resumes from heaven. "After these things, I saw, and, behold, a door opened in heaven, and the first voice which I heard, as of a trumpet speaking with me, saying, 'Come up hither, and I will show thee things which must come to pass after these.'"

Both the Common and the Revised Version have "hereafter." But this is vague. It would allow the prophecy that follows to be, after all, contemporaneous in its fulfillment with that of the addresses just completed. But the words are definite, and allow of no such idea. In the first chapter, the apostle had been bidden to "write the things which thou hast seen, and the things which shall be after these;" and now he is reminded that he is come to this distinct division of his prophecy—"the things which must come to pass after these." The prophecy is orderly and successive, at least thus far.

Looking at the addresses to the churches, therefore, as depicting the phases of the professing church during the present dispensation, the meaning of the words would be, "The things which must come to pass *after the history of the Church is ended.*" If, then, such an interpretation of the two previous chapters is correct, the time we have reached is clearly enough defined. And how significant, at this point, the translation of the seer from earth to heaven! The voice with its trumpet-call is the first voice which he had heard—the voice of Jesus. No longer occupied with His lamps of testimony upon earth, He calls His servant up to Himself above.

And "immediately," he says, "I became in the Spirit." The distinctness of the new beginning is evident. Just so had he been, rapt in this ecstatic state, when he had had the former vision. It had not continued throughout, but now began afresh, his whole being absorbed in that which the Spirit of God communicated. He is, as it were, not in the body, as another apostle says of visions that he had received, that whether he was in the body or out of the body, he could not tell. (2 Cor. xii. 2): the Spirit of God was, so to speak, eyes and ears and all else to him.

And now by the Spirit he is rapt into heaven,—a new thing for a prophet, and as such, exceptional to John alone. Doubtless the heavens had opened before, even in Old-Testament times, though with reserve, and never to invite an entrance. Enoch, and afterward Elijah, had been taken there indeed, and comfort and blessing it was to know this. Still this was not an opening of it to men on earth. Heavenly visitants had appeared too among men, but they had no disclosures to make of the unseen sanctuary from which they came. Even in Job one might read also how the "sons of God came to present themselves before the Lord, and Satan came also among them." And Micaiah at a much later day could say, "I saw the Lord sitting on His throne, and all the host of heaven standing by Him, on His right hand and on His left." Ezekiel, moreover, after this, that "the heavens were opened, and I saw visions of God." All this betokened, indeed, heaven's interest in earth, but it only serves to make evident the contrast with what we find here—a witness taken into heaven to bear testimony of what he found there.

The opening of the heavens is characteristic of New-Testament times. At the outset, the heavens are indeed, in the truest sense, opened when the Son of God lies in the manger of Bethlehem. And as He who reveals the Father is revealed, we are brought into communion with what spiritually constitutes heaven—with the Father and the Son. At the Lord's death, the vail of the sanctuary is rent asunder for us, and when He has ascended up, our Representative and Forerunner, the Holy Ghost sent down becomes in us the witness and earnest of heavenly things.

But the earnest shows that we have not yet possession, which John anticipatively brings us into. Paul also had been caught up into the third heaven—into paradise—and heard unspeakable things, which it is not lawful for a man to utter. (2 Cor. xii. 4.) But John finds utterance: he carries his writer's inkhorn into heaven, and reports what it was he saw there. He is bidden "Write," lest in his entrancement he should forget it. And how has the power of these communications been felt by those who have become heirs since to what has been thus written! Even those that have known least, have they not felt much? And how much more, then, should flow from deeper knowledge!

But then the character of this prophecy before us, in the very charm of its face-to-face vision, may assure us of what it speaks of and anticipates. It is our own call home this call of the prophet up to heaven, and how well it may thrill our hearts and gladden them as we listen to it!

Enter, then! Heaven is before us. Enter! It is the sanctuary. Not speculation do we seek, but enjoyment—

holy and hallowing enjoyment. Not a thing here forbidden to us, and not a thing upon which the lusts of the flesh can fasten! To breathe this pure air, is to live indeed. To abide here is to make all the world can proffer an unmeaning emptiness, to brighten the dullest heart into glory, and make the tongue of the dumb to sing for joy.

Heaven! And the first thing the apostle sees is "a throne," and "One sitting on the throne."

It is the first necessity for all blessing, for all stability, for all rest of heart. It is the assurance of order, of peace, of concord, of congruity: over all, a real, personal, living, and sovereign God. Not a democracy, but an absolutism; not laws which execute themselves, but the will of the All-wise, All-holy: fixed rule in free hands. It is this that sin would have overturned, and which has proved itself impossible to be overturned; whose eternity alone insures the absolute security of all else. Well may all crowns be cast before this throne, by which all are sustained and served. The sovereignty of God is surely the joy and triumph of every redeemed soul.

He who sits upon the throne is not and cannot be pictured, and the jasper and sardine stone to which He is compared have as yet yielded but little to the interpreter. As jewels, like those of the high-priest's breastplate, they represent, no doubt, the "Lights and Perfections" (Urim and Thummim) of God, unchanging, but seen, not in the inapproachable light itself, but in manifestations such as can be given to His creatures, and which display to them a various beauty they could not otherwise enjoy. "God is light," and the "*Father* of *lights*." The one colorless beam, broken up into the various colored prismatic rays, clothes the whole earth with its beauty. And the precious stones enshrine and crystallize these various rays.

If the "jasper" here be rather the *diamond*, as many believe, then there does seem to be in it a most appropriate thought, and one it is hard to give up after having received it. The diamond is the brightest of gems, the nearest to the pure ray of light in its lustre, the most indestructible in character,—eminently fitted (as one might think) to be a symbol of the glory of Deity. But these are not its chief points of significance after all. The diamond is, as every one knows, but crystallized *carbon*, which we find in a pure form as graphite, the black-lead of our pencils. Carbon exists in these so opposite conditions, the symbol of divine glory (as it might be) on the one hand might on the other be that of evil and ruin and sin. And has not divine grace wrought in the transformation of our ruined humanity into the brightest display of divine glory? And could there be any thing of which we could be more fitly reminded here?*

God has forever displayed Himself in Christ, His perfect and glorious manifestation. He is "the effulgence of His glory, the express image of His substance." (Heb. i. 3.) It is not meant by that, what some have argued from it, that we shall see the Father only in Him. Scripture speaks of those who "in heaven always behold the face of the Father who is in heaven." (Matt. xviii. 10.) But the cross will not on that account lose its significance, nor the glory of the incarnate Son be the less needful for us.

And when we look on to the end of the book, and see the "city which hath foundations" in her eternal beauty, not only do we find the jasper as the first of these foundations, but the light—the lustre—of the city also is "like unto a stone most precious, as it were a jasper stone, clear as crystal." (xxi. 11.)

This is at least all perfectly consistent. Its consistency and beauty may well plead for its acceptance by us, until, at least, something that more commends itself can be produced.

---

*Carbon is also the element characteristic of all organic products; so that organic chemistry has been called "the chemistry of the carbon compounds." It is thus connected with living forms, whether vegetable or animal. And I add, though this be a distinct thought, that crystallization is, as it were, the organization of the mineral.

The "sardine stone," or rather "sardius," is our carnelian, a stone much prized by the lapidary, and especially in the east, its most valued form being an unmixed bright red. The association with the jasper or diamond would suggest an association of thought; the diamond flashing with the red hues of the carnelian would necessitate almost the idea of the cross. Incarnation and redemption unite to make known the sovereign God.

It is not an objection, I believe, that in the next chapter we find explicitly the Lamb slain. The connection there is different, and God is never weary of Christ. Here it is the One upon the throne who is declared; and apart from Christ He could not be declared to us. The full radiance of divine glory are thus in the jasper and the sardine stone, or, as we have taken them to be, the diamond and the carnelian. The connection of the two throws light upon each, and the truth of its interpretation must rest on its verisimilitude.

Thus the One who sits upon the throne is declared to us. It is the "God of our Lord Jesus Christ," perfectly known and alone revealed in Him. The throne is *His* throne; the supreme will and power are His: and this is what makes us delight in that supremacy. Absolute in power and control, there is no mere arbitrary will in Him. Omnipotence never acts but with omniscient wisdom, perfect righteousness, holiness, and love. His pleasure is *good* pleasure: "*Worthy* art Thou, O Lord," is the adoring cry of the hosts of heaven.

The One who sits upon the throne is disclosed and characterized for our hearts before the throne is. And when we come now to the throne itself, we find as the first thing, what is addressed to our hearts no less, "a rainbow round about the throne, in sight like unto an emerald." The natural and historical associations here are full of precious suggestions.

The bow we all know as the token of God's covenant with the earth, and with every creature in it. The flood had just passed over the earth and desolated it, and now the sun was shining out in the retreating storm of judgment. God declares He will no more destroy, as He had destroyed. If He bring a cloud, it shall be for purification and blessing, not any more "a flood to destroy all flesh."

Where we see it now, the bow is used symbolically, of course, and therefore with a wider, deeper meaning. It is still of the earth it speaks, where alone storms are purificatory and for blessing; but these are no longer merely natural. It is not limited to this or that divine act, but characterizes the throne in its general action. Blessing for men, and rest of which the emerald speaks, with the suggestion of the springing grass after the rain, are to be accomplished; even the judgment may be the necessary means of their accomplishment. And in this, too, God will manifest Himself in the glory of the light which He is, as the prismatic colors of the bow symbolically display it.

To those who realize the character of the period which follows the present one, nothing could be plainer than the language of this bow-encircled throne. God is *now* calling out for heaven the objects of His grace. And while He is doing this, the fulfillment of His promises as to the earth is suspended; the earthly people are set aside: it might seem as if He had forgotten that which fills the pages of the Old-Testament prophets. So much so, that as if in despair of their accomplishment, men would turn them all into figures of other things. The knowledge of dispensational truth, so little regarded even yet by most Christians, relieves the whole difficulty, and puts every thing into its own place. Ours is a heavenly calling; ours are "all spiritual blessings in heavenly places in Christ Jesus." (Eph. i. 3.) When we are, according to His promise, gathered up to Him, then the Old-Testament promises will be fulfilled to Israel, to whom they belong (Rom. ix. 4), and the predicted time will come when the "earth shall be filled with the knowledge of the glory of the Lord as the waters cover the sea." (Heb. ii. 14.)

For this the "sons of God," now in suffering and sorrow, must be revealed in glory when Christ our life shall appear, and we shall appear with Him in glory. "The earnest expectation of the creature waiteth for the revealing of the sons of God. For the creation was subjected to vanity, not of its own will, but by reason of Him who subjected it, in hope that the creation should itself also be delivered from the bondage of corruption into the liberty of the glory of the children of God." (Rom. viii. 19–21, *R. V.*)

The bow of promise for creation, girdling the throne of God in heaven, speaks, then, of God's covenant with the earth remembered in a way which goes far beyond the letter of it. He is going now to bring it into perpetuity of blessing through another judgment, in which His glory will be displayed in a peculiar way. It will soon be said among the nations that the Lord reigneth, and the world be established that it cannot be moved. "Let the heavens be glad, and let the earth rejoice; let the sea roar, and the fullness thereof. Let the field exult, and all that is therein; then shall all the trees of the wood sing for joy before the Lord: for He cometh, for He cometh to judge the earth; He shall judge the world with righteousness, and the peoples with His truth." (Ps. xcvi. 10–13.)

Thrones Around the Throne. (Chap. iv. 4.)

This rainbow-girdled throne is a throne of judgment: "Out of the throne proceeded lightnings and voices and thunders." Mercy may and does restrain judgment within fixed limits, or use it sovereignly to fulfill purposes of widest, deepest blessing. None the less is it plain that the "throne of grace," to which it is the part of faith *now* to "come boldly, that we may obtain mercy, and find grace to help in time of need," is not here before us. Even the bow of promise itself speaks of a "cloud over the earth," which might seem to threaten ruin as by another deluge. The promise to Philadelphia warned of an "hour of trial" which was to "come upon the whole world, to try them that dwell upon the earth," while it assured the overcomers there that the Lord would keep them out of this. And now before the lightnings are seen to issue from the throne, before the peal of judgment startles the world from its security, we find "round about the throne four and twenty elders sitting, clothed in white raiment, and on their heads crowns of gold." The promise has been fulfilled, and the "kings and priests" of God are around the throne of God.

That these are "thrones," not seats merely as in the common version, is not contested, so far as I know, by any one. That they are men, not angels,* who sit upon them, should be plain by many considerations. Their very title of "elders" speaks for it, and in Israel these were the representatives and rulers of the people. Their number, twenty-four, if to be illustrated by any thing in Scripture, can only be referred to the twenty-four courses into which David divided the priesthood. And this reference is confirmed by the priestly actions of these elders in the next chapter (v. 8). They are *crowned* priests,— "kings and priests,"—the "royal priesthood" of which Peter speaks (1 Pet. ii. 9). And when they act in that capacity, the angels stand in a separate company outside of them (v. 11).

They are therefore saints, not angels, as the general consent of interpreters acknowledges. There are "thrones" indeed among angelic powers, but no priests: for priesthood speaks of mediation and of sin which requires it, and no provision of this kind is needed by the holy or exists in behalf of the fallen angels. No doubt the angel-

---

* E. H. Bickersteth, the author of "Yesterday, To-day, and Forever," and Dr. Craven, American editor of Lange's Commentary on Revelation, are among those who advocate the angelic interpretation in the present day. The arguments of the latter are based entirely on the confusion of the multitudes of the redeemed in chaps. vii. and xiv. with the heavenly saints of the present and the past dispensations.

priest of the eighth chapter will be urged by some, but here it is in behalf of men he offers, and there is but One to whom it belongs to add to the prayers of the saints that which gives them efficacy. Christ, therefore, though presented in a mysterious manner, must be the Priest in this case. Nowhere else in Scripture is there the most distant thought of angelic priesthood.

But if the elders are saints, *how* are they represented to us in this picture? Not, plainly, as departed spirits, but as glorified beings, raised or changed, and evermore beyond the power of death. Not till Christ gets His human throne do His people get theirs (chap. iii. 21). All rewards proper wait till the day when we shall stand before the judgment-seat of Christ, and receive for the things done in the body (2 Cor. v. 10). Thus it is clear that the scene at which we are looking supposes resurrection come, and the voice of the Lord to have called us to Himself. Thus alone could the thrones around the throne be filled.

For the same reason we cannot conceive of any representation here of the position of Christians as now known to and enjoyed by faith. We are indeed "raised up together, and seated together in the heavenly places in Christ Jesus" (Eph. ii. 6); but this is a question of acceptance, not of reigning. Christ reigns, it is true, but in no wise has He taken that place as our representative. Seated upon the Father's throne, we are not seated *in* Him, nor ever shall be *with* Him there. Thus such a thought is absolutely forbidden to us, as that of a positional application of the vision before us.

More plausible would be the thought of *anticipation*,—a pledge and assurance for our encouragement of what is to be only at the end enjoyed. Such anticipations there are in the book before us. The multitude out of all nations, who are seen in the seventh chapter as already "come out of the great tribulation," present us, in fact, with such an anticipatory vision. The woman of the twelfth, clothed with the glory of the sun, is in some such features similarly anticipative. Thus the *principle* is one we cannot refuse, and which *might* apply in this case. We have only to ask, Is there any thing which in fact would prevent our so applying it?

Now, if we look at the white-robed multitude of the seventh chapter, which is the nearest in resemblance to the vision of the elders, if the latter be anticipative, we find one very marked difference between the two. The former is a complete whole, separated from the other visions which surround it, and not an integral part of the prophetic history. It forms no part of the events of the sixth seal, as it plainly forms none of the seventh, but, with its kindred vision of the Jewish remnant sealed, is inserted parenthetically between them. It *interprets* the course of the history, rather than forms part of it; and here the moral purpose of the interpretation is quite evident.

But suppose we had found, on the contrary, this company associated with the course of the prophecy throughout; present and worshiping when the Lamb takes the book; interpreting some of the after-visions; mentioned as present when other events take place: should we not look at it as strange and incongruous indeed to be told that it had no existence as such during this very time? that it was only anticipatively brought before us,—an encouraging vision, not an actual fact?

Such is the relation of the elders to the prophecy before us until the nineteenth chapter closes with the appearing of the Lord. They sing the song of redemption when the Lamb takes the book; they interpret as to the white-robed multitude; they worship again when the seventh trumpet sounds; in their presence the new song is sung which the one hundred and forty-four thousand alone can learn; and when Babylon the Great is judged, they fall down once more before the throne, saying, "Amen, Halleluiah." It is not till after this that the Lord appears.

Thus the elders in heaven are no transient vision, but

an abiding reality all through this long reach of prophecy. We must accept the fact of glorified saints enthroned around the throne of God from the commencement of the "things that shall be." With this, many other things are implied of necessity. The descent of the Lord into the air; the resurrection of the dead; the change of the living saints; the rejection of the rest of the (now merely) professing church; the close of the Christian dispensation. All this we have already found in Scripture to take place before the incoming "end of the [Jewish] age,"—the last week of Daniel's seventy. The internal evidence harmonizes completely with what is derived from the general consent of prophecy, in proving to us to what point in the dispensations we have here arrived.

Daniel had long before this spoken of thrones around the throne. "I beheld," he says, "till thrones were placed (*R. V.*), and One that was Ancient of days did sit" (chap. vii. 9). But he can tell us nothing more as to the occupants of these thrones. The earthly, and not the heavenly side is given to him to unfold. John not only shows us the occupants, but his vision antedates that of Daniel, and raises the thrones themselves to a higher elevation. We must pass on to the twentieth chapter of this book to find the scene which the Old-Testament prophet depicts, and there the character of rule is limited every way both as to time and place. "They lived and reigned with Christ a thousand years." This is earthly rule, and not yet the new earth; but it is just as plainly said of Christ's "servants" in the New Jerusalem, "they shall reign forever and ever." Here the limitation is gone, and the heirs of God, joint-heirs with Christ, are fully manifested.

The idea of a millennial reign, true and scriptural as it is, tends to get too large possession of the thoughts of those often styled "millennarians," a word which answers to the early "chiliasts,"—both derived from this "thousand years" of rule. And these, as shown in Papias, Justin, and Irenæus, conceived of it in a Jewish and earthly fashion, seriously conflicting with the Christian's heavenly hope. To this Old-Testament expectation many in the present day have swung round again, and we cannot too earnestly protest against it.

The truth is, that to those whose hope is the millennium, it is quite natural and necessary to go to the Old Testament for their views of it. But then they are in the line of Jewish promises, and an appropriation of these to a greater or less extent is to be looked for. This is the mode in which have been produced some of the most heterodox and evil systems of the day.

If we would "rightly divide the Word of God," it can be only by respecting the divisions which the Word itself has established for us. And if we ask ourselves, What has the New Testament to say of the millennium? for how much of our knowledge of it are we indebted to its pages? the answer will be impressive and should be enlightening.

In the New Testament we find, first of all, that it is a *millennium*,—that is to say, that it is *limited as a period.* It belongs not to eternity. It precedes the "new earth, wherein dwelleth righteousness;" closes with the judgment of the great white throne, and passing away of present things.

It is *not*, therefore, as so often represented, Sabbath-rest, but only the last day of man's work-day week, the last of the probationary dispensations. Its true type is the sixth day of the creative week when man and woman are put at the head of earthly government, and not the seventh day, which God hallows because He can rest. The merest glance at Rev. xx.,—the merest reference to the Old-Testament prophet, ought to make this so plain that there should be no need to spend another word in its defense.

But what, then, must be the effect of substituting for what is everlasting that which is temporal and transient merely? Certainly, it cannot be a light one. With many, it has perverted the whole future before them, and introduced into it elements destructive to Christianity. To any, it must be hurtful, just in proportion to their occupation with it. For the truth it is that sanctifies. Error demoralizes and despiritualizes. How much, if it touch that in which the heart is called to rest, as it were, looking forward and entering into it as that in which God shall rest eternally? What indeed we hope for, we practically reach after, and are controlled and fashioned by it.

The New Testament speaks of the binding of Satan during these thousand years, and of the deliverance of creation from the bondage of corruption into the liberty of the glory of the children of God. It speaks also—and this is the positive feature which it adds to the Old-Testament picture,—of the reign of the saints with Christ over the earth. This is expressed in the Lord's promise to the apostles that they should "sit upon twelve thrones, judging the twelve tribes of Israel" (Matt. xix. 28); in the authority given over ten or over five cities (Luke xix. 16–19); in the promise of the rod of iron (Rev. ii. 26, 27); and of sitting with the Son of Man upon His throne (iii. 21). In the twentieth chapter of this book, it is the one thing we find as to the millennium besides the fact of its being such, and the binding of Satan. These things are significant. The New-Testament blessings are "in heavenly places in Christ Jesus" (Eph. i. 3), and thus the book of Revelation adds but the heavenly side to the earthly picture. It shows us beyond the judgment of the dead the new heavens and earth, and the tabernacle of God with men; and then the prophecy closes with the description of the New Jerusalem, the heavenly city.

The millennial rule, characterized by the rod of iron which dashes in pieces the opposition of the nations, is a special, exceptional kingdom for a great purpose, which being accomplished, it is given up. Christ sits now at the right hand of God until He makes His foes His footstool; and this subjecting of His enemies goes on until death, the last enemy, is subdued. This is preparatory to the judgment of the great white throne, and after this Christ delivers up the kingdom to the Father, that God may be all in all (1 Cor. xv. 24-28).

The special kingdom closes, but this does not and cannot touch the blessed truth that the throne in the heavenly city remains, past all changes, the "throne of God and *of the Lamb;*" nor this, that " His servants shall serve Him . ... and shall reign forever and ever." The thrones around the throne abide forever. The joint-heirship with Christ—wonder of divine grace as it is—on that very account can be no passing thing. The rod of iron passes away. All that speaks of sin as present passes necessarily. The glory of the grace remains. In the ages to come He will show the exceeding riches of His grace in His kindness toward us through Christ Jesus (Eph. ii. 7).

The Living Ones. (Chap. iv. 5-11.)

As I have said, the character of the throne as a throne of judgment is not seen until the saints are seen upon their thrones around it. In fact, we may say, it does not assume this character until they are there. For the "lightnings and voices and thunders" which now proceed from it are plainly not the announcement of any special judgment, but of the throne as a judgment-throne. This entirely accords with the fact that the dispensation of grace is at an end, the Christian Church complete, and with the saints of past ages glorified.

On the other hand, when the kingdoms of the earth shall have become the kingdom of Christ, the throne will not be characterized as here it is. Righteousness will reign, but the fruit of it will be peace, and the effect, quietness and assurance forever (Isa. xxxii. 17).

Thus we have in the lightnings and thunders proceeding from the throne neither the attributes of the day of grace nor those of the kingdom of glory, but rather of that interval of time which we have been already considering, in which, God's judgments being upon the earth, the inhabitants of the world will learn righteousness (Isa. xxvi. 9). The bow of promise encircling the throne tells of the storm when it shall have passed —the effect designed from the beginning.

And before the throne, the seven lamps of fire bear witness of its action as suited to the character of Him who sits upon it. They are the sevenfold energy of the Spirit of God, who ever works out the divine purpose in the creature, whether it be in creation as at the beginning—when He brooded over the waters, or in sanctification—when we are new born of the Spirit, or in resurrection—when the work of grace ends in glory. And these seven spirits rest upon the Branch of Jesse when the government of the earth is put into His hand; "the Spirit of Jehovah shall rest upon Him; the spirit of wisdom and understanding, the spirit of counsel and might, the spirit of knowledge and of the fear of Jehovah; and He shall be of quick understanding in the fear of Jehovah : and He shall not judge after the sight of His eyes, neither reprove after the hearing of His ears; but with righteousness shall He judge the poor, and reprove with equity for the meek of the earth; and He shall smite the earth with the rod of His mouth, and with the breath of His lips shall He slay the wicked one" (Isa. xi. 2–4). Here is the same perfect character of government. In both we see "man's day" ended and the "day of the Lord" commencing its course. Nor shall its sun ever go down.

Before the throne, also, is "a sea of glass like unto crystal" Before the *typical* "heavenly places" among the shadows of the law, there stood in Solomon's day a "sea" of water, at which the priests washed their hands and feet before they went in to minister in the sanctuary. But the priests are now gone in; the defilements of earth are over, and there is no longer need of cleansing. The sea is therefore here a sea of glass.

Abiding purity has succeeded to constant purification. No wind can henceforth even ruffle it. The lightnings and thunder cannot disturb its rest,—to it are as if they were not. Thus the elders rest upon their thrones in peace.

Below, we shall find the meaning of the judgment-character assumed by the throne. The conflict between good and evil is nearing its crisis; the power of evil is rearing itself in gigantic forms; open blasphemous defiance of God is succeeding to secret impiety; men are loudly saying, "Let us break their bands asunder and cast away their cords from us," and it is time for God to put to His hand, and to meet His adversaries face to face.

As, therefore, the cherubim and the flaming sword united to bar fallen man from paradise,—as, when Israel had reached the limit of divine forbearance, Ezekiel saw the infolding fire and the cherubic forms of judgment,—so now once more, but without the wheels within wheels of providential use of earthly instruments (God not to speak by a Nebuchadnezzar, but in plain wrath from heaven), the cherubim are seen.

"And in the midst of the throne, and round about the throne, were four living creatures full of eyes before and behind. And the first living creature was like a lion, and the second living creature like a calf, and the third living creature had the face as of a man, and the fourth living creature was like a flying eagle. And the four living creatures, having each of them six wings, are full of eyes round about and within; and they have no rest day and night, saying, Holy, holy, holy, Lord God Almighty, who was, and is, and is to come."

The living creatures are in the midst of the throne, yet round about it,—identified with it, yet distinct. To picture this, as some have tried to do, may be difficult, and yet the idea involved in it is not difficult at all. The government of God is carried on, as Scripture represents it to us, largely at least, through created instruments. The Old Testament shows us thus angelic ministries in sway over the earth; the New Testament speaks of "thrones and dominions and principalities and powers" (Col. i. 16). They are thus creaturely, yet identified with the divine. Thus were the judges in Israel called "gods," and our Lord says, "He called them 'gods' unto whom the word of God came" (Jno. x. 35). Here we have the idea which the words as to the living creatures "in the midst of the throne and round about the throne" seem intended to convey.

The "living creatures" certainly show that they are "creatures;" although no stress can be laid upon this word as used by the *R.V.* here, in place of the objectionable one, "beasts," in the older translation. The Greek word is, "living ones," though generally used as the equivalent of our word, from the Latin, "animal," which literally means the same thing. But the forms are those of the heads of the animal creation,—the lion, of wild beasts; the calf or ox, of cattle; the eagle, of birds; and man, of all. Such symbols could not be— were forbidden to be—used of God Himself. Their six wings are intended, surely, to lead us back to Isaiah's vision of the seraphim, who cry, "Holy, holy, holy," also, just as these; and here "with twain they covered their face, and with twain they covered their feet," the suited reverence of creatures in the presence of God. They are not, then, direct symbols of God Himself.

That they are the angels as a class is more *like* the truth, as is plain from what we have already seen; yet in the fifth chapter they are broadly distinguished from the angels, who are seen in a separate company round the throne; while, if the elders represent the redeemed, they are in our present one distinguished from these also. That they are a distinct *class* among the angels has in itself no *scriptural* probability, though it is the favorite traditional view. That they are symbols can scarcely be doubted; hardly of a race of beings of whom elsewhere we have no trace. Lastly, that they symbolize the

Church, as distinct from other bodies of redeemed, is negatived by all the Old-Testament passages.

The view which alone harmonizes all that is conflicting in these is, that they are symbols of that government of God over the earth which may be exercised by angels, will be over the millennial earth by the redeemed associated with Christ Himself. The transition we shall find, in fact, in these very chapters of Revelation; while cherubim were, as we know, upon the tabernacle-vail, which the apostle declares to be the "flesh," or human nature, of Christ (Ex. xxvi. 31; Heb. x. 20).

Hence also—as having reference to the government of the earth—the living creatures are four in number, 4 being significant of earthly completeness, as in the "four corners of the earth." Their six wings speak of restless activity,—perhaps of restraint upon evil, for 6 speaks of this limit imposed by God. The eyes within and around show regard to God—for "within" is toward Him that sits upon the throne—and perfect, not partial, knowledge of things on every side. For the simple complete obedience of the creature would keep it free from displaying the short-sightedness of the creature.

Now, if we look at the appearance of the living creatures themselves, we shall find that each one furnishes us with some view of the divine government which supplements and balances the rest, and that the order also is significant, as in Scripture every thing is. What the Lord teaches us as to every jot and tittle of the law is true no less of the whole inspired Word.

How significant that the first form is that of a lion, the symbol of royal and resistless power! This is the first necessity for government, in which feebleness is only another name for failure. Christ's own name in the chapter following is, "Lion of the tribe of Judah," and when He acts in that character, no one will be able for a moment to resist Him. It will be the most absolute sovereignty that the world has ever seen.

But then, by itself, assuredly, this symbol would mislead. When John looks for the Lion of the tribe of Judah, he sees a "Lamb as it had been slain;" and when even wrath is ready to be poured out upon men, it is spoken of as the "wrath of the Lamb." Indeed, that is what makes it so terrible. It is the wrath of love itself. It is the judgment of One with whom judgment is a "strange work." It is judgment which is so unsparing because love energizes the arm and guides the blow. It is judgment for which there is no remedy,—which can alone fulfill the counsels of perfect wisdom and goodness; judgment which prayer cannot be offered to avert, but for which prayer is made and accepted by God.

Slow indeed it has been in coming! So the ages of misrule and evil, of oppression and wrong, would say. So murmur the down-trodden; so scoffs the infidel. The prophet cries, "How long?" The wicked, pursuing his successful wickedness, says, "God hath forgotten: He hideth His face; He will never see it." All are expecting from the government of God the rapid and decisive action which they think alone suited to Him in whose hands all power is.

Hence, the slow ox* follows the lion here; with strength equal to his, but used how differently! The ox is the symbol of patient labor, and which has man's good for its end. So the apostle uses it (1 Cor. ix. 9, 10). It is the mystery of apparent slowness that is here explained. "God is not slack, as some count slackness," but in all His government works out unfailingly counsels of wisdom in which man's blessing will surely at last be found. Not in the lion is the highest type of sovereignty. The lion's is brute force at the bidding of impulse merely. The ox works under the control of *mind*.

---

*"*Moschos*," translated in our version "calf," is so used in the Septuagint (Ex. xxi 33; xxii. 1, 9, 10, 30; Lev. iv. 10; ix. 4, etc.), which uses it in Ezek. i. 10, the parallel passage to this in Revelation. The idea is of a young, fresh animal, not galled yet with a yoke, nor jaded with over-labor, the fitted type, therefore, of divine working.

But there is more than this, which the next cherub speaks of: for now a human face greets us—"the third living creature had the *face of a man.*" And what strikes us first in this? Not mind merely, though there is mind, and in it lies the power he has—power which both the ox and lion own. But that only completes the thought which we have had already presented. Surely beyond this, and rather than this, what strikes us in a human face in the midst of such surroundings, is its *familiarity.* Here we have what we can understand in a way we cannot the lion or the ox; and as a symbol of divine government, it forces upon us irresistibly the conviction that in it God seeks to be known by us. Not only is He working out blessing in the end. He is meeting us also now, and giving us to know Himself. He is cultivating intimacy with us. And this every soul of His own can better understand in His personal dealings with himself, than in His ways at large—His public government of the world.

Here in our little world we can find, at least, if we will, how "tribulation worketh patience; and patience experience, and experience hope." Here the darkness and the sorrow, the night and the storm, yield (at least afterward) their "peaceable fruits." Here, if we "go down to the sea in ships, and have" our "business in the deep waters," we but the more "see the works of the Lord, and His wonders in the deep." And how sweetly assuring is this knowledge of a living God, for whose care we are not too little, and from whom no circumstance of our lives, no need of our souls, is hid. Would that we all knew this better, which the most exercised among us knows best! We shall find in it, what this "face of a man" may well prepare us for, that it is not necessarily in great and out-of-the-way occurrences that God most manifests Himself. He has here as elsewhere a way of taking up and magnifying what is little by putting Himself into connection with it; and thus (as in all His works) the microscope will convey as much to us, it may be more, than the telescope. For He is every where: "One God and Father of all, who is over all, and through all, and in all."

Yet because He is God, there will be that every where which will remind us in whose presence we stand. No where can we escape from the mystery which attends His presence. Nor would we if we realize this as its meaning. A God always comprehensible by us would be only such an one as ourselves: but magnify man into God you cannot. Still there will be the "light inaccessible, which no man can approach unto." Yet this is *light*, not darkness, and it makes nothing really dark, as men profess; rather in this light we see light,—the knowledge of God illuminates all other things.

And this is what is intimated, I believe, by the last of these living ones: "The fourth living creature was like a flying eagle"—an eagle on the wing. For the "way of an eagle in the air" is one of the four things of which the wise man speaks as "too wonderful" for him (Prov. xxx. 18, 19). And this is to be joined with what the eagle in itself conveys to us as a "bird of heaven,"—a type of what is heavenly; especially with its bold, soaring flight, for which the ancients assigned it to the apostle John as his emblem.

Thus, then, these cherubic figures speak to us, and in their praise they celebrate the holiness, power, and unchangeableness of the covenant-God. The Old-Testament names, as all the way through this part, come up again. It is this God who is our Father, but not as Father do we find Him here. He is our God, if Father: and as such the elders worship Him. For "whenever the living creatures give* glory and honor and thanks to Him that sitteth on the throne, to Him that liveth forever and ever, the four and twenty elders fall* down before Him that sitteth on the throne, and worship* Him that liveth forever and ever, and cast* their crowns before the throne, saying,

---

*These are all strictly futures, but the force seems better expressed in English by "whenever" with the present.

Worthy art Thou, our Lord and our God, to receive glory and honor and power; for Thou hast created all things, and because of Thy will they were, and were created."

How blessed is this worship! The constraint is that of the heart alone: the spirit of praise dictates the praise. They are intelligent, and give the reason of it; not here redemption, but creation. By and by they celebrate redemption also, but one theme does not displace another: all that God is and has done is worthy of Him, and they express their adoration as dependent on the will of Him who, for His glory, had created them. This perpetual worship of heaven is the witness of the perpetual freshness of abiding blessing traced by the happy heart to God as its source. May we learn better on earth this song of praise!

THE LION OF THE TRIBE OF JUDAH.
(Chap. v.)

AND now, in the right hand of Him that sits upon the throne there is seen a book, or scroll, completely filled* with writing, which is, however, as to decipherment, completely hid from sight. It is the book of the future, already and completely foreknown and settled in the divine counsels: no room for any thing to be afterward supplied. Thank God, no tittle of history that the future holds will put omniscience to shame, or show the book of God's counsels to have escaped out of the hand of enthroned omnipotence.

Yet if it remain there, who can penetrate it? The seven seals show it to be absolutely hidden from saint or angel. Let it be proclaimed with a voice mighty enough to reach all the inhabitants of heaven, earth, and

---

* "According to ancient usage, a parchment-roll was first written on the *inside*, and if the inside was *filled* with writing, then the *outside* was used, or back part of the roll; and if that also was covered with writing, and the whole available space was occupied, the book was called *opistho graphos* ('written on the back-side,' *Lucian Vit. Auct.* 9, *Plin. Epist.* iii. 5.)" (Wordsworth, quoted in Schaff's Lange.)

the underworld, there is nowhere any answer to the challenge, "Who is worthy to open the book?"

God's counsels imply blessing. It may be indeed through much tribulation — the light checkered with shadows—evening and morning together making up the day. Even so, we name it "day" from the light, not from the darkness. The conflict of good with evil must end in triumph, not in defeat. And who is worthy to proclaim that triumph? Only He who can insure it and carry it out; for this only it is, as we shall see, that opens the book. It is no longer, at the time to which this change brings us, a question of making prophetic announcements, but of manifesting God's purposes by decisive acts of power. True, *we* are enabled, as having the prophecy, in measure to anticipate what is to come. But that, with all its value for us, is not what we see in this picture. It is not the inditing of a book, nor the uttering of a prophecy, that we have before us, but the opening it by fulfillment.* Here, then, One alone can be found "worthy" to open it. And though we know well who it is, yet we must note the character in which He is introduced to us.

The prophet weeps because no one is "found worthy to open the book, neither to look thereon. And one of the elders saith unto me, 'Weep not : behold, *the Lion of the tribe of Judah*, the Root of David, hath prevailed to open the book and the seven seals thereof.'"

This is in complete and striking accord with what we have already seen as to the change of dispensation which the vision shows to be taking place. The time of gathering from heaven being fulfilled, the body of Christ completed, and the saints of the New-Testament period caught up with those of former times to meet the Lord in the air, the fulfillment of Old-Testament prophecy, long suspended, begins again, and in the forefront of the world's history Israel find their place as of old. The "Lion of the tribe

---

*We may note here, although it is not necessary to this interpretation, that "and to read" in ver. 4 is omitted by the editors.

of Judah" here announces One who is taking up once more their cause, to crown it with speedy and entire victory. Power is soon to manifest itself in that sudden outburst of irresistible righteous anger of which the second psalm warns the kings of the earth: "Be wise now, therefore, O ye kings! be instructed, ye that are judges of the earth! Serve the Lord with fear, and rejoice with reverence. Kiss the Son, lest He be angry, and ye perish from the way, when His wrath shall suddenly kindle."

In this title, "Lion of the tribe of Judah," the whole significance of Jacob's ancient prophecy flashes out. "Judah, thou art he whom thy brethren shall praise · thy hand shall be upon the neck of thine enemies; thy father's children shall bow down before thee. Judah is a lion's whelp; from the prey, my son, thou art gone up: he hath stooped, he hath couched as a lion, and as an old lion,— who shall rouse him up?"

From this we must not disjoin what follows: "The sceptre shall not depart from Judah, nor a lawgiver from between his feet, until Shiloh come; and to him shall the gathering of the people be" (Gen. xlix. 8-10).

Thus it is Christ that Jacob has in spirit before him, when he sees Judah assuming the lion-character. And when in David it actually rose up for a short time in the predicted manner, the brief glory of his kingdom only foretold and heralded the better glory of Christ's enduring one. And in this way the Lion of the tribe of Judah is not only the "Branch of David," springing out of the cut-down tree, but, as here, the *Root* also of David, from which David himself derives all real significance.

It is plain, then, that now the appeal of the eighty-ninth psalm is to be answered. David's throne is to be lifted up from the dust, and Judah's long-delayed hope is to expand into fruition. Strange is it to think how critics and commentators can, in the Lion of *Judah* opening the book of God's counsels, see only the general truth of

Christ upon the throne of providential government, when it is plain, according to the undoubted reference, that the thought of Judah's Lion is inseparably connected with that of *Judah* taking the prey, and then couching with a front of power which none will dare to excite: "*Judah*, thou art a lion's whelp; from the prey, my son, thou art gone up: he hath couched as a lion—who shall rouse him up?"

It is not only ignorance of Scripture, but also of the perfection of Scripture, which operates in these beclouding views of the great prophecy before us, in which every expression, every nicety of utterance, is to be marked and estimated at its worth, because it *has* worth. If not one jot or one tittle could pass from the law, as the Lord Himself declared, till all were fulfilled, how impossible, then, for prophecy to have an irrelevant jot or tittle which can be safely disregarded! Go on, with this character that Christ has now assumed present in the mind, and is it strange or doubtful what can be meant by the sealing out of the twelve tribes, in the seventh chapter, with the separate gathering of the Gentile multitude afterward, "come out of (not merely great, but specifically) *the* great tribulation? All is clear and consistent in detail when we have correctly the general thought.

It is the Lion of the tribe of Judah, then, who prevails to open the book. The hindrance to the blessing of Israel and the earth is now removed. Christ has overcome. But how then overcome? What could be the impediment to the execution of divine purposes of goodness toward men, and how alone could evil be met, subdued,—nay, made to minister to higher blessing? This is what is now to be declared.

"And I saw standing in the midst of the throne and of the four living creatures, and in the midst of the elders, a Lamb, as though it had been slain, having seven horns and seven eyes, which are the seven spirits of God, sent forth into all the earth."

The Lamb is not here represented as upon the throne, but in the midst of a circle formed by the throne, the living creatures, and the elders. Lamb as He is (and the word used emphasizes the connected thought of feebleness in some way), the attribute of perfect power is seen in the seven horns as that of omniscience is seen in the seven eyes, with the still more decisive interpretation given them. Still the feebleness is again marked, and to the extreme, in the note appended that it was "as though it had been slain." Weakness, then, we are to mark in the One depicted here as well as power, and the evident tokens of past suffering even to death, although alive out of death.

Evidently this is how He has prevailed. He has conquered death through dying, conquered it in its own domain by going into it, giving Himself a sacrifice, a vicarious offering, for the *lamb* was well known as that. Sin has been thus met by atonement; evil triumphed over by good, the might of pure love acting according to holiness, where power otherwise there was none, or it was against the Sufferer. This was the victory that opened the book.

But we must not read this as if it was meant to assure us that the Christian view of the Lamb has replaced or set aside or come as in a mystery to explain the Jewish conception of the Lion. This is the thought of many, but it is entirely wrong and hopelessly confusing. The Lion and the Lamb are but one blessed Person; and, moreover, One who remains, through whatever changes of position, wholly unchanging Himself,—" Jesus Christ, the same yesterday, to-day, and forever" (Heb. xiii. 8). This is true, and necessarily true, and it is our joy and consolation for all time; but it does not turn condemnation into salvation, or make the judgment of wrath a piping instead of mourning.

The Lion of the tribe of Judah is not a mere Jewish notion, but a true and scriptural conception. It is Jewish indeed—not Christian; and for that very reason cannot be the equivalent of the "Lamb as it had been slain." And yet it is in His victory over death that He acquires the power which as the Lion of Judah He displays. This is how the two views, in themselves so manifestly different, find their relation to one another.

Yet it is the Lamb that takes the book, and the Lion of the tribe of Judah who does so. As the first, He is the Interpreter of the counsels of redeeming love, as they embrace the whole circle of its objects. As the second, He takes up Israel specifically to deliver them from surrounding enemies and establish them in peace under the shield of His omnipotence. His title here has plainly to do with power displayed against the foes of His people. And this is what plainly gives the necessary stand-point from which we can see aright the meaning of the chapters which follow for the larger part of the remainder of the book.

Yet it is no wonder that up in heaven, among the redeemed, it is as the Lamb slain that the myriad voices celebrate Him, and the Lion of Judah seems to be forgotten. This is not really so; nor does it show that the one title is not to be distinguished from the other. When He acts according to the latter, we shall find how intense are the sympathies of this heavenly throng. To no act of His can there be indifference. But the praise and homage of heaven are to the Lamb slain. Redemption is what declares Him to the heart, and that a redemption by purchase, though redemption by power be its necessary complement. The Lamb slain gives the one side; the Lion of the tribe of Judah speaks of the other.

When the Lamb takes the book, the redemption-song is heard in heaven. "And when He had taken the book, the four living creatures and the four and twenty elders fell down before the Lamb, having every one of them a harp, and golden bowls full of incense, which are the prayers of the saints. And they sing a new song, saying, 'Worthy art Thou to take the book, and to open the seals thereof; for Thou wast slain, and didst purchase unto God with Thy blood out of every tribe and tongue and people and nation, and madest them unto our God a kingdom and priests, and they shall reign over the earth."

In this "new song," the living creatures and the elders are united. The angels we find in the verses succeeding these, worshiping in a circle outside and in other terms. This surely is another sign of what is taking place, and where the vision brings us. The symbols of administrative government, which the living creatures present to us, are now connected with redeemed men, and no longer with angels. " Unto angels hath He not put in subjection the world to come whereof we speak. But one in a certain place testified, saying, 'What is man, that Thou art mindful of him, or the son of man, that Thou visitest him? Thou madest him a little lower than the angels; Thou crownedst him with glory and honor; Thou didst set him over the works of Thy hands'" (Heb. ii. 5–8).

This is, of course, spoken of the Lord Jesus, but in Him *man*, according to the will of God, comes to the place of authority in the world to come, in which, in the book of Daniel, we find the angels. It is when the Son of Man takes His own throne that the saints reign with Him. Thus, in this song of redemption we have now "they shall reign over the earth." It is plain, then, that the vision here brings us to the eve of the millennial day.

Not only are the heavenly saints seen as about to enter on their reign over the earth; they are already in their character as priests, "having golden bowls full of incense, which are the prayers of the saints." It is not said that they are offering them: they are, in fact, at that moment in another attitude; and this seems pointed out as to them, as if to be another of the marks of the period which is now beginning. Observe, they are never looked at as themselves interceding. They are charged with the prayers of others, but add nothing to them. There are no supererogatory merits that they have acquired, to give efficacy to what they present; and the prayers themselves are the incense, not incense is added to them. Romanism finds here no atom of justification, such as some have alleged; but the statement of the text is plain, and we must abide by it. The risen saints are priests and kings to God. In the former capacity, they have the incense-prayers in their hand; in the latter, they are presently to reign over the earth, so that the cherubic living creatures and the elders are now seen together.

Thus the period of the vision is made as plain as possible, and the song of the redeemed is thus a "new" song, not because redemption itself was yet a new thing, but because it was now, as far as heaven itself was concerned, accomplished. Resurrection, the redemption of the body, was now accomplished, and the Lamb about to commence what He alone could undertake—the redemption by power of the earth also. At this point, the song of praise celebrates the completion of all as to the singers save the reign over the earth involved in what He is now taking in hand to do. Thus the song is new.

But is it their own redemption they are celebrating? The text as it used to be read made no doubt of this; but it is abandoned by the general consent of the editors, who accept substantially what the *R.V.* gives, except that, as to the last clause, there is still dispute whether it should be "they reign" or "they *shall* reign." I prefer the latter, as most according to the fact, authorities being divided. The result as to the whole is that the elders do not say, "Thou hast redeemed *us*, and *we* shall reign," but "Thou hast redeemed a people, and they shall reign." Instead of being specific, it is general, as to who the people are, although the last clause limits it to the heavenly family of the redeemed. The millennial saints do not *reign* over the earth. They inherit it in peace and blessing, but it is they who suffer with Christ who shall reign with Him (2 Tim. ii. 12).

The change puts emphasis upon the redemption, rather than upon the persons who are partakers of it; and this commends itself to spiritual apprehension. The Lamb and His wondrous work fill the souls of His own with rapture as they fall before His feet: "THOU wast slain, and hast redeemed to God." But there seems to me no ground for what some allege from this change of text, that the heavenly saints here are celebrating the redemption of others and *not* their own! Why should this be? The language does not necessitate it; for if we say, "Thou hast redeemed a people," even though we are speaking of ourselves, it is quite in order to say, keeping up the third person all through, "and *they* shall reign." I agree with those who hold the view with which I cannot agree, that there is a company of martyrs after this who are, as such, to be joined to this heavenly company, and who are seen in this way as added to them in chap. xx. 4-6. But to think that in the vision before us the saints are praising Christ solely for the redemption of another class than themselves, is, I venture to say, extreme and incongruous. Surely we should not think, in praising Christ for redemption, of wholly omitting the thought that we ourselves are among the subjects of it! Every consideration here, moreover, would forbid the supposition.

Outside the circle of the redeemed, the angels have now their place and their praise. It has been often and justly remarked that they do not "sing." Their peaceful lives, not subject to vicissitude, nor touched by sin, furnish no various tones for melody. The harps which we have above are tuned down here, where the Davids, signalized by their afflictions, are the sweet singers of Israel. Wondrous and eternal fruit of earth's sorrow, though by divine grace only, the redeemed among men will be the choir of heaven! Blessed be God!

"And I beheld, and I heard the voice of many angels round about the throne and the living creatures and the elders; and the number of them was ten thousand times ten thousand, and thousands of thousands, saying as with a great voice, 'Worthy is the Lamb that has been slain, to receive power and riches and wisdom and might and honor and glory and blessing.'"

Redemption has thus added to the angels' praise. It is not to the Creator only. And in this new praise, a new element of blessing, a new apprehension of God, has entered into their hearts. They are nearer, though in this outside circle, than they ever were before. In truth, though in some sense outside, our earthly idea of distance fails to convey the thought. Larger and smaller measures of apprehension there may be and will be, but true distance of the creature from the Creator is in heaven the one impossibility, where of the Father of our Lord Jesus Christ *every* family is named. "Whither shall I go from Thy presence?" is never whispered; and the whisper of it, even in heaven, would make it hell.

And now, in a wider sweep again,—

"Every creature which is in heaven, and on the earth, and under the earth, and such as are in the sea, even all that are in them, heard I saying, 'Blessing and honor and glory and power be unto Him that sitteth upon the throne, and unto the Lamb forever and ever.' And the four living creatures said, 'Amen,' and the elders fell down and worshiped."

This is the voice of the lower creation in echo to the praise of heaven. It is such a response as many of the psalms call for in view of the coming of the Lord; and is another mark of the time of the vision. The earth under the desolation of the fall has for the time lost its place, as it might seem, and wandered as a planet from its orbit into the starless silence around. Christ, as her central Sun, has come back to her after the long polar darkness, and her voices wake up as the spring returns. Blessed it is to realize (so simple and natural as it is) the response to this response on the part of the human elders, as this sound is heard. The governmental powers of earth—the living creatures—utter their glad "Amen" to it. Earth is to repay the long labor and service of rule at last. And the elders, with their own memories of sin and darkness (now forever but memories, though undying), hear it in a thrill of sympathetic joy that (as all the joy of heaven) melts into adoration: "The elders fell down and worshiped."

The Opening of the Seals: The First Four Seals. (Chap. vi. 1, 2.)

The Lamb having taken the book, the opening of the seals at once follows. When they are all loosed,—and not before,—then the book is fully opened. The seals then give us the introduction to the book, rather than (as many have imagined,) the complete contents. Beyond the seals lie the trumpets, contrasted with the seals in their nature: the latter are divine secrets opened to faith; the trumpets, loud-voiced calls to the whole earth. These go on to the setting up of the kingdom in the seventh trumpet; and after that, we have only separate visions giving the details of special parts, until in the nineteenth chapter we reach again a connected series of events, stretching from the marriage of the Lamb through the millennium to the great white throne.

The opening of the seals, then, gives us events introductory, as regards both time and character, to what follows, and which have their importance largely in this very fact. The opening of them is the key to the book; for when they are opened, the book is. Yet they only set us upon the threshold of the great events which precede the setting up of the kingdom of Christ, the time of the trumpets; while on the other hand they contain the germ and prophecy of these, which spring out of them as it were necessarily.

In the Lord's great prophecy of Matt. xxiv., which similarly sets before us the time of the end, we have, before the period of special tribulation connected with the abomination of desolation in the holy place, an order of things which has often been compared with what we find under the seals. Nor can we compare them without being struck with the resemblance. The Lord specifies here, as warning-signs of His coming, false Christs, wars, and rumors of wars, famines, pestilences, and earthquakes, and persecution of His people. In the first and second seals we have correspondingly war—that of conquest and civil war; in the third, famine; in the fourth, pestilence; in the fifth, the cry of the martyrs; and in the sixth, a great earthquake, though perhaps only as a symbol of national convulsion. Only the false Christs seem to be entirely omitted, and some have therefore imagined that the rider on the white horse in the first seal—coming, it must be admitted, in the right place to preserve the harmony with the gospel,—might fill the gap. But this we must look at later on. The correspondence is sufficiently striking to confirm strongly the thought that the seals refer to the same period as does the passage in the gospel, the time preceding and introducing the great tribulation of the end.

Looking again at the seals, we find they are divided, like most other septenary series, into four and three; the first four being marked from the rest by the horse and rider which is in each, and by the call of the living beings by which each is introduced. Their relation to each other is plainer (or more outward) than in the case of the last three, as may be observed also in such series generally. And how beautiful and reassuring is this rhythm of prophecy! The power of God every-where controlling with perfect ease the winds and waves in their wildest uproar, so as for faith to produce harmony where the natural ear finds only discord. Significant is it that in no other book of Scripture have we so much of these numberings and divisions and proportionate series as we have in the book of Revelation.

THE OPENING OF THE FIRST FOUR SEALS.   59

The call of the cherubim at the opening of the first four seals is also significant. It is to be noted that it is not addressed, as in our common version, to John, but to the riders upon the horses, who then come forth. It is not "Come and see," but "Come," as the *R.V.*, with the editors in general, now gives it. The living beings utter their call also in the order in which they have been seen in the vision: for although in the first instance it is said, "*one* of the four living beings," not "*the first*," yet in the case of the other seals they are named in order—second, third, and fourth. And we shall find a correspondence in each case between the living being and the one who comes forth at his call.

We have seen that the cherubic figures speak of the government of God, in the hands of those who are commissioned of Him to exercise it. And thus the vail of the holiest, the type of the Lord in manhood—"the vail, that is to say, His flesh" (Heb. x. 20)—was embroidered with cherubim. To Him they have peculiar reference as the King of God's appointment; and the four gospels, as has been seen by many, give in their central features these cherubic characters in the Lord, and again in the order in which the book of Revelation exhibits them. The Lion of Judah we find in Matthew's gospel, where Christ is looked at as Son of David. Mark gives us, on the other hand, the young bullock—the Servant's form. Luke meets us with the dear and familiar features of manhood,—the "face of a man;" while in John we have the bird of heaven—the vision of incarnate Godhead. These aspects of the Gospels I may assume to be familiar to my readers· here is not the place to consider them.

Now Christ has been seen in heaven in a double character:—the Lion of the tribe of Judah is the Lamb that was slain. It is the title under which He takes every thing, for it is that which shows Him as the One who has bought every thing by His surrender of Himself unto death. He is the "man" who, according to His own parable, having found in a field hidden treasure, went and sold all that he had, and bought that field. "The field," He says again Himself, "is the world."

But the Lord's death had also another side to it. It was man's emphatic rejection of God in His dearest gift to him,—just in his sweetest and most wonderful grace. While every gospel has a different tale to tell of what Christ is, every gospel has also, as an essential feature, the story of His rejection in that character. As Son of David, as the gracious Minister to man's need, as God's true Man, or as the only begotten Son from heaven, He is still the crucified One. Man has cast out with insult the divine Saviour,—has refused utterly God's help and His salvation. What must be the result? He must—if in spite of long-suffering mercy he persist in this,—remain unhelped and unsaved. He has cast out the Son of God; and why? Because he was His essential opposite: "the prince of this world cometh, and hath nothing in Me." The world which rejects Christ as finding nothing in Him naturally is the world which owns Satan as its prince. He who rejects Christ is ready for Antichrist; and so He says to the Jews, "I am come in My Father's name, and ye receive Me not: if another shall come in his own name, him ye will receive."

Thus man's sin foreshadows the judgment which must come upon him. This is no arbitrary thing. The law is the same physically and morally,—"Whatsoever a man soweth, that shall he also reap." In the true sense here, man is the maker of his own destiny.

And this will prepare us to understand the cherubim-call for judgment. If the living beings represent characters of God's government, and characters also which are found in Christ, we can find here a double reason why, Christ being rejected, the judgments come forth at the cherubim's call. A rejected Saviour calls forth a destroyer. The voice of the lion summons to his career the white-horsed conqueror.

THE OPENING OF THE FIRST FOUR SEALS.

This shows us, then, that it is not Christ who is thus represented. Many have supposed so, naturally comparing with it the vision of the nineteenth chapter, where Christ comes forth upon a white horse to the judgment of the earth. But the comparison really proves the opposite. We have not, certainly, under the first seal, already reached the time of Christ's appearing. And the symbol of judgment is unsuited for the going forth of the blessed gospel of peace. The gospel-dispensation is over now, and the sheaves of its golden harvest are gathered into the barn. Not peace is it now, but war. Peace they would not have at His hands: its alternative they have no choice as to receiving. Christ received would have been an enemy only to man's enemies. Power would have been used on his behalf, and not against him: that rejected, the foes that would have been put down rise up, and hold him captive.

This, then, is the key to what we have under the first seal: a few words must suffice for the present as to the other details.

The horse is noted in Scripture for its strength, and as the instrument of war: other thoughts believed to be associated with it seem scarcely to be sustained. It indicates, therefore, aggressive power, and a *white* horse is well known as the symbol of victory. In the *rider*, who of course governs the horse, there seems generally indicated an agent of divine providence, though it may be not merely unintentionally so, but even in spirit hostile. The rider here is not characterized save by his acts. His bow is his weapon of offense, which speaks not of hand-to-hand conflict, but of wounds inflicted at a distance. The crown *given him* seems certainly to imply, as another has said, that he obtains royal or imperial dignity as the fruit of his success, though by whom the crown is given does not appear. Altogether we have but a slight sketch of the one presented to us here, and one which might fit many of whom history speaks; but this is *divine* history, and the person before us must have an important connection with the purposes of God, to earn for him the leading place which he fills in the beginning of these visions of earthly doom.

We naturally ask, Can we find no intimations elsewhere of this conqueror? It appears to me we may; and I hope to give further on what I think Scripture teaches as to it, not as pretending to dogmatize as to what is obscure, but presenting simply the grounds of my own judgment for the consideration of others. If it be not the exact truth, it may yet lead in the direction of the truth.

Some preliminary points have, however, first to be settled; and for the present it will be better to content ourselves with noting the detail as to this first rider, and to pass on.

The second living creature is the patient ox. True figure of God's laborer, strength only used in lowly toil for man, it speaks to us of Him who on God's part labored to bring man back to Him, and plow again the channels back to the forsaken source, so that the perennial streams might fill them, and bring again to earth the old fertility. Yet here the ox calls forth one to whom it is "given to take peace from the earth, and that they should slay one another." Civil war is bidden forth by that which is the type of love's patient ministry. Yes, and how fitly! For just as if received, God having His place, all else would have its own; so, rejected, all must be out of joint and in disorder. Man in rebellion against God, the very beasts of the earth rebel in turn. Having cast off affection where most natural, all natural affection withers. Man has initiated a disorder which he cannot stop where he desires, but which will spread until all sweet and holy ties are sundered, and love is turned (as it may be turned) to deadliest opposition.

In the third seal the third living creature calls: the one with the face of a man. At his call, famine comes. We see a black horse, and he that sits on him has a pair of balances in his hand; and there is heard in the midst of

THE OPENING OF THE FIRST FOUR SEALS. 63

the living beings a voice which cries, "A quart of wheat for a denarius, and three quarts of barley for a denarius, and see thou hurt not the oil and the wine." A denarius, which was the ordinary day's earnings of a laboring man, would usually buy eight quarts of wheat, one of which would scarcely suffice for daily bread. It is evident, therefore, that this implies great scarcity.

The congruity of this judgment with the call of the living being is not so easy to be understood as in the former cases. Were we permitted to spiritualize it, and think of what Amos proclaims, "Not a famine of bread, nor a thirst of water, but of hearing the words of the Lord, such a famine would, on the other hand, suit well: for "the face of a man" reminds us how God has met us in His love, and revealed Himself to us, inviting our confidence, speaking in our familiar mother-tongue, studying to be understood and appreciated by us; and assuredly this familiar intercourse with Him is what we want for heart-satisfaction. "Lord, show us the Father, and it sufficeth us," was not an unintelligent request so far as man's need is itself concerned. The unintelligence was in what the Lord points out, "Have I been so long time with you, and hast thou not known *Me*, Philip? He that hath seen Me hath seen the Father."

Here, then, man's need is fully met. The hunger of his soul is satisfied. The bread from heaven is what the *Son of Man* alone gives, and it is meat that "endures to everlasting life." And this rejected,—the true manna loathed and turned from,—what remains but a wilderness indeed, a barren soil without a harvest?

But this gives only a hint of the real connection: for this seal following the other two, seems evidently to give a result of these. What more simple and natural than that after conquest and civil war,—above all, the latter,— the untilled soil should leave men destitute? Still more, that the oil and the wine, which do not need in the same way man's continual care, remain on the whole uninjured?

An ordinary famine seems to be intended, therefore; yet the connection has been hinted as already said: for the natural is every where a type of the spiritual, and depends on it, as the lesser upon the greater. Our common mercies are thus ours through Christ alone. Take away the one, the other goes. A natural famine is the due result of the rejection of the spiritual food. With the substance goes the shadow also.

That the third living creature calls for famine, then, may in this way be understood, and it shows how the greater the blessing lost, the deeper the curse retained. Christ rejected strikes every natural good.

And when we come to the fourth seal, and the flying eagle summons forth the pale horse with its rider Death, Hades following with him to engulf the souls of the slain, the same lesson is to be read, becoming only plainer. John's is the gospel to which this flying eagle corresponds, —the gospel of love and life and light, each fathomless, each a mystery, each divine. Blot this out—reject, refuse it, what remains? What but the awful eternal opposite, which the death here as from the wrath of God introduces to?

These initial judgments, then, are seen to speak of that which brings the judgment. The day of harvest is beginning, and man is being called to reap what he has sown. The darkness which begins to shut all in is the darkness not merely of absent, but rejected light.

This, in its full dread reality, no one that is Christ's can ever know. Yet before we leave it, it is well for us to realize how far for us also rejected light may be, *and must be*, darkness. We are in the kingdom of Christ, children of the light, delivered from the authority of darkness. Around us are poured the blessed beams of gladdening and enfranchising day. And yet this renders any real darkness in which we may be practically the more solemn. It too is not a mere negative, not a mere absence of light, but light shut out. And darkness itself is a kingdom, rebellious indeed, yet subject to the god of this world. To shut out the light—any light—is to shut in the darkness, and thus far to join the revolt against God and good.

And the necessary judgment follows,—for us, a Father's discipline, that we may learn, in our self-chosen way, what evil is, but learn it, that at last we may be what we must be, if we are to dwell with Him, "partakers of His holiness." But will it not be loss,—aye, even eternal loss, to have had to learn it so?

Who would force the love that yearns over us to chasten, instead of comforting,—to minister sorrow, when it should and would bring gladness only? THERE IS NO MERE NEGATIVE. In that in which we are not for Christ, we are against Him. To shut Him out is a wrong and insult to Him. And these quick-eyed cherubim, careful for the "holy, holy, holy God" they celebrate, will they not, must they not, call forth the judgment answering to the sin?

THE LAST THREE SEALS. (Rev. vi. 9–17; viii. 1.)

THE first four seals have thus shown to us judgments poured out upon the earth,— judgments which are the necessary result of the rejection of Christ, now completed by the refusal of the gospel for so many centuries of divine long-suffering. The fifth opens to us a very different scene: here are beheld "under the altar, the souls of them that were beheaded for the word of God and for the testimony which they held." Persecution has broken out against the people of God; for such there are still upon the earth, though the saints of the present time are with the Lord in glory. Heaven being filled, the Spirit of God has been at work to fill the earth with blessing; and here, as we know, God's ancient people are the first subjects of His converting grace. The remnant of that time could be fitly represented by those disciples of the Lord to whom He addressed the great prophecy of

His coming, Jewish as they were still in conceptions and in heart; and to these, after such warnings as had been fulfilled in the former seals, He says, "Then shall they deliver you up to tribulation, and shall kill you; and ye shall be hated of all the nations (the Gentiles) for My name's sake." The two passages agree with one another and with nature.

Woe unto those who in a day of wrath upon the world for the rejection of Christ go into it to insist upon His claim! And that is what is meant by "the gospel of the *kingdom*" which the Lord tells us "shall be preached in all the world for a witness to all the nations, and then shall the end come" (Matt. xxiv. 14). "Glad tidings" though it may be that the kingdom of righteousness at last is to be set up, and the King Himself is at hand,—to those who reject Him, it is the announcement of their doom. And we see under this fifth seal what will be the result. The Word of God will again have its martyrs, but whose cry will not be with Stephen, "Lord, lay not this sin to their charge!" but with the martyrs of the Old Testament, "The Lord look upon it, and require it!" "And they cried with a loud voice, 'How long, O Lord, holy and true, dost Thou not judge, and avenge our blood on them that dwell upon the earth?'"

The cry is now in place, as is the pleading for grace in a day of grace. Judgment is indeed to come, and the time when God "maketh inquisition for blood" (Ps. ix. 12); but though at hand, there is yet a certain delay, for, alas! even yet, the measure of man's iniquity is not reached. "And white robes were given unto every one of them; and it was said unto them that they should rest yet for a little season, until their fellow-servants and their brethren, who should be killed as they were, should be fulfilled."

Two seasons of persecution seem to be marked here, though with no *necessary* interval between them; though the crash that follows under the sixth seal, with the terror

THE LAST THREE SEALS.

thus (if but for awhile) produced, might well cause such a cessation of persecution for the time being. Whether this be so or not, the two periods are surely here distinguished. A much later passage (chap. xx. 4) similarly distinguishes them, while it enables us to recognize the latter of these periods as that of the beast under his last head: "And I saw thrones, and they sat on them"— those already enthroned in chap. iv. and v.,—"and the souls of those that were beheaded for the witness of Jesus and for the word of God,"—those seen under the fifth seal,—"and such as had not worshiped the beast, nor his image, and had not received his mark upon their foreheads or in their hands"—here are their "brethren that were to be slain as they were,"—"and they lived and reigned with Christ a thousand years."

The distinction between these two periods proves the introductory character of the seals, at least as far as we have gone. The time of the *great* tribulation is not come; just as, in Matt. xxiv. 9, the persecution prophesied of precedes it. Thus the martyrs here, while owned and approved, have yet to wait for the answer to their prayer. *Some* answer, it need not be doubted, the next seal gives; but plainly, it cannot be the full one: there are decisive reasons for refusing the thought entertained by many, that it is really the "great day of the Lamb's wrath" which is come. Men's guilty consciences make them judge it to be this; but that is only their interpretation, not the divine one.

A terrible break-up of the existing state of things it is: "And I beheld when he had opened the sixth seal, and lo, there was a great convulsion; and the sun became as sackcloth of hair, and the whole moon became as blood; and the stars of heaven fell unto the earth, as a fig-tree casteth her unripe figs when she is shaken of a great wind. And the heaven was removed as a scroll when it is rolled up, and every mountain and island were moved out of their places. And the kings of the earth, and the princes, and the chief captains, and the rich, and the strong, and every bondman and freeman, hid themselves in the caves and in the rocks of the mountains; and they say to the mountains and to the rocks, Fall on us, and hide us from the face of Him that sitteth on the throne, and from the wrath of the Lamb; for the great day of His wrath is come, and who shall be able to stand?"

Well may it seem to be so; and just such physical signs are announced in Joel (ii. 31 and iii. 15) before "the great and terrible day of the Lord shall come." Just so also the Lord speaks of what shall take place *after* the tribulation: "Immediately after the tribulation of those days shall the sun be darkened, and the moon shall not give her light, and the stars shall fall from heaven, and the powers of the heavens shall be shaken; and then shall appear the sign of the Son of Man in heaven; and then shall the tribes of the earth mourn, and they shall see the Son of Man coming in the clouds of heaven with power and great glory" (Matt. xxiv. 29, 30).

The sixth seal precedes the tribulation, however, as we have seen; except this could occur between the fifth and sixth, and were passed silently over. This would be a very violent supposition in view of what we have already seen, and of what follows the sixth seal itself, as we may see presently. The rolling up the heavens as a scroll, moreover, goes beyond the language of Joel or of the Lord, carrying us on, indeed, to the passing away of the heaven and earth which precedes the coming in of that "*new* heavens and earth in which dwelleth righteousness" (2 Pet. iii. 13). But this is impossible to be thought of as occurring in this place. The only other practicable interpretation, therefore, must be the true one,—the language is figurative, and the signs are not physical, though designedly given in terms which remind us of what indeed is swiftly approaching, though not yet actually come.

And in this way the general significance is not difficult to apprehend. The heavens in this way represent the

THE LAST THREE SEALS. 69

seat of authority. Nebuchadnezzar had to learn that the "heavens rule" (Dan. iv. 26). And they represent figuratively rule also on the part of man. In the Old-Testament prophets, we have similar pictures to that before us here (Isa. xiii. 10; xxxiv. 4), where the context shows that national convulsions are prophesied of. Here, it is evidently the collapse of governments, the shaking of all that seemed most settled and secure. All classes of men,—high and low, rich and poor, are involved in the effect of it, and their stricken consciences ascribe it as judgment to the wrath of God and the Lamb. In their alarm, they imagine He is just about to appear; but He does not, and the panic passes away. A new state of things is introduced, of which the features unfold themselves.

When we might now expect the opening of the seventh seal, we find instead the parenthetic visions of the seventh chapter; and there is a similar interruption in exactly the same place in the trumpet-series: the vision of the little book and the two witnesses comes in between the sixth and seventh trumpets. This exact correspondence claims our attention. One result of it is, to make the septenary series an octave, and to give, therefore, to the last seal and the last trumpet alike the character of a seventh and yet of an eighth division. Let us inquire for a moment into the significance of these numbers in this connection.

The numbers are, in their scriptural meaning, in some sense opposite to one another. "Seven" speaks of completion, perfection, and so cessation. Seven notes give the whole compass in music. On the seventh day God ended all His work which He had made, and rested. The eighth day is the first of a new week,—a new beginning. The eighth note is similarly a new beginning. The essential idea attaching to the number in its symbolic use in Scripture is that of what is new, in contrast with the old which is passed away,—as the new covenant, the new creation. As outside the perfect seven, it adds no other thought.

Now if we will remember the character of these seals, that they keep the book closed, it follows of course that the seventh seal opened opens for the first time really *the book itself*. This in fact introduces us therefore to what is a new thing. We were up to this time in the porch or vestibule merely. Immediately the last door is opened we are in the building itself.

Does not this account for the fact that on its opening there is simply a brief pause—"silence in heaven for the space of half an hour,"—and then come the trumpets? This is exactly according to the seven-eight character of the closing seal. One period is over, and with this we begin another. The last seal is open, and this discloses, not a bit more introduction, but *the book itself*.

The seventh trumpet will be found in these respects very like the seventh seal. It too is brief; and while closing the trumpet-series of judgment—in fact the three special woes,—opens into another condition of things, not woe at all, but the time long looked for, when "the kingdom of the world is become the kingdom of our Lord, and of His Christ, and He shall reign forever and ever" (chap. xi. 15). Thus the seven-eight structure justifies itself in both series, of seals and trumpets.

But before the seventh seal comes a parenthetic vision, which is not a part of the seals really, but a disclosure of what is in the mind of the Lord, His purpose of grace fulfilling steadfastly amid all the strife and sorrow and sin which might seem to prevail every where. Let us now give it our careful attention.

The Parenthetic Visions:—The Sealed of Israel. (Chap. vii. 1–8.)

An objection may be taken to our interpretation of the convulsion under the sixth seal,—that it is not in harmony with that which we have given of the earlier ones. In these, the "earth," for instance, was assumed to be

THE SEALED OF ISRAEL. 71

literally that; in the latter, it is taken in a figurative sense; and it may be urged that this want of uniformity in interpretation allows us to make of these visions very much what we will,—in fact makes their alleged meaning altogether inconsistent and unreliable.

This is a mistake, though a very natural one, and it needs to be examined and shown to be such, or else a serious difficulty will remain in the way of further progress, if such indeed be possible. For the same inconsistency, if it be really that, will appear again and again as we proceed with our study of the book before us; we shall be using the same terms now in a literal and again in a figurative sense, as it may appear, arbitrarily, but in fact as compelled by necessity to do so, or according to the law of the highest reason.

Figures pervade our common speech, even the most literal and prosaic,—disguised for us often by the mere fact that they are used so commonly. We employ them, too, with a latitude of meaning which in no wise affects their intelligibility to us. They are used with a certain freedom in which there is nothing arbitrary, but the reverse. They are used rather in the interests of clearness and intelligibility, the main end sought, which governs indeed their use. It is simple enough to say that the whole art of language is in clearness of expression, and that the right use of figures is therefore for this end.

Now, in visions, such as we have in Revelation, figures, it is true, have a much larger place: the meaning of the vision as a *whole* is symbolic—figurative. Yet this does not at all suppose that every feature in it is so, and in no case perhaps is this really true.

Take the fifth seal as a sufficient example,—where the altar is figurative, and so are the white robes, but the killing of their brethren is real and literal. This mingling of the literal and symbolic in one vision makes it plain that they may be and will be found mingled through the whole series of visions. And if it be asked, How, then, are we to discern the one from the other? the answer will be, that each case must be judged separately,—the sense that is simplest, most self-consistent, and agreeable to the context being surely the right one. God writes, as man does, to be understood, and *intelligibility* gives the law, therefore, to all the rest. It is reassuring indeed to remember this: plenty of deep things there are in the Word of God, and more perhaps than any where else are they to be found in the book of Revelation, but the mystery in them is never from mere verbal concealments or misty speech, but from defect in us,—spiritual dullness and incapacity. This most difficult of all Scripture-books God has stamped with the name of "REVELATION."

These thoughts are not an unnecessary introduction to the parenthetic visions between the sixth and the seventh seals, where just such questions have been asked as to the sealing of a hundred and forty-four thousand out of every tribe of the children of *Israel*. Is it in fact Israel literally, or a typical, spiritual Israel that we are to think of? The latter is the thought of expositors generally, though by no means all; and we are told (as by Lange, for instance,) that if we take Israel literally to be meant, then we must take all the other details,—the exact number sealed, etc., —literally also: to do which would not involve any absurdity, but which we have seen to be not in the least necessitated. We are free, as to all matters of the kind, to ask, What is the most suitable meaning? and to find in this suitability, the justification of one view or the other.

The *context* argues for the literal sense. The innumerable multitude seen afterward before the throne, "out of all nations and kindreds and peoples and tongues," shows us plainly a *characteristically* Gentile gathering, and that they are in some sense in contrast with the Israelitish one seems clear. Taken together, they throw light upon one another, and display the divine mercy both to Jews and Gentiles in the latter days. While the separateness of these companies, and the priority given to Israel, agree with the character of a time when the Christian Church being removed to heaven, the old distinctions are again in force. We are again in the line of Old-Testament prophecy, and of Jewish "promises" (Rom. ix. 4); "the *Lion of the tribe of Judah*" has taken the book.

Even apart from the context, (decisive as this is), the enumeration of the tribes would seem to make the description literal enough, even although Dan be at present missing from among them, and supposing no reason could be assigned for this.* Judah too is in her place as the royal tribe: not the natural birthright, but divine favor, controls the order here. Every thing assures us that it is indeed Israel, and as a nation, that is now in the scene.

Let us turn back now to see how she is introduced to us.

"After this, I saw four angels standing at the four corners of the earth, holding the four winds of the earth, that no wind should blow on the earth, or on the sea, or upon any tree. And I saw another angel ascend from the sunrising, having the seal of the living God; and he cried with a great voice to the four angels to whom it was given to hurt the earth and the sea, saying, 'Hurt not the earth, nor the sea, nor the trees, till we shall have sealed the servants of our God in their foreheads.'"

Here it is manifest that, terrible as have been the judgments already, far worse are at hand. The four winds— expressive of all the agencies of natural evil— are about to blow together upon the earth, under the control of spiritual powers (the angels) which guide them according to the supreme will of God. It is the "day of the Lord of Hosts upon every one that is proud and lofty, and upon every one that is lifted up; and he shall be brought low" (Isa. ii. 12). And as nothing *lifts itself* up as the tree does, so the "tree" is specially marked out here: the ax is laid at the root of it. The passage in Isaiah goes

---

*Dan and Zebulon are both omitted in the genealogical lists of 1 Chronicles.

on quite similarly: "And upon all the cedars of Lebanon that are high and lifted up, and upon all the oaks of Bashan" (*v.* 13).

But this becomes, as in the Baptist's lips, a general sentence upon man as man, from which none may escape but as in the Lord's grace counted worthy. Thus the sealing becomes quite evidently the counterpart of what we find in the ninth of Ezekiel, though there the range of judgment is more limited. "And He called to the man clothed in linen, which had the writer's inkhorn by his side; and the Lord said unto him, 'Go through the midst of the city, through the midst of Jerusalem, and set a mark upon the foreheads of the men that sigh and cry for all the abominations that be done in the midst thereof.' And to the others He said in mine hearing, 'Go ye after him through the city, and smite; let not your eye spare, neither have ye pity; slay utterly old and young, both maids and little children and women, but come not near any man upon whom is the mark.'"

The sealing is as evidently preservative as the "mark" is. They are both upon the forehead,—open and manifest. If we look on to the fourteenth chapter here, we shall find upon the hundred and forty-four thousand there (a company as to the identity of which with the present one it is not yet time to ask the question,) the name of the Lamb's Father written, and the seal marks thus undoubtedly to whom they belong.

Let us notice also that we are just approaching the time here in which the beast also will have his mark, if not always on the forehead, at least in the hands (chap. xiii. 16). The time of unreserved confession of one master or the other will then have come; and no divided service will be any longer possible. The beast "boycotts" (they have already invented both the *thing* and the expression for him,) those who do not receive his mark: those who do receive it are cast into the lake of fire (chap. xiii. 17; xiv. 9, 10).

The sealing is angelic,—a very different thing therefore from present sealing with the Holy Ghost, and from any power or gift of the Spirit. No angel could confer this, and the creaturehood of the angel here is manifest from his words, "Till *we* have sealed the servants of *our* God in their foreheads." The "we" shows that more than one execute the ministry, and they that do this speak of God as "our God." This is decisive, apart from all dispensational considerations. But in what the sealing consists it seems scarcely possible to say: the effect is, that the people of God are manifested as His, and preserved thus from the judgments which are ready to be sent upon it.

"The seal of the *living* God" seems along with this to imply their preservation as living men against all the power of their adversaries—His, and therefore theirs. True, that the power of the living God is shown more victoriously in resurrection than in preservation merely; true also that to the souls under the altar it has been foretold of others of their brethren to be slain as they were, and who are no less marked as His by the deaths they die for Him than any others can be : yet the "seal of the living God" may clearly manifest its power in securing preservation of natural life, and the connection seems to imply this here; while thus alone do the two companies of this parenthetic vision,—the Jewish and the Gentile, — supplement each other, as is their evident design. This also to some will not be apparent, for the Gentile multitude are commonly taken to be risen saints in heaven. But the consideration of this must be reserved for the present.

Certainly the enumeration of the tribes speaks for their connection with God's purposes for Israel nationally upon the earth, where her future is. In heaven, as a nation, she has no place, but on earth ever preserves it (Isa. lxvi. 22). And here the connection of both these companies with a series of events on earth is evident. It may be said that the souls under the altar find similarly their place in connection with the seals, and yet are passed from earth: but these are introduced to show the prevalence of persecution, the unchanged enmity to God manifesting itself thus after the first periods of judgment have run their course; while they bring on, as it would seem by their prayers, the crash which follows under the sixth seal.

No *such* connection can be seen here, but the saints here are to be sheltered from the judgments coming on the earth—being themselves on it, an Israelitish company, inferring national revival, significant enough for earth, but not at all for heaven.

Leaving this for the present, we must give our attention to the number so definitely stated, and so earnestly repeated, of this sealed company. The enumeration, so held up before us, and emphasized by repetition, cannot be a point of little consequence. Of each tribe distinctly it is stated that there are twelve thousand sealed. What, then, is the meaning of this number? It is evidently made up of 12 and 10, the latter raised to its third power, the number of government and of responsibility. But we must look at these a little further.

Ten is the measure of responsibility, as in the ten commandments of the law; raised to the third power, it seems to me to be responsibility met in grace with glory; while the number 12 speaks, as I have elsewhere sought to show, of *manifest* government. If I read the meaning right, the two together speak of special place conferred upon this company in connection with the Lamb's government of the earth; and this, it seems to me, is confirmed by other considerations.

That they are not the whole remnant of Israel preserved to be the stock of the millennial nation is evident from the one fact before mentioned, that the tribe of Dan has no place among them, and yet certainly has its place in the restored nation. In Ezekiel (xlviii. 1), Dan has

THE SEALED OF ISRAEL. 77

his portion in the extreme north of the land. Thus the hundred and forty-four thousand here are clearly a special company, and not the whole of the saved people.

But the case of Dan has further instruction for us in this connection; and we shall find it, if we turn back to the blessing of the tribes by Jacob in the end of the book of Genesis. Jacob himself tells us here that he is speaking of what should befall them in the *"last days;"* and it is to these last days plainly that Revelation brings us: so that the propriety of the application cannot be doubted. Let us listen, then, to what the dying patriarch has to say of Dan.

"*Dan shall judge his people as one of the tribes of Israel.* Dan shall be a serpent by the way, an adder in the path, that biteth the horse-heels, so that his rider shall fall backward. *I have waited for Thy salvation, O Lord."*

Abrupt, fragmentary, enigmatic, as the words are, with just this passage of Revelation before us, they startle us by the way in which they seem to meet the questionings which have been awakened by it. We are looking upon a sealed company, "a hundred and forty-four thousand of all the tribes of the children of Israel." But Dan is not found among them! Can this tribe, we ask, have been suffered to drop out of God's chosen earthly family, so as to have no part in the final blessing? The voice from of old answers the question decisively: "*Dan shall judge his people as one of the tribes of Israel.*" No! the Lord's grace prevails over all failure: Dan does not lose his place. It cannot be that a tribe should perish out of the chosen people.

But more,—the company before us, if we have read its numerical stamp aright, is a company having a place of rule under the Lamb in the day of millennial blessing; and among these, assuredly, Dan is *not* found. How the old prophecy comes in here once more with its assurance, "Dan shall *judge his people*"! The staff of judicial authority is not wholly departed; but simply as what is necessary to tribal place he retains it, "as one of the tribes of Israel,"—nothing more.

The patriarch's first words as to Dan imply, then, a low place—if not the lowest place—for Dan, even as his portion in Ezekiel is on the extreme northern border of the land. He retains his place as part of the nation, that is all. And if we naturally ask, Why? the answer is given in what follows :—

"Dan shall be a serpent by the way, an adder in the path, that biteth the horse-heels, so that his rider falleth backward."

Plainly these are characters which associate him in some way with the power of the enemy; for the "serpent," the "adder," speak of this. Jacob's words would show that in the apostasy of the mass of the nation under Antichrist, in the days to which we are here carried, Dan has a more than ordinary place. If the antichrist be, as every thing assures us, a Jew himself, what would be more in accordance with all this than the ancient thought that he will be of Dan?

And here how natural the groan, yet of faith, on the part of the remnant which breaks out in the next words of the prophecy, "I have waited for Thy salvation, O Lord"!

In Gad, therefore, the conflict finds its termination: "A troop shall overcome him, but he shall overcome at the last." Then in Asher and Naphtali the blessing follows, and Joseph and Benjamin show us in whom the blessing is. Upon all this, of course, it would be impossible to dilate now.

But all is confirmatory of the thought of this hundred and forty-four thousand being a special Israelitish company, destined of God to fill a place (but an earthly one,) in connection with the Lord's government of the world in millennial days. We have now to look at the Gentile company in the next vision.

THE PALM-BEARING MULTITUDE. (Rev. vii. 7-17.)

The hundred and forty-four thousand have been sealed before the winds of heaven have been let loose upon the earth. Before the next vision they have spent their violence, the great tribulation is passed, and an innumerable company of people are seen as come out of it. This expression, "the great tribulation," is one that rules in the interpretation of this scene as should be evident. When people simply read, "out of great tribulation," it was natural to think of all the redeemed of all generations as being included here, and the multitude and universality of the throng thus gathered would confirm the idea; but now it ought to be no longer possible. That it is "the *great* tribulation" is even emphasized in the original—"the tribulation, the great one,"—to forbid all generalizing in this way. We are reminded of one specific one, which as thus named we are expected to know; and he who will take Scripture simply will surely find without difficulty the one intended. We have already gone over this ground, and there is scarcely need to remind our readers that the "great tribulation" of which our Lord spoke to His disciples, "such as was not from the beginning of the world to this time, no, nor ever shall be," which is shortened by divine grace, for otherwise "no flesh should be saved," and at the close of which "they shall see the Son of Man coming in the clouds of heaven," must needs be that out of which the multitude before us come.

That the tribulation is thus immediately followed by the coming of the Lord from heaven makes it easier to understand another thing, that their standing before the throne, as the prophet sees them, does not necessitate the thought of their being in heaven. There is no hint of their being raised from the dead, or having died at all. Simply they are "*before* the throne of God, and serve Him day and night in His temple." Here again it is natural to the common habits of thought to suppose that the temple of God must be in heaven, and passages from this very book would doubtless be cited in support of this (chap. xi. 19; xv. 5): these will come naturally before us for consideration in their own place; but here it is sufficient to say that it is not said "in heaven," and that *on earth* there is yet to be a temple, as Ezekiel shows. Isaiah also declares that also of the Gentiles the Lord will "take for priests and Levites" (lxvi. 21).

With this view at least let us look at the scene before us, and see what we can gather more. That they have "white robes" shows simply their acceptance; the palms in their hands speak of rest in victory; their words ascribe their salvation to God and to the Lamb, but they "cry,"—it does not say "sing." The angels and the elders stand "around" the throne; they simply stand "*before*" it.

One of the elders now raises the question with John, "Who are these?" He, unable to say who they can be, refers back the question to the speaker, and he answers it. But note the strangeness of such a question upon the ordinary view, and the greater strangeness of John's inability to answer. Plainly they were a company of saved ones giving praise for their salvation, and if it were the *whole* company, the very naturalness of the thought as accepted by so many would make us wonder at the question about it, still more at the apostle's speechlessness. But he had seen another company in heaven, who still kept their place before his eyes, and who had *sung* the new song, and at least with fuller praise. As to these, no question had been raised at all. It would seem, he might be trusted to make out who these were; and one of these elders was now accosting him! How could he miss the thought that here was a separate class of redeemed ones, and certainly upon a lower footing than those whose rapturous thanksgiving he had heard before?

Accordingly he hears that such is the fact. He is told

THE PALM-BEARING MULTITUDE.

they are those who come out of the great tribulation, and have washed their robes, and made them white in the blood of the Lamb. Not their sufferings have washed their robes white, but the Lamb's blood: and here again, though the expression is peculiar, they are on common ground with saints at all times.

And on this account they are before the throne of God, and serve Him day and night in His temple; (but in the new Jerusalem there is no temple: the "Lord God Almighty and the Lamb are the Temple of it;") and "He that sitteth on the throne shall spread His tabernacle over them." So rightly now the $R.\ V.$, and not, "shall dwell among them." It is like Isaiah (iv. 6), who similarly describes the condition of Jerusalem in the time to which this refers: "And there shall be a tabernacle for a shadow in the day-time from the heat, and for a place of refuge, and for a covert from storm and from rain." How plain that it is as protection and defense, from the words that follow here in Revelation: "They shall hunger no more, neither thirst any more, neither shall the sun strike upon them, nor any heat"! How suited to men still in the world is this assurance!

But it goes on: "For the Lamb which is in the midst of the throne shall be their Shepherd, and shall guide them to fountains of waters of life, and God shall wipe away every tear from their eyes."

Blessed as all this description is, it seems to fall short of the full eternal blessing, and certainly short of what is heavenly. The impression given is of the earth's warfare not yet over, sin and evil not completely banished, but themselves indeed effectually sheltered. The thought of shepherd-care suits this as well as does the tabernacle stretched over them. The thanksgiving expressed also is that of those emerging out of a trial great as that out of which it is said they come, and for whom the joy of deliverance as yet allows little else to be thought of. There is not even a song—and Scripture can be trusted to its least tittle of expression—they "cry with a great voice," but do not "*sing*."

We may well believe, then, that these are the priestly class taken from among the nations of which Isaiah speaks (lxvi. 21). I am aware that it is a matter of dispute whether "I will take of *them* for priests and Levites" is to be referred to the Israelites whom the Gentiles bring back or to the Gentiles who bring them back; but, as Delitzsch well says, "God is here certainly not announcing so simple a thing as that the priests among the returned people should be still priests." He has just declared that the Gentiles "shall bring all your brethren out of all the nations for an offering unto the Lord . . . as the children of Israel bring their offering in a clean vessel unto the house of the Lord." The Gentiles are here, therefore, this "clean vessel;" and being thus cleansed, He further promises as to them, "And of them also will I take for priests and Levites, saith the Lord."

The passages in Isaiah and Revelation mutually confirm each other in this application, and we see who are those honored to serve in the temple of the Lord, as we see also what temple it is in which they serve. All is in perfect harmony, and the multitude of Gentiles stands here in plain analogy with Israel's hundred and forty-four thousand, and upon a similar footing to them. The two together complete the picture of blessing for both Israel and the Gentiles, through the storm which is about to burst upon the earth. Neither group is heavenly; neither is the full number to be saved and enjoy the summer sunshine of millennial days; but they are the sheaf of first-fruits of the harvest beyond, in each case dedicated, therefore, in a peculiar manner to the Lord.

Let us pause here to notice the thought so characteristic of the book of Revelation, book as it is of the throne and of governmental recompense,—of "robes washed and made white in the blood of the Lamb." The figures of Scripture are perfectly definite and absolutely appropriate, never needing apology. Of them, as of all else in it, the words of the Lord are true: "Scripture cannot be broken." On the other hand, they are various, and with meaning in their variations, so that if we are not careful, we may easily force them into contradiction with each other and with the truth.

What, for instance, is the "robe" in which the saint appears before God? It is easy to answer, and absolutely scriptural to quote, "He hath covered me with the robe of *righteousness*" (Isa. lxi. 10). And how beautifully does the "robe" speak of that, by which the shame of our nakedness, which came in through sin, is put away!

But what *is* our righteousness? Here again we have most familiar texts, "This is the name whereby He shall be called, 'The Lord our righteousness'" (Jer. xxiii. 6); "Christ, who is made of God unto us . . . righteousness." And the prodigal's "best robe" reminds us here how the beauty of Christ upon us must transcend far the lustre of angelic garments.

Nevertheless, if we think we have got the one idea of Scripture in this matter, we shall be sorely perplexed when we come to this text in Revelation. Could we wash *this* robe, and make it white in the blood of the Lamb? Assuredly not: it would be impossible to apply this expression, in any way that can be imagined, to this robe, which is Christ.

The Revelation has its own distinct phraseology here, in perfect harmony with the line of truth which it takes up. The robe is still the symbol of righteousness, but in view of the recompense that awaits us, "the fine linen" with which the bride is clothed, "is the righteousnesses— the righteous *deeds*—of the saints" (chap. xix. 8). It is practical righteousness that is in question,—not something wrought by another for us, but wrought by our own hands. It is a completely different thought from that in the Lord's parable, and in no wise contradictory because so different. Assuredly "we shall all be *manifested* before the judgment-seat of Christ, that every one may receive for the things done in the body, whether it be good or bad" (2 Cor. v. 10).

For the saint, indeed, this is not to come *personally* into judgment. That, the Lord has assured us, personally we cannot do (Jno. v. 24, *R. V.*). God can raise no question as to a soul whom He has received, whether He has received him. The matter of reward is entirely distinct from that of personal acceptance; but it has its place. And here comes in this solemn and precious reminder of how the robe needs washing in the blood of the Lamb in order to be white. How else could any thing of ours find approval and recompense? Thus as the apostle tells us in his prayer for Onesiphorus (2 Tim. i. 18), that reward itself is "mercy:" "the Lord grant unto him that he may find *mercy* of the Lord in that day!"

These saints out of the great tribulation know at least that not *by* tribulation, but by the work of Another, can that which is best and holiest in their lives be accepted of God. "*They* have washed their robes." They have renounced the thought of any proper whiteness in their robes save that produced by the blood of the Lamb. On this ground they are as we, and we are as they.

Looking back at these visions now, and their connection with the seals, we see more fully than ever the introductory character the latter have, and how at the same time the seventh seal introduces to the open book itself. The sixth seal is not final judgment, prophetic of it as it may be. It is but as a zephyr compared with the storm-blast, for the winds have not yet been allowed to burst forth as they will. So too the brethren of the fifth-seal martyrs, which are to be slain as they were, have yet to give up their lives. But because the seventh seal, in opening the whole book, brings us face to face with this last and most awful period of the world's history ever to be known, therefore before it is opened, we are summoned apart for the succession of events, to see the gracious purposes which are hidden behind the coming judgments,—to see beyond it, in fact, to the clear blue sky beyond. And we see why these are not seals nor trumpets, but an interruption—a parenthetic instruction, which, coming in the place it does, pushes as it were the seventh seal on to be an eighth section, *itself filling the seventh place.* If numbers have at all significance, we may surely read them here. The seeming disorder becomes beauteous order: the seventh seal fills the eighth place, as introducing to the new condition of things, the earth's last crisis; *the seventh place is filled by that which gives rest to the heart* in God's work accomplished, a sabbatism which no restlessness of man can disturb! Let us too rest in thanksgiving, for these are the ways of God.

PART II.

The Trumpets. (Chap. viii. 2–xi. 18.)

The First Four Trumpets. (Chap. viii. 2–13.)

THE last seal is loosed, and the book of Revelation lies open before us; yet just here it is undoubtedly true that we have reached the most difficult part of the whole. As we go on, we shall find ourselves in the midst of scenes with which the Old-Testament prophets have made us in measure familiar—a part which can be compared in this very prophecy to "a little *open* book." In the seals, we have found also what was more simple by its very breadth and generality. We have here evidently predictions more definite, and yet the application of which may never be made known to us, as they do *not* seem to come into that "open book,"—do not seem to find their place where the Old Testament can shed its light in the same way upon them. Yet we are not left to that mere "private interpretation" which is forbidden us; and it is well to inquire at the beginning, what helps we have to interpretation from other parts of Scripture.

The series of trumpets is septenary, as we know—just as those of the seals and vials are. Not only so, but, as already said, the 7 here becomes, by the interposed vision between the sixth and seventh, in structure, an 8. And in this, the seals are plainly similar; the vials really, though more obscurely.

This naturally invites further comparison; and then at once we perceive that the vials are certainly in other respects also a parallel to the trumpets. In the first of each, the *earth* is affected; in the second, the sea; in the third, the rivers and fountains of waters; in the fourth, the sun; in the fifth, there is darkness; in the sixth, the river Euphrates is the scene: the general resemblance cannot be doubted.

No such resemblance can be traced if we compare the seals, however; though the similarity of structure should yield us something. The structure itself, so definite and plainly numerical, may speak to those who have ears to hear it, and we shall seek to gain from it what we can. But there is a third witness, whose help we shall do well to avail ourselves of, and that is, the historical interpretation, which just here—strangely as it may seem—is at its plainest. There is a very striking and satisfactory agreement among those of the historical school with regard to the fifth and sixth trumpets at least; and the harmony pleads for some substantial truth in what they agree about. We must at all events inquire as to this.

Strictly, according to the structure, the first five verses of this chapter belong to the seventh seal; but for our purpose it is more convenient to connect them with the trumpet-series, which they introduce. The judgments following they show us to be the answer of God to the cry of His people, though in His heart for them before they cry. This is what the order plainly teaches: "And I saw the seven angels which stand before God, and seven trumpets were given unto them." Thus all is prepared of God beforehand; yet He must be inquired of, to do it for them, and therefore we have next the prayers of all the saints ascending up to God. There is now a union of all hearts together: the common distress leads to united prayer; and He who has given special assurance that He will answer the prayer of two or three that unitedly ask of Him, how can He withdraw Himself from such supplication?

But we see another thing,—the action of the angel at the altar of incense: "And another angel came and stood at the altar, having a golden censer; and there was given unto him much incense, that he should offer it with the prayers of all saints upon the golden altar which was before the throne. And the smoke of the incense which came with the prayers of the saints ascended up before God out of the angel's hand." Thus the fragrance of Christ's acceptability gives efficacy to His people's prayers; a thing perfectly familiar to us as Christians, and which scarcely needs interpretation, but which, as pictured for us here, has this element of strangeness in it—the figure of an *angel*-priest. Why, if it be Christ who of necessity must take this place, why is He shown us as an angel? "For He taketh not hold of angels, but of the seed of Abraham He taketh hold. Wherefore in all things it behoved him to be made *like unto His brethren*, that He might be a merciful and faithful High-Priest in things pertaining to God." (Heb. ii. 16, 17.) If, then, to be the priest men need, He must be made like to men, why does He appear here as an angel, and not as a man?

There is no need for doubt that what has been answered by many is the true explanation, and that the angel-figure here speaks of personal distance still from those for whom yet He intercedes. We have many like examples in Scripture, and one which is of special interest in this connection. Those who appear in the eighteenth of Genesis as "men" to Abraham, go on to Sodom as "angels" in the nineteenth. They go there to deliver Lot, but are not able to show him the intimacy which they show to Abraham. "Just man" as he is, and "vexed with the filthy conversation of the wicked," he is yet one "saved so as through the fire." Found, not in his tent-door at Mamre, but in the "gate of Sodom," he is one of those righteous men but in an evil place, for whom Abraham intercedes with God, and when delivered, it is said of him that "God *remembered Abraham*, and sent Lot out of the midst of the overthrow, when He overthrew the cities in the midst of which Lot dwelt." (Gen. xix. 29.)

Lot may thus fitly represent this very remnant of Israel at the last, whose prayers are here coming up before God; who have had opportunity to have known the Church's pilgrim path, but have refused it, and to whom Christ is even yet a stranger, though interceding for them. If we remember the priestly character of the heavenly elders in the fifth chapter here, and "their vials full of odors, which are the prayers of saints" (*v*. 8) we may see further resemblance between these pictures so far apart. And how touching is it to see how in the troubles which encompass Lot in Sodom, these angels begin to appear as "men" again! (Gen. xix. 10, 12, 16.) Sweet grace of God, shining out in the very midst of the trial from which it could not, because of our need of it, exempt us!

Thus the angel-priest, in its very incongruity of thought, exactly suits the place in which we find it. It is "the time of Jacob's trouble,"—needed, because he is yet *Jacob*, but out of which he shall be delivered when its work is once accomplished. (Jer. xxx. 7.) Thus their prayers offered are heard; and, as inheriting on the earth,

THE FIRST FOUR TRUMPETS.

the answer to them involves the purging of the earth. "And the angel took the censer, and filled it with fire of the altar, and cast it unto the earth; and there were voices and thunderings and lightnings, and an earthquake. And the seven angels which had the seven trumpets prepared themselves to sound."

This fire, because from the altar, some have difficulty in believing to be judgment. They remember how a live coal from the altar purged Isaiah's lips, and cannot see how that which has fed upon the sacrifice can be any longer wrath against men. But this is easily answered; for while, where the heart turns to God, this is certainly true, it is in no wise true for those who do not turn. For them, there is no sacrifice that avails; rather it pleads *against* its rejecters: the wrath of God against sin has not been set aside, but demonstrated an awful reality by the cross; and where the precious blood has not cleansed from sin, the wrath of God rests only the more heavily on those who slight it. The signs of judgment following are therefore in perfect keeping with the fact that it is the fire of the altar that evokes them, as they are with their being the answer to the prayers of a people who cry (with the saints under the fifth seal, or with the widow to whom the Lord compares them,), "Avenge me of mine adversary." (Luke xviii. 3.)

Every thing finds its place when once we are in the track of the divine thoughts; and in all this there is no difficulty when we have learnt the period to which it applies. It is a suited introduction to the trumpets which follow, and in which, according to the old institution (Num. x. 9), God Himself now declares Himself in behalf of His people, and against their enemies.

There is much more difficulty when we come to consider separately the trumpets themselves.

"And the first sounded, and there followed hail and fire, mingled with blood, and they were cast upon the earth: and the third part of the earth was burnt up, and the third part of the trees was burnt up, and all green grass was burnt up."

Hail with fire we find in other parts of Scripture, as in nature also. It is one of the most solemn figures of the divine judgment which nature furnishes. It was one of the plagues of Egypt. In the eighteenth psalm it is found connected with similar judgment. "The Lord also thundered in the heavens, and the Highest gave His voice,—hailstones and coals of fire." Electricity and hail are products of the same cause, a mass of heated air saturated with vapor, rising to a higher level, and meeting the check of a cold current. It is a product of cold, the withdrawal of heat, as darkness is the absence of light; and light and heat, cold and darkness, are akin to one another. Cold stands (with darkness) for the withdrawal of God, as fire (which is both heat and light) for the glow of His presence, which, as against sin, is wrath. And both these things can consist together, however they may seem contradictory—"hailstones and coals of fire" be poured out together. God's forsaking is in anger necessarily, and thus what would be a ministry of refreshment is turned into a storm of judgment. There is a concord of contraries against those that cast off God; as for those who love Him, all things work together for good.

The blood mingled is of course a sign of death—a violent death,—and shows the deadly character of this visitation, by which a third part of the prophetic earth is desolated, a third part of the trees burnt up, and prosperity (if the green grass implies that,) every-where destroyed.

This judgment seems to affect, therefore, especially the lower ranks of the people, though, as necessarily would be the case, many of the higher also; but it does not affect especially those in authority. They have not escaped, as we have seen, in the general convulsion under the sixth seal;—nay, the heavens fleeing away might seem to intimate that the very possibility of true government

THE FIRST FOUR TRUMPETS. 91

was departed. Yet this might be while in fact govern·
ments go on, and we find in what follows here that they
do go on, although never really recovering themselves.
Under this trumpet now begins, as it would seem, what
shall really cause them to collapse. A people impover-
ished by that which spares the governing classes, who
does not realize the danger to these of such a state of
things? And the second trumpet seems to show us in
reality what we might anticipate to grow out of this.

"And the second angel sounded, and as it were a great
mountain, burning with fire, was cast into the sea; and the
third part of the sea became blood; and the third part of
the creatures which were in the sea and had life died;
and the third part of the ships were destroyed."

The comparison of Babylon to such a mountain (Jer.
li. 25) may put us in the track of the meaning here. It
is a power mighty, firmly seated and exalted, yet full of
volcanic forces in conflict, by which not only her own
bowels shall be torn out, but ruin spread around. This
cast into the sea of the nations,—already in commotion,
as the "sea" implies—produces death and disaster beyond
that of the preceding trumpet. Human life is more
directly attacked by it. Such a state of eruption was in
France at the end of the last century, and may well
illustrate (as others have suggested) what seems intended.
The fierce outburst of revolt against all forms of mon-
archy, the fruit of centuries of insolent tyranny under
which men had been crushed, set Europe in convulsion.
History is full of such portents of that which shall be, and
we do well to take heed to them. Especially as the end
approaches may we expect to find it so: there is growth
on to and preparation for that which at last takes those
who have not received the warning by surprise.

The third part of the ships being destroyed would
seem naturally to imply the destruction of commerce to
this extent, the intercourse between the nations necessarily affected by the reign of terror around.

The third trumpet sounds, and a star falls from heaven, burning like a torch. "And it fell upon the third part of the rivers, and upon the fountains of waters. And the name of the star is called Wormwood: and the third part of the waters became wormwood; and many men died of the waters, because they were made bitter."

The heavens are the sphere of government, whether civil or spiritual; a ruler of either kind might be here indicated therefore, and the historical application is in general to Attila, king of the Huns; yet the fall from heaven, the poisoning of the sources of refreshment, as well as the parallel, if not the deeper, connection with the sixth trumpet, seem to point much more strongly to an apostate teacher, by whose fall the springs of spiritual truth should be embittered, causing men to perish. With all the misery that has hitherto been depicted as coming upon men under these apocalyptic symbols, we have not before had any clear intimation of this, which we know, however, to be a principal ingredient in the full cup of bitterness which will then be meted out to men. Because they have not received the love of the truth, that they might be saved, God will send them strong delusion, that they may believe a lie; and here would seem to be the beginning of this.

In the French revolution at the end of the last century, the revolt against the existing governments linked itself with an uprise against Christianity; and the socialistic and anarchical movements which have followed, with however little present success, are uniformly allied with infidel and atheistic avowals as extreme as any of that time. Russian "nihilism" fulfills its name in demanding "No law, no religion—*nihil!*" and as the first thing, "Tear out of your hearts the belief in the existence of God." Here is forestalled the one "who opposeth and exalteth himself above all that is called God, or that is worshiped;" nor is it a contradiction to this that one with such nihilism on his standard should exalt himself

THE FIRST FOUR TRUMPETS. 93

into the place of God: the atheist Comte devised for his followers a new worship, with forms borrowed from Rome, and a peremptory spirit, which have gained for it from a noted infidel of the day the title of "Catholicism *minus* Christianity." This was his proposition, as stated by himself: "The re-organization of human society, without God or king, through the systematic worship of humanity."

This was a delirium! True, but such dreams will come again, as the Word of God declares, in that fever of the world to which, with its quick pulse now, it is fast approaching. Apostasy is written already upon what men would fain have the dawn of a new day, and the being who has raised himself from the chattering ape to link the lightning to his chariot of progress, what shall stay him now? These are the words from the lips of Truth itself: "I am come in My Father's name, and ye receive Me not; if another shall come in his own name, him ye will receive."

We have already considered in a measure the doctrine of a personal antichrist yet to come, and we shall be repeatedly recalled to the consideration of it as we go on with Revelation. Here it is only the place to say that his birthplace in the book seems to be under this third seal, though his descent more strictly than his rise. He is born of apostasy, as the second epistle to the Thessalonians (chap. ii. 3) would lead us to anticipate.

And now, under the fourth trumpet, a scene occurs which may be compared with that under the sixth seal, but which in the comparison reveals important differences. Then, a convulsion affected (as would appear) the whole earth: now, it is only the governing powers that are affected by it; and that, not everywhere, but a third part of the sun and of the moon and of the stars, so that the day shines not for a third part of it, and the night likewise. These last words in connection with the similar limitation to a third part in the preceding seals, seem plain enough. The day does not shine in a third part of the sphere of its dominion, nor the night (in its moon and stars) either. Certainly this would not be the natural result of the darkening of a third part of sun and moon, and intimates to us that we have not here a literal phenomenon such as is represented, but figures of other things. Royal or imperial authority has collapsed, with its train of satellites, within such limits as a "third part" may designate; and with this, the first series of the trumpets ends. As ordinarily in these septenary series, the last three are cut off from these first four, which have a certain oneness of application, as the use of this "third part" employed in them throughout also would imply; for the next trumpet has no intimation of this kind. The sixth has it again, but the seventh refuses all such limitation.

The meaning of this trumpet, then, is simple; but its proper significance must be gained from its connection with the series of which it forms a part, and indeed with any prophecies elsewhere which by comparison may throw light upon it.

In general, also, the historical application attains here a consistency which claims attention; and that there is some substantial truth in it (though not the full truth) there is no need to doubt. The minds of so many of the Lord's people as have explored the book of Revelation by this light have not been left so utterly dark and untaught of the Spirit as to have allowed them to wander utterly astray. Scripture is larger in compass than we think, and this is by no means the only part of prophecy in which a certain fulfillment has anticipated and, as it were, typified the final and exhaustive one. In this very book, those who receive the addresses to the seven churches as prophetic of the history of the professing church at large can surely not deny, or seek to deny, a primary application to churches actually existing in the apostle's day. And here the foundation of the historical interpretation is already laid. The stream of prophecy in the seals and trumpets in this case naturally has its germinant fulfillment from that very time; and if we refuse it, we refuse not only the comfort we should gain from seeing the Lord's control of the whole course of man's spiritual history for so many centuries, but also lose for the final application a guiding clue with which the grace of God has furnished us. That it is not a full, exhaustive fulfillment will not in this case either affect its being *a* fulfillment. It will be in perfect keeping with its place that it shall not be a complete one; for were it this, no room for the final one would be left.

Now the general interpretation of the first four trumpets applies them to the breaking up of the Roman empire by the barbarian inroads of Goths, Vandals, and Huns, until its final extinction in the west by the hands of Odoacer. The eastern half survived to a latter day, but it was henceforth Grecian rather than Roman, Rome itself, with all that constituted its greatness,—nay, its being, in the days of its ancient glory, having departed from it. This application agrees with the unity of these trumpets, while it gives a sufficient reason for the series coming to an end, and the fifth and sixth trumpets turning now to judgments upon the eastern half, by the hands of Saracen and Turk, the seventh being in its character universal. The Roman empire, let us remember, as the last empire of Daniel's visions, and that which existed in the Lord's lifetime upon earth, and by the authority of which He was crucified, stands as the representative of the world-power in its rebellion against God. (Comp. Ps. ii. with Acts iv. 25–28.) No wonder, therefore, if its history should be given under these war-trumpets, the last of which gives the full victory of Christ over all the opposition.

It is consistent with this that Satan in the twelfth chapter of this book should as the dragon be pictured with the seven heads and ten horns of the Roman beast. He is the spiritual prince of this world, and in this way is clothed with the power of the world, which we see here again is *Roman*.

So again, the "earth," which both in Greek and Hebrew may mean "land," and is often by no means the equivalent of the world, seems almost constantly in these prophecies, till the final one, to be the Roman earth, the territory of the Roman empire in its widest, and of which the western part seems to be the "third part" mentioned in the trumpets. As to this third part, Mr. Elliott urges, that during the period of these early trumpets, "the Roman world was, in fact, divided into three parts,* viz., the *Eastern* (Asia Minor, Syria, Arabia, Egypt); the *Central* (Mœsia, Greece, Illyricum, Rhœtia); the *Western* (Italy, Gaul, Britain, Spain, north-western Africa); and that the third, or western, part was destroyed."

Others would make the "third part" equivalent to the territory peculiar to the third beast of Daniel, or the Greek empire; but this seems certainly not the truth: for in this case, according to the historical interpretation, the end of the *eastern* empire must be found under the fourth trumpet, whereas the fifth trumpet goes back before this, to introduce the Saracens!

Of all interpretations, that only seems consistent which applies the "third part" to the western part of the Roman earth, and in this way the term may have a further significance, as that part in which the Roman empire is yet to revive again, as it will revive for judgment in the latter days,—the "third" being very often connected in Scripture, as is well known, with the thought of resurrection.

The Roman empire has indeed long been extinct, both in the west and in the east, and it is of this very extinction that the historical interpretation of the trumpets speaks, yet the voice of prophecy clearly assures us that it must be existing at the time of the end, when, because of the words of the little horn, judgment comes down upon it.

---
* I quote from the American edition of Lange on Revelation, p. 201.

THE FIRST FOUR TRUMPETS. 97

(Dan. vii. 11.) The nineteenth chapter of this book unites with the book of Daniel in this testimony: for it is when the Lord appears that the beast is seen, along with the kings of the earth, arrayed in opposition against Him. Thus it is plain that the Roman empire must be existent at the end. It has yet, therefore, to rise again, and in the thirteenth chapter we see it, in fact, rising out of the sea: while in the seventeenth, where the woman Babylon has her seat upon it, it is said, "The beast that thou sawest was, and is not, and shall ascend out of the bottomless pit, and go into perdition." (*v.* 8.) So it is called, "The beast that was, and is not, and shall come." (*v.* 8., *R. V.*)

Nothing can be much plainer than the fact that the Roman empire will revive again.

But not only so; it is also declared by the same sure Word that it will revive to be smitten again in one of its heads, and apparently to death, yet its wound is healed and it lives. (chap. xiii 3, 12, 14.) It is after this that it becomes idolatrous, as Daniel has intimated to us it will, and all the world wonders after it. (*vv.* 3, 8, 12.) CHAP. 13 V. V.

It is not yet the place to go fully into this, but so much is clear as enables us to see how the historical interpretation of these trumpets points, or may point, to a future fulfillment of them. One other thing which the book of Revelation notes will make more complete our means of interpretation.

The beast, as seen in Revelation, has seven heads, or kings; and these are successive rulers—or forms of rule —over the empire: for "five," says the angel, "are fallen, and one is, and another is yet to come; and when he cometh, he must continue a *short* space." The heads, then, in this primary view, are seven, but five had passed away —commentators quote them from Livy—the sixth, the imperial power, existed at that time: the seventh was wholly future, and, in contrast with the long continuance of the sixth, would continue only a short space.

But there is an eighth head, and the beast himself is

this. The last statement has been supposed to mean that the head exercised the whole authority of the empire; but it would seem nothing strange for the head of empire to exercise imperial authority. Does it not rather mean that the beast that is seen all through these chapters is the beast of this eighth head?

But the seventh head, where does it come in? There are some things that would seem to give us help with regard to this. For the empire plainly collapsed under its sixth head, and the seventh could not be until the empire again existed. There are questions here that have to be settled with the historical interpretation; but in the meantime the course of the trumpets as we have already followed it, confirmed by their historical interpretation also, would suggest that we have in them, and indeed from the commencement of the seals, the history of the seventh head. The rider upon the white horse, to whom a crown is given, may well be the person under whom the empire is at first re-established. And of such an one Napoleon, though not (as some have thought) the seventh head himself, may be well the foreshadow. The sixth seal does not point to his overthrow: it is a wider, temporary convulsion which affects all classes—high and low together; and in the pause that follows, they would seem to recover themselves. The trumpets begin, however, at once to threaten overthrow. The very escape of the governing classes under the first trumpet seems to prepare the way for the outburst under the second, which is an eruption from beneath,—fierce with passionate revolt; to which is added, under the third, apostasy, the giving up of the restraint of divine government, soon to grow into the last, worst form of Christianity according to Satan— Antichrist: the opposition to incarnate Deity of deified humanity.

The result is, under the fourth trumpet, as it would appear, the imperial power smitten, the seventh head wounded to death, and with it the recently established empire overthrown beyond mere human power to revive again. But this brings in the help of one mightier than man—the awful power of Satan, working with an energy proportionate to the shortness of the time which is now his. The beast arises out of the abyss, its deadly wound is healed; the dragon gives him his power and throne and great authority; and all the world wonders and worships. (chap. xiii. 2–4.)

Then indeed it is "Woe! woe! woe! to the inhabiters of the earth."

THE FIRST WOE. (Chap. ix. 1–12.)

AT the sound of the fifth trumpet a star is seen, not to fall, as the common version puts it, but already fallen from heaven to earth. This seems naturally to connect thus with the apostasy under the third trumpet, nor is it likely that the apostasy of any other should be as noteworthy as his whose course is recorded here. At all events, it is an apostate, surely, that is before us, and to him is committed "the key of the abyss."

The force of the words have first of all to be considered. A "pit" is in the Old Testament often a synonym for a dungeon, and every thing unites to show this to be the meaning here; while the "abyss" is not other than the pit itself, but only a further definition of it *—the dungeon which is the abyss. So the demons pray that they may not be sent into the *deep*, or "abyss" (Luke viii. 31), and Satan is, in the twentieth chapter, shut up there. In the Old-Testament parallel to the same in Revelation, it is said, "They shall be gathered together as prisoners are gathered in the pit, and shall be shut up in prison." (Isa. xxiv. 22.) Here the abyss is the "pit," or prison, clearly. The key is used in this place as in the later one—here, the "key of the pit of the abyss;" there, simply "the key of the abyss."

The abyss is not, however, "hell"—the "lake of fire,"

---
* The genitive of apposition, as Jno. ii. 21, "the temple of His body."

—as we may see by the fact that it is, in one passage (Rom. x. 7), used in connection with the Lord: "Who shall descend into the deep (the abyss)?—that is, to bring up Christ again from the dead." Here, as the heavens are inaccessible to man for height, so is the abyss for depth. The literal meaning ("bottomless") must not be pressed, as our own use of the word shows, and the Greek was similar ; the Septuagint use it for the "deep" upon which darkness rested on the first day.

The connection of the "pit" with the state of the dead in the Old Testament is similar to that of the "abyss" here in the New. We have this again in Revelation, where the "beast," in its last phase, is said to come up out of the abyss. This seems naturally to refer to the wounding to death, and revival (chap. xiii. 3, 12, 14). Some have even contended, seeing the identification of the beast (the empire) with its last head (chap. xvii. 11), for the literal resurrection of a person in this case; but this is only a wild extravagance: for resurrection literally could only be from God, and the beast in its last form is wholly under the power of Satan. (xiii. 1, 2). The rising up out of the abyss is figurative, therefore, as the beast itself is; and indeed the use of the word seems figurative throughout.

Now Christ has "the keys of hades and of death" (chap. i. 18); and it is not to be imagined that He should give up into the hand of an apostate, whether man or spirit, any portion of His own authority. We must not think, therefore, (as has been done,) of a literal opening of hades, and an irruption of the spirits of the lost upon the earth. Fancies like these easily gain ascendency over a certain class of minds; and yet who could seriously maintain such an outbreak of wickedness on the part of those shut up, like the rich man in hades, to await judgment? Were it so, there would be "deeds done" out of the body, as well as "in the body," to give account of in the day of judgment. But, in fact, the locusts are not said even to come out of the pit. Nothing is said to come out of it but the smoke which darkens the sun and air; and out of the *smoke* the locusts come. It may be natural to think that, after all, they cannot be bred of the smoke, and that they must come with the smoke out of the pit; but naturalistic interpretations may easily deceive us, where the spiritual sense is the whole matter, and for the spiritual meaning there is no difficulty. The smoke is not, as in other places, the smoke of torment, but the fumes of malign spiritual influences which darken the air and the supreme source of light itself. Out of this darkness we can easily understand the locusts to be bred.

It is quite in accordance with their origin that their power should be represented as that of the scorpions of the earth—that is, in their poisonous sting—and their distinction from natural locusts is seen in this, that they do not touch the locusts' food, but are a plague only upon men, and these the unsealed. Remembering that it is in Israel that the sealing is found, the inference seems just that these unsealed ones are Israelites, and the sphere of this plague is in the east. They do not kill—as, in general, the scorpion does not,—but inflict torment to which death is preferable; and their power lasts five months.

We next find them pictured as warriors—a military power subordinated to what is their grand interest and aim, the propagation of poisonous falsehood. Thus "the shapes of the locusts were like horses prepared unto battle;" and, as in the certainty of triumph beforehand, "upon their heads were as it were crowns like gold." Little matter of real triumph had they, as the limiting words here show. "Their faces were as faces of men" also,—they had the dignity and apparent independence of such; while yet "they had hair as the hair of women," being in the fullest subjection to the dark and dreadful power that ruled over them. "Their teeth as the teeth of lions" show the savage, tenacious grip with which they can hold their prey; their breastplates of iron, perhaps, the fence of a hardened conscience; the sound of their wings, like that of the locust-hosts they resemble, conveys the hopeless terror which they inspire. Finally, we are again told of their scorpion-stings, and their power to hurt men five months.

They have a king over them—the angel of the abyss, whose name is given, almost exactly the same in meaning, in Hebrew and in Greek. The use of the Hebrew unites, with other indications we have had, to assure us that it is upon Israel that this woe comes, while the Greek no less plainly indicates that the angel here has also to do with the Gentiles: according to both, he is the "destroyer;" and it is natural to think of Satan in such connections, while it seems *not* probable that the angel of the abyss is the same person with the fallen star.

The historical application in this case is one in which there is great unanimity among interpreters. They apply it to Mohammed, and the Saracens, whose astonishing successes were manifestly gained under the inspiration of a false religion. They came in swarms from the very country of the locusts, and their turbaned heads with men's beards and women's hair, their cuirasses, the sparing of the trees and corn, and even of life where there was submission, with their time of prevalence, according to the year-day reckoning, one hundred and fifty years,— all these things have been pointed out as fulfillment of the vision. It has been objected, on the other hand, that such points as these are below the dignity of Scripture, and that the terms are moral. While this is surely true if we think of the full intention, it is to be considered, on the other hand, whether God does not allow and intend oftentimes a correspondence between such outward things and what is deeper, just as the face of a man may be a real index to his spirit. Just *because* they are external, they are well fitted to strike the imagination; and the parable is, as we know, a very common method of instruction every where in Scripture. Thus God would open our eyes to see what is indeed all around us; and to stop at what is external, or to ignore it, is alike an error.

In any case, and for reasons which we have already considered, we cannot take this Saracenic scourge as any complete fulfillment of the locust-vision. Nor can we, on the other hand, connect it as fully and certainly with other prophecy as would be necessary for very clear interpretation. What seems indicated, however, with regard to its final fulfillment in a time yet to come, is the rise and propagation of that delusion to which we know both the mass of mere Christian profession and of the unbelieving Jews will in the end surrender themselves. (2 Thess. ii.) The antichrist of that time will be, there is little doubt, both an apostate from Christianity and from the faith of his Jewish fathers (Dan. xi. 37); and his apostasy will remove (under divine permission) the present restraint upon the power of evil. It will be as if the abyss had opened its mouth to darken the light of heaven; a mist of confusion will roll in upon men's minds, which will under satanic influence soon find definite expression in forms of blasphemy and a host of armed adherents ready to force upon others the doctrines of the pit. As has been said, it is apparently with Israel that this trumpet has to do, but yet the Greek name of the leader seems to speak also of the connection with the Gentiles. If the application here made be the true one, then we know that the "wicked one" will not be a Jewish false Christ merely, but will also head the apostasy of Christendom. In this sense also it may be that the "beast" under its last head—the revived Roman empire—is said to come up out of the abyss, its actual revival being due to the dark and dreadful power which is presented to us here,—so exceeding in malignity all that has preceded it, that its advent is called, in the language of inspiration, "the first woe."

The Sixth Trumpet. (Chap. ix. 12–21.)

In these trumpet-judgments we are, as has been already seen, traversing some of the most difficult parts of the book of New-Testament prophecy. This is owing largely to the fact that the link with the Old Testament seems very much to fail us, and thus the great rule for interpretation which Peter gives us can be acted on only with proportionate difficulty. Moreover, in the case of symbols such as we have before us, the application is of the greatest importance to the interpretation, and the application is just the fitting of the individual prophecy into the prophetic whole. We have need, therefore, to look carefully, and to speak with a caution corresponding to the difficulty.

A certain connection of the trumpets among themselves, however, we have been able to trace, and this we should expect still to discover, every fresh step in this confirming the past and gaining for itself thus greater assurance. Moreover, the general teaching of prophecy will assist and control our thoughts, although we may be unable to show the relation to each other of single predictions, such as we find, for instance, in comparing the fourth beast of Daniel with the first of Revelation.

A voice from the horns of the golden altar brings on the second woe. It is natural at first sight to connect this with the opening of the eighth chapter, and to see in it an answer to the prayers of the saints with which the incense of the altar is offered up. But this view becomes less satisfactory as we consider it, if only for the reason that the *whole* of the seven trumpets are in answer to the prayers of the saints, as we have seen, and to make the sixth trumpet specifically this would seem in contradiction. Besides, a voice from the horns of the altar, or even from the altar, would scarcely convey the thought of an answer to the prayers that came up from the altar. The horns too were not in any special relation to the offering of incense, but were for the blood of atonement, which was put upon them either to make atonement for the altar itself, or for the sin of the high-priest or of the congregation of Israel. A voice of judgment from these horns,—still more emphatic if we read, as it seems we should do, "one voice from the four horns,"—so different from the usual pleading in behalf of the sinner, speaks of profanation of the altar, or of guilt for which no atonement could be found; and, one would say, of such guilt resting upon the professed people of God, whether this were Israel or that Christendom which Israel often pictures.

If with this thought in our mind we look back to what has taken place under the last trumpet, there seems at once a very distinct connection. If the rise of Antichrist be indeed what is represented there, then we can see how the horns of the altar, from which he has caused sacrifice and oblation to cease (Dan. ix. 27), should call for judgment upon himself and those who have followed him, whether Jews or Gentiles. In the passage just quoted from Daniel it is added, "And because of the wing of abominations there shall be a desolator." In the sixth trumpet we have just such a desolator.

The Euphrates was the boundary of the old Roman empire, and there the four angels are "bound"—"restrained," it may be, by the power of the empire itself, until, having risen up against God, their own hands have thrown down the barrier, and the hordes from without enter upon their mission to "slay the third part of men," a term which we have seen as probably indicating the revived Roman empire. Here, too, is the seat of the beast's supremacy and of the power of Antichrist. Thus there seems real accordance in these several particulars; and in this way the trumpet-judgments give us a glance over the prophetic field, if brief, yet complete, as otherwise they would not appear to be. Moreover, when we turn to the thirty-eighth and thirty-ninth chapters of

Ezekiel to find the desolator of the last days (chap. xxxviii. 17), we find in fact the full array of nations from the other side of the Euphrates pouring in upon the land of Israel, while the connection of that land with Antichrist and with the Roman empire is plainly shown us in Daniel and in Revelation alike. If the Euphrates be the boundary of the empire, it is also Israel's as declared by God, and the two are already thus far identified: their connection spiritually and politically we shall have fully before us in the more detailed prophecy to come.

But why *four* angels? and what do they symbolize? The restraint under which they were marks them sufficiently as opposing powers, and would exclude the thought of *holy* angels; nor is it probable that they are literal angels at all. They would seem representative powers, and in the historical application have been taken to refer to the fourfold division of the old Turkish empire into four kingdoms prior to the attack upon the empire of the East. If such an interpretation is to be made in reference to the final fulfillment, then it is noteworthy that "Gog, of the land of Magog, prince of Rosh, Meshech, and Tubal,"—as the *R.V.*, with most commentators, reads it now,—gives (under one head, indeed,) *four* separate powers as principal associates in this latter-day irruption. Others there are, but coming behind and apart, as in their train. I mention this for what it may be worth. It is at least a possible application, and therefore not unworthy of serious consideration, while it does not exclude a deeper and more penetrative meaning.

The angels are prepared for *the* hour and day and month and year, that they might slay the third part of men. The immense hosts, two hundred millions in number, are perfectly in the hand of a Master,—time, work, and limit carefully apportioned by eternal Wisdom, the evil in its fullest development servant to the good. The horses seem to be of chief importance, and are most dwelt upon, though their riders are first described, but only as to their "breast-plates of fire and hyacinth and brimstone." These answer to the "fire and *smoke* and brimstone" out of the horses' mouths: divine judgment of which they are the instruments making them thus invincible while their work is being done. The horses have heads like lions; destruction comes with an open front— the judgment of God: so that the human hands that direct it are of the less consequence,—divine wrath is sure to find its executioners.

God's judgment is foremost in this infliction, but there is also Satan's power in it: the horses' tails are like serpents, and have heads, and with these they do hurt. Poisonous falsehood characterizes this time when men are given up to believe a lie. Death, physical and spiritual, are in league together, and the destruction is terrible; but those that escape are not delivered from their sins, which, as we see, are, in the main, idolatrous worship, with things that naturally issue out of this. The genealogy of evil is as recorded in the first of Romans: the forsaking of God leads to all other wickedness; but here it is where His full truth has been rejected, and the consequences are so much the more terrible and disastrous.

The Little Open Book. (Chap. x.)

WE have already seen that in the trumpets, as in the seals, there is a gap, filled up with a vision, between the sixth and seventh, so as to make the seventh structurally an eighth section. This corresponds, moreover, to the meaning; for the seventh trumpet introduces the kingdom of Christ on earth, which, although the third and final woe upon the dwellers on the earth, is on the other hand the beginning of a new condition, and an eternal one. With this octave a chord is struck which vibrates through the universe.

The interposed vision is in both series, therefore, a *seventh*, with a meaning corresponding to the number of perfection. At least, so it is in the series of the seals, and we may be sure we shall find no failure in this case: failure in the book of God, even in the minutest point,—our Lord's "jot or tittle,"—is an impossibility. Nothing is more beautiful of its kind than the way in which all this prophetic history yields itself to the hand that works in all and controls all: thank God, we know *whose* hand.

But the vision of the trumpet-series is very unlike that of the seals, and its burden of sorrow different indeed from that sweet inlet into beatific rest. We shall find, however, that it vindicates its position none the less. As in the work, so in the word of God, with a substantial unity, there is yet a wonderful variety, never a mere repetition, which would imply that God had exhausted Himself. As you cannot find two leaves in a forest just alike, so you cannot find two passages of Scripture that are just alike, when they are carefully and intelligently considered. The right use of parallel passages must take in the consideration of the diversity and unity alike.

In the vision before us there is first of all seen the descent of a strong angel from heaven. As yet, no descent of this kind has been seen. In the corresponding vision in the seal-series, an angel ascends from the east, but here he descends, and from heaven. A more positive direct action of heaven upon the earth is implied, power acting, though not yet the *great* power under the seventh trumpet when the kingdom of Christ is come. This being, apparently angelic, is "clothed with a cloud,"—a vail about him, which would seem to indicate a mystery either as to his person or his ways. It does not say "*the* cloud," —what Israel saw as the sign of the presence of the Lord,—otherwise there could be no doubt as to who was here: yet in His actions presently He is revealed to faith as truly what the cloud intimates. It is Christ acting as Jehovah, though yet personally hidden, and in behalf of Israel, among whom the angel of Jehovah walked thus appareled. It is only the cloud; the brightness which is yet there has not shone forth : faith has to penetrate the cloud to enter the Presence-chamber : yet is He there, and in a form that intimates His remembrance of the covenant of old, and on His own part some correspondent action.

So also the rainbow (which we last saw round the throne of God) encircles His head. Joy is coming after sorrow, refreshing after storm, the display of God's blessed attributes at last, though in that which passes, a glory that endureth. And this is coming nearer now, in Him who descends to earth. But His face is as the sun : there indeed we see Him ; who else has such a face ? In our sky there are not two *suns:* our orbit is a circle, not an ellipse.

His face is above the cloud with which He is encircled: heaven knows Him for what He is ; the earth not yet ; though on the earth may be those who are in heaven's secret. But His feet are like pillars of fire, and these are what are first in contact with the earth, the indication of ways which are in divine holiness, necessarily, therefore, in judgment, while the earth mutters and grows dark with rebellion.

Now we have what reveals to us whereto we have arrived : "And he had in his hand a little book opened." The seventh seal opens a book which had been seen in heaven ; the seventh section here shows us another book now open, but a *little* book. It had not the scope and fullness of the other : we hear nothing of how the writing fills up and overflows the page. It is a little book which has been till now shut up, but is no longer shut up,— a book too whose contents, evidently connected with the action of the angel here, has to do with the earth simply, not with heaven also, as the seven-sealed book has. We have in this what should lead us to what the book is ; for the characteristic of Old-Testament prophecy is just this, that it opens to us the earthly, not the heavenly things. Its promises are *Israel's*, the earthly people (Rom. ix. 4), and it deals fully with the millennial kingdom, and the convulsions which are its birth-throes. Beyond the millennium, except in that brief reference to the new heavens and earth to which Peter refers, it does not go; and the "new heavens" are not our blessed portion, but the *earth*-heavens, as Peter very distinctly shows. There is no heavenly city there in prospect; there is no rule over the earth on the part of Christ's co-heirs, such as we have already found in the song of Revelation. All this the Christian revelation adds to the Old Testament; while in Revelation the millennium is passed over with the briefest notice. Here for the first time indeed we get its limits set, and see how short it is, while the main thing dwelt upon as to it is with whom shall be filled those thrones which Daniel sees "placed," but sees not the occupants (chap. vii. 9, *R.V.*). Thus it is plain how the book of Old-Testament prophecy is, comparatively with the New, "a *little* book."

It is fully owned and maintained that when we look, with the aid of the New Testament, beyond the letter, we can find more than this. Types there are and shadows, and that every where, in prophecy as well as history, of greater things. Earth itself and earthly things may be and are symbols of heaven and the heavenly. The summer reviving out of winter speaks of resurrection; the very food we feed on preaches life through death. And so more evidently the Old Testament: for Revelation, completing the cycle of the divine testimony, brings us back to paradise, as type of a better one; and the latest unfolding of what had been for ages hidden, shows us in Adam and his Eve Christ and the Church.

But this manifestly leaves untouched the sense in which Old-Testament prophecy may be styled "a little book." The application here is also easy. For in fact the Old-Testament prophecy as to the earth has been for long a thing waiting for that fulfillment which shall manifest and illumine it. Israel outcast from her land, upon whom the blessing of the earth waits, all connected with this waits. We may see now, indeed, as in some measure we see their faces set once more toward their land, that other things also are arranging themselves preparatory to the final accomplishment. But yet the proper fulfillment of them is not really begun.

In the meanwhile, though the Lord is fulfilling His purposes of grace, and taking out from among the Gentiles a people for His name, as to the earth, it is "man's day." (1 Cor. iv. 3, *marg.*) When He shall have completed this, and having gathered the heavenly saints to heaven, shall put to His hand in order to bring in the blessing for the earth, then the day of *the Lord* will begin in necessary judgment, that the inhabitants of the world may learn righteousness. (Is. xxvi. 9.) This *day* of the Lord begins, therefore, before the *appearing* of the Lord, for which it prepares the way : the dawn of day is before the sunrise.

The apostle, in warning the Thessalonians against the error of supposing that the day of the Lord was come (2 Thess. ii. 2, *R.V.*), gives them what would be a sign immediately preceding it: "For that day," he says, "shall not come except there come a falling away first, and that man of sin be revealed, the son of perdition, who opposeth and exalteth himself above all that is called God or that is worshiped, so that he sitteth in the temple of God, showing himself that he is God." The manifestation of the man of sin is therefore the bell that tolls in solemnly the day of the Lord.

This would seem to be the opening, then, of the "little book." Thenceforth the prophecies of the latter day become clear and intelligible. Now the apostasy has been shown, as it would seem, in its beginning under the fifth trumpet, and the man of sin may well be the one spoken of there : thus the little book may be fittingly now seen as opened, and in the continuation of the vision here we find for the first time the "beast," the "*wild* beast" of Daniel, in full activity (chap. xi. 7). All, therefore, seems connected and harmonious; and we are emerging out of the obscure border-land of prophecy into the place where the concentrated rays of its lamp are found.

We see too how rapidly the end draws near: "And he set his right foot upon the sea, and his left upon the earth; and he cried with a great voice, as when a lion roareth." It is the preparatory voice of Judah's Lion, as "suddenly his anger kindles;" and the seven thunders, —the full divine voice,—the whole government of God in action,—answers it; but what they utter has to find its interpretation at a later time.

Meanwhile, the attitude of the angel is explained: "and the angel which I saw standing upon the sea and upon the earth lifted up his right hand to heaven, and sware by Him that liveth forever and ever, who created the heavens, and the things that are therein, and the earth, and the things that are therein, and the sea, and the things that are therein, that there should be delay no longer; but in the days of the voice of the seventh angel, when he is about to sound"—when he shall sound, as he is about to do,—"then is finished the mystery of God, according to the good tidings which He hath declared to His servants the prophets."

All is of a piece: the prophetic testimony, (the testimony of the little open book,) is now to be suddenly consummated, which ends only with the glories of Christ's reign over the earth. Amid all the confusion and evil of days so full of tribulation, that except they were mercifully shortened, no flesh should be saved (Matt. xxiv. 22), yet faith will be allowed to reckon the very days of its continuance, which in both Daniel and Revelation are exactly numbered. How great the relief in that day of distress! and how sweet the compassion of God that has provided it after this manner! "He that endureth to the end shall be saved,"—shall find deliverance speedy and effectual, and find it in the coming of that Son of Man whose very title is a gospel of peace, and whose hand will accomplish the deliverance.

There has been an apparent long delay: "There shall be delay* no longer." Man's day has run to its end, and, though in cloud and tempest, the day of the Lord at last is dawning. Then the mystery of God is finished: the mystery of the first prophecy of the woman's Seed, and in which the whole conflict between good and evil is summarized and foretold. What a mystery it has been! and how unbelief, even in believers, has stumbled over the delay! The heel of the Deliverer bruised: a victory of patient suffering to precede and insure the final victory of power! Meantime, the persistence and apparent triumph of evil, by which are disciplined the heirs of glory! Now, all is indeed at last cleared up; the mystery of God (needful to be a mystery while patience wrought its perfect work,) is forever finished: the glory of God shines like the sun; faith is how completely justified! the murmur of doubt forever silenced.

Thus the sea and the land already, even while the days of trouble last, know the step of the divine angel, claiming earth and sea for Christ. And now faith (as in the prophet) is to devour the book of these wondrous communications, sweet in the mouth, yet at present bitter in digestion, for the last throes of the earth's travail are upon her. By and by this trouble will be no more remembered for the joy that the birth of a new day is come,—a day prophesied of by so many voices without God, but a day which can only come when *God* shall wipe away the tears from off all faces. And it comes; it comes quickly now: the voice heard by the true Philadelphian is, "I come quickly." Come, Lord, and "destroy the face of the covering that is cast over all peoples, and the vail that is spread over all nations;" come, and

---

* There is no doubt at all as to this being legitimate, and being so, although the *R. V.* still puts it into the margin, there should be no doubt as to its being the true rendering.

swallow up death in victory, and take away the reproach of Thy people from off all the earth; come, that faith may say in triumph, "Lo, this is our God: we have waited for Him, and He will save us: this is the Lord; we have waited for Him, we will be glad and rejoice in His salvation."

THE WITNESSES. (Chap. xi. 1–14.)

THE last words of the preceding chapter receive their explanation from what we have seen to be the character of the little open book. If this be Old Testament prophecy that is now "open," then we can see how John has at this point to "prophesy *again*," not "*before*," but "over,"—that is, "*concerning* many peoples and nations and tongues and kings." He is to take up the strain of the old prophets, not, of course, merely to echo their predictions, but to add to them a complementary and final testimony.

Accordingly we find now what carries us back to those prophecies of Daniel which were briefly reviewed in our introductory chapter. The mention of the "beast," and of the precise period of "forty-two months," or "twelve hundred and sixty days,"—that is, the half-week of his last or seventieth week, previous to the coming in of blessing for Israel and the earth, is by itself conclusive. This week we have seen to be, in fact, divided in this way by the taking away of the daily sacrifice in the midst of it (Dan. ix. 27). It is by this direct opposition to God also that the man of sin is revealed. Hence it would seem clear that it is with the last half of the week that we have here to do.

A reed like a staff is now given to the prophet that he may measure with it the temple of God. If a reed might suggest weakness, as in fact all that is of God lies at the time contemplated under such a reproach, the words, "like a staff" suggest the opposite thought. God's care for his people implied in this measurement is to unbelief indeed a mystery, for they seem exposed to the vicissitudes of other men, yet is it a staff upon which one may lean with fullest confidence. *His* measurement of things abides, perfect righteousness and absolute truth, abiding necessarily as such.

The temple of God is, of course, the Jewish temple, and though not to be taken literally, still, as all its connections here assure us, stands for Jewish worship, and not Christian, though a certain application, as in the historical interpretaion, need not be denied. The altar, as distinct from the temple proper, is, I believe, the altar of burnt-offering, upon which, indeed, for Israel, all depended. It was there God met with the people (Ex. xxix. 43), although, as we contemplate things here, the mass of the nation was in rejection, the court given up to the Gentiles,* the holy city to be trodden under foot by them, only a remnant of true worshipers acknowledged. It may be said that the altar of burnt-offering stood in the court ; but the idea connected with each is different. The court, however, being given up, the worshipers recognized must have the sanctuary opened for them: in the rejection of the mass, God brings the faithful few nearer to Himself. This is His constant grace.

"And the holy city shall they tread under foot forty and two months." The "holy city" can speak but of one city on earth ; nor can there be justifiable doubts as to the place in prophecy of this half-week of desolation. The mixture of literal and figurative language will be no cause of stumbling to any one who has carefully considered the style of all these apocalyptic visions, which are evidently not intended to carry their significance upon their face. All must be fully weighed, must be self-consistent, and fitting into its place in connection with the whole prophetic plan. Thus alone can we have clearness and certainty as to interpretation.

---

* Which shows, I think, that it is not the court of the Gentiles, which belonged to them of right.

As a man, then, who has been sunk in a long dream of sorrow, but to whom is now brought inspiriting news of a joy in which he is called to have an active part,—as an Elijah at another Horeb after the wind and the earthquake and the fire have passed and He whom he had sought—the Lord—is not in these, but who is aroused at once by the utterance of the "still, small voice,"—so the prophet here is bidden to rise and measure the temple of God. Not so unlike, either, to the measure given to the elder prophet, of seven thousand men that had not bowed the knee to the image of Baal. How speedy and thorough a relief when God is brought into the scene! and from what scene is He really absent? How animating, how courageous a thing, then, is faith that recognizes Him!

And where He is there must be a testimony to Him. We find it, therefore, immediately in this case: "And I will give power unto My two witnesses, and they shall prophesy a thousand, two hundred, and threescore days clothed in sackcloth. These are the two olive-trees, and the two candlesticks which stand before the Lord of the earth."

The reference is plain to Zechariah (chap. iv.), but there are also differences which are plain. There it is the thing itself accomplished, to which here there is but testimony, and in humiliation, though there is power to maintain it, spite of all opposition, till the time appointed. The witnesses are identified with their testimony—that to which they bear witness. Hence the resemblance. They stand before the Lord of the earth,—the One to whom the earth belongs, to maintain His claim upon it: in sackcloth, because their claim is resisted; a sufficient testimony in the power of the Spirit, a spiritual light amidst the darkness, but which does not banish darkness.

"And if any man desireth to hurt them, fire proceedeth out of their mouth and devoureth their enemies; and if any man shall desire to hurt them, in this manner must he be killed. These have power to shut the heaven that it rain not during the days of their prophecy; and they have power over the waters, to turn them into blood, and to smite the earth with every plague as often as they shall desire."

Here is not the grace of Christianity, but the ministry of power after the manner of Elijah and of Moses: judgment which must come because grace has been ineffectual, and of which the issue shall be in blessing, for "when Thy judgments are in the earth, the inhabitants of the world shall learn righteousness." (Isa. xxvi. 9.)

The association of Elijah with Moses, which is evident here, of necessity reminds us of their association also on the mount of transfiguration, wherein, as a picture, was presented "the power and coming of our Lord Jesus Christ." (2 Pet. i. 16–18.) They are here in the same place of attendance upon their coming Lord. It does not follow, however, that they are personally present, as some have thought, and that the one has had preserved to him, the other will have restored to him, his *mortal* body for that purpose.

The preservation to Elijah of a *mortal* body in heaven seems a thought weird and unscriptural enough, with all its necessary suggestions also. But the closing prophecy of the Old Testament does announce the sending of Elijah the prophet before the great and dreadful day of the Lord. Is not this proof that so he must come?

Naturally, one would say so; but our Lord's words as to John the Baptist, on the other hand,—"If ye will receive it, this is Elias, which was for to come,"—raise question. It has been answered that his own words deny that he was really Elias, and that Israel did not receive him, and so John could not be Elias to them. Both things are true, and yet do not seem satisfactory as argument. That he was not Elias literally, only shows, or seems to show, that one who was not Elias *could*, under certain conditions, have fulfilled the prediction. While other words of the Lord—"I say unto you that Elias is come already, and they have done unto him whatsoever they listed"—show even more strongly that for that day and generation he was Elias. Why, then, could not another, coming in his spirit and power, fulfill the prophecy in the future day?

This Revelation seems to confirm, inasmuch as it speaks of *two* witnesses who are both marked as possessing the spirit and power of Elias, and who stand on an equal footing as witnesses for God. Had it been one figure before the eyes here, it would have been more natural to say it is Elias himself; but here are two doing his work, nor can we think of a possible third behind and unnoticed and yet the real instrument of God in this crisis. The *two* form this Elias ministry, which is to recall the hearts of the fathers to the children, and of the children to the fathers, and who both lay down their lives as the seal of their testimony. Put all this together, and does it not seem as if Elias appeared in others raised up of God and indued with His Spirit, to complete the work for which he was raised up in Israel?

Much more would all this hinder the reception of the thought of any personal appearance of Moses, while there is no prediction at all of any such thing. Jude's words (which have been adduced) as to the contention of Michael with Satan about the body of the lawgiver may well refer to the fact that the Lord had buried him, and no man knew of his sepulcre. Satan may well, for his own purposes, have desired to make known his grave, just as God in His wisdom chose to hide it.

Yet the appearance of Moses and Elias in connection with the appearing of the Lord, as seen on the mount of transfiguration, seems none the less to connect itself with these two witnesses and their work,—both caught away in like manner into *the* "cloud," as the twelfth verse ought to read. And Malachi, just before the declaration of the mission of Elias, bids them, on God's part, "remember the law of Moses My servant." Moses must do his work as well as Elias; for it is upon their turning in heart to the law of Moses that their blessing in the last days depends; and thus we find the power of God acting in their behalf in the likeness of what He wrought upon Egypt: the witnesses "have power over waters, to turn them to blood." It is not that Moses is personally among them, but that Moses is in this way witnessing for them; and so the vials after this emphatically declare.

God thus, during the whole time of trouble and apostasy, preserves a testimony for Himself, until at the close the final outrage is permitted which brings down speedy judgment. For "when they shall have finished their testimony, the beast that cometh up out of the abyss shall make war with them, and overcome them, and kill them. And their dead bodies lie in the street of the great city, which spiritually is called 'Sodom' and 'Egypt,' where also their Lord was crucified. And from among the peoples and tribes and tongues and nations do men look upon their dead bodies three days and a half, and suffer not their dead bodies to be laid in a tomb. And they that dwell upon the earth rejoice over them and make merry; and they shall send gifts to one another; because these two prophets tormented them that dwell on the earth. And after the three days and a half, the breath of life from God entered into them, and they stood upon their feet; and great fear fell upon them which beheld them. And they heard a great voice from heaven saying unto them, 'Come up hither.' And they went up into heaven in the cloud; and their enemies beheld them. And in that hour there was a great earthquake, and the tenth part of the city fell; and there were killed in the earthquake seven thousand persons: and the rest were affrighted, and gave glory to the God of heaven."

If the twelve hundred and sixty days of the prophetic testimony agree with the last half of the closing week of

Daniel, they coincide with the time of the beast's permitted power, and the death of the witnesses is his last political act. That a certain interval of time should follow before his judgment, which takes place under the *third* and not the second woe, does not seem to conflict with chap. xiii. 5, where it should read, "power was given unto him to *practice*"—not "continue,"—"forty and two months." The last act of tyranny may have been perpetrated in the slaying of the witnesses; and indeed it seems a thing fitted to be the close of power of this kind permitted him. With this the storm-cloud of judgment arises, which smites him down shortly after.

If, however, the duration of the testimony be for the *first* half of the week, then the power of the beast begins with the slaughter of the witnesses, and the three and a half years' tribulation *follows*, which does not seem to consist with the judgment and its effects three and a half days afterward. Then, too, "the second woe is past" (*v.* 14), and the third announces the kingdom of Christ as having *come*. But we shall yet consider this more closely when we come, if the Lord will, to the interpretation of the vials.

Here, then, for the first time, the beast out of the abyss comes plainly into the scene. In Daniel, and in Rev. xiii., he does not come out of the abyss, but out of the sea; but in the seventeenth chapter he is spoken of as "about to come up out of the abyss," showing undeniably that it is the same "beast" as Daniel's fourth one,—the Roman empire. In the first case, as coming out of the sea, it has a common origin with the other three empires—the Babylonian, Persian, and Grecian—out of the heaving deep of Gentile nations. Then we find in Revelation what from Daniel we should never have expected, but what in fact has certainly taken place,—that the empire which is to meet its judgment at the coming of the Lord does not continue uninterruptedly in power till then. There is a time in which it ceases to be,—and we can measure this time of non-existence already by centuries,—and then it comes back again in a peculiar form, as from the dead: "the beast that was and is not, and shall be present." (Chap. xvii. 8.) This rising again into existence we would naturally take as its coming up out of the abyss,—out of the death state,—and think that we were at the bottom of the whole matter. The truth seems to be not quite so simple, but here is not the place to go into it further.

For the present, it is enough to say that the coming up out of the abyss is in fact a revival out of the death state, but, as a comparison with the fifth trumpet may suggest, revival by the dark and demon-influences which are there represented as in attendance upon the angel of the abyss. It is the one in whom is vested the power of the revived empire who concentrates the energy of his hatred against God in the slaying of the witnesses.

The place of their death is clearly Jerusalem : " Their dead bodies lie in the street of the great city, which spiritually is called ' Sodom ' and ' Egypt,' *where also their Lord was crucified.*" Certainly no other place could be so defined : and thus defined and characterized for its lusts as Sodom, for its cruelty to the people of God as Egypt, it is not now called the "holy," but the "great" city,—great even in its crimes. In its street their bodies lie, exposed by the malice of their foes which denies them burial, but allowed by God as the open indictment of those who have thus definitively rejected His righteous rule. The race of the prophets is at an end, which has tormented them with their claim of the world for God ; and the men of the earth rejoice, and send gifts to one another. Little do they understand that when His testimony is at an end, there is nothing left but for God Himself to come in and to manifest a power before which man's power shall be extinguished as flax before the flame.

And the presage of this quickly follows. "And after the three days and a half, the breath of life from God entered into them, and they stood upon their feet; and great fear fell upon them which beheld them. And they heard a great voice from heaven saying unto them, 'Come up hither.' And they went up into heaven in the cloud; and their enemies beheld them."

If this is the time of the addition of the saints martyred under the beast's persecution to the first resurrection, of which the vision in the twentieth chapter speaks, then it is plain that we are arrived at the end of the beast's power against the saints, and of the last week of Daniel. "Two" is the number of valid testimony (Jno. viii. 17), and these two witnesses may, in a vision like that before us, stand for many more,—nay, for this whole martyred remnant in Israel. We cannot say it *is* so, but we can as little say it is *not* so; and even the suggestion has its interest: for thus this appendix to the sixth trumpet seems designed to put in place the various features of Daniel's last week, the details of which are opened out to us in the seven chapters following, with many additions. And this we might expect in a connected chain of prophecy which stretches on to the end; for under the seventh trumpet the kingdoms of this world are become the kingdoms of the Lord, and of His Christ, and the "time of the dead to be judged" is at least contemplated.

The resurrection of the witnesses is not all: a great earthquake follows, "and the tenth part of the city fell; and there were killed in the earthquake seven thousand persons; and the rest were affrighted, and gave glory to the God of heaven."

Thus the sixth trumpet ends in a convulsion in which judgment takes, as it were, the refused tithe from a rebellious people. There is a marked similarity here between the trumpets and the vials, which end also in an earthquake and judgment of the great city: as to which we may see further in its place. The rest that are not slain give glory to the God of heaven. It is the unacceptable product of mere human fear, which has no practical result; for God is claiming the *earth*, not simply heaven, and for the affirmation of this claim His witnesses have died. They can allow Him heaven who deny Him earth. And judgment takes its course.

The second woe ends with this, and the third comes quickly after it.

The Kingdom. (Chap. xi. 15-18.)

The third woe is the coming of the kingdom!

Yes; that to greet which the earth breaks out in gladness, the morning without clouds, the day which has no night, and the fulfillment of the first promise which fell upon man's ears when he stood a naked sinner before God to hear his doom, the constant theme of prophecy now swelling into song and now sighed out in prayer, that kingdom is yet, to the "dwellers upon earth," the last and deepest woe.

The rod of iron is now to smite, and omnipotence it is that wields it. "And the seventh angel sounded, and there followed great voices in heaven, and they said, 'The kingdom of the world is become the kingdom of our Lord and of His Christ, and He shall reign forever and ever.'"

Few words and concise, but how pregnant with blessed meaning! The earth that has rolled from its orbit is reclaimed; judgment has returned to righteousness; He who has learned for Himself the path of obedience in a suffering which was the fruit of tender interest in man has now Himself the sceptre; nor is there any power that can take it out of His hand.

There are no details yet: simply the announcement, which the elders in heaven answer with adoration, prostrate upon their faces, saying, "We give Thee thanks, O Lord God the Almighty, who art and who wast, that Thou hast taken Thy great power, and hast reigned. And the nations were angry, and Thy wrath is come, and the time of the dead to be judged, and to give their reward to Thy servants the prophets, and to the saints, and to them that fear Thy name, small and great; and to destroy them that destroy the earth."

There is nothing difficult here in the way of interpretation, except that the "time of the dead to be judged" seems to come with the period of the earthly judgments which introduce millennial blessing. We find in the twentieth chapter full assurance that this is not to be. The explanation is that we have here the setting up of the kingdom in its full results, and that the *order* is one of thought and not of time. The judgments of the quick (or living) and of the dead are both implied in the reign of our Lord and of His Christ, though they are not executed together. God's wrath is mentioned first, because it is for the earth the pre-requisite of blessing, and because judgment is not what He rests in, but in His love. It is therefore put first, that the realization of the blessing may come after, and not give place to it. But this wrath of God which meets and quells the nations' wrath goes on and necessitates the judgment of the dead also. Death is no escape from it: the coming One has the keys of death and hades.

With this the holiness of God is satisfied, and the love in which He rests is free to show itself in the reward of prophets and saints, and those who fear His name, little as well as great. This seems as general in its aspect as the judgment of the dead on the other side unquestionably is. The foremost mention of the prophets, as those who have stood for God in testimony upon the earth, is in perfect keeping with the character of the whole book before us. And the destruction of those who destroy the earth is not noticed here apparently as judgment so much as to assure us of the reparation of the injury to that which came out of His hands at first, and in which He has never ceased to have tender interest, despite the permitted evil of "man's day."

PART III.

THE TRINITY OF EVIL, AND THE MANIFESTATION OF THE WICKED ONE.

COMMENCING FULFILLMENT OF THE FIRST PROMISE [TO THE WOMAN'S SEED]. (Chap. xi. 19–xii.)

THE trumpets, as we have seen, carry us to the end of all. What follows here, therefore, is not in continuation of them, but a new beginning, in which we find the development of details,—of course as to what is of primary importance, and involving principles of the deepest interest and value for us. Through all, the links between the Old Testament and the New are fully maintained, and we have the full light of the double testimony. On our part, we shall need on this account a more patient and protracted examination of that which comes before us.

The last verse of the eleventh chapter belongs properly to the twelfth. It characterizes what is to follow rather than what precedes, and, when we remember that Israel is upon the scene, is of greatest significance. The temple of God is opened in heaven, and there is seen in His temple the ark of His covenant. From the world below it had disappeared, and the temple itself been overthrown, —the testimony of His displeasure with an apostate people. Nor, though the temple were replaced, as after the Babylonish captivity had been the case, could the ark ever be restored by man's hand. It was gone, and with it the token of Jehovah's presence in the midst—a loss evidently irretrievable from man's side. Yet if Israel had no longer thus the assurance of what they were to Him, in heaven all the time, though in secret, the unchangeable goodness of God remained. The ark abode, as it were, with Him, and the time was now come to manifest this: the inner sanctuary of the heavens was opened, and there was the ark still seen.

To us who are accustomed to translate these types into the realities they represent, this is all simple. The ark is Christ, and, as the gold *outside* the shittim-wood declared, is Christ in glory, gone up after His work accomplished—the work which had provided the precious blood which had sprinkled the mercy-seat. Israel had indeed rejected the lowly Redeemer, and imprecated upon themselves the vengeance due to those who shed it. Yet, though the wrath came, Israel was neither totally nor finally rejected. The blood of Jesus speaketh better things than that of Abel, and is before God the justification of a grace that shall yet be shown them. The literal ark is passed away, as Jeremiah tells us, never to return; but instead of that throne of His of old, a more magnificent grace has declared that Jerusalem itself shall be called "the throne of the Lord; and all the nations shall be gathered unto it, to the name of the Lord, to Jerusalem; neither shall they walk any more after the imagination of their evil heart." (Jer. iii. 16, 17.)

The ark, then, seen in the temple in heaven is the sign of God's unforgotten grace toward Israel; but the nations are not yet ready to welcome that grace, nor indeed are the people themselves, save a remnant, who on that account pass through the bitterest persecution. To that the chapter following bears decisive testimony, as it does of the interference of God for them. Therefore is it that when the sign of His faithfulness to His covenant is seen in heaven, on the earth there ensue convulsion and a storm of divine wrath: "there were lightnings, and voices, and thunders, and an earthquake, and great hail."

And now a "great sign" appears in heaven, "a woman clothed with the sun, and the moon under her feet, and upon her head a crown of twelve stars; and she being with child cried, travailng in birth, and in pain to be delivered."

The sign appears in heaven, not because the woman is actually there, but because she is seen according to the mind of God toward her. Who the woman is should be quite plain, as the child she brings forth is He who is to rule all nations with a rod of iron. That is Christ, assuredly, and the mother of Christ is not the virgin, as we see clearly by what follows, still less the Church, of which in no sense is Christ born, but Israel, " of whom, as concerning the flesh, Christ came," says the apostle. (Rom. ix. 4.) Thus she is seen clothed with the glory of the sun,—that is, of Christ Himself as He will presently appear (Mal. iv. 2) in supreme power, for the sun is the ruler of the day. As a consequence, her glory of old, before the day-dawn, the reflected light of her typical system, is like the moon here under her feet. Upon her head the crown of twelve stars speaks naturally of her twelve tribes,—planets now around the central sun.

The next words carry us back, however, historically, to the time before Christ. She is in travail with Messiah,— a thought hard to realize or understand, except as we realize what the fulfillment of God's promise as to Christ involved in the way of suffering on the part of the nation. To them while under the trial of law, and with the issue (to man's thought, of course,) uncertain, Christ could not be born; the prosperous days of David must go by; the heirs of David be allowed to show out what was in their heart, and be carried to Babylon; humiliation, sorrow, captivity, fail to produce result, until the voice of prophecy even lapses with Malachi; until the long silence, as of death, is broken by the cry at last, "To us a child is born." Here is at least one purpose, as it would seem, of that triple division of the genealogy of the Lord in Matthew, the governmental gospel, in which the first fourteen generations bring one to the culmination of their national prosperity, the second is a period of decline to the captivity, the third a period of resurrection, but which only comes at last, and as in a moment, after the failure of every natural hope. Thus in the government of God Israel must have her travail-time.

But before we see the birth of the man-child, we are called to look at "another sign in heaven," "a great red dragon, having seven heads and ten horns, and seven diadems upon his heads." These heads and horns we shall presently find upon the fourth beast, or world-empire, but we are not left doubtful as to who the dragon is. Here we find the first in all this part of those interpretations which are given henceforth here and there throughout the book: the dragon is "that ancient serpent which is called the devil and Satan, which deceiveth the whole world." Thus as the dawn rises upon the battle-field the combatants are discerned. It is Satan who here as the "prince of this world" appears as if incarnate in the last world-empire. "Seven heads" show perfection of world-wisdom; and every one of these heads wears a *diadem*, or despotic crown. The symbolic meaning of the number does not at all preclude another meaning historically, as Scripture-history is every where itself symbolic, as is nature also. The ten horns measure the actual extent of power, and infer by their number responsibility and judgment.

The serpent of old has thus grown into a *dragon*—a monster—"fiery red," as the constant persecutor of the people of God, and he draws with his tail the third part of the stars of heaven, and casts them to the earth. The analogy of the action of the little horn in Daniel (viii. 10), as well as the scope of the prophecy before us, would lead us to think here of Jews, not Christians, and certainly not angels, as to whom the idea of casting them to the *earth* would seem quite inappropriate. The "tail" implies the false prophet (Isa. ix. 15), and therefore it is apostasy among the professing people of God that is indicated. False teaching is eminently characteristic of satanic power at all times, and far more successful than open violence.

And the dragon stood before the woman which was ready to be delivered, to devour her child as soon as it was born. And she was delivered of a son, a man-child, who is to rule all the nations with a rod of iron: and her child was caught up to God, and to His throne."

The power of Satan, working through the heathen empire of Rome, was thus, with better knowledge than Rome had, in armed watch against the woman and her seed. The census mentioned in Luke as to have gone into effect at the time of Christ's birth, and which was actually carried out after the sceptre had wholly departed from Judah, was in effect a tightening of the serpent-coil around his intended victim. Divine power used it to bring a Galilean carpenter and his wife to Bethlehem, and then, as it were without effort, canceled the imperial edict. Only from the nation itself could come the sentence which should, as far as man could do so, destroy it, and that sentence was in Pilate's handwriting upon the cross. But from the cross and the guarded grave the woman's Seed escaped victoriously: "her child was caught up to God, and to His throne."

All is thus far easy of interpretation. In what follows, there is more difficulty, although it admits of satisfactory solution. "And the woman fled into the wilderness, where she has a place prepared of God, that there they may nourish her a thousand, two hundred, and threescore days."

There Daniel's seventieth week comes in again, and evidently the last half of it. But the prophecy goes on immediately from the ascension of Christ to this time, not noticing a gap of more than eighteen centuries which has already intervened between these periods. How, then, can we explain this omission? and granting it can be explained, what is the connection between these two things that seem, in more than time, so far apart,—the ascension of Christ, and Israel's flight into the wilderness for this half-week of years?

The answer to the first question is to be found in a character of Old-Testament prophecy of which already we have had one example, and that in the prophecy of the seventy weeks itself. The last week, although part of a strictly determined time on Israel, is cut off from the sixty-nine preceding by a gap slightly longer than that in the vision before us, the sixty-ninth week reaching only to " Messiah the Prince." (Dan. ix. 25.) He is cut off and has nothing: the blessing cannot, therefore, come in for them; instead, there is a time of warfare—a controversy between God and the people which is not measured, and which is not yet come to an end. Of this the seventieth week is the conclusion, while it is also the time of their most thorough apostasy—the time to which we have come in this part of Revelation.

This lapse of prophecy as to Israel is coincident with the Christian dispensation, the period in which God is taking out of the earth (and characteristically out of the Gentile nations,) a *heavenly* people. True, there are Jews saved still,—"there is," as the apostle says, "at the present time also, a remnant according to the election of grace." But these are no longer partakers of Jewish hopes: blessed be God, they have better ones; but the nation as such in the meanwhile is given up, as Micah distinctly declares to them should be the case, while he also declares to them the reason of this, and the limit which God has appointed to it. His words are one of the clearest of Old-Testament prophecies to Christ, so clear that nothing can be clearer, and are those cited by the chief priests and scribes themselves in proof of "where Christ should be born." "They shall smite the Judge of Israel," says the prophet, "with a rod upon the cheek." It is His people who do this,—His own, to whom He came, and they "received Him not." Then he declares the glory of the rejected One: "But thou, Bethlehem-Ephratah, though thou be little among the thousands of Judah, yet out of thee shall He come forth unto Me, that is to be Ruler in Israel, whose goings forth have been of old, from everlasting." (Chap. v. 1, 2.) But what will be the result then of His rejection? This is answered immediately: "Therefore will He *give them up*, until the time that she which travaileth hath brought forth; *then* the remnant of His brethren shall return unto the children of Israel."

The last sentence of this remarkable prophecy is a clear intimation of what we know to be the fact, that in this time of national rejection there would be "brethren" —Jewish evidently—of this Judge of Israel, whose place would not be *with* Israel; while at the end of the time specified, such converted ones would again find their place in the nation. Meanwhile, Israel being given up, the blessing of the earth which waits upon theirs is suspended also: the shadow rests upon the dial-plate of prophecy; time is as it were uncounted. Christ is gone up on high, and sits upon the Father's throne: the kingdom of heaven is begun, indeed, but only its "mysteries," unknown to the Old Testament, "things which have been kept secret from the foundation of the world." (Matt. xiii. 11, 35.)

Here, then, where we return to take up the thread of Old-Testament prophecy, it is no wonder if the style of the Old Testament be again found. We have again the gap in time uncounted, the Christian dispensation treated as a parenthesis in God's ways with the earth, and the woman's Seed caught away to God and to His throne. Then follows, without apparent interval, the Jewish flight into the wilderness during the three and a half years of unequaled tribulation.

But this does not answer the second question—that as to the connection between the catching away of the manchild and the woman's flight. For this we must look deeper than the surface, and gather the suggestions which in Scripture every-where abound, and here only more openly than usual demand attention.

That which closes the Christian dispensation we have seen to be what is significantly parallel to that which opens it. In the Acts, the history of the Church is prefaced with the ascension of the Lord: that which will close its history is the removal of His people. This naturally raises the inquiry, If Christ and His people be so one as in the New Testament they are continually represented, may not the man-child here include both, and the gap be bridged over in this way? The promise to the overcomer in Thyatira links them together in what is attributed to the man-child—the ruling the nations with a rod of iron; and the mention of this seems to intimate the time for the assumption of the rod at hand.

This, then, completes the picture and harmonizes it, so that it may be well accepted as the truth; especially as this acceptance only recognizes that which is otherwise known as true, and makes no additional demands upon belief.

The man-child caught up to God and to His throne, the woman flies into the wilderness, into a place prepared of God, where they nourish her for the time of trouble. The woman is the nation as in the sight of God; not all Israel, nor even all the saints in Israel, but those who are ordained of God to continue, and who therefore represent it before Him. The apostate mass are cut off by judgment (Zech. xiii. 8, 9; Isa. iv. 3, 4). The martyred saints go up to heaven. Still God preserves a people to be the nucleus of the millennial nation, and this, of course, it is the special desire of Satan to destroy. They are preserved by the hand of God, though amid trial such as the "wilderness" naturally indicates, and which is designed of God for their purification.

And now there ensues that which in the common belief of Christians had long before taken place, but which in fact is the initial stage of final judgment,—Satan is cast out of heaven.

"And there was war in heaven: Michael and his angels fought against the dragon; and the dragon fought and his angels, and prevailed not; neither was their place found any more in heaven. And the great dragon was cast out,—that old serpent called the devil and Satan, which deceiveth the whole world: he was cast out into the earth, and his angels were cast out with him."

As I have said, the simplest interpretation of this is counter to the common belief of Christendom. Satan has, according to the thought of many, long been in hell, though he is (strangely enough) allowed to leave it and ramble over the earth at will. To these, it is a grotesque, weird and unnatural thought that the devil should have been suffered all this time to remain in heaven. Man has evidently been allowed to remain on earth, but then —beside the fact of death removing his successive generations—toward *him* there are purposes of mercy in which Satan has no part. The vision-character of Revelation may be objected against it also, so that the simplest interpretation may seem on that very account the widest from the truth. Does not our Lord also say that He saw "Satan fall as lightning from heaven"? (Luke x. 18.) And the apostle, that the angels which sinned, He cast down to hell? (2 Pet. ii. 4; Jude 6.) Such passages would seem with many decisively to affirm the ordinary view.

In fact, it is only the last passages that have any real force; and here another has said, "It seems hardly possible to consider Satan as one of these,"—the angels spoken of,—"for they are in chains, and guarded till the great day; he is still permitted to go about as the tempter and the adversary, until his appointed time be come."* As to our Lord's words, they are easily to be

---

*Principal Barry, in Smith's Dictionary. The question as to the class of angels here referred to, this is hardly the place to entertain.

understood as in the manner often of prophecy, "I saw," being equivalent to "I *fore*saw."

On the other hand, that the "spiritual hosts of wickedness" with which now we wrestle are "in heavenly places" is told us plainly in Ephesians (vi. 12, *R.V.*); and in the passage in Revelation before us, no less plainly. For the connection of this vision with what is still future we have already seen, and shall see further, and the application to Satan personally ought not to be in doubt. The "dragon" is indeed a symbol; but "the devil and Satan," is the interpretation of it, and certainly not as figurative as the dragon itself.

Scripture implies also in other ways what we have here. When the apostle speaks of our being "sealed with the Holy Spirit of promise, which is the earnest of our inheritance," he adds that it is to be that "until the redemption of the purchased possession,"—that is, until we get the inheritance itself (Eph. i. 14). But we get it then by redemption, not our own, but of the inheritance itself. Our inheritance has therefore to be redeemed, and this redemption takes place manifestly when the heirs as a whole are ready for it. Now redemption, it is plain, in this case, like the redemption of the body, is a redemption by power,—God laying hold of it to set it free in some sense from a condition of alienation from Himself, and to give his people possession. And if the man-child include "those who are Christ's at His coming," then the purging of the heavenly places by the casting of Satan and his angels out is just the redemption of the heavenly inheritance.

Elsewhere we read, accordingly, of the *reconciliation* of heavenly as of earthly things (Col. i. 20). And this is a phrase which, like the former, implies alienation previously. And here it is on the ground of the cross: "having made peace through the blood of the cross." In Hebrews, again, as "it was necessary that the patterns of things in the heavens"—as in the tabernacle—"should be purified with" sacrificial blood, so must "the heavenly things themselves with better sacrifices than these." (Heb. ix. 23.) The work of Christ having glorified God as to the sin which has defiled not the earth only but the heavens, He can come in to deliver and bring back to Himself what is to be made the inheritance of Christ and His "joint-heirs."

All is, then, of a piece with what is the only natural meaning of this war in heaven. The question of good and evil, every-where one, receives its answer for heaven as for earth, first, in the work of Christ, which glorifies God as to all, and then, as the fruit of this, in the recovery of what was alienated from Him, the enemies of this glorious work being put under Christ's feet. This now begins to be, though even yet in a way which to us may seem strange: strange to us it seems to hear of war in heaven,—of arrayed hosts on either side,—of resistance though unsuccessful, the struggle being left as it would seem to creature-prowess, God not directly interfering. "Michael and his angels fought with the dragon; and the dragon fought and his angels, and prevailed not."

After all, is it stranger that this should be in heaven than on the earth? Are not God's ways one? And is not all the long-protracted struggle allowed purposely to work out to the end thus, the superior power being left to show itself as the power resident in the good itself, as in that which is the key of the whole problem, the cross of the Son of Man? If God Himself enter the contest, He adapts Himself to the creature-conditions, and comes in on the lowest level,—not an angel even, but a *man.*

Let us look again at the combatants: on the one side is Michael—"Who is like God?"—a beautiful name for the leader in such a struggle! On the opposite side is he who first said to the woman, "*Ye* shall be as God;" and whose pride was his own condemnation (1 Tim. iii. 6). How clearly the moral principle of the contest is here defined! Keep but the creature's place, you are safe, happy, holy; the enemy shall not prevail against you: leave it, you are lost. The "dragon"—from a root which speaks of "keen sight"—typifies what seems perhaps a preternatural brilliancy of intellect, serpent-cunning, the full development of such "wisdom" as that with which he tempted Eve, but none of that which begins with the fear of God. He is therefore, like all that are developed merely upon one side, a monster. This want of conscience is shown in his being the devil—the "false accuser;" his heart is made known in his being Satan—the adversary.

These are the types of those that follow them; and Michael is always the warrior-angel, characterized as he is by his name, as Gabriel—"*man* of God"—is the messenger of God to men. If God draw near to men, it is in the tender familiarity of manhood that He does so. How plainly do these names speak to us!

In the time of distress that follows upon earth, Daniel is told that "Michael shall stand up, the great prince that standeth for the children of thy people; . . . and at that time thy people shall be delivered, every one that shall be found written in the book." Here in Revelation we have the heavenly side of things, and still it is Michael that stands up as the deliverer. The tactics of divine warfare are not various, but simple and uniform. Truth is simple and one; error manifold and intricate. The spiritual hosts fight under faith's one standard, and it is the banner of Michael, "Who is like God?" Under its folds is certain victory.

The dragon is cast out: the war in that respect is over; heaven is free. But he is not yet cast into hell, nor even into the bottomless pit, but to the earth; and thus the earth's great trouble-time ensues. Satan comes down with great wrath, because he knows that he has but a short time. How terrible a thing is sin! How amazing that a full, clear view of what is before him should only inspire this fallen being with fresh energy of hate to that which must all recoil upon himself, and add intensity of torment to eternal doom! Even so is every act of sin as it were a suicide; and he who committeth it is the slave of sin (Jno. viii. 34).

A great voice in heaven celebrates the triumph there. "Now is come the salvation and power and kingdom of our God, and the authority of His Christ; for the accuser of our brethren is cast down, who accused them before our God day and night." The salvation spoken of here is not, apparently, as some think, the salvation of the body; for it is explained directly as deliverance of some who are called "our brethren" from the accusation of Satan. The voice seems, therefore, that of the glorified saints, and the "brethren" of whom they speak, the saints on earth, who had indeed by individual faithfulness overcome in the past those accusations which are now forever ended. Satan's antipriestly power, as another has remarked, is at an end.

Yet he may, and does, after this, exercise imperial power, and stir up the most violent persecution of the people of God, and these still may be called not to love their lives unto death. It is not here, then, that his power ceases: they have conflict still, but not with "principalities and powers in *heavenly* places." (Eph. vi. 12.) Heaven is quiet and calm above them, if around is still the noise of the battle. And how great is the mercy that thus provides for them during those three and a half years of unequaled tribulation still to come! Is not this worthy of God that, just at the time when Satan's rage is greatest, and arming the world-power against His people, the sanctuary of the soul is never invaded by him: the fiery darts of the wicked one cease; he is no more "prince of the power of the air," but restricted to the earth simply, to work through the passions of men, which he can inflame against them.

Accordingly to this he gives himself with double energy:

"And when the dragon saw that he was cast unto the earth, he persecuted the woman who brought forth the man-child." But God interferes: "And there were given unto the woman the two wings of the great eagle, that she might fly into the wilderness, into her place, where she is nourished for a time and times and half a time, from the face of the serpent."

The words recall plainly the deliverance from Egypt. Pharaoh king of Egypt is called thus by the prophet, "the great dragon that lieth in the midst of his rivers," (Ezek. xxix. 3,) and is himself the concentration of the malice of the world-power; while God says to delivered Israel at Sinai, "Ye have seen what I did unto the Egyptians; and how I bare you on eagle's wings, and brought you to Myself." (Ex. xix. 4.) The reference here seems definitely to this: it is not, as in the common version, "a" great eagle, indefinitely, but *"the"* great eagle,—the griffon, perhaps, than which no bird has a more powerful or masterly flight. Clearly it is divine power that is referred to in these words: in the deliverance out of Egypt there was jealous exclusion of all power beside. Israel was to be taught the grace and might of a Saviour-God. And so in the end again it will be when He repeats, only in a grander way, the marvels of that old deliverance, and "allures" the heart of the nation to Himself.

Miracle may well come in again for them, and it may be that the wilderness literally will once more provide shelter and nourishment for them. Figure and fact may here agree together, and so it often is; the terms even seem to imply the literal desert here, just because it is evidently a place of shelter that divine love provides, and sustenance there; and what more natural than that the desert, by which the land of Israel is half encompassed, should be used for this?

That which follows seems to be imagery borrowed from the desert also. Like the streams of Antilibanus, many a river is swallowed up in the sand, as that is which is now poured out of the dragon's mouth. If it be an army that is pictured, the wilderness is no less capable of the absorption of a nation's strength. The river being cast out of his mouth would seem to show that it is by the power of his persuasion that men are incited to this overflow of enmity against the people of God, which is so completely foiled that the baffled adversary gives up further effort in this direction, and the objects of his pursuit are after this left absolutely unassailed.

But those who so escape, while thus securing the existence of the nation—and therefore identified with the woman herself,—are not the whole number of those who in it are converted to God; and "the remnant of her seed" become now the object of his furious assault. These are indeed those, as it would seem, with whom is the testimony of Jesus, which is, we are assured, "the spirit of prophecy." (Chap. xix. 10.) These are they, perhaps, who amid these times of trouble go forth, as from age to age the energy of the Spirit has incited men to go forth, taking their lives in their hand that they might bring the word of God before His creatures, and who have been ever of necessity the special objects of satanic enmity. They are the new generation of those who as men of God have stood forth prominently for God upon the earth, and have taken from men on the one hand their reward in persecution, but from God on the other the sweet counterbalancing acknowledgment. It is of such the Lord says, "Blessed are ye when they shall reproach and persecute you, and say all manner of evil against you falsely for My sake. Rejoice, and be exceeding glad; for great is your reward in heaven, for so persecuted they the prophets that were before you." (Matt. v. 11, 12.)

Noticeable it is that it is in heaven still this new race of prophets find their reward. The two witnesses whom we have seen ascend to heaven in a cloud belong to this number; and those who in Daniel as turning many to righteousness, shine as the stars for ever and ever (Dan.

xii. 3). Earth casts them out, and they are seen in our Lord's prophecy as brethren of the King, hungering and athirst, in strangership, naked and sick and in prison (Matt. xxv. 35, 36, 40). Heaven receives them in delight as those of whom the earth was not worthy,—a gleaning after harvest, as it were, of wheat for God's granary,—a last sheaf of the resurrection of the saints, which the twentieth chapter of the book before us sees added to the sitters upon the thrones, among the "blessed and holy" now complete. How well are they cared for who might seem left unsheltered to Satan's enmity! They have lost the earthly blessing, they have gained the heavenly; their light has been quenched for a time, to shine in a higher sphere forever. Blessed be God!

We may follow, then, the new development of satanic enmity without fear. We shall gain from considering it. Their enemy and ours is one and the same: it is Satan, the old serpent, the ancient homicide, and we must not be "ignorant of his devices." His destiny is to be overcome, and that by the feeblest saint against whom he seems for the present to succeed so easily.

The Resurrection of the Fourth Empire.
(Chap. xiii. 1-10.)

SATAN being now in full activity of opposition to the woman and her seed, we are carried on to see his further efforts to destroy them. Working, as from the beginning, through instruments in which he conceals himself, we find ourselves now face to face with his great instrument in the last days; in which too we recognize one long before spoken of in the prophets, especially by him to whom in the book of Revelation we have such frequent reference—the apocalyptic prophet of the Old Testament.

It is indeed the fourth beast of Daniel without dispute to which the word of inspiration now directs our attention. "I saw," says the apostle, "a beast coming up out of the sea, having seven heads and ten horns, and on his

THE TRINITY OF EVIL, ETC.

horns ten crowns, and on his heads the names of blasphemy."

The four beasts of Daniel's vision answer, as every one knows, to the *one* human figure seen by the king of Babylon. In his eyes there is in it at least the likeness of man, although there is no breath, no life. To the prophet afterward the world-empires appear on the other hand full of life, but *it is bestial*. One of the chapters between supplies the link between the two: for Nebuchadnezzar is himself driven out among the beasts, as we see in the fourth chapter, for a disciplinary punishment until he knows "that the Most High ruleth in the kingdom of men." In a pride which has forgotten God, he has become but a beast which knows none. He is therefore driven out among the beasts until seven times pass over him. The prophet sees thus the powers of the world to be but beasts—*"wild* beasts" indeed, as here.

As the fourth beast, moreover, the successor and heir to those that have been before it, the last empire not only shows still this bestial nature. It combines in itself the various characters of the first three. It is in general form like the leopard or Greek empire, agile and swift in its attack as the leopard is known to be. But it has the feet of the bear, the Persian tenacity of grasp, and the mouth of the lion, the Babylonian ferocity. Beast it is clearly, yet not in simple ignorance of God as the beast is: its seven heads are seen to have on each of them a name of blasphemy.

In its ten horns it differs from all before it; and these, we are explicitly told, (xvii. 17,) are "ten kings" which "give their power unto the beast." In the vision now we find these kings actually crowned. They are in existence when the beast rises from the sea, that is, from the commencement of the empire in some sense—not of old Rome, that is certain, for old Rome never commenced in such a manner. It must then be Rome as new-risen among the nations in the latter days.

The later chapter, to which we have just now referred, speaks plainly of a time when the beast that was "is not;" and for centuries, we are well aware, the empire has not existed. But the same prophecy assures us that it is to be again; and in the vision before us we find it accordingly risen up, as of old time, from the sea,—that is to say, the restless strife of the nations. As we have seen, however, that is not the only way in which it is seen to rise again: for in the history of the witnesses it has been spoken of as "ascending up out of the bottomless pit," and this is repeated in the seventeenth chapter, "the beast . . . shall ascend out of the bottomless pit, and go into perdition." Are these two ascents, then? or only one, looked at from two sides?

Again of its heads, one is said in the present chapter to be "wounded to death," but "its deadly wound was healed;" and afterward the beast is spoken of as having had the "wound by a sword" and living (*v.* 14). Are these still various ways of expressing the same thing, or not? and is there any way of deciding this?

Certainly, the long collapse of centuries during which the beast "was not" could hardly seem to be described as its having a wound and living, or as a deadly *wound* which could be healed. Let us look more closely at the prophecy, or rather at the different prophecies about this, and see what may be gathered.

In Daniel we have no mention of the time of non-existence, or of a plurality of heads upon the beast, but the ten horns show us that the empire is there before us also as it exists in the latter days; as it is plain also that it is in this form that the judgment there described comes upon it. But the prophet considering these ten horns, sees, rising up after them, another little horn in which are developed those blasphemous characters which bring down its final judgment upon the beast. It speaks great words against the Most High, and wears out the saints of the Most High, and thinks to change times and laws; and these are given into its hands until a time and times and the dividing of a time,—that is, for the last half week of Daniel's seventy, just before the Lord comes and the judgment falls.

Now this last horn rises up after the first ten are in existence, and therefore the empire in its latter-day form; and if this little horn be that whose "dominion" brings judgment upon the beast, then it would seem that the eleventh horn and the eighth head of Revelation must be the same.

The seven heads are not in Daniel, nor is the eleventh horn in Revelation. But we may learn in both of these details by means of which we can compare them. Thus, as to the heads, five had fallen when the angel spoke to John (xvii. 10): one existed, the imperial; another was to come and last but a short time, and then would be the eighth, or *the* beast in its final form, identified with its head here, as morally at least with the little horn in Daniel.

We have anticipated somewhat, and seem obliged for our purpose to anticipate, what is given us only in the seventeenth chapter, before the history of these latter days becomes in measure clear to us. Let us seek first to get hold of the point of time which the interpretation contemplates as present. When the angel says to John, "The woman which thou sawest is that great city which reigneth over the kings of the earth," we know that at the time of the revelation there was one city, and but one, to which his words could apply. It was Rome that ruled over the kings of the earth, even as Rome fills out his description also in another respect, being notoriously the seven-hilled city. That Rome is in fact the city spoken of, is, spite of the effort of a few to find another application, the verdict of the mass of commentators of all times, and this interpretation of the woman seems given by the angel as what would need no further explanation.

The ten horns, on the other hand, he states to be

future: "the ten horns are ten kings which have received no kingdom as yet." Here we see that the point of view is still that of the apostle himself. And when it is said of the heads, "five are fallen, and one is," Livy, as is well-known, has given the five different forms of government under which Rome had been before that sixth, the imperial, which existed in the apostle's day. The point of view seems here quite plain.

On the other hand, "the beast that was and *is not*" may seem to be opposed to this. But if that could not be said in the apostle's day, that the beast was not, it could be as little said of the day of the fulfillment of the vision. Thus, "was, is not, and shall be," merely pictorially presents the history of the beast, and does not at all give us the stand-point, as the other expressions do.

It is a curious coincidence, that if in Daniel's vision of the four beasts we connect the four heads of the leopard with the other three of the remaining ones, we have just seven, and it has been argued that these are, in fact, the seven heads upon the beast in Revelation; but then *six* should have fallen, and not five, when the angel spoke. The sixth also would be the last Grecian head, and the Roman would be future. That the heads are successive is quite plain, and there seems no room for any other application than that of the sixth head to the emperor of Rome.

The seventh would follow at an uncertain period in the future, and the application here has been various—to the exarchate of Ravenna, to Charlemagne, to Napoleon. It is not needful to enter into any elaborate disproof of these, as that putting together of prophecy, of the necessity of which the apostle warns us, will show sufficiently how inadmissible they are.

"The beast that was and is not, even he is the eighth, and is of the seven," says the angel: "*one* of the seven," Bleek with others takes it to mean; "*sprung* from the seven," says Alford. But the last, if we are to interpret the sixth as we have done, can scarcely be maintained. If we are to say, "one of the seven," then we may tentatively suppose it to be the seventh revived; and put in this way, other passages would seem to throw light upon it.

The seventh head was to continue but a little while; and *one* of the heads —it is not stated which—was to be wounded to death and live, as we have seen. It is on this account that the world wonders after the beast, and this is clearly at the end: so that it is either the eighth head itself that is wounded and revives, or else it is the eighth head which is the seventh revived, as we have just supposed. This thought unites then and makes plain the different passages.

The beast (under this eighth head) "practices" forty and two months, the last half week of Daniel's seventy. Yet the "prince that shall come" makes his covenant with the Jews for the *whole* last week, in the midst of which he breaks it (Dan. ix. 27). Does not this show that not only are the seventh and eighth heads as heads identical, but individually also? and does it not confirm very strongly as truth what at first appeared only to be supposition?

In this manner Daniel's prophecy of the little horn would seem to describe his second rise to power, after having fallen from being the seventh head of the beast to a rank below that of the ten kings. From this, partly by force, partly by concession, gained no doubt by the aid of him who discerns in the fallen ruler a fitting instrument for his devilish ends, he rises to his former pre-eminence over them all, filled with the animosity against God with which the dragon, "prince of this world," has inspired him, and the world wondering and ready to worship.

Thus the picture seems complete and the outline harmonious in all its details. It agrees well with what has been before suggested—the rise of the seventh head under the first seal, its collapse under the fourth trumpet, its revival through satanic influence under the sixth. Its judgment takes place under the seventh, but the details of this are unfolded in the latter part of Revelation. We see that the conspiracy of the second psalm, of the kings and rulers "against the Lord and His Anointed," is by no means over. Nay, the Gentile power that wrote defiantly His title on His cross is risen up again, and with even more than its old defiance. The long-suffering of the Lord has not been to it salvation. The exhortation, "Kiss the Son, lest He be angry, and ye perish from the way," has not been heeded. Rome still vindicates its title to its position as the head of a hostile world. "I gave her space to repent, and she will not repent," is as true of her in her civil as in her ecclesiastical character.

The revival of the last empire is Satan's mockery of resurrection; yet God is over it and in it, commanding her from her tomb for judgment. And with her, other buried nations are to revive and come forth to the light. Greece has thus revived. Italy has revived. Israel, as we well know, is reviving, and for her also there is not unmingled blessing, but solemn and terrible judgment that will leave but a remnant for the final promise surely to be fulfilled. Israel were foremost in the rejection of their Lord, when first He came to His own, and His own received Him not. It was they who used Gentile hands to execute the sentence which they lacked power to carry out. And it is strange indeed to find, in these awful last days of blasphemy and rebellion, the Jew still inspiring the Gentile in the last outburst of infidel pride and lawlessness: the second beast in the chapter before us is at once Jewish, and by its lamblike appearance and its dragon-voice, antichristian.

And this is that to which, unwarned by the sure word of prophecy, men are hurrying on. The swiftness of the current that is carrying them, owned as it is by all, is for them "progress," while it is but the power felt of the nearing cataract. "When they shall say, Peace and safety, then sudden destruction cometh upon them, as travail upon a woman with child, and they shall not escape!" So said the lips that uttered that lament over Jerusalem, which with added force may speak to us to-day, "How often would I have gathered your children together, even as a hen gathereth her chickens under her wing; and YE *would not!*"

ANTICHRIST. (Chap. xiii. 11-18.)

ALONG with the resurrection of the imperial power, we are now shown in the vision the uprise of another "wild beast," which we have nowhere else brought before us in this character. We shall have, therefore, more attentively to consider the description given, and what means we have for identification of the power or person who is described, so that the prophecy may be brought out of the isolation which would make it incapable of interpretation, and may speak at least with its full weight of moral instruction for our souls.

The one seen is "another wild beast," and this character is clear enough. The empires of Daniel are "beasts," in that they know not God; the thought of the *wild* beast adds to this that savage cruelty, which will, of course, display itself against those who are God's. Inasmuch as the other beasts are powers—empires,—it would seem as if here too were a power, royal or imperial; but this would not be certain, unless confirmed by other intimations.

It is seen rising up out of the *earth*, and not out of the *sea*. The latter symbol evidently applies to the nations, —the Gentiles; does not then this power rise out of the nations? It has been thought to mean a settled state of things into which the nations now had got,—a state of things unlikely at the period we are considering, and which would seem rather imageable as quiet water, than as "earth." Looking back to that first chapter of Genesis, in which we should surely get the essential meaning of these figures, and where typically the six days reveal the story of the dispensations on to the final Sabbath-rest of God, we shall find the earth, in its separation from the waters on the third day, speaking of Israel as separated from the Gentiles.* If this be true interpretation, as I doubt not, it is an *Israelitish* power with which we are here brought face to face. Political events to-day look to a Jewish resurrection, as something in the near future scarcely problematical. Daniel's words (chap. xii. 1) which apply to this, make it sure that this will not be all of God, but that "some" will rise "to shame and everlasting contempt." Prophecies that we have already to some extent considered, intimate that Jewish unbelief is yet to unite with an apostasy of Christendom, and culminate in a "man of sin, the son of perdition, who opposeth and exalteth himself above all that is called God, or that is worshipped, so that he sitteth in the temple of God, showing himself that he is God." (2 Thess. ii. 3, 4.) Thus we may be prepared to find here a blasphemous persecuting power rising up in the restored nation. And this may help us to the awful significance of what follows in Revelation—"and he had two horns like a lamb, and spake as a dragon."

"Two horns *like a lamb:*" the "Lamb" is a title so significant in the present book,—nay, of such controlling significance, that any reference to it must be considered of corresponding importance. The two horns, then, are of course an intimation that the power exercised by the one before us—for the "horn" is a well-known symbol of power—is twofold, in some sense like that of a lamb: how then? What is the twofold character of the power here? It seems as if there could be but one meaning: Christ's power is twofold, as manifested in the day that comes; He is a priest upon the throne,"—a royal Priest, with spiritual authority as well as kingly. This the blas-

---

* See "Genesis in the light of the New Testament," or "The Numerical Bible."

phemous usurper before us will assume; and this manifests him, without possibility of mistake that one can see, as ANTICHRIST.

He is betrayed by His voice: his speech is that of a dragon; he is inspired, in fact, by Satan. There is no sweet and gracious message upon His lips. It is not He who has been man's burden-bearer, and the sinner's Saviour. No gentleness and meekness, but the tyranny of the destroyer; no heavenly wisdom, but Satan's craft, utters itself through him. Arrogant as he is, he is the miserable tool of man's worst enemy, and his own.

"And he exerciseth all the power of the first beast in his presence." He is the representative of the newly constituted empire of the west, not locally merely, but throughout it; and thus, as standing for another, he is still the awful mockery of Him who is on the throne of the world, the Father's representative. This is developed by the next words to its full extent: "and he causeth the earth and them that dwell therein to worship the first beast, whose deadly wound was healed; and he doeth great signs, so that he maketh fire to descend from heaven upon the earth before men." Here the very miracle which Elijah once had wrought to turn back the hearts of apostate Israel to the true God he is permitted to do to turn men to a false one. Men are given up to be deceived: God is sending them (as it is declared in Thessalonians) "strong delusion, that they may believe the lie . . . because they received not the love of the truth." The Word of God, announcing this beforehand, would, of course, be the perfect safeguard of those that trusted it; and this very miracle as it would appear, would be a sign to the elect, not of Christ, but of Antichrist. But to the men that dwell upon the earth, a moral characteristic distinguishing those who as apostate from Christianity have given up all their hope of heaven, and who are all through this part specially pointed out, heaven itself would seem to seal the pretensions of the deceiver. "And he deceiveth the dwellers upon the earth, by means of the signs which it was given him to do in the presence of the beast, saying to the dwellers upon earth, that they should make an image to the beast who had the wound by the sword and lived. And it was given him to give breath to the image of the beast, that the image of the beast should both speak, and cause those that would not worship the image of the beast to be slain."

Is an actual image of the beast intended here? or is it some representative of imperial authority, such as the historical interpreters in general (though in various ways) have made it out to be? Against the latter thought there is in itself no objection, but rather the reverse, the book being so symbolical throughout. But it is the second beast itself that is the representative of the authority of the first beast; and on the other hand an apparent creation-miracle would not be unlikely to be attempted by one claiming to be divine. Notice, that it is not "life" he gives to it, as in the common version, nor "spirit," though the word may be translated so, but "breath," which as the alternative rendering is plainly the right one, supposing it be a literal image.

Our Lord's words as to the "abomination of desolation standing in the holy place" (Matt. xxiv. 15), are in evident connection with this, and confirm this thought. "Abomination" is the regular word in the Old Testament, to express what idolatry is in the sight of God; but here it is established in what was but awhile before professedly His temple. For until the middle of Daniel's seventieth week, from the beginning of it, sacrifice and oblation have been going on among the returned people in Jerusalem. This was under the shelter of the covenant with that Gentile "prince" of whom the prophet speaks as the "coming one." At first, he is clearly therefore not inspired with the malignity toward God which he afterwards displays. Now, energized by Satan, from whom he holds his throne, and incited by the dread power that holds Jerusalem itself, he makes his attack upon Jehovah's throne itself, and as represented by this image, takes his place in defiance in the sanctuary of the Most High.

The connection of this prophecy with those in Daniel and in Matthew makes plain the reason of the image being made and worshiped. The head of the Roman earth, and of this last and worst idolatry, is not in Judæa, but at Rome; and he who is in Judæa, of whatever marvelous power possessed, is yet only the delegate of the Roman head. Thus the image is made to represent this supreme power, and the worship paid to it is in perfect accordance with this. Here in Judæa, where alone now there is any open pretension to worship the true God,—here there is call for the most decisive measures. And thus the death-penalty proclaimed for those who do not worship. Jerusalem is the centre of the battle-field, and here the opposition must be smitten down. "And he causeth all, both small and great, both rich and poor, both free and bond, that they should give them a mark upon their right hand and upon their forehead, and that no one should be able to buy or sell except he have the mark, the name of the beast, or the number of his name."

Thus, then, is that "great tribulation" begun of which the Lord spoke in His prophecy in view of the temple. We can understand that the only hope while this evil is permitted to have its course is, that flight to the mountains which He enjoins on those who listen to His voice. Israel have refused that sheltering wing under which He would have so often gathered them, and they must be left to the awful "wing of abominations" (Dan. ix. 27, *Heb.*) on account of which presently the "desolator" from the north swoops down upon the land. Still His pity whom they have forsaken has decreed a limit, and "for His elect's sake, whom He hath chosen, He hath shortened the days."

Why is it that *breath* is given to the image? Is it in

defiance of the prophet's challenge of the "dumb idols," which "speak not through their mouth"? Certainly to make an image speak in such a place against the Holy One would seem the climax of apostate insolence. But it only shows that the end is indeed near.

What can be said of the "number of the beast"? The words, "Here is wisdom: let him that hath understanding count the number of the beast," seem directly to refer to those whom Daniel calls "the wise," or "they that understand among the people," of whom it is said, concerning the words of the vision "closed up and sealed till the time of the end," that "none of the wicked shall understand, but the wise shall understand." The "wise," or "they that understand," are in Hebrew the same word— the *maskilim*, and remind us again of certain psalms that are called *maskil* psalms, an important series of psalms in this connection, four of which (lii.–lv.) describe the wicked one of this time and his following; while the thirty-second speaks of forgiveness and a hiding-place in God, the forty-second comforts those cast out from the sanctuary, and the forty-fifth celebrates the victory of Christ, and His reign, and the submission of the nations. Again, the seventy-fourth pleads for the violated sanctuary; the seventy-eighth recites the many wanderings of the people from their God; the seventy-ninth is another mourning over the desolation of Jerusalem; the eighty-eighth bewails their condition under a broken law; and the eighty-ninth declares the "sure mercies of David. The hundred and forty-second is the only other *maskil* psalm.

Moll may well dispute Hengstenberg's assertion that these psalms are special instruction for the *Church*. On the other hand, the mere recital of them in this way may convince us how they furnish the very key-note to Israel's condition in the time of the end, and may well be used to give such instruction to the remnant amid the awful scenes of the great tribulation. In Revelation, it will not be doubtful, I think, to those who will attentively consider it, that we have in this place a *nota bene* for the *maskilim*.

Can we say nothing, then, as to the number of the beast?

As to the individual application, certainly, I think, nothing. We cannot prophesy; and until the time comes, the vision in this respect is "sealed up." The historical interpreters, for whom indeed there should be no seal, if their interpretation be the whole of it, generally agree upon *Lateinos* (the Latin), which has, however, an *e* too much, and therefore would make but 661. Other words have been suggested, but it is needless to speak of them: the day will declare it.

Yet it does not follow but that there may be something for us in the number of significance spiritually. The 6 thrice repeated, while it speaks of labor and not rest,—of abortive effort after the divine 7, declares the evil in its highest to be limited and in God's hand. This number is but, after all, we are told, "the number of a man;" and what is man? He may multiply responsibility and judgment; but the Sabbath is God's rest, and sanctified to Him: without God, he can have no Sabbath. This 6, 6, 6, is the number of a man who is but a beast, and doomed.

With this picture in Revelation, we are to connect the prophecies of Antichrist which we have elsewhere in the New Testament, and which we have briefly considered. The apostle John has shown us distinctly that he will deny the Father and the Son,—the faith of Christianity,—and (not that there *is* a Christ, but) that *Jesus* is the Christ. He is thus distinctly identified with the unbelief of Israel, as he is impliedly an apostate from the Christian faith, in which character the apostle plainly speaks of him to the Thessalonians. He is a second Judas, "the son of perdition," the ripe fruit of that "falling away" which was to come before the day of the Lord came,—itself the outcome of that "mystery of of iniquity" (or "lawlessness") then at work. He is the "wicked," or "lawless one,"—not the sinful *woman*, the harlot of Revelation, but the "*man* of sin."

Every word here claims from us the closest attention. The sinful *woman* is still professedly subject to the man, antichristian, because in fact putting herself in Christ's place, claiming a power that is His alone. Nevertheless, she claims it in His name, not in her own. The pope assumes not to be Christ, but the vicar of Christ. The real "*man* of sin" throws off this womanly subjection. He is no vicar of Christ, but denies that Jesus is the Christ. He sits in the temple of God, showing himself that he is God. Yet, even as Christ owns, and brings men to worship, the Father, so Antichrist brings men to worship another, as Revelation has shown us. There is a terrible consistency about these separate predictions, which thus confirm and supplement one another.

We see clearly now that the temple in which he sits is not the Christian church, but the Jewish temple, and how he is linked with the abomination of desolation, spoken of by Daniel and by the Lord, an abomination, which brings in the time of trouble lasting till the Son of Man comes in the clouds of heaven as Saviour of Israel and of the world.

The abomination is mentioned three times in Daniel, the only place that is equivocal in its application to the last days being that of the eleventh chapter (*v.* 31). The connection would refer it there to Antiochus Epiphanes, the Grecian oppressor of Israel, who, near the middle of the second century before Christ, profaned the temple with idolatrous sacrifices and impure rites. It is agreed by commentators in general that the whole of the previous part of the chapter details in a wonderful manner the strife of the Syrian and Egyptian kings, in the centre of which Judæa lay. From this point on, however, interpreters differ widely. The attempt to apply the rest of the prophecy to Antiochus has been shown by Keil and others to be an utter failure. The time of

THE TRINITY OF EVIL, ETC. 155

trouble such as never was, yet which ends with the deliverance of the people (chap. xii. 1) corresponds exactly with that which is spoken of in the Lord's prophecy on the mount of Olives ; and the "time, times, and a half" named in connection with the abomination of desolation, and which the book of Revelation again and again brings before us, are alone sufficient to assure us that we have here reached a period future to us to-day. The connection of all this becomes a matter of deepest interest.

That the whole present period of the Christian dispensation should be passed over in Old-Testament prophecy is indeed not a new thing to us ; and the knowledge of this makes the leap of so many centuries not incredible. If, however, the "time, times, and a half," or twelve hundred and sixty days, from the setting up of the abomination, contemplate *that* abomination set up by Antiochus, more than a century and a half before Christ, then the reckoning of this time is an utter perplexity. Yet, what other *can* be contemplated, when in all this prophecy there is none other referred to? To go back to chaps. viii. or ix. to find such a reference, overlooking what is before our eyes, would seem out of question. What other solution of the matter is possible?

Now we must remember that the book is shut up and sealed until the "time of the end,"—a term which has a recognized meaning in prophecy, and cannot apply to the times of Antiochus, or to those of the Maccabees which followed them. It assures us once more that the prophecy reaches on to the days of Matt. xxiv.; and that the abomination of desolation there must be the abomination here. Yet how can it be? Only, surely, in one way : if the application to Antiochus, while true, be only the partial and incipient fulfillment of that which looks on to the last days for its exhaustive one, then indeed all is reconciled, and the difficulty has disappeared. This, therefore, must be the real solution.

What we have here is only one example of that double

fulfillment which many interpreters have long since found in Scripture prophecies, and of which the book of Revelation is the fullest and the most extended. There may be a question here as to how far the double fulfillment in in this case reaches back. With this we have not to do, for we are not primarily occupied with Daniel. It is sufficient for our purpose, if we are entitled to take the abomination of desolation here (as it certainly appears that we are bound to take it,) as in both places the same, and identical with that which we find in the New Testament.

Going on in the eleventh chapter, then, to the thirty-sixth verse, we find the picture of one who may well be the same as the second "beast" of Revelation. If at the first look it might appear so, a further consideration, it is believed, will confirm the thought of this. We must quote the description in full.

"And the king shall do according to his will; and he shall exalt himself, and magnify himself above every god, and shall prosper till the indignation be accomplished, for that that is determined shall be done. Neither shall he regard the God of his fathers, nor the Desire of women, nor regard any god; for he shall magnify himself above all. But in his estate shall he honor the god of forces; and a god whom his fathers knew not shall he honor with gold and silver, and with precious stones, and pleasant things. Thus shall he do in the most strong holds with a strange god, whom he shall acknowledge and increase with glory; and he shall cause them to rule over many, and shall divide the land for gain."

If we take the prophecy as closely connected, at least from the thirty-first verse,—and we have seen that there seems a necessity for this,—then this king is described in his conduct after the abomination of desolation has been set up in the temple; and this strange, and it might seem contradictory character that is ascribed to him, would seem to mark him out sufficiently, that he sets himself up

above every god, and yet has a god of his own. This is
exactly what is true of the antichristian second beast:
and there can scarcely be another at such a time, of whom
it can be true. But let us look more closely.

First, he is a king; and the place of his rule is clearly,
by the connection, in the land of Israel. Thus he fills the
identical position of the second beast. Then he does according to his own will, is his own law—"lawless," as in
Thessalonians. His self-exaltation above every god
naturally connects itself with blasphemy against the God
of gods, spite of which he prospers till the indignation is
accomplished,—that is, the term of God's wrath against
Israel, a determinate, decreed time. This is the secret of
his being allowed to prosper, that God wills to use him
as a rod of discipline for His people. Israel's sins give
power to their adversaries.

The next verse intimates that he is a Jew himself, an
apostate one, for he regards not the God of his fathers.
It is not natural to apply this to any other than the true
God, and then his ancestry is plain. Then too the "desire of women," put as here among the objects of worship, is the Messiah, promised as the "woman's seed."
Thus his character comes still more clearly out.

Yet, though thus exalting himself, he has a god of his
own, the "god of forces," or "fortresses." And we have
seen the second beast's object of worship is the first
beast; a political idol, sought for the strength it gives, a
worship compounded of fear and greed. Thus it is indeed a god whom his fathers knew not, none of the old
gods of which the world has been so full, although the
dark and dreadful power behind it is the same: the face
is changed, but not the heart.

Indeed strongholds are his trust, and he practices against
them with the help of this strange god: this seems the
meaning of the sentence that follows. "And whosoever acknowledges him he will increase with glory, and cause him
to rule over the multitude, and divide the land for gain."

In all this we find what agrees perfectly with what is elsewhere stated of the "man of sin." There are no doubt difficulties in interpreting this part of Daniel consistently all through, especially in the connection of the "king" here spoken of with the setting up of the abomination in the thirty-first verse. For it is the *king of the north* who there seems to inspire this; and the king of the north is throughout the chapter the Grecian king of Syria, and the part he plays is clearly that which Antiochus did play. From this it is very natural that it should be conceived (as by some it is) that the king of the north and Antichrist are one. If this were so, it would not alter any thing that has been said as to the application of the prophecy, although there might be a difficulty as to a Grecian prince becoming a Jewish false Christ.

But there is no need for this; nor any reason that I am aware why the perpetration of the awful wickedness in connection with Jehovah's sanctuary should not be the work of more than even the two beasts of Revelation. It is certainly striking that in chap. viii., where the rise of this latter-day Grecian power is depicted, the taking away of the daily sacrifice is linked in some way with his magnifying himself against the Prince of the host (*v.* 11). It may not be positively asserted that it is done by him, (as most translators and interpreters however give it,) yet the connection is so natural, one might almost say, inevitable, that, had we this passage alone, all would take it so. How much more would one think so when the eleventh chapter seems so entirely to confirm this?

Let it be remembered that Greece was one of the provinces of the Roman empire, and as such would seem to be subject to it upon its revival, whether or not the bond with it be broken before the end. Why not a combination of powers and motives in the commission of this last blasphemous crime, even as in the cross Jew and Gentile were linked together?

The instrument is no doubt the antichristian power in

Judæa, but the Grecian power may none the less have its full part, and both of these be in subordination to the head of the western empire.

PART IV.

THE EARTH-TRIAL. (CHAP. XIV.)

"First-Fruits." (*vv.* 1-5.)

THE manifestation of evil is complete; we are now to see God's dealings as to it. These acts of Satan and his ministers are a plain challenge of all His rights in Israel and the earth; and further patience would be no longer patience, but dishonor. Hence we find now, as in answer to the challenge, *the Lamb upon Mount Zion*, —that is, upon David's seat; and as the beast's followers have his mark upon them, so the followers of Christ, associated with Him here, have His and His Father's name upon their foreheads. What this means can scarcely be mistaken.

Zion is not only identified in Scripture with David and his sovereignty, but very plainly with the sovereign grace of God, when everything intrusted to man had failed in Israel, priesthood had broken down, the ark gone into captivity in the enemy's land, and although restored by the judgment of God upon the Philistines, was no more sought unto in the days of Saul. He, though Jehovah's anointed king, had become apostate. All might seem to have gone, but it was not so; and in this extremity, as the seventy-eighth psalm says, "Then the Lord awaked as one out of sleep, . . . and He smote His adversaries backward. Moreover, He refused the tent of Joseph, and chose not the tribe of Ephraim, but chose the tribe of Judah—the Mount Zion which He loved. . . . He chose also David His servant." Nor was this a temporary choice: as a later psalm adds, "For Jehovah hath chosen Zion; He hath desired it for His habitation. This is My rest forever: here will I dwell, for I have desired it." (Ps. cxxxii. 13, 14.)

Thus, though the long interval of so many centuries may seem to argue repentance upon God's part, it is not really so: "God is not man, that He should lie; nor the son of man, that He should repent." The Lamb on Zion shows us the true David on the covenanted throne, and Zion by this lifted above the hills indeed. The vision is of course anticipative, for by and by we find that the beast still exists. The end is put first, as it is with Him who sees it from the beginning, and then we trace the steps that lead up to it.

But who are the hundred and forty-four thousand associated with the Lamb? Naturally one would identify them with the similar number sealed out of the twelve tribes in the seventh chapter, and the more so that the Lamb's and His Father's name upon their foreheads seems to be the effect of this very sealing, which was upon the forehead also. No other mark is given us as to them in the former vision, of whom we read as exempted from the power of the locusts afterward. Here, if it is not directly affirmed that these are sealed, yet it seems evident, a seal having been often a stamp with a name: and the purpose of the sealing in the former case being to mark them out as God's, this is manifestly accomplished by the name upon them. This open identification with Christ in the day of His rejection might seem to be what would expose them to all the power of the enemy, yet it is that which in fact marks them for security. In reality, what a protection is the open confession of Christ as the One we serve! There is, in fact, no safer place for us than that of necessary conflict under the Lord's banner; and the end is glory. Here they stand—these confessors, openly confessed by Him on His side; and their having been through the suffering and the conflict is just that which brings them here upon the mount of royalty: it is "if we suffer, we shall also reign with Him."

Another inestimable privilege they have got, though clearly an earthly, not a heavenly company: they are able to learn a song that is sung in heaven. "And I heard a voice from heaven, as a voice of many waters, and as a voice of great thunder; and the voice which I heard was of harpers harping with their harps; and they sing a new song before the throne, and before the four living beings and the elders: and no one was able to learn the song, except the hundred and forty-four thousand that were purchased from the earth."

It is clear that the company here occupy a place analogous to that of the Gentile multitude of the seventh chapter, who stand before the throne and the living ones also. The vision in either case being anticipative, we can understand that earth and heaven are at this time brought near together, and that "standing" before the throne and "singing" before the throne involve no necessary heavenly place for those who sing or stand there. Here they *stand* upon Mount Zion while they *sing* before the throne,—if, that is, the singers are primarily the hundred and forty-four thousand, as many think. What seems in opposition to this is that the voice is heard from heaven, and that the company on Mount Zion are spoken of as *learners* of the song. On the other side, the difficulty is in answering the question, Who are these harpers, plainly human ones, who are distinguished from the elders, yet in heaven at this time? Remembering what the time is may help us here. May they not be the martyrs of the period with which the prophecy in general has to do,— those seen when the fourth seal is opened, and those for whom they are bidden to wait—the sufferers under the beast afterward? two classes which are seen as completing the ranks of the first resurrection in the twentieth chapter. These would give us a third class, evidently—neither the heavenly elders nor the sealed ones of Israel; and *yet in closest sympathy with the latter.* It could not be thought strange that these should be able to learn *their* song. And at the time when the Lamb is King on Zion, this third class would certainly be found filling such a place as that of the harpers here.

This seems to meet every difficulty, indeed: for their song would clearly be a new song, such as neither the Old Testament nor the revelation of the Church-mystery could account for; while the living victors over the beast would seem rightly here to enter into the song of others, rather than to originate it themselves.

But they have their own peculiar place, as on Mount Zion, first-fruits of earth's harvest to God and to the Lamb, purchased from among men, (grace, through the blood of Christ, the secret of their blessing, as of all other,) but answering to that claim in a true undefiled condition, in virgin-faithfulness to Him who is afresh espousing Israel to Himself. In their mouth thus no lie is found, for they are blameless: and these last words we shall surely read aright when we remember that to those who have not received the love of the truth, "God will send strong delusion, that they may believe *the* lie" (2 Thess. ii. 11), and the apostle's question, "Who is *the* liar, but he that denieth that Jesus is the Christ?" and that "he is the antichrist who denieth the Father and the Son." (1 Jno. ii. 21, 22.) The names of the Lamb and of His Father are on the foreheads of these sealed ones.

The Everlasting Gospel. (*vv.* 6, 7.)

It is a foregleam of the day that comes that the first vision of this chapter shows us: but, although the day is coming fast, we have first to see the harbingers of judgment, and then the judgment, before it can arrive. Righteousness, unheeded when it spoke in grace, must now speak in judgment, that "the work of righteousness" may be "peace; and the effect of righteousness, quietness and assurance forever." (Isa. xxxii. 17.)

In this way it is that we come now to what seems to us perhaps a strange, sad gospel, and yet is the everlasting one, which an "angel flying in mid-heaven," preaches to the inhabitants of the earth. And this is what his voice declares: "Fear God, and give glory to Him; for the hour of His judgment is come; and worship Him who made heaven and earth and the sea and the fountains of waters."

How any one could confound this gospel of judgment with the gospel of salvation by the cross would seem hard to understand, except as we realize how utterly the difference of dispensations has been ignored in common teaching, and how it is taken as a matter of course that the "gospel" must be always one and the same gospel; which even the epithet "everlasting" is easily taken to prove. Does it not indeed assert it?—that the same gospel was preached, of course, in a clearer or a less clear fashion, all through the dispensation of law and before it?

No doubt the everlasting gospel must be that which from the beginning was preached, and has been preaching ever since, although it should be plain that "the hour of His judgment is come" is just what with truth no one in Christian times *could* say. Plain it is too that the command to worship God the Creator is not what any one who *knew* the gospel could take as that. In fact, the gospel element, or glad tidings, in the angel message is just found in that which seems most incongruous with it to day—that the "hour of His judgment is come." What else in it is "tidings" at all? That certainly is; and if serious, yet to those who know that just in this way deliverance is to come for the earth, it is simple enough that the coming of the delivering judgment is in fact the gospel.

Listen to that same gospel, as a preacher of old declared it. With what a rapture of exultation does he break out as he cries,—

"Oh sing unto the Lord a new song!
Sing unto the Lord, all the earth.
Sing unto the Lord, bless His name;
Show forth His salvation from day to day!
Declare His glory among the nations,
His marvelous works among all the peoples!

* * * * * *

Tremble before Him, all the earth!
Say among the nations that the Lord reigneth;
The world also is established, that it cannot be moved:
He shall judge the peoples with equity.
Let the heavens be glad, and let the earth rejoice!
Let the sea roar, and the fullness thereof!
Let the field exult, and all that is therein!
Then shall all the trees of the wood sing for joy before
 the Lord;
For He cometh, for He cometh, to judge the earth.
He shall judge the world with righteousness,
And the peoples with His truth!" (Ps. xcvi.)

Here is a gospel before Christianity; and it has been sounding out all through Christianity, whether men have heard it or have not. And it is but the echo of what we hear in Eden, before the gate of the first paradise shuts upon the fallen and guilty pair,—that the seed of the woman shall crush the serpent's head. That is a gospel which has been ringing through the ages since, and which may well be called the everlasting one. Its form is only altered by the fact that now at last its promise is to be fulfilled. "Judgment" is now to "return to righteousness." The "rod" is "iron," but henceforth in the Shepherd's hand. Man's day is past, the day of the Lord is come; and every blow inflicted shall be on the head of evil, the smiting down of sorrow and of all that brings it. What can he be but rebel-hearted, who shall refuse to join the anthem when the King-Creator comes into His own again? The angel-evangel is thus a claim for worship from all people, and to Him that cometh every knee shall bow.

The Fall of Babylon. (*v.* 8.)

THAT the message of judgment is indeed a "gospel" we find plainly in the next announcement, which is marked as that of a "second" angel, a "third" following, similar in character, as we shall see directly. Here it is announced that Babylon the Great has fallen: before, indeed, her picture has been presented to us, which we find only in the seventeenth chapter. The name itself is, however, significant, as that of Israel's great enemy, under whose power she lay prostrate seventy years, and itself derived from God's judgment upon an old confederation, the seat of which became afterward the centre of Nimrod's empire. But that was not Babylon *the Great*, although human historians would have given her, no doubt, the palm; with God, she was only the type of a power more arrogant and evil and defiant of Him than the old Chaldæan despot, and into whose hands the Church of Christ has fallen,—the heavenly, not the earthly people. It is an old history rehearsed in a new sphere and with other names,—a new witness of the unity of man morally in every generation.

The sin on account of which it falls reminds us still of Babylon, while it has also its peculiar aggravation. Of her of old it was said, "Babylon hath been a golden cup in the Lord's hand that made all the earth drunken: the nations have drunk of her wine; therefore the nations are mad." (Jer. li. 7.) But it is not said, "the wine of the fury of her fornication." This latter expression shows that Babylon is not here a mere political but a spiritual power. One who belongs professedly to Christ has prostituted herself to the world for the sake of power. She has inflamed the nations with unholy principles, which act upon men's passions, (easily stirred,) as we see, in fact, in Rome. By such means she has gained and retained power; by such, after centuries of change, she holds it still. But the time is at hand when they will at last fail her, and this is what the angel declares now to have come. Babylon is fallen, and that fall is final: it is the judgment of God upon her; it is retributive justice for centuries of corruption; it is a note of the everlasting gospel, which claims the earth for God, and announces its deliverance from its oppressors. But we have yet only the announcement: the details will be given in due place.

The Warning to the Beast-Worshipers.
(vv. 9-13.)

A THIRD angel follows, noted as that, and belonging, therefore, to the company of those that bring the gospel of blessing for the earth. That it comes in the shape of a woe, we have seen to be in no wise against this: Babylon is not the only evil which must perish that Christ may reign; and Babylon's removal only makes way at first for the full development of another form of it more openly blasphemous than this. The woman makes way for the man,—what professes at least subjection to Christ, for that which is open revolt against Him. Here, therefore, the woe threatened is far more sweeping and terrible than in the former case; there are people of God who come out of Babylon, and who therefore were in her to come out (chap. xviii. 4). But the beast in its final form insures the perdition of all who follow it: "If any man worship the beast and his image, and receive his mark in his forehead or in his hand, the same shall drink"—or "he also shall drink"—"of the wine of the wrath of God which is poured out without mixture into the cup of His indignation; and he shall be tormented with fire and brimstone in the presence of the holy angels, and in the presence of the Lamb; and the smoke of their torment ascendeth up forever and ever; and they have no rest, day nor night, who worship the beast and his image, and whosoever receiveth the mark of his name."

It is the beast who destroys Babylon, after having for a time supported her: his own pretension tolerates no divided allegiance, and in him the unbelief of a world culminates in self-worship. Here God's mercy can only take the form of loud and emphatic threatening of extreme penalty for those who worship the beast. In proportion to the fearful character of the evil does the Lord give open assurance of the doom upon it, so that none may unknowingly incur it. Here "the patience of the saints" is sustained in a "reign of terror" such as has never yet been.

Faith too is sustained in another way, namely, by the special consolation as to those who die as martyrs at this time: "And I heard a voice from heaven saying unto me, 'Blessed are the dead that die in the Lord *from henceforth.*'" That is clearly encouragement under peculiar circumstances. All who die in the Lord must be blessed at any time; but that only makes it plainer that the circumstances must be exceptional now which require such comfort to be so expressly provided for them. Something must have produced a question as to the blessedness of those that die at this time; and in this we have an incidental confirmation—stronger because incidental—that *the resurrection of the saints has already taken place.* Were *they* still waiting to be raised, the blessedness of those who as martyrs join their company could scarcely be in doubt. The resurrection having taken place, and the hope of believers being now to enter alive into the kingdom of the Son of Man at His appearing,—as the Lord says of that time, "He that shall endure to the end, the same shall be saved" (Matt. xxiv. 13),—the question is necessarily raised. What shall be the portion of these martyrs, then, must not remain a question; and in the tenderness of divine love the answer is here explicitly given. Specially blessed are those who die from henceforth: they rest from their labors; they go to their reward. The Spirit seals this with a sweet confirming "yea"—so it is. Earth has only cast them out that heaven may receive them; they have suffered, therefore they shall reign with Christ. Thus accordingly we find in the twentieth chapter, that when the thrones are set and filled, those that have suffered under the beast are shown as rising from the dead to reign with the rest of those who reign with Him. Not the martyrs in general, but these of this special time are marked distinctly as finding acknowledgment and blessing in that "first resurrection," from which it might have seemed that they were shut out altogether.

It may help some to see how similar was the difficulty that had to be met for the Thessalonian saints, and which the apostle meets also with a special "word of the Lord" in his first epistle. They too were looking for the Lord, so that the language of their hearts was (with that of the apostle), "*We* who are alive and remain unto the coming of the Lord." They had been "turned to God from idols, to serve the living and true God, and to wait for His Son from heaven;" and with a lively and expectant faith they waited.

But then what about those who were fallen asleep in Christ? It is evident that here is all their difficulty. He would not have them ignorant concerning those that were asleep, so as to be sorrowing for them, hopeless as to their share in the blessing of that day. Nay, those who remained would not go before these sleeping ones: *they* would rise first, and those who were alive would then be "caught up *with them*, to meet the Lord in the air." This for Christians now is thus the authoritative word of comfort. But the sufferers under the beast would not find this suffice for *them;* for them the old difficulty appears once more, and must be met with a new revelation.

How perfect and congruous in all its parts is this precious Word of God! And how plainly we have in what might seem even an obscure or strange expression —"blessed *from henceforth*"—a confirmation of the general interpretation of all this part of Revelation! The historical interpretation, however true, as a partial anticipatory fulfillment, fails here in finding any just solution.

The Harvest and the Vintage. (*vv.* 14-20.)

In the next vision the judgment falls. The Son of Man upon the cloud, the harvest, the treading of the wine-press, are all familiar to us from other Scriptures, and in connection with the appearing of the Lord. We need have no doubt, therefore, as to what is before us here.

The "harvest" naturally turns us back to our Lord's parable, where wheat and tares represent the mingled aspect of the kingdom, the field of Christendom. "Tares" are not the fruit of the gospel, but the enemy's work, who sows not the truth of God, but an imitation of it. The tares are thus the 'children of the wicked one,' deniers of Christ, though professing Christians. The harvest brings the time of separation, and first the tares are gathered and bound in bundles for the burning, and along with this the wheat is gathered into the barn. In the interpretation afterward we have a fuller thing: the tares are *cast into the fire*, and the righteous *shine forth* as the sun in their Father's kingdom.

Here the general idea of harvest would be the same, though it does not follow that it will be a harvest of the same nature. In the harvest-time there are crops reaped of various character: the thought is of discriminative judgment, such as with the sheep and goats of Matt. xxv. There is what is gathered in, as well as what is cast away, and hence the Son of Man is here as that. The vintage-judgment is pure wrath: the grapes are cast into the great wine-press of the wrath of God, and thus it is the angel out of the altar, who has power over the fire, at whose word it comes. The vine of the earth is a figure suitable to Israel as God's vine (Is. v.), but apostate, yet cannot be confined to Israel, as is plain from the connection in which we find it elsewhere. But it represents still apostasy, and thus what we have seen to have its centre at Jerusalem, though involving Gentiles also far and near. Thus the city also outside of which the wine-press is trodden is Jerusalem, as the sixteen hundred furlongs is well known to be the length of Palestine. Blood flows up to the bits of the horses for that distance—of course, a figure, but a terrible one.

Both figures—the harvest and the vintage—are used in Joel, with reference to this time: "Proclaim ye this among the nations; prepare war: stir up the mighty men; let all the men of war draw near; let them come up. Beat your plowshares into swords, and your pruning-hooks into spears: let the weak say, I am strong. Haste ye, and come, all ye nations round about, and gather yourselves together: hither cause *Thy* mighty ones to come down, O Lord! Let the nations bestir themselves, and come up to the valley of Jehoshaphat: for there will I sit to judge all the nations round about. Put ye in the sickle, for the harvest is ripe: come, tread ye, for the wine-press is full, the vats overflow; for their wickedness is great. Multitudes, multitudes in the valley of decision! for the day of the Lord is near in the valley of decision. The sun and the moon are darkened, and the stars withdraw their shining. And the Lord shall roar from Zion, and utter His voice from, Jerusalem; and the heaven and the earth shall shake: but the Lord will be a refuge unto His people, and a stronghold to the children of Israel."

Thus comes the final blessing, and the picture upon which the eye rests at last is a very different one. "So shall ye know that I am the Lord your God, dwelling in Zion My holy mountain: then shall Jerusalem be holy, and there shall no strangers pass through her any more. And it shall come to pass in that day, that the mountains shall drop down sweet wine, and the hills shall flow with milk, and all the brooks of Judah shall flow with waters, and a fountain shall come forth of the house of the Lord and water the valley of Shittim. . . . And I will cleanse their blood that I have not cleansed: for the Lord dwelleth in Zion."

PART V.

THE VIALS OF WRATH. (Chap. xv., xvi.)

The Character of the Judgment Coming.
(Chap. xv)

THE visions of the last chapter plainly reach to the end of judgment in the coming of the Lord Himself. The vials, therefore, cannot come after these or go beyond them: in fact, the coming of the Lord is not openly reached in them, though it may seem implied, for in the vials is filled up the wrath of God. But the coming of the Lord, although necessary to complete the judgment, is yet so much more than this, that it would seem even out of place in a vial of wrath. In the fourteenth chapter, where it is the Lamb's answer to the challenge of the enemy, He does indeed appear: He comes out Himself to answer. But in this also there is more than judgment. The manifestation of Antichrist is met by the manifestation of Christ, as the day antagonizes and chases away the night; but the day then is come. In the vials there is simply the destruction of the evil; and while the previous visions classify in a divine way the objects of wrath, the vials give us rather the history in detail,—the succession of events; though this, of course, like all else, has divine meaning in it. All history has: the difficulty is, with what is common history, to get the facts distinctly and in proportion, which the inspiration of Scripture-history secures for us. But along with this, we have here, what is obscured so much to men, heaven's action in earth's history; and heaven is acting in a more direct manner now that the end is at hand, and the wrath stored up for many generations is to burst upon the earth at last.

"And I saw another sign in heaven, great and marvelous,—seven angels having seven plagues—the last; for in them is finished the wrath of God."

The one bright word here is "FINISHED." For the earth at large, it is indeed so. Judgment comes, as we shall see, at the close of the millennium, upon a special, though, alas! a numerous class; but it is, nevertheless, not earth that rebels, nor can the hand that holds the sceptre be any more displaced. How the voice of the "everlasting gospel" sounds in that word, "finished"! But in proportion as the judgment is final now, so must it be complete, conclusive. All limitations are now removed: the rod of iron thoroughly does its work. As in the Lord's answer to His disciples' question as to this very period: "Wheresoever the carcass"—the corruption that provokes God's anger—"is, there will the eagles be gathered together."

But first—and this is the style of prophecy, as we have seen,—before the judgment strikes, the gathering clouds are for a moment parted, that we may see, not the whole good achieved, but the care of God over His own, who in this scene might seem to have found only defeat and forsaking. Only *one* righteous Man was ever really forsaken. And we are permitted to see how, in fact, He has but hidden in His own pavillion, from the strife of men, those who amid the battle drop down and are lost to sight. "And I saw as it were a sea of glass, mingled with fire; and those that had gotten the victory over the beast, and over his image, and over the number of his name, standing upon the sea of glass, having harps of God. And they sing the song of Moses, the servant of God, and the song of the Lamb, saying, 'Great and marvelous are Thy works, Lord God Almighty; just and true are Thy ways, Thou King of ages. Who shall not fear, O Lord, and glorify thy name? for Thou only art holy; for all nations shall come and worship before Thee; for Thy righteous acts have been made manifest.'"

The sea of glass answers to the brazen sea—the laver

of the temple; but it is glass, not water: purification is over, with the need of it; the fire mingled with it indicates what they have passed through, which God has used for blessing to their souls. That they are a special class cannot be questioned,—martyrs under the beast, who have found victory in defeat, and are perfected and at rest before the throne of God.

They sing a mingled song—of Moses and of the Lamb, conquerors as those who were delivered out of Egypt, but by the might of Him who goes forth as a "man of war" for the deliverance of His people. The song of the Lamb looks to the victories recorded in this book, in which the "works" of the Lord God Almighty of the Old Testament are repeated by Him who as King of the ages manifests thus His "ways" as true and righteous throughout the dispensations.*

Divine promises are being fulfilled: God is once more taking up the cause of His ancient people, while the sufferers in Christian times are no less being vindicated, and their enemies judged. Great Babylon, with the blood of the prophets in her skirts, comes into remembrance before God. He has not slept, when most He seemed to do so; and now acts in judgment that makes all men fear. Ripened iniquity, come to a head, wherever we may look, claims the harvest-sickle. The open challenge of the enemy brooks no delay in answering it. It is the only hope for the earth itself, which will learn righteousness when His judgments are in it. While the New Testament here coalesces with the voice of prophecy in the Old, and the cycle of the ages is completed and returns into itself, only with a *Second* Man, a new creation and the paradise of God. Truly Christ is "King of the ages."

---

*There is an alternative reading accepted by most editors,—"*nations*," found in the Alexandrian and Vatican MSS., with the Ethiopic and Coptic versions. "*Ages*" is found in the Sinaitic and Ephræmi MSS., with the Vulgate. The Revised Version, with Westcott & Hort, prefer the latter, which has the oldest authority in its favor, and, I judge, the spiritual sense.

And now the temple of the tabernacle of testimony is opened, where the ark of His covenant has been already seen. Faithful to that covenant now, in which Israel and the earth are together ordained to blessing, the seven angels with the seven last plagues issue forth as the result of that faithfulness. Thus they are arrayed in pure white linen, and girded with golden girdles: it is the glory of God in behalf of which they serve, as the bowls or vials are also golden, and filled with *His* wrath. From the glory of God and from His power smoke fills the temple. None can therefore approach to intercede. There can be no more delay: long-suffering patience is exhausted: "no one was able to enter into the temple until the seven plagues of the seven angels were fulfilled."

The Vials of Wrath. (Chap. xvi.)

The vials of wrath are now poured out upon the earth at the bidding of a great voice from the temple. The wrath of God is no mere ebullition of passion that carries away the subject of it. It waits the word from the sanctuary; and at length that eventful word is spoken. Completing the divine judgments, the range of the vials is not narrower than that of the prophetic earth, and in this, differ from the trumpet-series which otherwise they much resemble. Another resemblance which is significant is to the plagues of Egypt, which were at once a testimony to the world and for the deliverance of Israel. Israel is here also in her last crisis of trouble, and waiting for deliverance, for which these judgments, no doubt, prepare the way, though that which alone accomplishes it, the coming of the Lord Himself, is not plainly included.

The first vial is poured out distinctively, in contrast with the sea and rivers, etc., upon the *earth*, like the first trumpet-judgment; but the effect is different: an evil and grievous sore breaks out upon those that have the mark of the beast, and that worship his image. In Egypt such a plague routed their wise men so that they could not stand before Moses. According to the natural meaning of such a figure, it would speak of inward corruption which is made now to appear outwardly in what is painful, loathsome, and disfiguring; those who had accepted the beast's mark being thus otherwise marked and branded with what is a sign of their moral condition. As the apostle shows (Rom. i.) idolatry is itself the sign of corruption which would degrade God into creature semblance in order to give free rein to its lusts. Here it is openly the worship of the image of him whom Scripture stamps as the "beast," which those branded with his mark give themselves up to. The excesses of the French revolution, when God was dethroned to make way for a prostitute on the altar of Notre Dame, if they be not, as some have thought them, the fulfillment of this vial, may yet sufficiently picture to us how it may be fulfilled in a time of trouble such as never was before, and, thank God, such as never will be afterward.

The second vial is poured out on the sea, and the sea becomes like the blood of a dead man, and every living soul dies in the sea. Here we have the second trumpet in its effect upon the sea, but without the limitation there. And there seems a difference also, in that the blood is as of a dead man. It cannot be that it is merely dead blood, for all blood shed becomes that almost at once, and the sea turned into blood would by itself suggest death without the addition. Would it not rather seem to be, that the blood of a dead man, while it is indeed dead blood, is also that which has *not* been shed? Life has not been violently taken, but lost though disease or natural decay. Thus in the law that which had died of itself was forbidden as food, because it spoke of internal corruption, as the life still vigorous when the blood was shed did not. If this thought be the true one, then the state imaged under the second vial is not that of strife and bloodshed among the nations, but of professed spiritual life gone, which the addition, "Every living soul died in the sea," affirms as complete. Life there might be in hunted and outlawed men, no longer recognized as part of the nations; but the mass was dead. This seems to me the only thought that gives consistently the full force of the expressions.

The third vial is poured out upon the rivers and fountains of waters, the sphere affected by the third trumpet; but in the trumpet they are made bitter, now they become blood, which, as owned to be the judgment of God upon persecutors, seems clearly to speak of bloodshed: they are given blood to drink. Where naturally there should be only sources of refreshment, as perhaps in family life, there are found instead strife and the hand of violence. The angel of the waters may be in this case the representative of that tender care of the Creator over the creature-life, which in this case comes to be against the persecutor and applauds His judgments; as the altar does, upon which the lives of the martyrs have been poured out to God.

This seems to consist well with what has been given as the interpretation of the second seal.

The fourth angel pours his vial upon the sun, and it scorches men with its heat; but they only blaspheme God's name, and repent not. Here, as often, the head of civil authority seems to be represented; and Napoleon's career has been taken as in the historical application the fulfillment of it. In him after the immorality, apostasy, and bloodshed of that memorable revolution, imperial power blazed out in a destructive fierceness, that might well be symbolized as scorching heat. There was splendor enough, but it was not "a pleasant sight to behold the sun:" the nation over which he ruled was oppressed with "glory," and soon manifested how its vitality had been exhausted by its hot-house growth. His career was brief; and briefer still in proportion to its intensity will be the closing despotism, which will be followed by the kingdom of the Son of Man, and the display of a true glory unseen by the world before. Then shall that be fulfilled which is written: "the Sun shall not smite thee by day," and how great will be the joy of this that is added, "thy Sun shall no more go down; . . . the Lord shall be thine everlasting Light." (Is. lx. 20.)

The fifth vial is poured out, and the meteoric blaze is passed. Poured on the throne of the beast, darkness spreads over his kingdom. It is the foreshadow of that final withdrawal of light, the "outer darkness" of that awful time, when they who have so often bidden God withdraw from them will be taken at their word. But who out of hell can tell what that will be? The sun has ascribed to it by the science of the day more than ever was before done; but who at any time could have said to the glowing sun, Depart from me: I desire darkness? Yet this is what they say to God.

Nor does the darkness work repentance: "They gnawed their tongues for pain, and blasphemed the God of heaven, because of their pains and sores, and repented not of their deeds." Such is the hardening character of sin; and such is the impotence of judgment in itself to break the heart and subdue the soul to God.

So far, spite of the general character of the vials, they seem to have to do almost entirely with the beast and his followers; and these are, as we know, the principal enemies of Israel, and the boldest in defiance of God, at the time of the end. Nevertheless there are other adversaries besides those of the new risen empire of the west. The king of the north or of Greece is evidently in opposition at the close to the "king in the land of Israel, who is the viceroy of the beast in Judea. (Dan. xi.) This king of Greece also, if mighty, is so "not by his own power." (Dan. viii. 24.) There is behind him, in fact, a mightier prince, who in Ezek. xxxviii.–xxxix, comes clearly into view as head of many eastern nations, Gog, of the land of Magog, the prince of Rosh, Meshech and Tubal; Persia, Cush and Phut with the house of Togarmah, (Armenia,) being confederate with him. This is not the place to look at the people to whom all these names refer. Magog, the first of them, by common consent, stands for the Scythians, who, "mixed with the Medes," says Fausset, "became the Sarmatians, whence sprang the Russians." Rosh is thus by more than sound connected with Russia, as Meshech and Tubal may have given their names, but slightly changed, to Moscow and Tobolsk. The connection with Persia and Armenia, and with Greece no less, is easily intelligible at the present day.

Here are powers, then, outside the revived Roman empire, which we find in relation with Israel at the time of the end, and which will find their place in the valley of Jehoshaphat ("Jehovah's judgment") in the day when the Lord sits there to judge all the nations round about. (Joel iii. 12.) Accordingly now, under the sixth vial, the way is prepared for this, and the gathering is accomplished. The sixth vial is poured out upon "the great river Euphrates," the effect being that the water is dried up, "that the ways of the kings of the east may be prepared." The Euphrates is the scene also of the sixth trumpet, which would seem to give but a previous incursion of the same powers that are contemplated here, the door being now set widely open for them by the drying up of the river, the boundary of the Roman empire in the past. In the trumpet there was but an inroad upon the empire; now there is much more than this: it is the gathering for the great day of God Almighty!

Accordingly all the powers of evil are at work: three unclean spirits like frogs come out of the mouth of the dragon, out of the mouth of the beast, and out of the mouth of the false prophet; for they are the spirits of demons, working miracles, who go forth unto the kings of the whole world, to gather them together unto the war of the great day of God Almighty! . . . And they gathered them together unto the place which is called in Hebrew Har-Magedon."

The frogs are creatures of slime and of the night, blatant, impudent impotents, cheap orators, who can yet gather men for serious work. Here, those brought together little know whom they go to meet; but this is the common history of men revealed in its true character. The cross has shown it to us on the one side; the conflict of the last days shows it on the other. The vail of the world is removed, and it is seen here what influences carry them: the dragon, the spirit of a wisdom which, being, "earthly," is "sensual, devilish" (Jas, iii. 15,); the "beast," the influence of power, which apostate from God is bestial (Ps. xlix. 20,); the "false prophet," the inspiration of hopes that are not of God: so the mass are led.

Har-magedon is the "mount of slaughter." We read of Megiddo in the Old Testament as a "valley," not a mountain; whether it refers to this or no, the phrase seems equivalent to the "mountain of the slain," a mountain of heaped up corpses. To this, ignorant of what is before them, they are gathered.

A note of urgent warning is interjected here: no need of declaring the Speaker! "Behold, I come as a thief. Blessed is he that watcheth and keepeth his garments, lest he walk naked, and they see his shame." It is to the world Christ's coming will be that of a thief; for "in such an hour as ye think *not*, the Son of Man cometh." "Blessed is he that watcheth" is, as we see by the closing words, a solemn warning to the heedless. Who will be ready at this time to hear? In any case, wisdom will utter its voice; and none shall go out to meet unwarned the doom of the rebellious. Good it is to find just in this place, whether heeded or not, the pleading of mercy. Not the less terrible on that account the doom that comes.

And now the seventh angel pours his vial into the air. Of "the power of the air" Satan is the prince (Eph. ii. 2), and all Satan's realm is shaken. A great voice breaks out of the throne, saying, It is done; and there are lightnings, and voices, and thunders,—the "voices" showing the lightnings and thunders between which they come to be no mere natural tempest, but divinely guided judgment. There is an unparalleled convulsion; and the great city (Babylon or, as it is applied here, Rome) is divided into three parts, and the cities of the nations generally fall. It is added as to a special object of the divine judgment,—"And Babylon the great was remembered before God, to give unto her the cup of wine of the fierceness of His wrath." This is in brief what is given presently in detail. Babylon has only once before been named in Revelation; but the two following chapters treat of it in full.

Then "every island fled away:" as I suppose, there is no isolation of any from the storm; "and the mountains were not found:" no power so great but it is humbled and brought low. "And a great hail, every stone about a talent weight, fell down from God out of heaven upon men: and men blasphemed God because of the plague of the hail; for the plague thereof was exceeding great."

In the hail the effect of God's withdrawal from men is seen in judgment. The source of light and heat are one; and for the soul God is the source: the hail speaks not of mere withdrawal, but of this becoming a pitiless storm of judgment which subdues all, except, alas! the heart of man which, while his anguish owns the power from which he suffers, remains in its hard impenitency the witness and justification of the wrath it has brought down.

PART VI. (Chap. xvii.–xix. 4.)

BABYLON AND HER OVERTHROW.

BABYLON is already announced as fallen in the fourteenth chapter, and as judged of God under the seventh vial; but we have not yet seen what Babylon is, and we are not to be left to any uncertainty: she has figured too largely in human history, and is too significant a lesson every way, to be passed over in so brief a manner. We are therefore now to be taught the "mystery of the woman."

For she is a mystery; not like the Babylon of old, the plain and straightforward enemy of the people of God: she is an enigma, a riddle, so hard to read that numbers of God's people in every age have taken her, harlot as she is, for the chaste spouse of the Lamb. Yet here for all ages the riddle has been solved for those who are close enough to God to understand it. And the figure is gaudy enough to attract all eyes to her—seeking even to do so. Let us look with care into what is before us in these chapters, in which the woman is evidently the central object, the beast on which she is sitting being only viewed in its relation to her.

It is one of the angels of the vials who exhibits her to the apostle, and his words naturally show us what she is characteristically as the object of divine judgment. As described by him, she is "the great whore that sitteth upon many waters, with whom the kings of the earth have committed fornication, and the inhabitants of the earth have been made drunk with the wine of her fornication."

As brought into sharp contrast with the beast that carries her, we see that she is a woman, has the human form, as the beast has not. A beast knows not God; and in Daniel we have found the Gentile power losing the human appearance which it has in the king's dream to take the bestial, as in the vision of the prophet. In Nebuchadnezzar personally we see what causes the change;—that it is pride of heart which forgets dependence upon God. The woman, on the other hand, professedly owns God, and moreover, as a woman, takes the place of subjection to the man,—in the symbol here, to Christ. When she is removed by judgment, the true bride is seen, to whom she is in contrast, and not (as so many think) to the woman of the twelfth chapter, who is mother, not bride, of Christ, and represents Israel.

But the woman here is a harlot, in guilty relation with the kings of the earth. Her lure is manifestly ambition, the desire of power on earth, the refusal of the cross of Christ,—the place of rejection; and the *wine*—the intoxication—of her fornication makes drunk the "dwellers upon earth." These we have already seen to be a class of persons who with a higher profession have their hearts on earthly things. (Phil. iii. xix.; Rev. iii. 10; xi. 10; xiii. 8.) These naturally drink in the poison of her doctrine.

To see her, John is carried away, however, into the wilderness; for the earth is that, and all the efforts of those who fain would do so cannot redeem it from this. There he sees the woman sitting on a scarlet-colored beast, full of names of blasphemy; easily identified as the beast of previous visions by its seven heads and ten horns.

The beast is in a subjection to the woman which we should not expect. It is the imperial power, but in a position contrary to its nature as imperial, in this harmonizing with the interpretation of the angel afterward,— the " beast that was, and *is not*." In some sort it is; in some sort it is not; and this we have to remember, as we think of its heads and horns. If the beast "is not," necessarily its heads and horns are not. These are for identification, not as if they were existing while the woman is being carried by it. In fact, *she* is now its head, and reigns over its body, over the mass that *was* and that *will be* again the empire, but now "is not."

What are we to say of the scarlet color and the names of blasphemy? Are they prospective, like the horns? The latter seems so, evidently, and therefore it is more consistent to suppose the former also. The difficulty of which may be relieved somewhat by the evident fact, that of these seven heads, only one exists at a time, as we see by the angel's words: the seven seen at once are again for identification, not as existing simultaneously. The scarlet color is that which typifies earthly glory which is simply that: the beast's reign has no link with heaven. That it is full of *names*, not merely *words*, of blasphemy, speaks of the assumption of titles which are divine, and therefore blasphemous to assume. Altogether we see that it is the beast of the future that is presented here, but which could not really exist while carrying the woman. She could not exist in this relation to him, he being the beast that he is, and thus the expression is fully justified, —really alone explains the matter—the "*beast that is not, and will be.*"

There is clearly an identification of a certain kind all through. While the woman reigns, that over which she reigns is still in nature but the beast that was, and that after her reign will again be. There is no fundamental change all through. The Romanized nations controlled by Rome are curbed, not changed. And breaking from the curb, as did revolutionary France at the close of the last century, the wild beast fangs and teeth at once display themselves.

But we are now called to the consideration of the woman, who, as reigning as the professed spouse of Christ over what was once the Roman empire, is clearly seen to be what, as a system, we still call Rome: "that great city which reigneth over the kings of the earth;" which did so even in John's time, although to him appearing in a garb so strange that when he sees her he wonders with a great wonder.

She is appareled in purple and scarlet, for she claims spiritual as well as earthly authority, and these are colors which Rome, as we know, affects, God thus allowing her even to the outward eye to assume the livery of her picture in Revelation. She is decked too with gold and precious stones and pearls, figures of really divine and spiritual truths, which, however, she only outwardly adorns herself with, and indeed uses to make more enticing the cup of her intoxication : "having a *golden cup* in her hand," says the apostle, "full of abominations and filthiness of her fornications." Now we have her name : "And upon her forehead was a name written, ' Mystery, Babylon the Great, the Mother of Harlots and Abominations of the Earth.' "

Her name is Mystery, yet it is written in her forehead. Her character is plain if only you can read it. If you are pure, you may soon know that she is not. If you are true, you may quite easily detect her falsehood. In lands where she bears sway, as represented in this picture, she has managed to divorce morality from religion, that all the world knows the width of the breach. Her priests are used to convey the sacraments, and one need not look at the hands too closely that do so needful a work. In truth it is an affair of the hands, with the magic of a little breath, by means of which the most sinful of His creatures can create the God that made him, and easily new create another mortal like himself. This is a great mystery, which she herself conceives as "sacrament," and you may see this clearly on her forehead then. It is the trick of her trade, which without it could not exist. With it, a little oil and water and spittle become of marvelous efficacy, a capital stock at least out of which at the smallest cost the church creates riches and power, and much that has unquestionable value in her eyes.

"Babylon the great" means "confusion the great."

Greater confusion there cannot be than that which confounds matter and spirit, creature and Creator, makes water to wash the soul, and brings the flesh of the Lord in heaven to feed literally with it men on earth. Yet to this is the larger part of Christendom captive, feeding on ashes, turned aside by a deceived heart, and they cannot deliver their souls, nor say, "Is there not a lie in my right hand?" (Is. xliv. 20.)

Nay, this frightful system has scattered wide the seed of its false doctrine, and the harlot mother has daughters like herself: she is the "mother of harlots and abominations of the earth." Solemn words from the Spirit of truth, which may well search many hearts in systems that seem severed far from Rome, as well as those that more openly approach her. Who dare, with these awful scriptures before them, speak smooth things as to the enormities of Rome? To be protestant is indeed in itself no sign of acceptance with God, but *not* to be protestant is certainly not to be with God in a most important matter. This Roman Babylon is not, moreover, some future form that is to be, though it may develop into worse yet than we have seen. It is that which has been (in the paradoxal language which yet is so lively a representation of the truth) seated upon the beast while the beast " is not." It is Popery as we know it and have to do with it; and woe to kings and rulers who truckle to it, or (again in the bold Scripture words) commit fornication with it! "Come out from her, my people, that ye be not partakers of her sins, and that ye receive not of her plagues!"

"And I saw the woman drunk with the blood of the saints and the blood of the martyrs of Jesus; and when I saw her," says the apostle, "I wondered with a great wonder."

Romish apologists have been forced by the evidence to admit that it is Rome that is pictured here; but they say, and some Protestant interpreters have joined them in it, that it is *pagan* Rome. But how little cause of wonder to

John in his Patmos banishment, that the heathen world should persecute the saints! That this same Rome, professing Christianity, should do it, this would be indeed a marvel. With us it is simple matter of history, and we have ceased to wonder; while, alas! it is true that many to-day no longer remember, and many more think we have no business to remember, the persecutor of old. It was the temper of those cruel times of old, many urge: nineteenth century civilization has tamed the tiger, and Rome now loves her enemies, as the Christian should. But abundant testimony shows how false is this assertion. Here, just before her judgment, the apostle pronounces her condemnation for the murder of God's saints still unrepented of.

The angel now explains the mystery, and begins with the beast. "The beast that was and is not" is clearly from the point of view of the vision,* as has been said. The rule of the woman necessarily destroys beast-character, while it lasts. But the beast will awake from its long sleep: it is "about to come up out of the abyss, and to go into perdition." This coming up out of the abyss, however, as has been elsewhere said, does not seem to be merely the revival of the empire: the key of the abyss in the hands of the fallen star under the fifth trumpet, and the angel of the abyss being the person who by the two languages of his name is the "destroyer" of both Jew and Gentile, would lead us to believe that there was in it the working of satanic power. This is strengthened by the connection of this ascent with the "going into perdition" of that which comes up.

The previous revival under the seventh head would thus be passed over; and the prophecy hastens on to what is most important, the beast pictured here being identified

---

* This is contrary, however, to the view taken of it when considering the thirteenth chapter. But the difficulty of the "beast that *is not*" and the "one *is*," spoken of the heads of the beast, seems in this way to find a better solution. The paragraph as to this in the former place may therefore be considered canceled.

in fact, in the prophecy itself, with its own eighth head. (*v.* 11.) That it has only seven, as seen in the vision, is not against this if the seventh and eighth heads are the same person.

The unhappy "dwellers upon the earth" wonder at this revival, whose names have not from the foundation of the world been written in the book of the Lamb slain. Divine grace is that alone which makes any to differ; and of this we are reminded here. The power that works in the revival of the beast is plainly beyond that of man; and how many in the present day seem to take for granted that what is more than human power must be divine. This is the essence of the "strong delusion" which God sends upon those who have not received the love of the truth that they might be saved. Powers and signs and lying wonders confirm the imperial last head in his pretension; and that they are "*lying*" means, not that they are mere juggling and imposition, but that they are made to foster lies. They shall wonder, "seeing how that the beast was and is not and shall be present [again]."

And "here is the mind that hath wisdom,"—the divine secret for an understanding heart. First, as to the woman: "The seven heads are seven mountains on which the woman sitteth." Surely there need not be much doubt about the application of this; although some would apply it to a new Babylon yet to be built on the Euphrates, and others would make the interpreting word "mountains" to be still a figure of something else. They might indeed easily build Babylon again, that is merely looking at things from a human stand-point; but how could it be said of this new city that "in her was found the blood of prophets and saints, and of all the slain upon the earth"?

That Rome was the seven-hilled city is familiar to every school-boy; and its being a "geographical" mark need not make it unsuited to be one, as Lange believes. It makes it plain, as God would have it surely for His saints whose blood it would shed, and who would need the comfort of knowing that He was against this "Mother and Mistress of churches," with all her effrontery and the crowd that followed her.

God has even, if one might say so, gone out of the way to give a needed plain mark of identification. For it is not easy as a symbol to understand how the heads of the beast should be the seat of the woman. But this does not make it harder for identification, while it seems to illustrate the more the tender thought of God for His people, of which the tokens can never be too many, and in a place like this, of what special value!

But the heads are also seven kings,—consecutive, not contemporaneous rulers; for five had already fallen, one was, and another was yet to come, only to exist for a short time, the beast himself being the final one. Five forms of government have been given by the historians as preceding the imperial in Rome, this last being evidently the existing one in the apostle's day. "One is" we must take as applying to the apostle's day; for at the time of the vision the beast itself "is not," as we have seen. The only other time present would be the time in which the apostle lived himself.

The imperial head came to an end necessarily when the empire as a whole broke up under the attacks of the barbarians; and to make, as Barnes and others do, the exarch of Ravenna the seventh head of the *world*-empire is either to overlook the plain terms of the prophecy, or else to pervert the simple facts of history. The exarchate lasted about two hundred years, which Barnes considers (comparatively) but a "short time;" and the papacy he considers the eighth head. This falls with the exarchate; for the papacy would then be but the seventh, and nothing would correspond.

The seventh head began, according to Elliott, when Diocletian, already emperor, assumed the diadem,—the symbol of despotic sovereignty after the eastern fashion; and he quotes Gibbon's words, that, "like Augustus, Dio-

cletian may be considered the founder of a new empire."
But if this were the seventh head, there was a gap between it and the papacy; and this must have been the time when the beast "was not." This is better in some respects than Barnes, and may be really an anticipative fulfillment, such as we find in the "historical" interpretation generally. But it fails when we come to apply it consistently all through, as where Elliott has to make the burning of the woman with fire by the ten horns to be merely the devastation of the city and the Campagna prior to their giving power to the beast, whereas it is really effected by the beast and the horns together, and is the complete end of the ecclesiastical system which the woman represents. It would be manifestly incongruous to suppose the papacy to hate and consume the Roman Catholic church.

The scheme of prophecy involved in all this, if taken as a whole, would destroy entirely the interpretation of Revelation which has been given in these papers, and is negatived by all the considerations that substantiate this. I do not propose, therefore, to go more fully into it. When the papacy ruled the empire, it had ceased to be in a proper sense, the empire, and then it was that according to the chapter before us, the beast "was not." The true bestial character could not co-exist with even the profession of Christianity.

The beast is necessarily, therefore, secular, not ecclesiastical. When the secular empire fell, the beast was not; though in that contradictory condition the woman might ride it. Since that fall there has been no revival, and therefore as yet no seventh head. The seventh head is constituted that, as I believe, by the union of ten portions of the divided territory to give him power; and the preponderance of Russia in Europe might easily bring about a coalition of this kind. The new imperial head lasts but a short time, is smitten with the sword, possibly degraded to the condition of a "little horn," is revived by the dreadful power of Satan acting through the antichristian second beast of the thirteenth chapter, assumes the blasphemous character in which we have already seen him, and thus goes into perdition at the appearing of the Lord.

This is the beast, as Revelation contemplates him generally, identified with the eighth head, but who is of the seventh, in fact, the seventh, which had the wound by the sword, yet lived. Thus seen, all the passages seem to harmonize,—a harmony which is the main argument for the truth of such an interpretation of them.

"And the ten horns which thou sawest are ten kings which have received no kingdom as yet, but they receive authority as kings one hour with the beast. These have one mind, and give their power and authority unto the beast." Alas! they are united against God and against His Christ: "These shall make war with the Lamb, and the Lamb shall overcome them, for He is Lord of lords, and King of kings; and they that are with Him, called, and chosen, and faithful."

Here we have anticipated the conflict of the nineteenth chapter. These that are with Christ are His redeemed people, as is plain. Angels might be "chosen and faithful," but only *men* are "called;" and when He comes forth as a warrior out of heaven, they, as "the armies that were in heaven, follow Him." The rod of iron which He has Himself is given to His people, and the closing scene in the conflict with evil sees them in active and earnest sympathy with Him.

The waters where the harlot sat are next interpreted as "peoples and multitudes and nations and tongues." With another meaning and intent than where it is spoken of Israel, "her seed is in many waters." Her influence is wide-reaching and powerful; but it is brought to an end: "and the ten horns which thou sawest *and* the beast;"—. so, and not "*upon* the beast," all authorities give it now— "these shall hate the harlot, and make her desolate and naked, and shall eat her flesh, and burn her up with fire." That surely is not a temporary infliction, but a full end; and beast and horns unite in it. She has trampled upon men, and, according to the law of divine retribution, it is done to her. This has been partially seen many times in the history of Rome, and the end of the last century was a dreadful warning of what is soon to come more terribly still upon her. The very profession of Christianity which she in time past used for purposes of gain and power over men will no doubt, by the same retributive law, become at last the mill-stone round her neck forever. And no eye will pity her. For it is God who has "put into their hearts to do His will, and to come to one mind, and to give their kingdom to the beast, until the words of God should be accomplished."

How good to know amid all that day of terror that God is supreme above all, *in* all, the devices of His enemies! Still "He maketh the wrath of man to praise Him, and the remainder of it He restraineth." And this is the time which will most fully demonstrate this. It is the day of the Lord upon all the pride of man to bring it low. It is the day when every refuge of lies shall be swept away, and all the vanity of his thoughts shall be exposed. "The idols He shall utterly abolish." Yea, those who have been their slaves shall fling them to the moles and to the bats. "And the Lord alone shall be exalted in that day." Then the way is prepared for blessing, wide in proportion to the judgment which has introduced it.

The eighteenth chapter gives the judgment from the divine side. The question has been naturally raised, Is it another judgment? There is nothing here about beast or horns,—nothing of man's intervention at all,—and there are signs apparently of another and deeper woe than human hands could inflict. It is this last which is most conclusive in the way of argument, and we shall examine it in its place.

Another angel descends out of heaven, having great authority: and the earth is lighted with his glory. Earth is indeed now to be lighted, and with a glory which is not of earth. Babylon is denounced as fallen,—not destroyed, as is plain by what follows, but given up to a condition which is a spiritual desolation, worse than the physical one of Babylon of old under which she has long lain, and from which the terms seem derived. She has become the dwelling-place of demons—"knowing ones;" Satan's underlings, with the knowledge of many centuries of acquaintance with fallen men, and serpent-craft to use their knowledge; a "hold of every unclean spirit, and a hold of every unclean and hateful bird." The parable of the mustard-seed comes necessarily to mind; and without confining the words here to that, it is amazing to see how deliberately filthy and impure Rome's system is. She binds her clergy to celibacy, forces them to pollute their minds with the study of every kind of wickedness, and then by her confessional system teaches them to pour this out into the minds of those to whom she at once gives them access and power over them in the name of religion itself!

What has brought a professing Christian body into so terrible a condition as this bespeaks? We are answered here by reference once more to her spiritual fornication with the nations and with the kings of the earth, and to the profit which those make, who engage in her religious traffic. As worldly power is before all things her aim, and she has heaven to barter in return for it, the nations easily fall under her sway, and are intoxicated with the "wine of the fury"—the madness—"of her fornication." First of all, it is the masses at which she aims, and only as an expedient to secure these the better, with the kings of the earth. Thus she can pose as democratic among democrats, and as the protector of popular rights as against princes. In feudal times, the church alone could fuse into herself all conditions of men, turning the true and free equality of Christians into that which linked all together into vassalage to herself; and so the power grew which was power to debase herself to continually greater depths of evil. Simoniac to the finger-ends, with her it is a settled thing that the "gift of God can be purchased with money." And with her multiplicity of merchandise, which is put here in catalogue, there will naturally be an abundant harvest for brokers. With these, who live by her, she increases her ranks of zealous followers.

Another voice now sounds from heaven,—"Come forth from her, my people, that ye partake not of her sins, and that ye receive not of her plagues; for her sins have heaped themselves to heaven, and God hath remembered her unrighteousnesses."

Even in Babylon, and thus late, therefore, there are those in her who are the people of God. But they are called to separation. Rome is a false system which yet retains what is saving truth. Souls may be saved in it, but the truth it holds cannot save the false system in which it is found. Truth cannot save the error men would ally with it, nor error destroy the truth. There are children of God, alas! that "suffer Jezebel," but Jezebel's true children are another matter: "I will kill them with death" is God's emphatic word. The testing-time comes when the roads that seemed to lie together are found to separate, and then the necessity of separation comes. Truth and error cannot lead to the same place, and he that pursues the road to the end will find what is at the end.

"Recompense to her as she recompensed; according to her works, double to her double: as she hath glorified herself, and lived luxuriously, so much torment and sorrow give her. For she said in her heart, I sit a queen, and am no widow, and shall see no sorrow. Therefore in one day shall her plagues come on her,—death and sorrow and famine; and she shall be burned up with fire: for strong is the Lord God who hath judged her."

The government of God is equal-handed, and for it the day of retribution cannot be lacking. "God hath remembered" Babylon at last. In truth, He never lost sight of her for a moment. But the wheels of His chariot seem often slow in turning, and there is purpose in it : " I gave her space to repent," He says pitifully: but pity is not weakness,—nay, it is the consciousness of strength that may make one slow. There is no possibility of escape. No height or depth can hide from Him the object of His search:—no greatness, no littleness. The day of reckoning comes at last, and not an item will be dropped from the account.

Then follows the wail of the kings of the earth for her, while they stand off in fear for the calamity that is come upon her, more sentimental than the selfish cry of the merchants, whose business with regard to her has slipped out of their hands. And then comes the detail of it, article by article,—all the luxuries of life, each of which has its price, and ending with "slaves, and souls of men." If one had skill to run through the catalogue here, he would doubtless find that each had its meaning ; but we cannot attempt this now. The end of the traffic is at hand, and the Canaanite is to be cast out of the house of the Lord.

The lament of so many classes shows by how many links Rome has attached men to herself. Her vaunted unity is large enough to include the most various adaptations to the character of men. From the smoothest and most luxurious life to the hardest and most ascetic, she can provide for all grades, and leave room for large diversities of doctrine also. The suppleness of Jesuitism is only that of her trained athletes, and the elasticity of its ethics is only that of the subtlest ethereal distillation of her spirit. But though she may have allurements even for the people of God, she has yet no link with heaven; and while men are lamenting upon earth, heaven is bidden to rejoice above, because God is judging her with the judgment that saints and apostles and prophets have pronounced upon her.

Finally, and reminding us of the prophetic action as to her prototype, "a strong angel took up a great mill-stone, and cast it into the sea, saying, 'Thus with a mighty fall shall Babylon the great city be cast down, and shall be found no more at all.'" And then comes the extreme announcement of her desolation. Not merely shall her merchandise be no more, there shall be no sign of life at all,—no pleasant sound, no mechanic's craft, no menial work, no light of lamp, no voice of bridegroom or of bride; and then the reason of her doom is again given: "For thy merchants were the princes of the earth; for with thy sorcery were all nations deceived. And in her was found the blood of prophets and of saints, and of all that have been slain upon the earth."

Interpretation is hardly needed in all this. The detail of judgment seems intended rather to fix the attention and give us serious consideration of what God judges at last in this unsparing way. Surely it is needed now, when Christian men are being taken with the wiles of one who in a day of conflict and uncertainty can hold out to them a rest which is not Christ's rest; who in the midst of defection from the faith can be the champion of orthodoxy while shutting up the word of life from men; who can be all things to all men, not to save, but to destroy them: at such a time, how great a need is there for pondering her doom as the word of prophecy declares it, and the joy of heaven over the downfall of the sorceress at last.

Heaven indeed is full of joy and gratulation and worship: "After these things, I heard as it were a great voice of a great multitude in heaven, saying, 'Halleluiah! salvation and honor and glory and power belong to our God; for true and righteous are his judgments; for He hath judged the great harlot which did corrupt the earth with her fornication, and hath avenged the blood of his servants at her hand.' And a second time they say,

'Halleluiah!' And her smoke goeth up forever and ever. And the four and twenty elders fell down and worshiped God, saying, 'Amen: halleluiah!'"

We may now briefly discuss the question of how far there is indication here of a divine judgment, apart from what is inflicted by the wild beast and its horns. These, we have read, "shall hate the harlot, and shall make her desolate and naked, and eat her flesh, and burn her up with fire." In the present chapter, we have again, "And she shall be burned up with fire; for strong is the Lord God who hath judged her." The kings of the earth "wail over her when they look upon the smoke of her burning, standing afar off for the fear of her torment." And so with the merchants and the mariners. And finally we read, "Her smoke goeth up forever and ever." Nothing in all this forces us to think of a special divine judgment outside of what is inflicted by human instruments, except the last. The last statement, I judge, does. It cannot but recall to our minds what is said of the worshipers of the beast and false prophet in the fourteenth chapter, where the same words are used; but this is not a judgment on earth at all: could indeed "her smoke goeth up forever and ever" be said of any earthly judgment? The words used are such as imply strict eternity: no earthly judgment can endure in this way; and the language does not permit the idea that the persistency is only that of the effects. No, it is eternity ratifying the judgment of time, as it surely will do; and it is only when we have taken our place, as it were, amid the throng in heaven, that this is seen.

But thus, then, we seem to have here no positive declaration of any judgment of Babylon on earth, save by the hands of the last head of western empire and his kings. Yet the eighteenth chapter, we have still to remember, says nothing of these kings: all is from God absolutely, and at least they are not considered. It has been also suggested that it is the "city" rather than the woman (the ecclesiastical system) that is before us in this chapter; but much cannot be insisted on as to this, seeing that the identification of the woman with the city is plainly stated in the last verse of the previous one, and also that the terms even here suppose their identity.

On the other side, there is in fact no absolute identity; nor is it difficult to think of the destruction of the religious system without its involving at all that of the city; nor, again, would one even suppose that the imperial head, with his subordinates, would utterly destroy the ancient seat of his own empire. Here a divine judgment, strictly and only that, taking up and enforcing the human one as of God, becomes at least a natural thought, and worthy of consideration.

Outside of the book of Revelation, Scripture is in full harmony with this. The millennial earth, as we may have occasion to see again, when we come to speak more of it, is certainly to have witnesses of this kind to the righteous judgment of God upon the objects of it. In it, as it were, heaven and hell are both to be represented before the eyes of men, that they may be fully warned of the wrath to come. During the present time, it is objected, there is not sufficient witness; in the millennium, therefore, there shall be no room left for doubt. Therefore while the cloud and fire rest as of old, but with wider stretch, as of sheltering wings, over Jerusalem (Isa. iv. 5, 6; comp. Matt. xxiii. 37), we have, on the other side, the open witness of the judgment upon transgressors which the Lord Himself renders as a type of the deeper judgment beyond. (Isa. lxvi. 23, 24, comp. Mark ix.)

Beside this, Edom remains desolate, and, to come near to what is before us, Babylon also. (Isa. xiii. 20; xxxiv. 9, 10.) How suitable that Rome, the seat of a power far worse and of far longer continuance should be so visited! Such a judgment would fill out the prophecy most fully and exactly. What a picture of eternal judgment is that of Idumea, in that "year of recompenses for the controversy of Zion"! "And the streams thereof shall be turned into pitch, and the dust thereof into brimstone, and the land thereof shall become burning pitch. It shall not be quenched night nor day; the smoke thereof shall go up forever." Rome is the great Edom as it is the great Babylon, and it would be really strange if there were not to be in her case a similar recompense. Barnes quotes from a traveler in Italy in 1850 what is only a striking confirmation of the story told by all who with eyes open have visited the country: "I behold everywhere, in Rome, near Rome, and through the whole region from Rome to Naples, the most astounding proofs, not merely of the possibility, but the probability, that the whole region of central Italy will one day be destroyed by such a catastrophe. The soil of Rome is *tufa*, with a volcanic subterranean action going on. At Naples, the boiling sulphur is to be seen bubbling near the surface of the earth. When I drew a stick along the ground, the sulphurous smoke followed the indentation. . . . The entire country and district is volcanic. It is saturated with beds of sulphur and the substrata of destruction. It seems as certainly prepared for the flames as the wood and coal on the hearth are prepared for the taper which shall kindle the fire to consume them. The divine hand alone seems to me to hold the fire in check by a miracle as great as that which protected the cities of the plain till the righteous Lot had made his escape to the mountains."

That Rome's doom will be as thus indicated, we may well believe. And it is in awful suitability that she that has kindled so often the fire for God's saints should thus be herself a monumental fire of His vengeance in the day in which He visits for these things!

PART VII. (Chap. xix. 5-xxii.)

THE CONSUMMATION.

The Marriage of the Lamb. (Chap. xix. 5-10.)

THE harlot is now judged. The judgment of the whole earth is at hand. Before it comes, we are permitted a brief vision of heavenly things, and to see the heirs of the kingdom now ready to be established in their place with Him who is about to be revealed. A voice sounds from the throne: "Give praise to our God, all ye His servants,—ye that fear Him, small and great." It is not, of course, a simple exhortation to what in heaven can need no prompting, but a preparation of hearts for that which shall furnish fresh material for it. The response of the multitude shows what it is: "Halleluiah! for the Lord our God, the Almighty, reigneth." The power that was always His He is now going to put forth. Judgment is to return to righteousness. Man's day is at an end, with all the confusion that his will has wrought. The day of the Lord is come, to abase that which is high and exalt that which is low, and restore the foundations of truth and righteousness.

The false church that would have antedated the day of power, and reigned without her Lord, has been already dealt with; and now the way is clear to display the true Bride. "The marriage of the Lamb is come, and His wife hath made herself ready." But the Church has been some time since caught up to meet the Lord: how is it that only now she is "ready"? In the application of the blood of Christ, and the reception of the best robe, fit for the Father's house assuredly, if any could be, she was *then* quite ready. Likeness to her Lord was completed when the glorified bodies of the saints were assumed, and they were caught up to meet Him in the air. The eyes from which nothing could be hid have already looked upon her, and pronounced her faultless: "Thou art all fair, My love: there is no spot in thee." What, then, can be wanting to hinder the marriage? A matter of divine government, not of divine acceptance; and this is the book of divine government. Earth's story has to be rehearsed, the account given, the verdict rendered, as to all "deeds done in the body." Every question that could be raised must find its settlement: the light must penetrate through and through, and leave no part dark. We must enter eternity with lessons all learnt, and God fully glorified about the whole course of our history.

What follows explains fully this matter of readiness: "And it was given unto her that she should array herself in fine linen, bright and pure; for the fine linen is the *righteous acts* of the saints." We see by the language that it is grace that is manifest in this award. We learn by a verse in the last chapter *how* grace has manifested itself: "Blessed are they that have *washed their robes* (*R.V.*), that they might have right to the tree of life, and enter in through the gates into the city." But what could wash deeds *already done?* Plainly no reformation, no "water-washing by the Word." (Eph. v. 26.) The deed done cannot be undone; and no well-doing for the future can blot out the record of it. What, then, can wash such garments? Revelation itself, though speaking of another company, has already given us the knowledge of this: "They have washed their robes, and made them white *in the blood of the Lamb*." (Chap. vii. 14.) Thus the value of that precious blood is found with us to the end of time, and in how many ways of various blessing!

It is not, then, the best robe for the Father's house: *that* robe never needs washing. It is for the kingdom, for the world, in the governmental ways of God with men, that this fine linen is granted to the saints. Yet they take their place in it at the marriage supper of the Lamb; for

Christ's love it is that satisfies itself with the recognition
and reward of all that has been *done for love of Him.*
This is what finds reward; and thus the hireling principle
is set aside.

"And he saith unto me, 'Write, Blessed are they that
are bidden to the marriage supper of the Lamb.'"
Blessed indeed are they that are bidden now! Alas!
they may despise the invitation. But how blessed are
they who, when that day comes, are found among the
bidden ones! I leave for the present the question of who
exactly make up the company of those that form the Bride;
but the Bride assuredly sits at the marriage supper, and
the plural here is what one could alone expect in such an
exclamation as this. There seems, therefore, no ground
in such an expression for distinguishing separate companies as the Bride and the "friends of the Bridegroom."
The latter expression is used by the Baptist in a very
different application, as assuredly *he* had no thought of
any bride save Israel.

"And he saith unto me, 'These are the true words of
God.'" Of such blessedness, it would seem, even the
heart of the apostle needed confirmation. Then, as if
overcome by the rapture of the vision, "I fell down at his
feet," says John, "to worship him. And he saith unto
me, 'See thou do it not: I am a fellow-servant with thee
and with thy brethren that have the testimony of Jesus:
worship God: for the testimony of Jesus is the spirit of
prophecy.'"

All prophecy owns thus and honors Jesus as its subject.
All that own Him, the highest only the most earnestly,
refuse other honor than that of being servants together
of His will and grace. How our hearts need to be en-
larged to take in His supreme glory! and how ready are
we in some way, if not in this, to share the glory which is
His alone with some creature merely! Rome's coarse
forms of worship to saints and angels is only a grosser
form of what we are often doing, and for which rebuke

will in some way come; for God is jealous of any impairment of His rights, and we of necessity put ourselves in opposition to the whole course of nature as we derogate from these. "Little children, keep yourselves from idols."

JUDGMENT OF THE LIVING AT THE APPEARING OF CHRIST. (Chap. xix. 11–21.)

THE prophecy pauses not further now to dilate upon the blessing. There is needed work to be done before we can enter upon this; and the work is the "strange work" of judgment. The vision that follows is as simple as can be to understand, if there are no thoughts of our own previously in the mind to obscure and make it difficult. And this is the way in which constantly Scripture *is* obscured.

Revelation, as the closing book of the inspired Word, supposes indeed acquaintance with what has preceded it, and the links with other prophecy are here especially abundant. The kingdom of Christ is the final theme of the Old Testament, upon which all prophetic lines converge; and the judgment which introduces it is over and over again set before us. The appearing of the Lord, and His personal presence to execute this, are also so insisted on, that nothing but the infatuation of other hopes could prevail to hide it from men's eyes. In the New Testament, the same things face us continually. As we are not considering it for the first time here, it will be sufficient to examine what is in the passage before us, with whatever connection it may have with other scriptures, needful to bring out fully the meaning of it.

Heaven is seen opened, the prophet's stand-point being therefore now on earth, and a white horse appears, the familiar figure of war and victory. It is upon the Rider that our eyes are fixed. He is called "Faithful and True" —known manifestly to be that—and in righteousness He judges and wars: His warring is but itself a judgment. For this, His eyes penetrate as a flame of fire; nothing escapes them. Many diadems—the sign of absolute authority—are on His head. And worthily, for His name in its full reality—name expressing (as always in Scripture) nature—is an incommunicable one, beyond the knowledge of finite creatures. But His vesture is dipped in blood, for already many enemies have fallen before Him. And His name is called—has been and is, as the language implies,—"The Word of God." The gospel of John shows us that in creation already He was acting as that; and now in judgment He is no less so.

Is this revealed name any thing else than His incommunicable one? It would seem not. The thought would appear to be in direct refutation of the skeptical denial of the knowledge of the Infinite One as possible to man. We cannot know infinity, but we can know the One who is infinite,—yea, know Him to *be* infinite: know His name, and not know His name. The Infinite One, moreover, Christ is declared here to be,—no inferior God, but the Highest.

In the power of this, He now comes forth; the armies that are in heaven following their white-horsed Leader, themselves also upon white horses, sharers with Him in the conflict and the victory, clothed in fine linen, white and pure. It is this fine linen which we have just seen as granted to the Bride, and which needed the blood of the Lamb to make it white. It is therefore undoubtedly the same company here as there, only here seen in a new aspect, even as the Lord Himself is seen in a new one. It is communion with Himself that is implied in this change of character. What He is occupied with, they are occupied with; what is His mind is their mind: so, blessed be God, it will be entirely then. None then will be ignorant of His will; none indifferent or half-hearted as to it. Alas! now to how much of it are even the many willingly strangers! and it is this willing ignorance that is so invincible: for all else there is a perfect remedy in the Word of God; but what for a back turned upon that Word?

The Lord comes then, and all the saints with Him. How impossible to think of a providential coming merely here! "When Christ, who is our Life, shall appear," says the apostle, "then shall ye also appear with Him in glory" (Col. iii. 4.) "Know ye not that the saints shall judge the world?" he asks elsewhere. Judgment is now impending: "out of His mouth goeth a sharp sword, that with it He may smite the nations." So Isaiah: "He shall smite the earth with the rod of His mouth, and with the breath of His lips shall He slay the wicked." (Chap. xi. 4.) It needs but a word from Him to cause their destruction; while it is judgment no less *according* to His Word: it is that long and oft threatened, slow to come, but at last coming in the full measure of the denunciation. Patience is not repentance.

"And He shall rule them with an iron rod"—"shepherd" them, to use a scarcely English expression. This is, of course, the fulfillment of the prophecy of the second psalm, and decides against the still retained "break them" of the Revised Version. It is the shepherd's rod—this rod of iron, used in behalf of the flock: as He says in Isaiah again, "The day of vengeance is in My heart, and the year of My redeemed is come; and I looked, and there was none to help, and I wondered that there was none to uphold: therefore Mine own arm brought salvation unto Me, and My fury, it upheld Me." (Chap. lxiii. 4, 5.) This is distinctly in answer to the question, "Wherefore art Thou red in Thine apparel, and Thy garments like him that treadeth in the wine-fat?" and to which He answers, "I have trodden the wine-press alone." Here also "He treadeth the wine-press of the fierceness and wrath of Almighty God."

Would it be believed that commentators have referred this to the cross, and the Lord's own sufferings there? And yet it is so; though the iron rod, with which the treading of the wine-press is associated in this place, is something that is promised to the overcomer in Thyatira (chap. ii. 27)—"To him will I give power over the nations, and he shall rule them with a rod of iron, even as I received of My Father." We have but with an honest mind to put a few texts together after this manner, and all difficulty disappears.

"And He hath on His vesture and on His thigh a name written—'King of kings and Lord of lords."

Now, in terrible contrast to the invitation lately given to the marriage supper of the Lamb, an angel standing in the sun bids the birds of the heaven to the "great supper of God," to feast upon earth's proudest and all their following. Immediately after which the beast and the kings of the earth and their armies are seen gathered together to make war against Him who sits upon the horse, and against His army. We are no doubt to interpret this according to the Lord's words to Saul of Tarsus,—"Saul, Saul, why persecutest thou Me?" But we have seen the idol thrust into Jehovah's temple, and know well that Israel's persecutors rage openly against Israel's God. They are taken thus banded in rebellion, and judgment sweeps them down; the beast and the false prophet that wrought miracles before him (the antichristian second beast of the thirteenth chapter) being exempted from the common death, only to be cast alive into a lake of fire burning with brimstone, where at the end of the thousand years of the saints' reign with Christ we find them still.

The vision is so clear in meaning, that it really has no need of an interpreter; and we should remember this as to a vision, that it is not *necessarily* even symbolic, though symbols may have their place in it, as here with the white horses of that before us, while the horses whose flesh the birds eat are not at all so. The "beast and the kings of the earth" furnish us with the same juxta-position of figure and fact, the figure not at all hindering the general literality of fact. In these prophecies of coming judgment, the mercy of God would not permit too thick a vail over the solemn truth. This is the end to which the world is hastening now, and God is proportionally taking off the vail from the eyes upon which it has been lying, that there may be a more urgent note of warning given as it draws nigh. "Who hath ears to hear, let him hear!"

The Restraint upon Satan. (Chap. xx. 1–3.)

The judgment upon living men is followed by that upon Satan their prince, though not yet is it final judgment. This partial dealing with the great deceiver means that the end of man's trial is not even yet reached. He is shut up in the abyss, or bottomless pit, of which we have read before, but not in hell (the lake of fire). As restraint, it is complete ; and with the devil, the host of fallen angels following him share his sentence. This is not merely an inference, however legitimate. Isaiah has long before anticipated what is here (chap. xxiv. 21–23): "And it shall come to pass in that day that the Lord shall punish the host of the high ones on high, and the kings of the earth upon the earth. And they shall be gathered together as prisoners are gathered in the pit, and shall be shut up in the prison, and after many days they shall be visited. Then the moon shall be confounded and the sun ashamed; for the Lord of Hosts shall reign in Mount Zion, and in Jerusalem, aud before His ancients gloriously."

Here the contemporaneous judgment of men and angels at the beginning of the millennium is clearly revealed, and just as clearly, that it is not yet final. The vision in Revelation is also clear. The descent of the angel with the key and chain certainly need not obscure the meaning. Nor could the shutting up of Satan mean any thing less than the stoppage of all temptation for the time indicated. The "dragon," too, is the symbol for the explanation of which we are (as in the twelfth chapter,) referred to Eden, "the ancient serpent," and then are told plainly, "who is the devil and Satan." It is simply inexcusable to make the interpretation of the symbol still symbolic, and to make the greater stand for the less —Satan the symbol of an earthly empire or any thing of the sort. What plainer words could be used? which Isaiah's witness also abundantly confirms. God has been pleased to remove all vail from His words here, and it does look as if only willful perversity could misunderstand His speech.

That after all this he is to be let out to deceive the nations is no doubt at first sight hard to understand. It is all right to inquire reverently why it should be; and Scripture, if we have learnt Peter's way of putting it together,—no prophecy to be interpreted as apart from the general body of prophecy,—will give us satisfactory, if solemn, answer. The fact is revealed, if we could give no reason for it. Who are we to judge God's ways? and and with which of us must He take counsel? It should be plain that for a thousand years Satan's temptations cease upon the earth; and then they are renewed and successful, the nations are once more deceived.

What makes it so difficult to understand is that many have a false idea of the millennial age, as if it were "righteousness *dwelling*" on the earth instead of "righteousness *reigning*" over it. It is said indeed of Israel, after they are brought to God nationally, "My people shall be *all* righteous" (Is. lx. 21); but that is not the general condition. The eighteenth psalm, speaking prophetically of that time, declares, "The strangers shall submit themselves unto Me," which in the margin is given as "lie," or "yield feigned obedience." They submit to superior power, not in heart; and so it is added, "The strangers shall fade away, and be afraid out of their close places." (Comp. lxvi. 3; lxxxi. 15.) And Isaiah, speaking of the long length of years, says, "The child shall die a hundred years old," but adds, "and the sinner being a hundred years old shall be accursed." (lxv. 20.) So Zechariah pronounces the punishment of those who do not come up to Jerusalem to worship the glorious King (xiv. 17).

The millennium is not eternal blessedness; it is not the Sabbath, to which so many would compare it. It answers rather to the sixth day than the seventh,—to the day when the man and woman (types of Christ and the Church) are set over the other creatures. The seventh is the type of the rest of God, which is the only true rest of the people of God (Heb. iv. 9). The millennium is the last period of man's trial, and that is not rest: trial in circumstances the best that could be imagined, righteousness reigning, the course of the world changed, heaven open overhead, the earth filled with the knowledge of the glory of God, the history of past judgment to admonish for the future; the question will then be fully answered, whether sin is the mere fruit of ignorance, bad government, or any of the accidents of life to which it is so constantly imputed. Alas! the issue, after a thousand years of blessing, when Satan is loosed out of his prison, will make all plain; the last lesson as to man will only then be fully learned.

THE RESURRECTION AND REIGN OF THE SAINTS.
(Chap. xx. 4–6.)

AND now we have what requires more knowledge of the Word to understand it rightly; and here, more distinctly than before, there are vision and the interpretation of the vision, so that we will be inexcusable if we confound them. The vision is of thrones, and people sitting on them, judgment (that is, rule) being put into their hands. "The souls of those beheaded for the witness of Jesus and the word of God" are another company separate from these, but now associated with them; and "those who have not worshiped the beast" seem to be still another. All these live and reign with Christ a thousand years, and the rest of the dead do not live till the thousand years are ended.

That is the vision. The interpretation follows: "This,"

we are told, "is the first resurrection;" and that "blessed and holy is he who hath part in the first resurrection: upon these the second death hath no power; but they shall be priests of God and of Christ, and shall reign with Him a thousand years."

We must look carefully at all this, and in its order. First, the thrones, aud those sitting on them: there should be no difficulty as to who these are, for we have already seen the elders crowned and seated in heaven, and before that have heard the Lord promise the overcomer in Laodicea that he should sit with Him upon His throne. That being now set up upon the earth, we find the saints throned with Him. In the interpretation, it is said they reign with Him a thousand years. The vision is thus far very simple.

Daniel has already spoken of these thrones: "I beheld," he says, "till the thrones were placed," (as the Revised Version rightly corrects the common one,) "and the Ancient of days did sit." (Chap. vii. 9.) But there was then no word as to the occupants of the thrones. It is the part of Revelation to fill in the picture on its heavenly side, and to show us who these are. They are not angels, who, though there may be "principalities" among them, are never said to reign with Christ. They are redeemed men,—the saints caught up at the descent of the Lord into the air (1 Thess. iv.), and who as the armies that were in heaven we have seen coming with the white-horsed King to the judgment of the earth.

This being so, it is evident that the "souls" next spoken of are a separate company from these, though joined to them as co-heirs of the kingdom. The folly that has been taught that they are "souls" simply, so that here we have a resurrection of souls, and not of bodies,—together with that which insists that it is a resurrection of truths or principles, or of a martyr-"spirit"—bursts like a bubble when we take into account the first company of living and throned saints. In the sense intended, Scripture never speaks of a resurrection of *souls*. "Soul" is here used for "person," as we use it still, and as Scripture often uses it; and the word "resurrection" is found, not in the vision, where its signification might be doubtful, but in the explanation, where we have no right to take it as other than literal. What is the use of explanation, except to *explain?*

The recognition of the first company here also removes another difficulty, which troubled those with whom the "blessed hope" revived at the end of the last century, that the first resurrection consisted wholly of *martyrs*. The *second* company does indeed consist of these, and for an evident reason. They are those who, converted after the Church is removed to heaven, would have their place naturally in earthly blessing with Israel and the saved nations. Slain for the Lord's sake, during the tribulation following, they necessarily are deprived of this: only to find themselves in the mercy of God made to fill a higher place, and to be added, by divine power raising them from the dead, to the *heavenly* saints. How sweet and comforting this assurance as to the sufferers in a time of unequaled sorrow!

When we look further at this last company, we find, as already intimated, that it also consists of two parts: first, of those martyred in the time of the seals, and spoken of under the fifth seal; and secondly, the objects of the beast's wrath, as in chap. xiii. 7, 15. This particularization is a perfect proof of who are embraced in this vision, and that we must look to those first seen as sitting on the thrones for the whole multitude of the saints of the present and the past. To all of which it is added that "the rest of the dead lived not again till the thousand years were finished," when we find in fact the resurrection of judgment taking place (*vv.* 11–15). All ought to be simple, then. The "first resurrection" is a literal resurrection of all the dead in Christ from the foundation of the world, a certain group which might seem not to belong to it being specialized, as alone needing this. The first resurrection is "first" simply in contrast with that of the wicked, having different stages indeed, but only one character: "Blessed and holy is he that hath part in the first resurrection! upon such the second death hath no power, but they shall be priests of God and of Christ, and shall reign with Him a thousand years."

To suppose that this passage stands alone and unsupported in the New Testament is to be ignorant of much that is written. "Resurrection *from* the dead," as distinct from the general truth of "resurrection *of* the dead," is special New-Testament truth. The Pharisees knew that there should be "a resurrection of the dead, both of the just and unjust." (Acts xxiv. 15.) But when the Lord spake of the Son of Man rising from the dead, the disciples question among themselves what the rising from the dead could mean (Mark ix. 9, 10.) Christ's own resurrection is the pattern of the believer's. The "order" of the resurrection is distinctly given us: "Christ the firstfruits; afterward, *they that are Christ's* at His coming" (1 Cor. xv. 23): not a general, but a selective resurrection. Such was what the apostle would by any means gain: not, as in the common version, "the resurrection *of*," but "the resurrection *from* the dead." (Phil. iii. 11.)

In his epistle to the Thessalonians, the same apostle instructs us more distinctly as to it, speaking in the way of special revelation, by "the word of the Lord:" "For this we say unto you by the word of the Lord, that we which are alive and remain unto the coming of the Lord shall not prevent"—or, as the Revised Version, "precede"—"them that are asleep. For the Lord Himself shall descend from heaven with a shout, with the voice of the archangel, and with the trump of God: and the dead in Christ shall rise first; then we which are alive and remain shall be caught up together with them in the clouds, to meet the Lord in air; and so shall we ever be with the Lord." (1 Thess. iv. 15-17.) Thus before He appears shall His saints be with Him; and, of course, long before the resurrection of the lost.

But the Lord Himself has given us, in His answer to the Sadducees, what most clearly unites with this vision in Revelation (Luke xx. 34-36). They had asked Him of one who had married seven brethren: "Whose wife shall she be in the resurrection?" meaning, of course, to discredit it by the suggestion. "And Jesus said unto them, 'The children of this world marry, and are given in marriage; but they which shall be accounted worthy to obtain that world, and the resurrection *from* the dead, neither marry nor are given in marriage; neither can they die any more; for they are equal unto the angels; and are the children of God, being the children of the resurrection.'"

Clearly this asserts the fact and gives the character of the special resurrection which the vision here describes. It is one which we must be "accounted worthy" to obtain, not one which nobody can miss: it is grace that acts in giving any one his place in it. Those who have part in it are by that fact proclaimed to be the "children of God," thus again showing that it cannot be a general one. They die no more: that is, (as here) they are not hurt of the second death. They are equal to the angels: above the fleshly conditions of this present life. Finally, it is the resurrection *from* the dead, not *of* the dead merely. All this is so plain that there should be no possibility of mistaking it, one would say; and yet it is no plainer than this scene in Revelation.

How dangerous must be the spell of a false system, which can so blind the eyes of multitudes of truly godly and otherwise intelligent persons to the plain meaning of such scriptures as these! And how careful should we be to test every thing we receive by the Word, which alone is truth! Even the "wise" virgins slumbered with the rest. Which shows us also, however, that error is connected with a spiritual condition, even in saints themselves. May we be kept from all that would thus cloud our perception of what, as truth, alone has power to bless and sanctify the soul!

The Little Season. (*vv.* 7-10.)

Of the millennial earth, not even the slightest sketch is given us here. The book of Revelation is the closing book of prophecy, with the rest of which we are supposed to be familiar; and it is the *Christian* book, which supplements it with the addition of what is heavenly. Thus the reign of the heavenly saints has just been shown us: for details as to the earth, we must go to the Old Testament.

In the millennium, the heavenly is displayed in connection with the earthly. The glory of God is manifested so that the earth is filled with the knowledge of it as the waters cover the sea. Righteousness rules, and evil is afraid to lift its head. The curse is taken from the ground, which responds with wondrous fruitfulness. Amid all this, the spiritual condition is by no means in correspondence with the outward blessing. Even the manifest connection of righteousness and prosperity cannot avail to make men love righteousness, nor the goodness of God, though evidenced on every side, to bring men to repentance. At the "four corners of the earth," retreating as far as possible from the central glory, there are still those who represent Israel's old antagonists, and thus are called by their names—"Gog and Magog." Nor are they remnants, but masses of population, brought together by sympathetic hatred of God and His people,—crowding alike out of light into the darkness: a last and terrible answer to the question, "Lord, what is man?"

The Gog, of the land of Magog, whose invasion of Israel is prophetically described in the book of Ezekiel (xxxviii., xxxix.), is the prototype of these last invaders. There need be no confusion, however, between them; for the invasion in Ezekiel is premillennial, not postmillennial, as that in Revelation is. It is then that Israel are just back in their land (xxxviii. 14), and from that time God's name is known in Israel, and they pollute His holy name no more (xxxix. 7). The nations too learn to know Him (xxxviii. 16, 23). There needs, therefore, no further inquiry to be sure that this is not after a thousand years of such knowledge.

But the Gog and Magog here follow in the track of men who have long before made God known in the judgment He executed,—follow them in awful, reckless disregard of the end before them. This is clearly due to the loosing once more of Satan. While he was restrained, the evil was there, but cowed and hidden. He gives it energy and daring. They go up now on the breadth of the earth—from which for the moment the divine shield seems to be removed, and compass the camp of the saints about, and the beloved city. The last is of course the earthly Jerusalem. The "camp of the saints" seems to be that of the heavenly saints, who are the Lord's host around it. The city is of course impregnable: the rebels are taken in the plain fact of hostility to God and His people; and judgment is swift and complete: "fire came down from God out of heaven, and devoured them." The wicked are extinct out of the earth.

The arch-rebel now receives final judgment. "And the devil, that deceived them, was cast into a lake of fire and brimstone, where the beast and the false prophet are; and they shall be tormented day and night for the ages of ages."

These words deserve most solemn consideration. They are plain enough indeed; but what is there from which man will not seek to escape, when his will is adverse? The deniers of eternal punishment, both on the side of restitution and that of annihilation, are here confronted with a plain example of it. Two human beings, cast in alive into the lake of fire a thousand years before, are found there at the close of this long period still in existence! How evident that this fire is not, therefore, like material fire, but something widely different! All the arguments as to the action of fire in consuming what is exposed to it are here at once shown to be vain. That which can remain a thousand years in the lake of fire unconsumed may remain, so far as one can see, forever; and it is forever that they here are plainly said to be tormented.

But it is objected that there is, in fact, no verb here: the sentence reads simply, "where the beast and the false prophet," and that to fill up the gap properly we must put "*were cast*," which would say nothing about continuance. But what, then, about the concluding statement, "and *they*"—for it is a plural,—"and *they* shall be tormented day and night for the ages of ages"?

Finding this argument vain, or from the opposite interest of restitution, it is urged that "day and night" do not exist in eternity. But we are certainly brought here to eternity, and "for the ages of ages" means nothing else. It is the measure of the life of God Himself (iv. 10). No passage that occurs, even to the smoke of Babylon ascending up, can be shown to have a less significance.

Growing desperate, some have ventured to say that we should translate "*till* the ages of ages." But the other passages stand against this with an iron front, and forbid it. We are, in this little season, right on the verge of eternity itself. The same expression is used as to the judgment of the great white throne itself, which is *in* eternity. It will not do to say of God that He lives *to* the ages of ages, and not *through* them. The truth is very plain, then, that the punishment here decreed to three transgressors is, in the strictest sense, eternal.

Whether the same thing is true of all the wicked dead, we now go on to see.

The Judgment of the Dead.

THE millennium is over: "And I saw a great white

throne, and Him that sat on it, from whose face the earth and the heaven fled; and there was found no place for them. And I saw the dead, great and small, standing before the throne, and books were opened; and another book was opened, which is the book of life: and the dead were judged out of those things that were written in the books, according to their works. And the sea gave up the dead which were in it; and death and hades delivered up the dead which were in them: and they were judged every one according to their works. And death and hades were cast into the lake of fire. This is the second death, the lake of fire. And whoever was not found written in the book of life was cast into the lake of fire."

This is the judgment of the dead alone, and must be kept perfectly distinct in our minds from the long previous judgment of the *living*. The judgment in Matt. xxv., for example, where the "sheep" are separated from the "goats," is a judgment of the living,—of the nations upon earth when the Lord comes. It is not, indeed, the warrior-judgment of those taken with arms in their hands, in open rebellion, which we have beheld in the premillennial vision. The nations are gathered before the Son of Man, who has just come in His glory, and all the holy angels with Him; and that coming, as when elsewhere spoken of throughout the prophecy, is unquestionably premillennial. As mankind are divided into the three classes, "the Jew, the Gentile, and the Church of God," so the prophecy in relation to the Jew is to be found in chap. xxiv. 1–42; that in relation to the professing Church, to the thirtieth verse of the next chapter; and the rest of it gives us the sessional judgment of the Gentiles, so far as they have been reached by the everlasting gospel. The judgment is not of all the deeds done in the body: it is as to how they have treated the brethren of the Lord (*v.* 40) who have been among them, evidently as travelers, in rejection and peril. The Jewish point of view of the prophecy as a whole clearly points to Jewish messengers, who as such represent Israel's King (comp. Matt. x. 40). There is not a word about resurrection of the dead, which the time of this judgment excludes the possibility of as to the wicked. It is one partial as to its range, limited as to that of which it takes account, and in every way distinct from such a *general* judgment as the large part of Christendom even yet looks for.

Here in the vision before us there is simply the judgment of the dead; and although the word is not used, the account speaks plainly of resurrection. The sea gives up the dead which are in it, as well as by implication also, the dry land. Death, as well as hades, deliver up what they respectively hold; and as hades is unequivocally the receptacle of the soul (Acts ii. 27), so must "death," on the other hand, which the soul survives (Matt. x. 28), stand here in connection with that over which it has supreme control—the body.

The dead, then, here rise; and we have that from which the "blessed and holy" of the first resurrection are delivered—the "resurrection of judgment." (Jno. v. 29, *R. V.*) From *personal* judgment the Lord expressly assures us that the believer is exempt (*v.* 24, *R. V.*) Here, not only are the *works* judged, which will be true of the believer also, and for lasting blessing to him, but *men* are judged *according to* their works—a very different thing. Such a judgment would allow of no hope for the most upright and godly among mere men.

And this would seem to show that though a millennium has passed since the first resurrection, yet no *righteous* dead can stand among this throng. The suggestion of the "book of life" has seemed to many to imply that there are such; but it is not said that there are, and the words, "whoever was not found written in the book of life was cast into the lake of fire," may be simply a solemn declaration (now affirmed by the result) that grace is man's only possible escape from the judgment. May it not even be intended to apply more widely than to the dead here, and take in the *living* saints of the millennium negatively, as showing how in fact they are not found before this judgment-seat?

At any rate, the principle of judgment—"according to their works"—seems to exclude absolutely any of those saved by grace. And there are intimations also, in the Old-Testament prophecies, as to the extension of life in the millennium, which seem well to consist with the complete arrest of death for the righteous during the whole period. If "as the days of a tree shall be the days of" God's "people" (Is. lxv. 22), and he who dies at a hundred years dies as a child yet, and for wickedness: because there shall be no more any one (apart from this) that shall not fill his days (*v.* 20), it would almost seem to follow that there is no death. And to this the announcement as to the "sheep" in the judgment-scene in Matthew —that "the righteous shall go away into life eternal," strikingly corresponds. For to go into life eternal is not to possess life in the way that at present we may; in fact, *as* "righteous," they already did this: it means apparently nothing less than the complete canceling of the claim of death in their case.

And now death and hades are cast into the lake of fire, —that is, those who dwelt in them are cast there. These exist as it were but in those who fill them; and thus we learn that there is no exemption or escape from the last final doom for any who come into this judgment. The lake of fire is the *second* death. The first terminated in judgment man's career on earth; the second closes the intermediate state in adjudged alienation from the Source of life. The first is but the type of the second. As we have seen, it is not extinction at all; and indeed a resurrection merely for the sake of suffering before another extinction would seem self-contradictory. In fact, death—what we ordinarily call that—is now destroyed. "It is appointed unto man *once* to die, but after this the judgment," which is thenceforth, therefore, undying (Heb. ix. 27).

With the great white throne set up, the earth and the heavens pass away, and there come into being a "new heaven and a new earth in which dwelleth righteousness." (2 Pet. iii. 13.)

The Earth's Final State. (Chap. xxi. 1-8.)

Before the face of Him who sits upon the great white throne "the earth and the heaven fled away, and there was found no place for them." (Chap. xx. 11.) We have now a complementary statement: "And I saw a new heaven and a new earth." It is clear, therefore, that an earthly condition abides for eternity. It is a point of interest as to which Scripture seems to give full satisfaction, whether this new earth is itself a "new *creation*," or the old earth remodeled and made new. At first sight, one would no doubt decide for the former; and this was the view that at one time almost held possession of the field, the new earth scarcely being regarded by the mass as "earth" at all. Practically, the earth was simply believed to exist no more, and in contrast with it all was to be heavenly: the double sphere of blessing, earth *and* heaven, was lost sight of, if not denied.

Lately, for many, reaction has set in, and the pendulum has swung past the point of rest to the other extreme. The prophecies of the Old Testament rightly understood as to be literally taken, and delivered from the glosses of a falsely called "spiritual" interpretation, seemed to agree with the apostle Peter and the book of Revelation in making the earth to be the inheritance of the saints,—the earth in a heavenly *condition*, brought back out of its state of exile, and into true relation with the rest of the family of heaven, not alienated from their original place. Contrast between earth and heaven as an eternal existence was again, but from the other side of it, denied.

The whole web and woof of Scripture is against either of these confusions: the point of rest can only be in accepting the distinction of earthly from heavenly as fundamental to all right understanding of the prophetic word. The Old-Testament "promises," which have in view the earth as a sphere of blessing, are, as the apostle declares (Rom. ix. 1–4), Jewish, not Christian. The New Testament emphasizes that the blessings of the Christian are in "heavenly places." (Eph. i. 3.) Nor can this last possibly apply to earth made heavenly. The Lord has left us with the assurance (Jno. xiv.) that in His Father's house are many mansions,—permanent places of abode,—that He was going to prepare a place there for us, and that He will come again to receive us to Himself, that where He is, there we may be also. As well assure us that the Lord's permanent abode is to be on earth and not in heaven, as that our own is to be here, not there.

Each line of truth must have its place if we are to be "rightly dividing the word of truth." The heavenly "bride of the Lamb" is not the earthly; "Jerusalem which is above" is not the Palestinean city; the "church of first-born ones, who are written in *heaven*" are not that "Israel," declared God's "first-born" as to the earth; the promise of the Morning Star is not the same as that of the "Sun of Righteousness," although Christ assuredly is both of these. Discernment of such differences is of necessity for all true filling of our place, and practical rendering of Christian life.

Let us look now, however, at the question of continuity between the earth that flees away and the earth that succeeds it. At first sight we should surely say, they cannot be identical. The well-known passage in the epistle of Peter would seem to confirm this (2 Pet. iii. 10, 12). There we learn that "the heavens shall pass away with a great noise, and the elements shall melt with fervent heat; the earth also, and the works that are therein, shall be burned up." And it is repeated, and thus emphasized by repetition, that "the heavens being on fire shall be dissolved, and the elements shall melt with fervent heat."

Yet, as we look more closely, we shall find reason to

doubt whether more is meant than the destruction of the earth as the place of human habitation. In the deluge, to which it is compared (*vv.* 5-7), "the world that then was *perished;*" yet its continuity with the present no one doubts. Fire, though the instrument of a more penetrating judgment, yet does not annihilate the material upon which it fastens. The melting even of elements implies rather the reverse, and dissolution is not (in this sense) destruction.

Yet the heavens and the earth pass away,—that is, in the form in which now we know them; or, as the apostle speaks to the Corinthians, "the *fashion* of this world passes away" (1 Cor. vii. 31): and that this is the sense in which we are to understand it, other scriptures come to assure us.

A "new" earth does not necessarily mean *another* earth, except as a "new" man means *another* man,—"new" in the sense of renewed. And even the words here, "there was no more sea," naturally suggest another *state* of the earth that now exists. This fact is a significant one: that which is the type of instability and barrenness, and condemns to it so large a portion of the globe, is gone utterly and forever. At the beginning of Genesis we find the whole earth buried under it; emerging on the third day, and the waters given their bounds, which but once afterward they pass. Now they are gone forever, as are the wicked, to whom Isaiah compares it: "The wicked are like the troubled sea when it cannot rest, whose waters cast up mire and dirt." This last is the effect of chafing against its bounds, as the "mind of the flesh" is "not subject to the law of God, neither indeed can be." (Rom. viii. 7.)

These analogies cannot fail to illustrate another which the Lord Himself gives us, when He speaks of the millennial kingdom as the "regeneration,"—"Ye who have followed Me, in the *regeneration*, when the Son of Man shall sit on the throne of His glory, ye also shall sit

upon twelve thrones, judging the twelve tribes of Israel."
(Matt. xix. 28.) Here, let us note that it is the Lord's
kingdom that is the regeneration of the earth. That reign
of righteousness which is the effectual curb upon human
wickedness, not the removal of it, answers thus to what—
"regeneration" is for him who is in this sense in the
Lord's kingdom now. Sin is not removed; the flesh
abides even in the regenerate; but it has its bound—it
does not reign, has not dominion. In the perfect state,
whether for the individual or the earth, righteousness
dwells, as Peter says of the latter: sin exists no more.
How striking does the analogy here become when we remember that the change, perhaps dissolution, of the body
comes between the regenerate and the perfect state, just
as the similar "dissolution" of the earth does between the
millennium and the new earth! Surely this throws a
bright light upon the point we are examining.

The new heavens are, of course, only the *earth*-heavens,
the work of the second of the six days. They are of great
importance to the earth which they surround, and to
which they minister. More and more is science coming
to recognize how (in natural law at least) the heavens rule.
Yet who but an inspired writer, of the time of Peter or
John, would have made so much of the new heavens?
And these only, as Peter reminds us, develop a much
earlier "promise." This we find in Isa. lxv. and lxvi., a
repeated announcement, the second time explicitly connected with the continuance of Israel's "seed" and
"name:" "For as the new heavens and the new earth
which I will make shall abide before Me, saith the Lord,
so shall your seed and your name remain." Thus even
in the new earth there will be no merging of Israel in the
general mass of the nations. The first-born people written
on earth will show still how "the gifts and calling of God
are without repentance," as will the "church of the firstborn who are written in heaven." These different circles
of blessing, like the principalities and powers in heavenly

places, are quite accordant with what we see everywhere of God's manifold ways and ranks in creation. Why should eternity efface these differences, which of course do not touch the unity of the family of God as such, while they are abiding witnesses of divine mercy in relation to a past, of which the lessons are never to be lost?

Earth, then, itself remains, but a "new" earth; and as the seal upon its eternal blessedness, "I saw," says the prophet-evangelist, "the holy city, new Jerusalem, coming down from God out of heaven, prepared as a bride adorned for her husband. And I heard a great voice out of the throne, saying, 'Behold, the tabernacle of God is with men, and He shall tabernacle with them, and they shall be His people, and God Himself shall be with them, their God.'" Here is the promise in Immanuel's name made finally good to the redeemed race: and he who is privileged to show us the glory of the Only-begotten of the Father tabernacling among men when the Word was made flesh, is the one who shows us the full consummation. Of the new Jerusalem we have presently a detailed account; here, what is emphasized is, that it is the link between God and men; God Himself is with men, in all the fullness of blessing implied in that.

We must not, however, pass over any thing: the less even that is said, the more should we ponder that which *is* said. Let us see, then, what is here, putting it in connection with what seems most naturally to throw light upon it elsewhere. Standing where we are—at the end of time, we stand indeed whither the whole stream of time has been conducting us; and therefore with the countless voices of the past sounding prophetically to us. What will it be to be actually there, at the end of the ways which, though through the valley of Baca, lead up to the city of God!

First, here, we are shown that He has prepared for us a city—"the holy city." The new Jerusalem is surely, what its earthly type is, a "city of habitation:" it is not simply a figure for the saints themselves. The patriarchs of old, content to await in patient faith the end of their pilgrim-journey, "looked for a city which hath foundations, whose builder and maker is God;" and He will not disappoint their expectations,—" He hath prepared for them a city." (Heb. xi. 10, 16.) At the very beginning of the world's history we find, in one who manifested a totally opposite spirit, still the desire of the human heart which this promise meets. Cain went out from the presence of the Lord, fugitive and vagabond as he was, to build a city. Without faith or patience, he only shows the natural craving of the heart, but not in itself evil because natural. Ever since, the history of man has connected itself mainly with its cities. From Babel on to Rome, these have been the centres of power and progress ever, and (the world being what it is) they have exhibited in the most developed way its opposition to God. But God too has His city, and makes much of it, "beautiful for situation, the joy of the whole earth," and with it associates (Ps. lxxxvii.) the One great name which eclipses that of all others.

The tendency of the day is toward cities, and in these, for good or for ill, we find the greatest development of man; only, man being fallen, the development is monstrous. When the day of the Lord has put down, however, all human thoughts, it is only to exalt Jerusalem upon the earth, and to make way for the display of that better Jerusalem that is here before us.

The city is the expression of human need, and the provision for it. In the midst of strife and insecurity, men gather together for protection; but that is only a small part of what is implied in it. There are other needs more universal than this, as that of coöperation, the division of labor, the result of that inequality of aptitudes by which God has made us mutually dependent. Our social nature is thus met, and there are formed and strengthened the ties by which the world is bound together; while the intercourse of mind with mind, of heart with heart, stimulates and develops every latent faculty. "Iron sharpeneth iron; so a man sharpeneth the countenance of his friend." (Prov. xxvii. 17.)

The eternal city implies for us association, fellowship, intercourse, the fullness of what was intimated in the primal saying, "It is not good for man to be alone," but which in respect of the bride city, which this is, has still a deeper meaning. Here, the relationship of the saints to Christ, who as the Lamp of divine glory enlightens it, alone adequately explains all. "Alone" can we nevermore be. "With Him" our whole manhood shall find its complete answer, satisfaction, and rest.

This is necessarily, therefore, the "*holy* city." Cain's has but too much characterized every city hitherto. Where shall we find as in the city the reek of impurity and the hotbed of corruption? There poverty and riches pour out a common flood of iniquity, out of which comes ever increasing the defiant cry of despair. But here at last is a "HOLY CITY," the new Jerusalem, "foundation of peace;" not, like Babel of old, towering up to heaven, but coming down from heaven, the way of all good, of all blessing for men. The tabernacle of God is with men. God Himself tabernacles with them. His own hand removes every trace of former sorrow, every effect of sin. His own voice proclaims what his hand accomplishes: "Behold, I make all things new."

Here, that we may be fully assured, a confirmatory word is added. And along with this, and in view of it, in the name of Him who is Alpha and Omega, beginning and end, the sweet invitation of the gospel is once more published, the free gift of the water of life to every thirsty soul is certified; and the inheritance to the overcomer, for it is reached by the way of conflict and of triumph,— grace securing, not evading, this: "He that overcometh shall inherit these things; and I will be his God, and he shall be My son."

Just here too, with no less earnestness, and in eternity, past all the change of time, the doom of the wicked is pronounced: "But the fearful"—too cowardly to take part with Christ in a world opposed to Him,—"and unbelieving, and abominable, and murderers, and whoremongers, and sorcerers, and idolaters, and all liars, shall have their part in the lake which burneth with fire and brimstone, which is the second death."

The Holy City.

The last vision of Revelation is now before us: it is that of the city of God itself. But here, where one would desire above all to see clearly, we become most conscious of how feeble and dull is our apprehension of eternal things. They are words of an apostle which remind us that "we see through a glass darkly"—*en ainigmati*, in a riddle. Such a riddle, then, it is no wonder if the vision presents to us: the dream that we have here a literal description, even to the measurements, of the saints' eternal home, is one too foolish to need much comment. All other visions throughout the book have been symbolic: how much more here! how little need we expect that the glimpse which is here given us into the unseen would reveal to us the shape of buildings, or the material used! Scripture is reticent all through upon such subjects; and the impress to be left upon our souls is plainly spiritual, not of lines and hues, as for the natural senses. "Things which eye hath not seen" are not put before the eye.

On the other hand, that the "city" revealed to us here is not simply a figure of the saints themselves, as, from the term used for it, "the Bride, the Lamb's Wife," some have taken it to be, there are other scriptures which seem definitely to assure us. "Jerusalem, which is above, which is our mother" (Gal. iv.) could hardly be used in this way, though the Church is indeed so conceived of in patristic and mediæval thought. But even thus it would not be spoken of naturally as "*above.*"

In Heb. xii. we have a still more definite testimony. For there the "Church of the first-born ones which are written in heaven," as well as "the spirits of just men made perfect"—in other words, both Christians and the saints of the Old Testament—are mentioned as distinct from "the city of the living God, the heavenly Jerusalem;" and this will not allow them to be the same thing, although, in another way, the identification of a city with its inhabitants is easy.

We are led in the same direction by the mention of the "tree of life in the midst of the paradise of God,"—something to which the apostle thought he might have been caught even bodily (2 Cor. xii.)—and here is the tree of life in the midst of the city beside the "river of the water of life" which flows from the throne of God. Figurative language all this surely; yet these passages combine to give us the thought of a heavenly abode, already existing, and which will be in due time revealed as the metropolis of the heavenly kingdom—what Jerusalem restored will be in the lower sphere. Indeed the earthly here so parallels and illustrates the heavenly as to be a most useful help in fixing, if not enlarging, our thoughts about it,—always while we realize, of course, the essential difference that Scripture itself makes clear to be between them. But this we shall have to look at as we proceed.

"The holy city, Jerusalem," is certainly intended to be a plain comparison with the earthly city. But that is the type only; this is the antitype, the true "foundation of peace," as the word means. What more comforting title, after all the scenes of strife, the fruit of the lusts that war in our members, which we have had to look upon! Here is "peace" at last, and on a foundation that shall not be removed, but that stands fast forever. For this is emphatically "the city that *hath* foundations," and "whose builder and maker is God." (Heb. xi. 10.) How blessed it is, too, that it should be just one of the seven angels that had the seven last plagues that shows John the city! for no mere executioner of judgment we see is he: judgment (as with God, for it is God's) is also *his* "strange work." It had to come, and it has come: there was no help, no hope without it; thus the stroke of the "rod of iron" was that of the shepherd's rod; it was the destruction of the destroyers only. But it is past, and here is the scene wherein his own heart rests, to which it returns with loyalty and devotion: here, where the water of life flows from the throne of God,—eternal, from the Eternal; refreshment, gladness, fruitfulness, and power are found in obedience.

But the city is the "Bride, the Lamb's wife." In the Old Testament, the figure of marriage is used in a similar way. Israel was thus Jehovah's "married wife" (Is. liv. 1, Jer. xxxi. 33), now divorced indeed for her unfaithfulness, but yet to return-(Hos. ii.), and be received and reinstated. Her Maker will be then once more her husband, and more than the old blessing be restored. In the forty-fifth psalm, Israel's King, Messiah, is the Bridegroom; the Song of Solomon is the mystic song of His espousals. Jerusalem thus bears His name: "This is the name whereby she shall be called: 'Jehovah our Righteousness.'" (Jer. xxxiii. 16, comp. xxiii. 6.) The land too shall be "married." (Is. lxii. 4.)

In the New Testament, the same figure is still used in the same way. The Baptist speaks of his joy as the "friend of the Bridegroom," in hearing the Bridegroom's voice (Jno. iii. 29); and in the parable of the virgins (Matt. xxv.), where Christians are those who go forth to meet the Bridegroom, they are by that very fact not regarded as the Bride, which is still Israel, (according to the general character of the prophecy,) though not actually brought into the scene. Some may be able to see also in the marriage at Cana of Galilee (Jno. ii. 1) the vailing of the same thought.

All this, therefore, is in that earthly sphere in which Israel's blessings lie; our own are "in *heavenly* places" (Eph. i. 3), and here it is we find, not the Bride of *Messiah* simply, but distinctively "the Bride of the *Lamb*." The "Lamb," as a title, always keeps before us His death, and that by violence, "a Lamb as it had been *slain*" (Rev. v. 6); and it is thus that He has title to that redemption empire in which we find Him throughout this book. But "the Bride of the Lamb" is thus one espoused to Him in His rejection, sharer (though it be but in slight measure) of His reproach and sorrow, trained and disciplined for glory in a place of humiliation. And so it is said that "*if we suffer*, we shall also reign with Him;" and again, "If so be we suffer with Him, that we may be also glorified together." (2 Tim. ii. 12; Rom. viii. 17.)

The saints in the millennium have no heritage of suffering such as this; even those who pass through the trial which ushers it in, have not the same character of it, although we must not forget those associated with the Lamb upon Mount Zion, who illustrate the same truth, but upon a lower platform. Even these are not His Bride.

Ephesians, the epistle of the heavenly places, shows us the Church as Eve of the last Adam, whom Christ loves, and for whom He gave Himself. Formed out of Himself and for Himself, He now sanctifies and cleanses her with water-washing by the Word, that He may present her to Himself a holy Church, not having spot or wrinkle or any such thing. In another aspect, this Church is His body, formed by the baptism of the Spirit as at Pentecost, complete when those who are Christ's are caught up to meet Him in the air. The doctrine of this is, of course, not in Revelation: the difficulty is in seeing the conformity of Revelation with it.

Outside of Revelation even, there is a difficulty in the connection (if there *be*, as one would anticipate, a connection) between the Church as the body of Christ *now*, before our presentation to Him, and the "one flesh" which is the fruit of marriage. Israel was the married wife, and will be, though now for a time "desolate," as one divorced. The Church is "espoused" (2 Cor. xi. 2), not married. Thus the "one body" and the "great mystery" of "one flesh," of which the apostle speaks (Eph. v. 29) must be distinct.

Looking back to Adam, to whom as a type he there refers us, we find that Eve is taken out of his side,—is thus really his "flesh" by her very making. Thus, as one with him in nature, she is united to him,—a union in which the prior unity finds its fit expression. The two things are therefore in this way very clearly and intimately connected. The being of Christ's body is that, then, which alone prepares and qualifies for the being of His bride hereafter; and body and bride must be strictly commensurate with each other.

The mystery here is great, as the apostle himself says; nor is it to be affirmed that the type in all its features answers to the reality. It is easily seen that this could not be; yet there is real correspondence and suitability thus far: according to it, the Church of Christ alone, from Pentecost to the rapture, is scripturally only (in a strict sense) the "Bride of the Lamb."

Yet can we confine the new Jerusalem to these? There would of course in this case be no difficulty as to the character of a city which it is given in this vision. A city is commonly enough identified with its inhabitants, so that the same term covers both place and persons. But are none to inhabit the new Jerusalem except the saints of Christian times? Are none of those so illustrious in the Old Testament to find their place there? Abraham, Isaac, and Jacob are among those with whom the Lord assures us we are to sit down in the kingdom of God (Luke xiii. 28, 29);—are they to be outside the heavenly city?

This is positively answered otherwise, as it would seem,

in Revelation itself. For while the general account of those who enter there is that they are those "written in the Lamb's book of life" (xxi. 27), "without" the city are said to be only "dogs, and sorcerers, and whoremongers, and murderers, and idolators, and whosoever loveth and maketh a lie" (xxii. 15).

In the eleventh of Hebrews, moreover, in a verse already quoted, "the city which hath foundations, whose builder and maker is God," for which the patriarchs looked and waited, can surely be no other than that which we find here; and it is added that they desired "a better country,—that is, a heavenly; wherefore God is not ashamed to be called their God : for He hath prepared for them a city." It could not be the New-Testament Church for which Abraham looked; for this was as yet entirely hidden in God. (Eph. iii. 9.) Another and larger meaning for the new Jerusalem must surely, therefore, be admitted.

And why should there not be in it the inclusion of both thoughts? Why should it not be the bride-*city*, named from the bride *church*, whose home it is, and yet containing other occupants? This alone would seem to cover the whole of the facts which Scripture gives us as to it; and the Jewish bride is in like manner sometimes a wider, sometimes a narrower conception ; sometimes the city Jerusalem, sometimes the people Israel. Only that in the Old Testament the city is the narrower, the people the wider view; while in the New Testament this is reversed. And even this may be significant: the heavenly city, the dwelling-place of God, permitting none of the redeemed to be outside it, but opening its gates widely to all. A Bride-City indeed, ever holding bridal festival, and having perpetual welcome for all that come : its freshness never fading, its joy never satiating ; blessed are they whose names are written there!

As before, the city is seen "descending out of heaven from God." We shall find, however, here, that the present vision goes back of the new heavens and earth to the millennial age,—that is, that while itself eternal, the city is seen in connection with the earth at this time. Not yet has it been said, "The tabernacle of God is with men, and He will dwell with them." The descending city is not, therefore, in that settled and near intimacy with men outside of it in which it will be. A significant and perfect note of time it is that the leaves of the tree of life are for the healing of nations (xxii. 2). Tender as this grace is, the condition it shows could not be eternal.

All the nearer does it bring this vision of glory and of love, no more to be banished or dimmed by human sin or sorrow. The city has the glory of God; and here is the goal of hope, complete fruition of that which but as hope outshines all that is known of brightness elsewhere. It cannot be painted with words. We cannot hope even to expand what the Holy Ghost has given us. But the blessedness itself we are soon to know.

The holy city descends from heaven, "having the glory of God." She is the chosen vessel of it, to display it to the universe, being the fruit of Christ's work, the fullest witness of abounding grace. Her shining is "like a most precious stone, as a crystal-like jasper-stone," or diamond, as we have already taken it to be.* The carbon crystallized into this lustrous brilliant, which still shines with a light not its own, is a fit representation of the "glory" that is to be "in the Church in Christ Jesus unto all generations of the age of ages." (Eph. iii. 21.) This glory which God manifests through His creatures, He manifests *to* His creatures, satisfying His own love in bringing them thus nigh unto Himself. How blessed to be a means of such display!

The wall of the city clearly speaks of its security: it has "a great and high wall;" for "salvation hath God appointed as walls and bulwarks." (Is. xxvi. 1.) And in

---

* See on chap. iv. 3.

the wall, which has four sides, there are twelve gates,— three gates on every side, for egress and ingress, home as this is of a life which is unceasing activity. The number 12 is upon all the city, 12 being an expanded 7, with the same factors (4×3 instead of $4 + 3$), and the symbol of manifest divine government, God being here manifestly supreme. This is perfection in its deepest analysis; and the numbers are thus one in fact.* The 12 here is plainly the usual 4×3; the 3 still speaking of divine manifestation, while the 4 shows it to be universal, the sides facing also every way.

At the gates are twelve angels; upon them the names of the twelve tribes of Israel. As the tabernacle of God, a reference to the tabernacle of old is surely in place here, though to that there was but one entrance, for a simple and beautiful reason, Christ being seen in it as the only way of approach to God. Now there are twelve gates, answering to the twelve tribes which in the wilderness also were grouped in similar threes around the tabernacle. Ezekiel, in his last vision of the future (chap. xlviii.), shows us what more exactly answers to what is here, though speaking of the earthly city restored, and not the heavenly; and there the gates are appropriated, one to each particular tribe. Israel are here, as it would seem, their own representatives, as in the vision of the seventh chapter; and we are reminded of their being in nearest connection upon earth with the heavenly city. In the *heavenly* sphere, at the gates are angels. The heavenly and earthly relations of the city are thus declared.

There are twelve foundations of the wall of the city also; but on these are the names of the twelve apostles of the Lamb. They have *laid* the foundations, and their names are stamped upon their work. We are surely not to imagine any individualizing here, as if any one foundation could be appropriated to any one apostle, or indeed that

---

* See "Spiritual Law in the Natural World," pp. 73-5.

the number 12 itself is any thing but characteristic. This connects itself also with the question of the presence or absence of Paul's name from the number. It is remarkable that almost the same difficulty connects with the *twelve* tribes of Israel, which often exclude and often include the tribe of Levi. Taking Ephraim and Manasseh, the two sons of Joseph, as tribal heads, equal in this respect to Jacob's other sons, (and this is the place that they are given in the history,) yet they are none the less always counted twelve. Why may not the apostles, in spite of the addition of Paul to their number, be counted here as twelve?

The measurements of the city and the wall are next given. The city is a cube, twelve thousand furlongs every way; the wall, a hundred and forty-four cubits high. The number 12 still governs everywhere. The cube speaks of substance, reality. The sanctuary in the tabernacle and in the temple were both cubes. This is the eternal sanctuary, and the full fruition of every hope of the saint. The measurements further, though surely symbolic, await yet their interpretation.

The building of the wall is of jasper (or diamond). The divine glory is itself a safeguard of the eternal city. What can touch that which God has ordained for His own praise? The city itself is pure transparent gold,—pure, permanent, radiant,—not hindering, but welcoming the enraptured sight. The foundations of the wall are adorned with every precious stone,—all the attributes of God displayed in that upon which rests the salvation of the people of God. The stones, in their separate meanings, are again a mystery. The twelve gates are twelve pearls—the picture of such grace as has been shown in the Church (Matt. xiii. 45, 46). These gates stand open all the unending day. The street of the city is, again, "pure gold, like transparent glass." The street—especially in the east—is the place of traffic, the meeting-place constantly of need and greed. But here, all circumstances, all intercourse, the whole environment, is absolute holiness and truth, fit for and permeated by the felt presence of God.

And this leads us directly to the next statement, that because the city is *all* sanctuary, there is no more any special one. The presence of God is the temple of the city: there is no other; and the Lamb is He who characterizes for us, and will always characterize, this otherwise ineffable Presence. There is no distance; there is nothing that can produce distance; there never can be more. It is that which the presence of Jesus among us—now nearly nineteen centuries since—implied and pledged to us: it is Immanu-El—"God with us"—in full reality, and in the highest and most intimate way.

It is true we have not the Father spoken of as such: it is "the Lord (or Jehovah) God Almighty"—the God of Old-Testament revelation,—with "the Lamb," in whom we have the revelation of the New. Nothing less, surely, is meant than God in full display, so far as the creature can ever be made to apprehend Him. There is a glory of the Light always inaccessible,—not hid in darkness, but in light, which no human eye can ever penetrate. None can fully know God but God. This is only to say that the creature remains the creature; but the limitation of faculties does not mean distance, as if kept back. "The Lamb" shows, on the one hand, the desire of God to be known, while implying, in the very fact of manhood taken for this revelation, that God purely as God could not be known.

Thus it is immediately added that the glory of God lightens the city, and "the Lamb is the lamp thereof." The lamp sustains the light. It adds nothing to it, for to divine glory nothing can be added: if any thing could be, it would no longer be divine. But the light is "put upon a candlestick (or lamp) that they who enter in may see the light." (Luke viii. 16.) So will Christ always be the One in whom the Father is made known: nay the sacrificial word ("Lamb") assures us that we shall always have need of the past also for this. But this does not at all mean that there will not be what the Lord has assured us the angels of the little children enjoy continually: "Their angels do always behold the face of My Father who is in heaven."

This, then, is the glory of the heavenly city, in the light of which the nations of the earth themselves walk; while the kings of the earth bring their glory unto it. As another has said, "They own the heavens and the heavenly kingdom to be the source of all, and bring there the homage of their power." And "they bring the glory and honor of the nations unto it." That is, "Heaven is seen as the source of all the glory and honor of this world." The nations are, as we shall see directly, undoubtedly the millennial nations; and it is no question of these entering themselves into the heavenly city: their glory and honor it is they bring, and though the words in the original admit the force of "into," they by no means compel it. The mention of the continually open gates speaks indeed of peaceful and constant intercourse, and we must remember that here is the abode of those who reign with Christ over the earth. Whether these are the "kings of the earth" meant is, however, a question: if it were so, the "into" might be still the true sense.

The next statement as to the city regards those who do enter therein,—that is, have part in the blessedness which is here depicted. In opposition to all defilement, one class alone has title here: it is "they who are written in the Lamb's book of life." This surely shows that the whole of the Old-Testament saints enter into the city. No one is excluded whose name is there. While, on the other hand, the millennial saints have as clearly their portion on earth—the new earth—in connection, indeed, with the "tabernacle of God," but not in it. The heavenly city remains always heavenly, and when it descends from heaven, has then received its inhabitants. These distinctions, which indeed are gathered from elsewhere, are nevertheless to be kept in remembrance here, or all will be confusion.

We have next before us the "paradise of God," in which the city lies. Man's paradise of old could not yet have the city; and when the city came, it was outside of paradise altogether. Here at last the two things are united.

We are of necessity reminded also of one of the closing visions of Ezekiel, while a comparison easily shows also the difference between the earthly and the heavenly in these pictures,—the one being indeed the shadow, but no more than the shadow, of' the other. John here sees "a river of water of life, bright as crystal, proceeding out of the throne of God and of the Lamb." And in Ezekiel, the life-giving waters issue forth from the house of the Lord, and thus is specially noted in connection with the fruit of the trees that are nourished by it: "And by the river, upon the bank thereof, on this side and on that side, shall grow all trees for meat, whose leaf shall not fade, neither shall the fruit thereof be consumed: it shall bring forth new fruit according to its months, because their waters, they issued out of the sanctuary; and the fruit thereof shall be for meat, and the leaf thereof for medicine." How like the account in Revelation is to this, no one can fail to understand: even the language might seem to be taken from it: "In the midst of the street of it, and on this side of the river and on that, was there the tree of life, which bare twelve [manner of] fruits, and yielded its fruit every month: and the leaves of the tree were for the healing of the nations."

But in Ezekiel all is distinctly earthly, and the blessing is not yet full. The waters go down into the salt sea and heal it, so that a great multitude of fish are in its waters; but there are miry places and marshes that are not healed, but given over to salt. With both the Old-Testament prophet and the New, we see that the earth is yet in the millennial, not the eternal condition; for the leaves of the tree are for medicine in both alike; there is, in both, need of healing yet.

The waters are in both cases from the sanctuary, for that is the character of the whole city of God. In Revelation, they are specifically from the throne of God; for here the one blessedness is, as we have seen, that God reigns,—God revealed in that perfect grace that is expressed in Christ,—the throne of God being also that of the Lamb. Thus the water is the type, as always in its highest meaning, of the fullness of the Spirit, the power of life and sanctification, indeed the power of God in all creation. The *tree* of life bears witness, as in the earthly paradise at first, of dependence upon Another, of life in dependence; but all the plenteous and varied fruits of this could not even be symbolized in the time of old; fresh fruits and abundant: who can tell the blessed meaning? or what Christ is to those that have their life in Him?

"And there shall be no more curse, but the throne of God and of the Lamb shall be in it; and His servants shall serve Him. And they shall see His face; and His name shall be in their foreheads." Thus He is openly theirs; they too are openly His. Service is taken up afresh in glory according to the fullness of that open-eyed and open-faced communion which is here so assured. It is indeed, when it has its proper character, communion itself. The love that serves us all is the love of God Himself, and of this Christ is the perfect expression. How is it possible to be in communion with Christ without the diligent endeavor to serve Him in the gospel of His grace, and in ministry to His people? In heaven, service will not for a moment cease; although some precious possibilities of the present will have passed away indeed. Would that this were more realized, with the Lord's estimate of greatness in the kingdom of which He is greatest of all!

But the light! and our inheritance is in the light. To

this the vision returns, and ends with it: "And there shall be no night there; and they need no candle, nor light of the sun; for the Lord God giveth them light, and they shall reign for the ages of the ages." Thus the reign of the saints is not for the millennium only, nor simply as partakers of the power of the rod of iron. "If by one man's offense death reigned through one, much more shall they who receive abundance of grace and of the gift of righteousness reign in life by One, Jesus Christ." (Rom. v. 17.) Reigning is, for the heavenly saints, inseparable from the life they enter into in the coming day. The new Jerusalem is a city of kings and priests,—the bridal city of the King of kings. Here the eternal reign seems associated necessarily with the glory in which all here live and move. For those who were once sinners,— slaves of Satan, and of the lusts by which he inthralled them, to be delivered and brought, by the priceless blood of Jesus, into such communion as is here shown with the Father and the Son,—how can their condition be expressed in language less glowing than this—needing no candle, nor light of the sun, because the Lord God giveth them light,—than that they reign forever and ever?

Closing Testimonies. (Chap. xxii. 6-21.)

The series of visions is thus completed. What remains is the emphasizing of its authority for the soul, with all that belongs to Him whose revelation it is, and who is Himself coming speedily. Thus the angel now affirms that "these words are faithful and true:" necessarily so, because of Him whose words they are. "The Lord God of the spirits of the prophets hath sent His angel to show unto His servants things which must soon come to pass." Here we return to the announcement of the first chapter. The book is, above all, a practical book. It is not for theorists or dreamers, but for servants,—words which are to be *kept*, and to have application to their service in the Church and in the world.

The things themselves were soon to come to pass. In fact, the history of the Church, as the opening epistles depict it, could be found imaged, as we see, in the condition of existing assemblies. The seeds of the future already existed, and were silently growing up, even with the growth (externally) of Christianity itself. As to the visions following the epistles also, from the sixth chapter on, we have acknowledged the partial truth of what is known as the historical fulfillment of these. It is admitted that there has been an anticipative fulfillment in Christian times of that which has definite application to the time of the end, although it is the last only that has been, in general, dwelt upon in these pages.

Historicalists will not be satisfied with such an admission, and refusing on their side (as they mostly do) the general bearing of the introductory epistles upon the history of the Church at large, insist upon such affirmations as the present as entirely conclusive that the historical interpretation is the only true one. In fact, the view which has been here followed brings nearest to those in the apostles' days the things announced, as well as makes the whole book far more fruitful and important for the guidance of servants. For how many generations must they have waited before the seals and trumpets would speak to these? And when they did, how much of guidance would they furnish for practical walk? The application of Babylon the great to Romanism is fully accepted, and that of Jezebel in the same way insisted on, so that as to the errors of popery, we are as *protestant* as any, if in the "beasts" of the thirteenth chapter we find something beyond this. But nothing of this could have been intelligible to the saints of the early centuries, while the fulfillment of Ephesus, Smyrna, and even Pergamos, would soon be of the first importance.

"The Lord God of the *spirits* of the prophets"—the reading now generally admitted to be right—emphasizes for us the presence of the living God as what was for these the constant realization, in all the shifting scenes of human history. And so it is for those whose spirit is in harmony with them. God in past history, God in the events happening under our eyes, His judgment therefore of every thing, while controlling every thing, for His own glory and for the blessing of His people,—in this respect how blessed to be guided by those wondrous revelations! While the future, to be learnt from the same infallible teaching, is not only that which animates our hopes, but is necessary for the judgment of the present, no less. All lines lead on to the full end, there where the full light gives the manifestation of all.

"And behold, I come quickly." This is for the heart: future as long as we are down here; and yet to govern the present. "Blessed is he that keepeth the words of the prophecy of this book."

Here we are warned of the mistakes that may be made by the holiest of men in the most fervent occupation with heavenly things. John falls at the angel's feet to worship him; but the angel refuses it, claiming no higher title than to be a fellow-servant with John himself, with his brethren the prophets, and with those also who keep the words of this book. And he adds, "Worship God:"—worship, that is, no creature.

Unlike Daniel's prophecies, the words of the prophecy of this book are not to be sealed up, for the time is near. To the Christian, brought face to face with the coming of the Lord, the end is always near. What time might actually elapse was another question. In fact, some eighteen centuries have elapsed since this was written: but while Daniel was taught to look on through a vista of many generations to the end before him, Christians, taught to be always in an attitude of expectation, have before them no such necessary interval, and are brought into the full light now, though unbelief and wrong teaching may obscure it. But nothing in this way is under a vail, save the moment whose concealment is meant to encourage expectation. How good for us, and fruitful such concealment, may be measured by the goodness and fruitfulness of the expectation itself.

The solemn words are just ready to be uttered which proclaim the close of the day of grace to those who have refused grace. It is just ready to be said, "Let him that doeth unrighteously do unrighteously still; and let the filthy make himself filthy still; and let him that is righteous do righteousness still; and he that is holy, let him be sanctified still." And when this applies is shown clearly in the next words, "Behold, I come quickly, and My reward with Me, to render to every one as his work shall be: I, the Alpha and the Omega, the Beginning and the End, the First and the Last." The last affirmation here shows the irrevocable character of this judgment. He sums up in Himself all wisdom, all power: "none can stay His hand, or say unto Him, What doest Thou?"

The way of life and the way of death are now put in contrast: "Blessed are they that wash their robes, that they may have right to the tree of life, and may enter in through the gates into the city." Here is the condition of blessing stated according to the character of Revelation, in terms that have been used before. Our robes must be washed in the blood of the Lamb, as those of the redeemed multitude in the vision under the seals, in order to be arrayed in the *white* garments that are granted to the Lamb's wife. A very old corruption in this text is that exhibited in the common version, "Blessed are they that do His commandments;" but which is the true reading ought to be apparent at once. It is not by keeping commandments than any one can acquire a *right* to the tree of life. On the other hand, condemnation is for committed evil: "without are dogs, and sorcerers, and fornicators, and murderers, and idolaters, and every one that loveth and maketh a lie."

Again it is repeated, "I, Jesus, have sent Mine angel

THE CONSUMMATION.

to testify these things unto you in the assemblies;" and then He declares Himself in the two relations among men in which the book has spoken of Him: "I am the Root and the Offspring of David"—the Jewish relation, the divine incarnate King of Israel,—"the bright and Morning Star,"—the object of expectation for the Christian. But immediately He is named—or rather names Himself in this way, the heart of the Bride, moved by the Spirit, awakes: "And the Spirit and the Bride say, 'Come!'" But because it is yet the day of grace, and the Bride is still open to receive accessions it is added, "And let him that heareth say, 'Come!'" And if one answer, "Ah, but my heart is yet unsatisfied," it is further said, "And let him that is athirst come; he that will, let him take the water of life freely."

Blessed is this testimony. The precious gifts of God are not restricted in proportion to their preciousness, but the reverse. In nature, sunlight, fresh air, the waterbrooks, things the most necessary, are on that account bestowed freely upon all. And in the spiritual realm there is no barrier to reception of the best gifts, save that which the soul makes for itself. Not only so, but men are urged to come,—to take,—to look,—with no uncertainty of result for those who do so. The stream that makes glad the city of God is poured out for the satisfaction of all who thirst, and will but stoop to drink of it. This is the closing testimony of the gospel in this book, and that with which it is associated adds amazingly to its solemnity.

There is now another warning, neither to add to, nor to take from the words of the prophecy of this book. Scripture has many similar admonitions, but here the penalty is an unutterably solemn one. To him that adds, God shall add the plagues that are written in this book. From him who takes away, God shall take away his part from the tree of life and from the holy city. Yet men are now not scrupulous at least to take away many of the words of Scripture, and of Revelation among the rest. Every *word* is claimed here by the Lord Himself for God; and if this is not a claim for verbal inspiration, what is it? As manifestly the closing book of New-Testament scripture, what may we not infer as to the verbal inspiration of other parts? And what shall be the woe of those who dare presumptuously to meddle with that which is the authoritative communication of the mind of God to man? Is it not being done? and by those who own that somewhere at least—and they cannot pretend to know exactly the limit,—Scripture *contains* the Word of God?

This announcement of penalty is Christ's own word: "He who testifieth these things saith, 'Surely, I come quickly.'" Is it not when His Word is being thus dealt with that we may more than ever expect Himself? When the testimony of Scripture is being invalidated and denied, is it not then that we may most expect the Faithful and True Witness to testify in person? And especially when this arises in the most unlooked for places, and Church-teachers laboriously work out a theology of unbelief?

And the promise abides as the hope of the Church, although it be true that the Bridegroom has tarried, and the virgins have slept! That—true or false—a cry has been raised, "Behold, the Bridegroom cometh!" is notorious. That many have stirred and taken up the old attitude of expectancy is also true. All these things should surely be significant also. But whatever one's *head* may say,—whatever the doctrine we have received and hold as to the coming of our Lord and Master,—the *heart* of the truly faithful must surely say with the apostle here, "Even so, come, Lord Jesus."

It is the only response that answers to the assurance of His love on His departure to the Father: "In My Father's house are many mansions; if it were not so, I would have told you; I go to prepare a place for you.

And if I go, I will come again, and receive you unto Myself, that where I am, ye may be also."

The Lord's coming—the *parousia*—is just the "presence" of the Lord Himself. Nothing short of this could satisfy the hearts of those who looked up after Him, as He ascended with His hands spread in blessing over them; and were reassured by the angels' voices, that this same Jesus would come again. Just in proportion as we too have learnt by the Spirit the power of the love of Jesus, we too shall be satisfied with this, and with this alone. May we learn more deeply what is this cry of the Spirit and the Bride : "Amen, come, Lord Jesus."

F. W. G.

www.ingramcontent.com/pod-product-compliance
Lightning Source LLC
Chambersburg PA
CBHW052047290426
44111CB00011B/1654